T0350653

Capitalizing China

**A National Bureau of
Economic Research
Conference Report**

Capitalizing China

Edited by **Joseph P. H. Fan and Randall Morck**

The University of Chicago Press

Chicago and London

JOSEPH P. H. FAN is professor of finance and codirector of the Institute of Economics and Finance at the Chinese University of Hong Kong. RANDALL MORCK holds the Stephen A. Jarislowsky Distinguished Chair in Finance and is the Distinguished University Professor at the University of Alberta Business School, and is a research associate of the National Bureau of Economic Research.

The University of Chicago Press, Chicago 60637
The University of Chicago Press, Ltd., London
© 2013 by the National Bureau of Economic Research
All rights reserved. Published 2013.
Printed in the United States of America

22 21 20 19 18 17 16 15 14 13   1 2 3 4 5
ISBN-13: 978-0-226-23724-4 (cloth)
ISBN-13: 978-0-226-23726-8 (e-book)

Library of Congress Cataloging-in-Publication Data

Capitalizing China / edited by Joseph P. H. Fan and Randall Morck.
     pages cm. — (National Bureau of Economic Research
conference report)
     Includes bibliographical references and index.
     ISBN 978-0-226-23724-4 (cloth : alkaline paper) — ISBN
978-0-226-23726-8 (e-book) 1. Mixed economy—China. 2. China—
Economic conditions—1976–2000. 3. China—Economic
conditions—2000– 4. China—Economic policy—1976–2000.
5. China—Economic policy—2000– I. Fan, Joseph P. H., editor.
II. Morck, Randall, editor. III. National Bureau of Economic
Research, sponsoring body. IV. Series: National Bureau of Economic
Research conference report.
HC427.95.C365 2012
330.951—dc23

                                                           2012009461

Relation of the Directors to the
Work and Publications of the
National Bureau of Economic Research

1. The object of the NBER is to ascertain and present to the economics profession, and to the public more generally, important economic facts and their interpretation in a scientific manner without policy recommendations. The Board of Directors is charged with the responsibility of ensuring that the work of the NBER is carried on in strict conformity with this object.

2. The President shall establish an internal review process to ensure that book manuscripts proposed for publication DO NOT contain policy recommendations. This shall apply both to the proceedings of conferences and to manuscripts by a single author or by one or more co-authors but shall not apply to authors of comments at NBER conferences who are not NBER affiliates.

3. No book manuscript reporting research shall be published by the NBER until the President has sent to each member of the Board a notice that a manuscript is recommended for publication and that in the President's opinion it is suitable for publication in accordance with the above principles of the NBER. Such notification will include a table of contents and an abstract or summary of the manuscript's content, a list of contributors if applicable, and a response form for use by Directors who desire a copy of the manuscript for review. Each manuscript shall contain a summary drawing attention to the nature and treatment of the problem studied and the main conclusions reached.

4. No volume shall be published until forty-five days have elapsed from the above notification of intention to publish it. During this period a copy shall be sent to any Director requesting it, and if any Director objects to publication on the grounds that the manuscript contains policy recommendations, the objection will be presented to the author(s) or editor(s). In case of dispute, all members of the Board shall be notified, and the President shall appoint an ad hoc committee of the Board to decide the matter; thirty days additional shall be granted for this purpose.

5. The President shall present annually to the Board a report describing the internal manuscript review process, any objections made by Directors before publication or by anyone after publication, any disputes about such matters, and how they were handled.

6. Publications of the NBER issued for informational purposes concerning the work of the Bureau, or issued to inform the public of the activities at the Bureau, including but not limited to the NBER Digest and Reporter, shall be consistent with the object stated in paragraph 1. They shall contain a specific disclaimer noting that they have not passed through the review procedures required in this resolution. The Executive Committee of the Board is charged with the review of all such publications from time to time.

7. NBER working papers and manuscripts distributed on the Bureau's web site are not deemed to be publications for the purpose of this resolution, but they shall be consistent with the object stated in paragraph 1. Working papers shall contain a specific disclaimer noting that they have not passed through the review procedures required in this resolution. The NBER's web site shall contain a similar disclaimer. The President shall establish an internal review process to ensure that the working papers and the web site do not contain policy recommendations, and shall report annually to the Board on this process and any concerns raised in connection with it.

8. Unless otherwise determined by the Board or exempted by the terms of paragraphs 6 and 7, a copy of this resolution shall be printed in each NBER publication as described in paragraph 2 above.

To Stephen Jarislowsky

Contents

Acknowledgments   xi

**Translating Market Socialism with Chinese
Characteristics into Sustained Prosperity**   1
Joseph P. H. Fan, Randall Morck, and
Bernard Yeung

I. Financial System and Its Governance

    1. **The Governance of China's Finance**   35
       Katharina Pistor
       Comment: Zheng Song

    2. **China's Financial System: Opportunities
       and Challenges**   63
       Franklin Allen, Jun "QJ" Qian,
       Chenying Zhang, and Mengxin Zhao
       Comment: Chenggang Xu

II. Governance of Stock Markets

    3. **Assessing China's Top-Down Securities Markets**   149
       William T. Allen and Han Shen
       Comment: Qiao Liu

    4. **Institutions and Information Environment
       of Chinese Listed Firms**   201
       Joseph D. Piotroski and T. J. Wong
       Comment: Li Jin

III. Capital Accumulation

5. **Why Are Saving Rates So High in China?**   249
Dennis Tao Yang, Junsen Zhang,
and Shaojie Zhou
Comment: Leslie Young

6. **The Chinese Corporate Savings Puzzle:
A Firm-Level Cross-Country Perspective**   283
Tamim Bayoumi, Hui Tong,
and Shang-Jin Wei
Comment: Ning Zhu

IV. Public Finance

7. **Financial Strategies for Nation Building**   313
Zhiwu Chen
Comment: Jiahua Che

8. **Provincial and Local Governments in China:
Fiscal Institutions and Government Behavior**   337
Roger H. Gordon and Wei Li
Comment: Zhigang Li

Contributors   373
Author Index   377
Subject Index   383

Acknowledgments

This volume is the result of a research project, "Capitalizing China," co-organized by the National Bureau of Economic Research and the Institute of Economics and Finance (IEF) of the Chinese University of Hong Kong. We thank the IEF for funding the project and organizing the project and conference.

Translating Market Socialism with Chinese Characteristics into Sustained Prosperity

Joseph P. H. Fan, Randall Morck, and Bernard Yeung

I.1 Introduction

Capitalizing China examines the accumulation, distribution, and governance of capital in China. According to Vladimir Lenin (Yergin and Stanislaw 1998), capitalists control "the commanding heights" of a capitalist economy and the Communist Party must control the "commanding heights" of a socialist economy. In the transition economies of Eastern Europe and the former Soviet Union, the party ceded this ground to capitalists—though sometimes the same people continued in residence there.

China often seems to be embracing capitalism, but unwilling to admit this. Recent estimates correctly attribute 70 percent of GDP to its private sector (Nee and Opper 2012), and millions of entrepreneurs are starting new businesses (Khanna 2008). But many of those entrepreneurs rely critically on local or central party connections, and terms like *hybrid sector* or *non-state-owned enterprise sector* might more aptly describe all but the smallest of these enterprises, whose CEOs and boards benefit from the advice of their dedicated enterprise-level party secretaries and party committees.

Joseph P. H. Fan is professor of finance and codirector of the Institute of Economics and Finance at the Chinese University of Hong Kong. Randall Morck holds the Stephen A. Jarislowsky Distinguished Chair in Finance and is the Distinguished University Professor at the University of Alberta Business School, and is a research associate of the National Bureau of Economic Research. Bernard Yeung is the Stephen Riady Distinguished Professor and Dean of Business at the National University of Singapore.

We are grateful to the Institute of Economics and Finance of the Chinese University of Hong Kong for funding, to P. W. Liu and T. J. Wong for their comments and suggestions, and to Jun Huang for excellent research assistance. For acknowledgments, sources of research support, and disclosure of the authors' material financial relationships, if any, please see http://www.nber.org/chapters/c12067.ack.

The studies in this volume reveal that China is not copying free market institutions, but trying something substantially different: market socialism with Chinese characteristics is a genuinely unique system.[1] A host of its formal reforms emulate the institutional forms of a market economy, often in painstaking detail. But its heart remains resolutely socialist: strategically placed state-owned enterprises (SOEs), SOE-controlled pyramidal business groups, and ubiquitous party cells, party Secretaries, and party committees leave Lenin's "commanding heights" firmly and exclusively under the control of the Chinese Communist Party (CCP), and consign much of the rest to provincial and local party cadres. This system also retains unique Chinese characteristics, relying on China's ancient tradition—at least in historical eras of relatively good government—of an insuperable, but meaningfully meritocratic and internally competitive, Imperial Civil Service to gather and process information, and to manage the economy. The result is a to-date successful stir-fry of markets, socialism, and traditional China that is fully none of the three, but mixes in bits and pieces of each—all tossed together over very high heat.

The chapters in this volume analyze this recipe in detail. Some of the ingredients the chapters highlight appeal to Western tastes. These include a commercial banking system replete with multiple regulators, inspectors, capital requirements, and disclosure rules, augmented by all the finery of a G7 financial regulatory system. Other ingredients less palatable to Western tastes include the CCP Organization Department (CCP OD) managing all senior promotions throughout all major banks, regulators, government ministries and agencies, SOEs, and even many officially-designated non-SOE enterprises. The party promotes people through banks, regulatory agencies, enterprises, governments, and party organs, handling much of the national economy in one huge human resources management chart. An ambitious young cadre might begin in a government ministry, join middle management in an SOE bank, accept a senior party position in a listed enterprise, accept promotion into a top regulatory position, accept appointment as a mayor or provincial governor, become CEO of a different SOE bank, and perhaps ultimately rise into upper echelons of the central government or CCP (Macgregor 2010)—all by the grace of the CCP OD. The chapters in this volume describe state-of-the-art financial regulations, corporate gov-

---

1. In this chapter, we follow the government of the People's Republic of China and the Chinese Communist Party in using the terms "market socialism with Chinese characteristics," or more briefly, "market socialism" or "socialist market economy" to describe the economic system used in China from the early 1980s on. We recognize that the appropriateness of both "market" and "socialism" as attributes of this system does not accord with some scholars' usage of these terms in economics, finance, and political economy. Nonetheless, these are the English words chosen by state and party officials, and presumably reflect the intentions of the system's architects—Deng Xiaoping and his successors. Moreover, the words are defensible, in that the Chinese economy genuinely combines a powerful command and control apparatus with an admixture of market forces.

ernance codes, bankruptcy laws, taxation, and accounting and disclosure rules. But they also raise scores of concerns about market socialism's basic socialist and Chinese ingredients, leaving market economy reforms as little more than a garnish.

So far, China's fusion economy is an unquestionable success. In 1978, the People's Republic of China posted a per capita GDP of US$155; a sparse and dangerously dilapidated network of narrow roads; infrequent, unreliable, and dangerous air connections between small, decaying airports; essentially no real health-care system; mouldering universities; and a dispirited cynical populace. In 2009, People's China boasts a per capita GDP of US$2,200—over US$3,700 at purchasing power parity (PPP), perhaps more given some estimates of black and grey market income (Wang and Woo 2011), a rapidly expanding network of divided highways, modern commercial airline service between sleek new airport terminals, an expanding modern health-care system, and even the world's only magnetic levitation train, connecting Shanghai to its airport. Maddison and Wu (2008) estimate China's GDP surpassing America's in 2015.

But this divides across some 1.3 billion people, so China's per capita GDP remains far below typical Organization for Economic Cooperation and Development (OECD) levels, and unlikely to catch up for many years yet. For example, Japan's 2009 per capita GDP, at PPP comparably measured, was just under US$40,000; and America's was approximately US$46,000. Market socialism with Chinese characteristics has delivered on early-stage industrialization and modernization, and this may well suffice to make China the largest economy in the world. After all, with some four times the population of the United States, China can attain that status by exceeding one-fourth of America's per capita. But this would still leave China numbered among low- to middle-income countries. Propelling China's rise into the ranks of high-income economies will demand far more of its institutions.

The chapters in this volume collectively address how China's unique market socialist institutions are designed, how they facilitate the accumulation and allocation of capital, how they contribute to economic growth, and how they are beginning to have some interesting and potentially problematic side effects. Each of the subsequent chapters deals with these issues from a different angle. Pistor (chapter 1) examines the governance of China's banking system. Allen et al. (chapter 2) chronicle the development of the financial system. Allen and Shen (chapter 3) focus on the workings of China's securities markets. Piotroski and Wong (chapter 4), explore the financial transparency of China's business enterprises. Yang, Zhang, and Zhou (chapter 5) examine China's remarkable savings rate, and Bayoumi, Tong, and Wei (chapter 6) examine savings by China's listed business enterprises. Chen (chapter 7) recounts the history of China's rulers' attitudes toward public finance, and Gordon and Li (chapter 8) examine the finances of China's multiple levels of government.

The remainer of this chapter connects the dots to show how, while each chapter addresses these questions from a different perspective, their findings are profoundly interconnected, and in ways foreigners, especially those well-schooled in modern economics, often have considerable difficulty grasping. Charting these connections requires placing the various chapters in the context of broader research on China, especially recent research into public and private sector governance. Once these interconnections become clear, the chapters coalesce into a comprehensive picture of the uniquely Chinese institutions that characterize its market socialism, and present a fascinating picture of the inner workings of the world's soon-to-be largest economy.

I.2   Market Socialism's Achievements and Potential

Continued economic growth under market socialism with Chinese characteristics is clearly important not only to China, but to the world. If the Chinese achieved the per capita GDP South Koreans currently enjoy, just over US$17,000, its 1.33 billion people would produce a total GDP of almost US$23 trillion—far more than the current $14 trillion total GDP of the United States. Were the Chinese to match Japan's US$40,000 per capita GDP, China's total GDP would amount to some US$53 trillion—almost four times that of the United States.

China's per capita GDP now is roughly where South Korea's was thirty years ago, when China began its market socialism experiment in 1978, so using the South Korean per capita GDP to estimate China's in 2040 is not unreasonable as a first pass. Such simple arithmetic can be illustrative, but hardly definitive. That an industrialized and fully developed China's GDP will level off at precisely that of South Korea, Japan, or America is highly unlikely. America's GDPs will continue to grow; shifting age dependency ratios will come into play, educational attainments will change as new generations enter and old generations leave; and numerous other considerations will further complicate unfolding events. But that China will end up somewhere in that range if it succeeds in becoming a developed economy is true by definition. China would also perhaps endure multiple economic crises as it pulls abreast of today's leading economies, but so did South Korea.

As China develops, its effects on other countries' economies are becoming evident. Freeman (2006) estimates that the integration of China (and other formerly nonmarket economies) roughly doubles the global market economy's labor force, but increases its capital by much less, depressing wages across the board. Khanna (2008), more optimistically, stresses how the same union increases the scope and scale for entrepreneurship, and thus for global prosperity.

A fully developed China would dwarf the rest of the world as thoroughly as the United States did in the late 1940s. The entire US economy would match the combined economies of three or four large provinces of a high-income China, and today's other G7 countries would match the economies of individual provinces of various sizes. Dealings between a fully developed China and the United States might plausibly resemble those between the United States and Britain, France, or Italy today. Designing international political and economic institutions, treaties, and precedents capable of constructively shaping such a future might merit serious contemplation by policymakers in today's developed economies (Jacques 2009).

That contemplation would obviously begin by assessing the realism of such a scenario. Meiji Japan, South Korea, and other late industrializers all ultimately embraced capitalism and liberal democracy—albeit after initial inconsistency, incompetence, compromise, and backsliding. China has not done this, and its leaders demonstrate no intention of doing this. Thus far, they are breaking a new trail.

The chapters in this volume argue that China's embrace of free markets is at best tentative and at worst insubstantial. China is not embracing free markets as presented in Western economics textbooks. China is not emulating Anglo-American free markets, nor German nor even Meiji Japan or postwar South Korean market economies. Market socialism with Chinese characteristics is not Newspeak for "capitalism," but an economic experiment of unproven sustainability. This makes China's economic rise a qualified scenario: contingent upon either the current system's continued adaptability or its ultimate abandonment for genuine market economy institutions. This also makes China intensely interesting to economists.

I.3   Markets, Socialism, and Chinese Characteristics

China remains a democratic dictatorship of the proletariat: the CCP leadership, elected representatives of the proletariat, rules the economy's "commanding heights" without opposition. The legitimacy of the CCP thus depends on its success in this. Since 1978, success has been gauged by sustained and broad-based economic prosperity.

The omnipresence of the CCP in China's business enterprises tends to surprise foreign observers. The CCP controls the careers of all government officials and senior SOE managers, and appoints cadres to key party positions in many large non-SOEs. Provincial and local party cadres similarly advise many smaller non-SOEs. Promotions depend on success in promoting economic growth and loyalty to the party hierarchy. The party's power to reward or punish aspiring bureaucrats and executives has grown stronger since the 1990s (Macgregor 2010).

Within these constraints, the system is a substantial meritocracy (Landry 2008). Cadres who oversee higher investment, rising per capita GDP, and other measurable signs of improved prosperity gain promotions to higher positions in the civil service, enterprise management, or the Party itself—if they also obey Party policies and directives (Macgregor 2010; Allen and

Shen, chapter 3, this volume; Pistor, chapter 1, this volume). Promotions are outcomes of an explicitly competitive tournament based substantially on quantitative, if imperfect and pliable, performance metrics (Lü 2000; Li et al. 2008). Career advancement based on meritocracy, rather than solely on ideological purity, deviates starkly from China's Maoist era, but recalls the examination-based civil service meritocracies that governed more flourishing eras in its Imperial past (Spence 1999).

These promotions need not be vertical. The SOE managers can be promoted into government or party positions, and cadres can be promoted into positions of influence in SOEs or non-SOEs (Allen and Shen; Li and Zhou 2005; Lü 2000; Landry 2008; Pistor). For example, on April 3, 2011, state media reported the promotion of Su Shulin from chairman of China Petroleum and Chemical Corp (SINOPEC) to Fujian provincial party leader. On April 8, the CCP OD announced that Fu Chengyu, then chairman of China National Offshore Oil Corp (CNOOC) was replacing Su at Sinopec, and that Wang Yilin, the former top manager of China National Petroleum Corp (CNPC), the parent of PetroChina, was replacing Fu at CNOOC. When the music stopped, much to the consternation of foreign suppliers and customers, the CCP OD had rotated the top managers of China's major oil companies.

Such rotation plausibly broadens cadres' connections networks and, perhaps most importantly, fosters cadres' loyalty to the party, rather than to specific localities, government agencies, enterprises, or shareholders. This is not utterly different from what happens in other countries. American investment bank CEOs become treasury secretaries and bank regulators, Canadian government auditors become corporate tax accountants, and the *président et directeur général* (PDG) of a French corporation is often a former civil servant from the ministry responsible for regulating that industry (Bertrand et al. 2010; Heilbrunn 2005; Kramarz and Thesmar 2006; Smith 2004). Career moves from government to business are sufficiently commonplace to justify the *Académie Française* sanctioned *pantouflage* (literally, "shuffling wearing indoor slippers") and the Japanese *amakudari* (literally, "descent from heaven"). But such a system can invite corruption and entrench weak governance (Huang 2008; Xu 2011).

I.3.1   Market Socialist CEOs

Pistor reveals Chinese financial sector pantouflage operating differently from French, Japanese, or American elite networks. China's centrally coordinated multiple bidirectional pantouflage is under overt party control, and above criticism. America, France, and Japan are robust democracies, where abuses are exposed by an aggressively free press and constrained by open economies. The workings of the CCP OD better recall the Imperial Civil Service in premodern China, and its ready acceptance by the Chinese people perhaps accords with such a historical continuity. Western observers might understandably find this system bizarre; but many Chinese—even Western-educated economists—seemingly regard it as such a self-evident part of the background as to hardly merit mention.

Cadres' success in overseeing economic growth depends on access to capital, and successive rounds of reform unfailingly preserved CCP control over the financial sector. All major banks are either SOEs or under tight control. In theory, at least, this lets SOE bankers direct capital to the SOE and non-SOE enterprises with the best prospects. But China is hardly unique in this: large SOE banks dominate other economies too (La Porta, Lopez-de-Silanes, and Shleifer 2002).

The CCP also provides ongoing and intensive training to promising cadres. The Party School and Civil Service School both teach modern management. Moreover, though China now boasts of numerous business schools, the Party School and Civil Service School are peerless for the connections and institutional knowledge their graduates obtain. But again, elite educational institutions and programs specifically designed for civil servants exist elsewhere. France's École Nationale d'Administration and other grandes écoles fast-track promising students into elite government and business positions, as do Japan's Imperial Universities and, legacy admissions aside, America's Ivy League colleges. China today evokes Veblen's (1921) concept of superstar engineers running a finely tuned precisely designed economic machine.

The scope for government failure problems in such a system is substantial, and is developed explicitly later. However, its potential for genuine economic development should not go unrecognized. The CCP's use of career incentives, capital allocation, and training to promote economic growth allows the sort of economic engineering called for in Big Push industrialization (Rosenstein-Rodan 1943; Murphy, Shleifer, and Vishny 1989). Each party or government organ and every SOE or non-SOE top management team strives for economic success, but central party coordination puts the focus on national economic success, rather than local or individual enterprise performance. Highlighting that this, not a covert adoption of capitalism, became the goal of party pragmatists, Pistor explains tensions now distorting the Chinese economy and likely to loom larger as China develops. In particular, if growth is to persist, China's leaders must sustain a genuine meritocracy in a culture that esteems family ties, and must overcome Hayek's (1945) argument that information flows less freely through command and control structures as they grow larger and more complex.

I.3.2   Market Socialist Corporate Governance

Several chapters examine reforms to the regulation and governance of China's listed enterprises, and a synthesis of their findings again highlights that something unique is happening. Listed firms have CEOs and dual boards, organized along German lines, with requirements for outside director participation in the full board and in key committees and many other features associates with tidy corporate governance. However, all this is likely at best a sideshow.

Parallel this corporate governance system, each enterprise also has a Communist Party Committee, headed by a Communist Party Secretary. These advise the CEO on critical decisions, and are kept informed by party cells throughout the enterprise that also monitor the implementation of party policies. Indeed, the party secretary plays a leading role in major decisions, and can overrule or bypass the CEO and board if necessary (Deng et al. 2011).

For example, foreign independent directors on the board of CNOOC reportedly first learned of that enterprise's takeover bid for Unocal, an American oil company, from news broadcasts (Macgregor 2010). Directors often also learn of such major strategic moves, and of equally major personnel moves—such as the rotation of oil company top managers described earlier—after the fact. Despite their formal powers, CEOs and boards are thought to welcome party advice, and any directors likely to have reservations are kept out of the loop to preserve harmony—especially if issues the CCP views as strategically important are involved. Party intervention in less strategic sectors, and in smaller enterprises, may well be less direct and overt, and the priorities of provincial and local party cadres can deviate from those of top CCP cadres in Beijing.

Listed enterprises' party secretaries and committees are difficult to ignore. When the Shenzhen and Shanghai stock exchanges began trading in the 1990s, large SOEs were instructed to populate them with listed joint stock companies. The SOEs consequently organized subsidiaries whose financial ratios met the exchanges' listing requirements, and floated minority interests in these via equity carve-out initial public offerings (IPOs). Both stock markets still feature many listed enterprises with vast total market capitalizations and miniscule public floats.

Control blocks in these were retained by various government ministries or other state or party organs, or by other listed SOEs in pyramidal holding company structures, and these blocks were designated as inalienable *nontraded* shares. Reforms in the 2000s unified each listed enterprise's traded and nontraded shares into a single alienable class, effectively turning full market capitalizations into potential public floats. Because this greatly increased the total quantity of equity available to savers, because nontraded shares owned directly by the central government were not required to pay dividends to the government until 2008, and (perhaps most importantly) because blocks of nontraded shares were reserved for employees and managers, valuations fell (Bayoumi, Tong, and Wei, chapter 6) and existing traded shareholders were compensated.

Equity unification, by letting the governments and government agencies that previously held nontraded shares sell out, could transform the large

SOE and SOE subsidiaries that still dominate both stock markets into fully privately-owned firms—albeit still assisted by their party secretaries and party committees.

To date, Allen and Shen find little evidence of a widespread substantial increase in private share ownership, and conclude that government and party officials retain control blocks in most listed enterprises, either directly or through pyramiding, especially in strategically important sectors such as banking. To illustrate, they examine Industrial and Commercial Bank of China (ICBC), China's second-largest bank, and find that a scant 4.3 percent of its domestically traded shares are in private hands (ICBC has a class of "H shares" traded in Hong Kong that appear largely foreign-owned). The H shareholders cannot outvote domestic shareholders. Consequently, the CCP continues to control most of the voting power in most listed firms' shareholder meetings.

Nonetheless, genuinely private ownership is rising. Allen and Shen find officially designated *listed SOEs* constituting over two-thirds of listings and including most very large enterprises. The remaining less than one third of listings, officially designated *listed non-SOEs,* consists of listed SOEs' controlled subsidiaries and privately-owned corporations. The CEOs and boards of listed SOEs are appointed by their parents' CEOs, advised by their parents party secretaries. The CEOs and boards of all major listed non-SOEs and SOEs are advised directly by their own party secretaries and party committees (Yu 2009).

Much of China's private sector consists of unlisted enterprises: local state-controlled cooperatives (township and village enterprises, or TVEs), many of which lease control rights to managers in transactions referred to as management buy-outs (MBOs). The sector also includes many joint ventures with multinationals, and numerous small single proprietorships, often of uncertain legal status. Preferring the term hybrid sector, Allen et al. and Gordon and Li examine local government-controlled enterprises, and suggest that their governance may be unexpectedly strong. Of course, all but the very smallest facilitate the organization of party cells, and their CEOs value the advice of their party secretaries, whose connections and influence with regulators, officials, and SOE banks and business partners can be critical.

The pause Allen and Shen observe in the transition of listed SOEs into fully privately-owned firms could allow time for other reforms—either to facilitate their efficient regulation and corporate governance or to safeguard party influence over their governance, or both. Allen and Shen, Allen et al. and Pistor describe the development of China's financial regulations. All question the real traction of these reforms in doing what financial regulations do in capitalist economies, given corporations' parallel governance systems.

For example, China's fully modern Corporate Governance Code authorizes shareholder derivative lawsuits and assigns fiduciary duties to directors and officers, though not party secretaries or party committee members. Judges are party appointees, and their careers turn on their respect for party policies and acceptance of party guidance. Moreover, court rulings are enforced at the discretion of party officials. For example, Allen et al. find bankruptcy rulings are rarely enforced because central government circulars applicable to SOE bankruptcies supersede the law, because local governments can halt cases, and because SOE banks prefer to avoid write-downs triggered by formal bankruptcies. Xu (comment, chapter 2, this volume), in reviewing this chapter, suggests that, despite CCP OD control over executives' careers, banks' financial operations are decentralized and subnational government and party influence may be more salient to local branch decisions regarding debt forgiveness. Allen et al. conclude that "for insolvent SOEs, what triggers the bankruptcy procedure is not their financial status per se, but whether they can get preferential treatment from the government." Finally, court rulings need not protect creditors. Although the Supreme People's Court ordered lower courts not to process bankruptcies designed solely to nullify debts in 2002, Garnaut, Ligang, and Yang (2006) report that 90 percent of SOE CEOs surveyed believe bankruptcy to be "a feasible channel to evade bank debts."

Piotroski and Wong suggest that weak regulation and discretionary enforcement render Chinese corporate financial reporting unreliable, leaving listed enterprises opaque to outside investors. This prevents outside shareholders and creditors from questioning managerial decisions, but also prevents capital market forces from channeling people's savings to their highest value uses. Jin (comment, chapter 4, this volume) argues that public investors may not demand transparency because central government policies, not enterprise policies, are the main drivers of stock prices.

All this surely diminishes marginal shareholders' valuations. Rational investors would discount the future dividend streams to account for governance and regulation deficiencies, and buy if share prices subside enough. The continued existence of Chinese stock markets is thus not threatened by such deficiencies, and investors can presumably expect fair risk-adjusted returns. But the governments and SOEs that sell their control blocks to investors will receive less per share, all else equal.

More importantly, the social purpose of a stock market is not to persist, nor even to fill the coffers of privatizing governments, but to direct savings to their highest value uses (Tobin 1984; Wurgler 2000). Intrusive party involvement in corporate governance would dam off market forces and entrust this task to cadres. The CCP is far more professional than in the past, and ideologues are largely replaced by pragmatists, so party guidance may well substitute for market forces—effectively turning China's listed enterprises into industrial policy tools. In other countries, state-led industrial policies often manage spurts of high early-stage growth, but then fail because capital allocation becomes more difficult in later stage growth, when creativity and productivity enhancement matter more than capacity expansion, and because political rent-seeking consumes ever-increasing resources (Easterly 2006). Perhaps this time is different.

I.3.3   Market Socialist Bankers

The Panic of 2008 and subsequent recession leave Anglo-American stock market-based capitalism in some disrepute. In theory, information-laden share prices guide capital toward firms with sound investment opportunities and away from firms that look ill-run; and well informed bank loan officers lend to firms with sound business plans and deny loans to dodgy firms (Tobin 1984). In practice, financial bubbles and crises misallocate capital, but most developed capitalist economies' financial systems appear to perform these tasks tolerably efficiently most of the time (Rajan and Zingales 1998; Wurgler 2000). Nonetheless, legitimate concerns attach to relying on stock markets to allocate capital in developing economies (Morck, Yeung, and Yu 2000; Jin and Myers 2006). If China largely disconnects its stock markets from capital allocation decisions, its banks might nonetheless channel market forces.

Allen et al. show most bank lending flowing to SOEs, rather than the hybrid sector they find better equipped to generate wealth—despite SOEs' ongoing accumulation of nonperforming loans. Their findings suggest that politics and connections dominate financial viability in bank loan allocation decisions, sheltering banks from market forces as well. Unsurprisingly, simultaneous capital shortages and surpluses ensue—excess capital being wasted in some sectors and firms while, simultaneously, chronic capital shortages blocks needed growth in other sectors and firms. The capital shortage in the hybrid sector is due to the lending bias of state-controlled banks, which prefer to lend to large state-controlled enterprises; frequent government intervention in the financial system merely reinforces this bias. In consequence, an informal financial sector—arguably, a shadow banking sector with Chinese characteristics—has arisen to provide credit to the many hybrid enterprises the banks neglect. In a prior paper, Allen, Qian, and Qian (2008) argue that the informal sector can substitute for the formal banking sector, and the chapters in this volume do not contradict this. However, the informal financial sector's sources of capital are opaque, rendering meaningful assessment of the sector's size, stability, and efficiency highly problematic. Moreover, the high interest the sector charges hybrid enterprises, most of which are small and median sized operations, and the sometimes severe consequences they suffer for missing a payment, suggest that the informal financial sector provides very costly capital. This may well be commensurate with high lending risks, but again, a quantitative assessment is stymied by the sector's opacity. China's shadow banking system, like America's in previous years, may well conceal hidden sources of instability and inefficiency.

Pistor utilizes the tools of network analysis to document webs of personal ties between party cadres in charge of China's banks and financial regulators. This dense network of linkages centered on cadres in key CCP organs contrasts vividly with banks' formal chains of accountability designed along Western lines. While individual banks, business enterprises, and regulatory agencies appear distinct on paper, they are actually highly integrated because the CCP OD handles human resource management (HRM) decisions throughout all of them (Macgregor 2010). The future careers of top bankers and bank regulators thus depend on how cadres in the CCP OD assess their performance. If the quality of lending decisions predominates in these assessments, an increasingly professionalized and pragmatic party might tolerably well incentivize bankers to lend efficiently. But if ideological purity, faction loyalty, or outright corruption take precedence, massive capital misallocation is likely.

Pistor finds that the prominence of the CCP OD is not a Maoist holdover awaiting reform, but a solution CCP cadres designed and built to safeguard the party's control over Lenin's commanding heights as reforms progressed. Thus, China complies fully with World Trade Organization (WTO) requirements to liberalize and deregulate, even as the CCP OD integrates top personnel at banks, borrower enterprises, regulatory bodies, governments, and the party itself, with loyalty and job performance, in uncertain balance, the criteria for promotion throughout.

These considerations lead Pistor to interpret Chinese pantouflage as qualitatively different from its French, Japanese, or American cognates, though she does not preclude the possibility that future reforms might lead to convergence. As countries grow richer, tolerably efficient capital allocation becomes both more urgent and more difficult. If China persists with its current system, regulatory capture problems (Stigler 1971) seem likely to defeat even the best de jure financial regulations. Allen and Shen, Allen et al., and Pistor argue that reforms effectively separating banks from their regulators would substantially improve the quality of capital allocation over the longer term. However, Song (comment, chapter 1, this volume) argues that the system Pistor describes could minimize systemic shocks while delivering politically acceptable growth for some years yet (see also Deng et al. 2011).

I.3.4   Market Socialist Tycoons and Entrepreneurs

Forbes Magazine lists more US dollar millionaires in China in 2011 than anywhere else save the United States itself. Wang and Woo (2011) argue that China's official data vastly underestimate rising Chinese inequality over the past two decades. Forsaking Maoist orthodoxy, China heeded Deng Xiaoping's call to "let a few people get rich first" as a prelude to broader development.

Faster economic development may well cause greater inequality, for a time at least, because the talents needed to organize an economy's resources efficiently are scarce and command high prices in the free market (Kuznets

1955). Persons possessing exceptional judgement (Knight 1921), foresight (Hayek 1941), creativity (Schumpeter 1911), technological skills (Veblen 1921), organizational ability (Coase 1937), or other rare and valuable skills accumulate wealth first, aggravating inequality, before their businesses create a large affluent middle class that mitigates inequality.

However, inequality per se need not cause development. If a nation enriches an elite largely bereft of these unique talents, inequality can lock in stagnation (Morck, Wolfenzon, and Yeung 2005). This is because an inadequately talented elite rationally fears development, for this would require its displacement by a talented elite, and uses its political power to preserve the status quo (Olson 2000). Such low-level poverty traps well characterize much Latin American history (Haber 2000; Edwards 2010).

The talents of China's nouveaux riches—its Communist millionaire class—are thus important. If market socialism with Chinese characteristics reliably entrusts capital to appropriately talented people, development can progress and inequality can abate. But if spoiled princelings, gray apparatchiks, ideological zealots, or scheming sycophants rise to the top more reliably, China risks emulating the Ottoman Empire, twentieth century Latin America, or Tsarist Russia, and combining brutal inequity with chronic economic lassitude.

The various chapters document how China's business elites owe their positions to party favor, or at least forbearance. But even very small-scale private businesses are subject to party guidance. Any enterprise employing more than three party members must allow a Communist Party Cell to organize and select a secretary. This allows the CCP in Beijing to keep up-to-date on any rising firm's business operations and plans, provide important advice at critical junctures, and assist its CEO in complying with regulatory constraints or negotiating exemptions with government officials or party cadres.

All this raises fundamental questions about China's business elite: are they primarily entrepreneurs or apparatchiks? Allen et al. argue that many are entrepreneurs. Defining the *hybrid sector* as all non-SOE unlisted firms, including privately-owned businesses and enterprises partially owned by local governments—including Township and Village Enterprises (TVEs)—they see competition between local governments mitigating inefficiency. This, they argue, makes TVEs and other local government-controlled enterprises resemble purely private businesses more closely than large SOEs and SOE subsidiaries.

Even if not entirely free of state influence, the hybrid sector likely has the greatest potential for fostering economic, rather than political, entrepreneurship (Baumol 1990; Murphy, Shleifer, and Vishny 1991). Its success is thus an important public policy issue. The corporate tycoons who run the SOEs, listed SOEs' subsidiaries, and ex-SOEs that constitute China's big business sector are largely career cadres. The party strives to select the best and brightest, and provides ongoing high-quality training, but bureaucratic hierarchies are generally ill-suited to rewarding creativity. Economic entrepreneurship thus appears dependent on the financial system identifying and backing promising entrants and upstarts in the hybrid sector.

Consistent with corporate savings primarily arising in small non-SOE businesses, the hybrid sector finances most of its capital investment out of enterprise savings—60 percent for the sector overall and 90 percent for purely private businesses—with informal debt, such as trade credit, making up much of the remainders. The hybrid sector's high dependence on retained earnings for expansion indicates that China's major banks have yet to make major inroads in financing economic entrepreneurs. Allen et al., documenting the entrance of new non-SOE banks and intermediaries, discern a diminution of the big SOE banks' supremacy. That entrant banks might better channel capital to economic entrepreneurs remains to be seen.

In explaining this reticence in lending to hybrid-sector businesses, Allen et al. highlight the nonperforming loan (NPL) of the major SOE banks. Arguing that these NPLs are largely a "policy burden"—the banks extended loans under political pressure—and that the burden is greater than a cursory inspection of the banks' balance sheets indicates, they argue that if the CCP desires continued high growth, a more complete immunization of the big SOE banks' NPL problem might be warranted. They argue that purchases of banks' equity by the Central Huijin Investment Company, a sovereign wealth fund initially capitalized by the People's Bank of China, helped solidify the banks' capital bases, but did not entirely solve their NPL problems. Moreover, the share purchases left the large SOE banks even more firmly under party control and SOE bankers still jittery about risky lending.

These findings suggest that market socialism with Chinese characteristics does not allocate national savings to the most efficient users of capital. Because hybrid sector enterprises rely on trade credit (rather than financial institutions and markets) for capital, they are subject to their suppliers' and customers' terms and conditions. Trade credit in Western economies tends to be an expensive source of capital.

In summary, China's tycoons, its barons of big business, are predominantly career bureaucrats and ex-bureaucrats: cadres the CCP Organization Department promoted through top positions in large SOEs and SOE subsidiaries. China's banking system appears well suited to channeling capital to these cadre-tycoons. China's entrepreneurs, who appear most often in the hybrid sector, rely largely on savings, somewhat on trade credit, and seemingly very little on the financial system.

I.3.5   Market Socialist Capital

Market socialism with Chinese characteristics is nonetheless capitalizing China rapidly—in the sense of eliciting an extraordinarily high and rising savings rate. As Prasad (2009) notes, investment pushes growth in China to an unprecedented extent, and consumption constitutes the lowest fraction of GDP ever recorded in any major economy.

This presents a dual puzzle to Yang, Zhang, and Zhou (chapter 5, this volume). Since the 1978 advent of market socialism, China's savings rate never dipped below 34 percent—far above the savings rates typical of other countries, developed or developing. Why is China's savings rate so high? From 2000 on, China's savings rate climbed steadily so that Chinese now save roughly one yuan out of every two. This is 3.3 times the average savings rate for other low income countries and 2.4 times the global average. Why, they ask, is China's unprecedentedly high savings rate yet rising?

Young's discussion argues that Chinese consumers and enterprises have much higher incomes than the data show because of inadequate exchange rate adjustments to purchasing power parity, and consequently only appear to save much more than foreigners. This corroborates Wang and Woo's (2011) contention that official Chinese aggregate consumption figures are vastly understated because they omit gray market transactions. Citing low-cost loans from SOE banks and ubiquitous debt forgiveness and the fact that SOE dividends are not actually paid in many cases, Young argues that many enterprises' actual costs are far below the nominal costs reported in their annual reports. Adding that local governments are awash in incomes from land lease sales, and ought not to spend all these proceeds at once, he is also unsurprised by high government savings rates.

China's national income accounts display other irregularities. For example, provincial GDPs in past years typically summed to more than national GDP. Lequiller and Blades (2006, c. 13) ties such anomalies to the Material Products System (MPS), an input-output framework for monitoring production quota attainment under central planning still used to track enterprise and regional economy performance. Tying data collection to performance evaluation plausibly encourages inflated production reports: for example, exaggerated agricultural production reports are blamed for excessive exports and rural starvation during the Great Leap Forward (Lü 2000; Yang 2008). The central government's statistics, which adjust MPS data using surveys, may be more reliable than the provincial numbers, which typically do not; however, broader surveys by the central government finding its official figures on GDP to be too low triggered major upwards adjustments in 2005 (Lequiller and Blades 2006, 377). Wu (2006) posits politics, not statistical accuracy, driving these adjustments. While China's national income accounting is flawed, the data are not meaningless. Other countries at similar stages of development quite plausibly have similar or worse data, yet do not display comparable anomalies. Maddison and Wu (2008) painstakingly dissect Chinese national income accounts and report distortions, but not futility.

Accepting China's national income accounts at face value, Yang et al. scrutinize its rapid and accelerating pace of capitalization, and weigh alternative explanations of it. They consider, but ultimately dismiss, a cultural explanation: savings rates tend to be high across East Asia, where traditional values extol savings. But traditional Asian values are not obviously stronger in China than elsewhere in the region, and are not obviously becoming even stronger in China faster than elsewhere. Moving on to economics-based explanations, they divide savings into enterprises, governments, and households. This reveals more patterns.

First, this exposes a long-run trend. In the early years of market socialism, government and enterprise savings were large and household savings were small. But as China developed, household savings rose steadily, while the other categories waned. But after 2000, all three surged, with government savings soaring fastest.

Government savings rose because tax revenues rose faster than government spending. Yang et al. link this to an ongoing "rich country–poor people" controversy, arguing that pressure for more spending on public goods and services is likely to reverse this trend. However, Chen disagrees, arguing that party leaders view government wealth accumulation as a pure policy objective. Yang et al. also suggest that demography may warrant a high government savings rate: the one-child policy means a low child dependency ratio now, but a very high seniors' dependency ratio in the future.

Enterprise savings are an ambiguity because many enterprises remain state controlled. The distinction between government and enterprise savings, though clear for accounting purposes, is somewhat blurry for economic conclusions. Nominal enterprise earnings rose sharply from the 1990s on, probably reflecting a confluence of favorable developments. New technology and better management improved productivity. Weak domestic competitive pressure and WTO access to foreign markets sustained revenues. Subsidized loans from SOE banks and largely de jure illegal migration of labor from the countryside contained capital and labor costs, as did a generally unresponsive party stance against labor unrest. These conditions let enterprises accumulate savings; however, the chapter argues that price competition will likely erode enterprise savings as reforms progress.

In terms of market share concentration, competition appears robust in China (Nee and Opper 2012). But the financial system's indisposition to allocate capital to hybrid sector enterprises (chapter 3; chapter 2) may well be a high barrier to entry for unconnected would-be entrepreneurs. The true strength of competition in China is thus ambiguous, and competition could be a public policy problem despite relatively low concentration.

Yang et al. explain how household savings rose markedly—from 6 to 7 percent in 1978 to 22 percent in 2007—with a rising propensity to save with income, as in Chamon, Liu, and Prasad (2010). Yang et al. find China's age-savings profile, previously "hump shaped" as in a life-cycle savings theory (Modigliani and Brumberg 1954), inverting after 2000. That is, just as China's savings rate shoots skyward, the curve flips: households headed by very young and very old people now save more than households headed by middle-aged people. Reviewing the literature on dependency ratios and savings, they argue in support of Chamon and Prasad (2008) who, reporting a similar pattern, present a "buffer-stock" model of savings: younger households save to buy homes; older households save for medical expenses and old age security.

Expanding this, Yang et al. advance another more subtle demographic explanation: competitive savings. China's one-child policy greatly skewed its gender ratios, and marriageable women are now in short supply. Families might therefore save to help their sons attract wives, an idea initially raised by Wei and Zhang (2011). Confirming this suggestion, they find markedly higher savings rates in provinces with fewer females. While alternative explanations are possible—for example, these might also be provinces where traditional values are strongest—the possibility of unfolding unintended economic consequences to the venerable Chinese preference for sons is intriguing, and deserves further investigation.

Noting that prior unemployment does not greatly increase savings, they dismiss an augmented precautionary savings motive due to middle-aged SOE employees' job insecurity. However, they are unable to preclude broader effects associated with the private provision of education, health care, and housing. Student loans, mortgages, and private health insurance remain largely inaccessible privately, and the government has yet to provide universal health care. Allen et al. document a stunted insurance industry, so households have little alternative but to manage health and other risks with aggressive precautionary savings. All this is consistent with Chamon and Prasad (2008): young households may be saving to buy homes, cars, and appliances because mortgages and consumer loans are not generally available; old households may be frantically saving in anticipation of looming health-care costs because insurance is not generally available. The rising savings rate in recent years also fits the narrative in Chamon and Prasad (2008) and Yang et al.: housing prices rose sharply in the same period as pension replacement rates fell. The chapter predicts that future reforms to remedy these gaps are apt to reduce China's savings rate.

I.3.6 Market Socialist Profits

Yet another reason for high savings could be that individuals do not consider the savings of business enterprises to be relevant to their personal well-being. In a country with widely held corporations, an efficient stock market, and strong shareholder rights, savings by business enterprises can be expected to translate into future dividends to individuals. However, most large Chinese listed enterprises have tiny, often single-digit public floats. Most of their shares belong to government or party organs, directly or through intermediary SOE holding companies. Moreover, most Chinese individuals do not own shares. A sort of Ricardian equivalence might nonetheless prevail: individual Chinese might expect high future dividends payable to state organs to lower individual tax rates in the future. However, cynicism about the efficiency of this indirect savings method might well disconnect enterprise savings from individuals' consumption-savings decisions.

China's national income accounts suggest high enterprise savings, and Bayoumi et al. reexamine China's savings puzzle using financial data disclosed by enterprises trading on the Shanghai and Shenzhen stock markets. Their startling, and very robust, conclusion is that listed Chinese enterprises do not retain substantially more earnings than comparable listed firms elsewhere. Moreover, the data show substantial declines in listed enterprises' savings after 2000. This result, combined with the findings in Yang et al. imply either that unlisted enterprises savings drive both the high overall enterprise savings rate and the post-2000 surge in enterprise savings. Yang et al. discern in macroeconomic data, or that something is seriously amiss with Chinese data. Accepting the validity of both firm-level and macroeconomic data, despite the reservations of Piotroski and Wong regarding the former and the problems in China's national income accounts data raised earlier, several reconciliations are possible.

Most obviously, as Zu's discussion contends, listed enterprises may be qualitatively different in numerous dimensions from unlisted enterprises, making different savings rates unremarkable. One set of differences likely to matter is access to capital. Listed enterprises, able to issue shares, can raise funds readily to finance new growth opportunities as they arise; while unlisted enterprises, unable to tap equity markets, must pile up retained earnings as corporate savings accounts to be drawn down in the future as needed. Or, the top executives of listed enterprises may have stronger personal connections to SOE bankers, or to party and government officials capable of influencing SOE bank lending decisions. Thus, unlisted firms might need savings because they lack access to credit, while listed firms' well-connected insiders might make enterprise savings unnecessary. The strength of such insiders' connections varies across enterprises, and can be measured (Fan, Wong, and Zhang 2007). Bayoumi et al. confirm that listed enterprises with stronger party connections have lower savings rates; though they link this to lower net earnings, not higher retained earnings.

Either reconciliation incriminates financial system infirmities for China's high macroeconomic enterprise savings rate, specifically fingering relatively financially isolated and politically unconnected unlisted enterprises. If so, reforms that would let capital market forces allocate savings impartially to their highest value uses are a likely policy option to make high growth sustainable. Allen and Shen, Allen et al., and Piotroski and Wong elaborate on such reforms.

Still another possible reconciliation is that unlisted enterprises, shielded from public view and foreign criticism, have more flexibility allocating their retained earnings. If so, listed firms might tunnel (Johnson et al. 2000) income to their unlisted parents, or to other entities from which insiders can readily move capital to where they feel it is needed. Tunneled funds could appear as costs in the subsidiaries' financial statements and retained earnings in those of their parent SOEs. Amid rapid economic development, this freedom of action can be justified as a means of overcoming network externalities, first mover hold-up problems, and other coordination problems that arise in early stages of industrialization (Rosenstein-Rodan 1943; Morck and Nakamura 2007; Morck 2011). However, the same freedom of action also creates scope for corruption on a grand scale, and raises the possibility that high earnings retentions by unlisted enterprises might be bookkeeping entries concealing unaccountably enriched insiders.

I.3.7   Market Socialist Debts

Allen et al. document a very rapid growth in government bond issues, with outstanding bonds totaling some RMB (Renminbi) 10 trillion (US$1.44 trillion) by December 2008. Virtually all is government debt: about 50 percent is government bonds, about 37 percent are the bonds of SOE policy banks, and the remaining 13 percent are the debts of large Chinese enterprises, virtually all of which are either SOEs or subsidiaries of SOEs. The absence of fully private-sector bonds is quite plausibly due to China's politicized bankruptcy process (Allen et al.).

Chen (chapter 7, this volume) examines China's government debt, but from the viewpoint of creditors. In December 2004, China's national debt stood at RMB 2.96 trillion—just under 22 percent of GDP. Of this, 97 percent was owned to domestic lenders, and only 3 percent was owed to foreigners. The total was 21.6 percent of GDP, well below the internationally-recognized warning limit of 60 percent. In 2003, interest payments on the national debt cost RMB 300 billion, about 14 percent of fiscal revenue. These figures, Chen argues, probably greatly understate the real debt payments because they do not adjust for SOE banks' NPLs. Citing estimates ranging from 29 percent to 36 percent of GDP for these, Chen reestimates China's total national debt as somewhere between 50 percent and 58 percent of GDP. This, he notes, approaches the 60 percent threshold, above which creditors begin sounding alarms.

The high government savings documented by Yang et al. need reconciliation with a large government debt. Yang et al. net Chinese government inflows and outflows and assess government savings in 2003 at RMB 944.5 billion, roughly one-tenth of bonds outstanding. Consistent with government savings and debts partially offsetting each other, Chen reports a RMB 200 billion rise in government bond issues (from RMB 400 billion in 2000), even as Yang et al. report government savings rising by about RMB 620 billion (from 325.5 billion in 2000). Clearly, accumulated government savings cannot be explained by bond issue proceeds, but the simultaneous accumulation of debts and savings remains incompletely explained.

Chinese officials' motives for borrowing and saving simultaneously, and both on very large scales, are harder to square. One possibility is that the central government might be borrowing and local or regional governments might be saving. Alternatively, the two might reflect an underlying unity. For example, the central government might be borrowing during a period of low international interest rates to accumulate capital for future needs; or borrowing in one currency and saving in another to control the exchange rate. This puzzle requires more work.

Contemplating China's large government debt, Chen sees a stark deviation from traditional characteristically Chinese policies. Throughout the Ming and Qing dynasties, China's rulers equated good government with the accumulation of vast silver hoards, to be drawn down should natural disaster or war arise. In these mercantilist aims, China resembled most premodern governments, Asian and European (Macdonald 2003). Emperors typically increased taxes and debased or inflated the currency to supplement drained silver hoards. As in medieval Europe, forced lending to princes who dwelt above the law ultimately elevated credit risk sufficiently to destroy the market. Confirming this, financially strapped nineteenth-century Qing rulers defaulted on the forced loans they extracted from a nascent banking industry (Morck and Yang 2011).

Chen accepts Macdonald's (2003) argument that limited governments can borrow more readily because they can less readily nullify their debts, and that this induces a positive feedback loop wherein governments, concerned about tapping bond markets, act more responsibly, which elevates their reputations, which government officials come to value, and so on. This virtuous circle, Macdonald argues, let Western governments borrow to finance infrastructure, war, and other expenditures; while China traditionally had to save up for such things.

Of course, bond market discipline is not the only possible check on irresponsible government spending. Profligate local and provincial governments that run up unmanageable debts may invite scrutiny by the CCP OD, and the career opportunities of those deemed responsible might be curtailed—especially if the meritocratic aspects of market socialism with Chinese characteristics persist and deepen. Alternatively, an unwillingness to acknowledge errors might keep China from achieving this virtuous confluence. China's public debt is mostly owed to domestic creditors, who still have few other savings options—basically bank accounts, domestic (mostly SOE or SOE-related) stocks, and a few SOE-run mutual funds. While irresponsible government policies might increase China's borrowing costs, its creditors' power to discipline the government and the party is limited. Even if a bond market develops, Chinese bondholders are unlikely to become prominent on the economy's commanding heights. The CCP discipline seems more feasible, if less certain, at least in the foreseeable future.

I.3.8   Market Socialist Public Finance

Gordon and Li (chapter 8, this volume) examine public finance under market socialism with Chinese characteristics more generally. Noting that China's economy has grown extraordinarily rapidly despite multiple checks on market forces, they posit a role for something akin to Tiebout (1956) competition, wherein competition for taxpayers forces governments to provide public goods and services efficiently.

Tiebout competition achieves this if taxpayers can either vote out incumbent politicians or exit, carrying their tax checks to other jurisdictions that provide more or better public goods per yuan of taxes. At present, contested elections are restricted to village councils, so incumbents' fear of voter wrath is an unlikely force for public sector efficiency.

Exit is also a limited option because individual taxpayers cannot freely relocate. Recapitulating traditional feudal labor mobility restrictions, the People's Republic of China's hukou system, established in 1949 and reorganized into its current form in 1958, assigns each individual to a locality, designates his or her residence as either urban or rural, and is hereditary. Changing one's hukou requires the permission of officials in both the old and new jurisdiction, and is currently difficult—especially for relatively unskilled people—because of concerns about a brain drain from poor regions, exploding populations in attractive cities, rising costs of public goods provision in those cities, and shanty towns developing in high growth provinces. A skill-based point system is coming into use among migrant-receiving provinces. Unregistered (unchanged hukou) migrants are becoming commonplace, but cannot send their children to state high schools or utilize other government services, raising the spectre of an entrenched urban underclass. At present, the migration of individuals is unlikely to contribute to strong Tiebout competition.

However, Gordon and Li argue that, even though individual mobility may be hampered, many business enterprises' activities are mobile across regions, and respond to competitive incentives offered both by *and to* village, township, municipal, province-level city, provincial, and regional (hereinafter "local" for brevity) government officials. Most obviously, local officials whose administrations provide better public goods for lower tax and regulatory costs attract firms to tax. If local officials cause their jurisdictions to compete for business activity, and cause the enterprises they govern to maximize their profits, something akin to social welfare maximization might theoretically ensue.

Moreover, local officials, often doubling as top executives of the hybrid enterprises their jurisdictions established, also have direct incentives to ensure those enterprises maximize profits—including by moving operations to jurisdictions that offer prospects of higher profits. This is because, between 1978 and 1994, local governments received both profits and tax revenue from all the enterprises they established, and their local government officials had free hand to spend much of that revenue as they liked. After a major tax reform in 1994, local governments still remained the de facto residual claimants to those enterprises' after-tax earnings net of mandated spending, and local government officials remained largely free to spend these funds as they chose. Local government officials thus gain larger discretionary budgets by ensuring that the hybrid enterprises they control generate higher profits by allocating resources more efficiently (Gordon and Li 1995; Li 1997).

If local officials' discretionary cash flow maximization induces local governments to compete for business activity and induces hybrid enterprises to maximize their residual cash flows, something approaching efficient resource allocation might ensue. However, some caveats are clearly in order. Local government officials, striving to maximize the residual earnings of enterprises that provide them with discretionary cash flow, might distort local policies to favor those enterprises to the disadvantage of the general citizenry. For example, such officials might skew local taxes, fees, or regulations, or might press local managers of state-owned banks to favor enterprises whose residual budgets they control, or for other private purposes. The social welfare benefits of such policies are far from clear. In addition, fattened local government coffers need not translate into more or better public goods—a problem epitomized as China's "rich nation–poor people" dichotomy. Indeed, in something akin to the "free cash flow" agency problems Jensen (1986) documents in cash-rich US firms with unaccountable CEOs, fiscal revenues excess to basic spending commitments were dispensed by essentially unaccountable local officials. Cash-rich subnational governments, it is now widely recognized, actually provided very poor public goods and services. In response to the "rich nation–poor people" problem, further mid-1990s reforms shifted influence over bank lending from local to central government and party officials who, it was hoped, would more reliably allocate public funds to provide badly needed public goods. Gordon and Li point out that many local governments switched to raising revenues from land lease sales, but remark that this is an exhaustible source of revenues.

Finally, Li, in discussing this chapter, argues that local officials care more about promotions, which affect their long-term earnings, than about their current discretionary budgets, and are therefore guided primarily by party dictates from Beijing.

Nonetheless, China has grown far more impressively than its widely panned institutions would seem to warrant. The premise of Gordon and Li, that market socialism with Chinese characteristics has unappreciated efficiency, is thus clearly worth pursuing. To explore this premise, they develop a simple yet elegant model of local public finance under these reforms, assuming local bureaucrats maximize tax revenue net of spending on public goods. This is defensible, in that top local bureaucrats have substantial discretion over how their governments' revenues are spent once mandated public goods are provided. The model treats local governments as profit maximizing entities that can attract business activity by providing public goods more efficiently.

With competitive elections unlikely in the foreseeable future, Gordon and Li consider options that the CCP might consider should it wish to strengthen public sector efficiency, weighing the pros and cons of retail sales taxes, value-added taxes, and property taxes under market socialism. They further suggest user fees as an option. To the extent that local governments compete for users who value the public goods those fees finance, a more efficient local government—that is, one that provides more or better public goods for lower user fees—earns higher tax revenues, all else equal. However, they caution, user fees evoke inequality problems. Poorer families might not send their children to school if school user fees appear prohibitive, for example, planting the seeds of future economic and social problems.

Hukou reform, they argue, is most likely consistent with improved resource allocation. Because rural-to-urban and poor-to-rich region migration is already occurring, they argue that integrating migrants and educating their children should be a priority if the government wishes to avoid entrenching inequality problems. They suggest that hukou reform and the formalization of farm land ownership and sales would allow migrants to arrive better positioned to contribute to their new communities and the rationalization of land use in rural areas. After hukou reforms, the original Tiebout (1956) model would apply directly. In competing for taxpaying residents, local governments would be incentivized to provide whatever public goods residents were willing to pay for, and to provide them at the lowest possible cost in terms of taxes, fees, and other burdens.

I.4   Market Socialist Market Forces

China has made a substantial start toward full-fledged economic development under an economic model unfamiliar to Western economic historians. That system, market socialism with Chinese characteristics, is not "capitalism in a Mao suit," despite popular reports of China's alleged embrace of capitalism. Extensive regulatory, legal, and administrative reforms that evoke developed market economies' institutions are deliberately superficial. While market forces function, to an extent, these reforms cloak an economy whose commanding heights remain unambiguously subject to party control. That control flows through a traditional Chinese command and control mechanism, an unassailable civil service.

This system is delivering rapid economic growth, thereby restoring legitimacy to the CCP after disastrous misadventures such as the Anti-right Movement, the Great Leap Forward, and the Cultural Revolution, and troubling incidents such as the student protests of 1989 and increasingly commonplace labor unrest since 2000. The socialist and Chinese aspects of

China's economic system, at least as much as its market aspects, are seen by top party cadres as crucial to this success (Macgregor 2010).

The socialist foundation of China's economic system is the unconditional supremacy of the Chinese Communist Party. Consistent with Marxist-Leninist tradition, the party directs the law. Regulations, laws, and administrative rulings are applied in accordance with current party policy. Just as a party position corresponds directly to each key position in government, a party hierarchy parallels corporate governance in banks, SOEs, listed non-SOEs, hybrid enterprises, joint ventures, and sufficiently large private businesses. Party cells throughout business enterprises constitute parallel internal accountability systems to those established by enterprises themselves, keeping an enterprise's party secretary and party committee up-to-date and able to provide timely guidance to its CEO and board. Imported corporate governance regulations, mandating independent directors and the like, essentially ignore party involvement in enterprise governance.

The most uniquely Chinese characteristic of Market Socialism with Chinese Characteristics is the CCP's reliance on compensation and promotion incentives throughout an all-encompassing civil service to effect party policies. Presiding over a more prosperous village, township, city, SOE, non-SOE, province, or industry appears genuinely important in advancing a cadre's career. Luck may be imperfectly distinguished from good governance, and loyalty may too often trump competence; but a degree of genuine meritocracy is evident in empirical studies of promotions (Landry 2008), and party training programs are increasingly rigorous and technocratic. These developments may explain why China's seemingly weak institutions deliver better economic results than do other countries with seemingly equivalently weak institutions.

Market forces affect economic decisions, in that most prices are no longer centrally administered and SOEs no longer receive production quotas from central planners. Profits motivate the allocation of many resources and the organization of much economic activity; and entrepreneurs can set up new businesses where demand arises if they can find financial backing. But the ongoing proletarian dictatorship of the CCP and party oversight of human resource management decisions throughout the economy make China a severely qualified market economy. "Market" is rightly a mere adjective and only one-fifth of market socialism with Chinese characteristics.

High-income market economies depend on high-quality government to set limits, arbitrate disputes, and enforce rules (North 1991). Elsewhere, this entails checks and balances on officials to prevent abuse. China's leaders appear interested in developing such checks and balances, but while retaining the party's primacy. That this choice is feasible remains unclear.

This may not matter greatly for a time. China's economy is still catching up. Huge potential for growth requires capital only for more off-the-shelf technology to produce consumer goods, housing, and automobiles of acceptable quality for an expanding middle class. China validates the argument of Aghion, Meghir, and Vandenbussche (2006) that catch-up growth demands less of business leaders than does the sustained growth of a high-income economy. Passably talented party cadres can import foreign machinery, produce generic goods amid passably restrained corruption, and still greatly improve living standards for many years. But ultimately, China will find itself where South Korea and other nouveaux riches Asian economies now stand. Off-the-shelf is no longer good enough: Korean firms must now produce innovations—technologically superior cars, appliances, or electronics—to continue growing. That requires capital for innovators, rewards for creativity, a tolerance for disruptive innovation, and acceptance of the destruction of stagnant business so their resources can be reallocated to better uses (Acemoglu, Aghion, and Zilibotti 2006; Fogel, Morck, and Yeung 2008).

That the CCP OD might reliably do this raises reservation (Aghion, Meghir, and Vandenbussche 2006). Bureaucracies typically resist innovation and instability (Wilson 1989), yet accommodating both seems the essential element behind capitalism's sustained success (Schumpeter 1911). Can market socialism with Chinese characteristics do this too? Or must China's leaders decide between sustained economic growth and preserving the party's leading role?

Several chapters—chapter 2, chapter 3, and chapter 4—see this binary choice approaching. Allen et al. argue that, if China's leaders desire a permanent place for their country amid the ranks of developed economies, then embracing capitalism fully is likely to be the most attractive policy. They argue that more efficient capital allocation can be achieved if China privatizes its large banks so as to render their lending decisions meaningfully independent of government policy. They add full-fledged bankruptcy reform as another key element of the efficiency-enhancing policy because even thoroughly independently run banks' lending decisions will accord with officials' preferences, rather than economic fundamentals, if government and party officials continue determining whether or not, and how severely, the bankruptcy code is to be applied on a case-by-case basis. They echo Allen and Shen and Piotroski and Wong in concluding that China's stock markets remain incapable of allocating capital efficiently, and perceive this deficiency important even if banks are privatized because bank financing is less agile than stock market at capitalizing new industries.

Many in China's media and leadership seemingly concur, calling for "deeper structural reform." The chapters argue that this is the simpler path because it is a well-trodden one. Liberal economics and democratic politics are far from perfect: their stock markets and banking systems undergo occasional manias and panics, and their politics can go badly awry. But they are the only proven path to high living standards sustained over the long run (Fukuyama 1992).

Stock markets allocate capital by raising and lowering firms' share prices. Higher share prices, all else equal, let firms raise capital more cheaply (Tobin 1984). If a stock market is to allocate capital efficiently, investors must have access to low cost information about firms whose shares they must value (Rajan and Zingales 1998; Wurgler 2000). China's disclosure regime looks sophisticated, but Piotroski and Wong argue that actually leaves listed firms profoundly opaque because politics prevents uniform adherence to disclosure rules and consistent penalization for their violations. If stock markets are to promote prosperity, shareholders must peer into firms so they can put their money into ventures they deem profitable. Different firms' top managers provide different choices to shareholders in developed capitalist economies by devising unique, creative, and idiosyncratic strategies, products, and policies. If China's leaders desire more efficient capital allocation, they might loosen party over corporate decision making so individual firms can pursue genuinely new and different paths that shareholders can genuinely evaluate, and either endorse or spurn.

A thoroughgoing conversion to free markets is only one possible option. Moreover, as Allen and Shen stress, such a conversion would have to be epiphanic. The party would have to cede the economy's commanding heights, entrusting the allocation of capital, labor, and other resources to market forces, delegating the rule of law to an independent and impartial judiciary, and authorizing regulatory powers to an independent civil service. Even such basic concepts as a CCP OD promoting people through top positions in banks, companies, regulatory agencies, and governments would be at risk, relegating managers' careers to a market for talent.

Is acquiescence to capitalism only a matter of time? Looking forward, even if SOE banks are not privatized, Allen et al. foresee foreign banks and credit cooperatives as a potentially impartial source of loans to the hybrid sector. They also argue that China's growth might be furthered by US-style private equity and venture capital funds, also capable of capitalizing that sector. But none of their suggestions seem feasible as incremental adaptations within the current framework of market socialism with Chinese characteristics. For example, the rule that any business with more than three employees who are party members must accept a party cell would surely apply to venture capital or private equity financed firms. Venture capital and private equity fund would presumably also benefit from party secretaries, party committees, and party cells. Foreign banks, for example, must accept party cells and heed advice from party cadres. Fully privatized banks would still have party committees and party secretaries, and the party cannot presume to retain the economy's commanding heights without retaining control over the judiciary.

A more likely scenario, in the view of most authors in this volume, is that China will persist in forging its own path toward sustainable prosperity under the continuing guidance of the party. Market socialism with Chinese characteristics has delivered—so far. But Hayek's (1941, 1945) essential critique of socialism stands unrefuted: information and coordination costs rise faster with scale and complexity in a command and control economy than in a market economy.

Pistor describes a broader range of capitalisms than most Anglophone economists usually consider. For example, postwar France achieved three decades of dramatic recovery while scorning Anglo-Saxon naïvety about market forces. The French did almost everything "wrong." They entrusted the governance of large business enterprises to ex-civil servants, corporate investment decisions to industry-level ministry personnel, and corporate finance to SOE banks. While the system now shows growing strain—high youth and minority unemployment, aging capital assets, entitled public sector unions, and so on (Smith 2004)—France sustains a high per capita GDP and an enviable quality of life. Were China to attain similar success from a like system, much of its populace would celebrate.

But is this feasible? Postwar France was an open economy, a founding member of the precursor to today's European Union. Regulations, politicized approval processes, and the omnipresent helpful supervision of party cells and party secretaries perhaps allow the Chinese government latitude for poor policy that European integration denied France. Postwar France also had competitive democratic governments, with rival parties vocally criticizing each others' policies despite sharing a common corporatist vision, and a free press that enthusiastically skewered sufficiently egregious corruption, waste, or fraud. Though China now allows contested elections at the lowest levels of municipal government and tolerates a degree of media dissent unthinkable under Mao, it remains a one-party state with a controlled press. The postwar French civil service was a genuine meritocracy: entry depended only on academic evaluation, and success depended on performance. China seems intent on something along these lines too, but party loyalty still counts for much.

Allen et al. argue that other Chinese characteristics of China's institutional syncretism—Confucian behavioral norms, traditional dispute resolution, and cultural standards lauding family and reputation—also help explain China's success, and often substitute effectively for formal legal codes and regulations. However, this constrains economic activity to channels in which these traditional mechanisms operate, enhancing the importance of connections and kinship.

If aging Communist leaders increasingly overtly favor their "princeling" sons, a meritocracy may become unsustainable. China's leadership appears to appreciate problems arising from party "princelings" disgracing their stalwart parents, but business princelings growing to resemble preliberation bourgeois and aristocrats is a more difficult problem. If China develops fully in a single generation, as South Korea did, entrenched princelings might matter little. But Korea ultimately embraced the full complement of free market institutions, which China thus far declines. If China's heretofore successful economic trailblazing ultimately takes longer, unqualified business princelings could become an entrenched oligarchy more reminiscent of Latin America than of France or South Korea.

The end of the Cold War and the failure of third world Middle Ways, such as Latin American corporatism and India's License Raj, leaves variants of free market economics the only off-the-shelf choices on offer (Fukuyama 2011). Even the US financial crisis of 2008, despite evoking voluble calls for better regulation, inspires no visionary new alternatives to capitalism. Even France, hailing European integration and driven by fiscal necessity, is slowly shedding its postwar system. Pragmatism may well push China toward more genuine free market economics, and recognition of the information problems inherent in centralized bureaucratic control may well render market socialism's characteristics progressively less Chinese.

Institutional change often requires a crisis to dislodged entrenched interest groups (Olson 2000), so Allen et al. (see also Allen and Gale 2004, 2007) may well correctly foresee successive internal crisis reforming and strengthening of Chinese institutions. In this context, Xu's discussion of this chapter, which highlights China's relative immunity to both the 1997 and 2008 financial crises, may bode ill for China's long-term prosperity. Xu argues that a guarded embrace of capitalism might be warranted for stability's sake. But Olson (2000) argues that efforts to promote stability often inhibit efficient resource allocation, and thus has costs. Hsieh and Klenow (2009) estimate that China's mean firm-level total factor productivity would have grown 2 percent faster every year were Chinese firms relocated to the United States.

Nonetheless, a common denominator throughout the chapters in this volume is the overarching public policy objective of safeguarding uncontestable party control over the commanding heights of the Chinese economy. The chapters in this volume caution that a range of increasingly serious economic inefficiencies are likely if the party assigns an overarching value to the persistent stability of the current regulatory system. Alternative approaches to regulation merit consideration if the party wishes to enhance the economic efficiency of financial markets (Alen and Shen, chapter 3; Allen et al., chapter 2), the banking system (chapter 2), information intermediation (Piotroski and Wong, chapter 4), public goods provision (Chen, chapter 7), corporate governance (Pistor, chapter 1), labor allocation (Gordon and Li, chapter 8), and risk-taking (chapters 2 and 3; Bayoumi et al., chapter 6; Yang et al., chapter 5).

The chapters of this volume also largely concur that market socialism with Chinese characteristics is a surprisingly unique and innovative economic system that has achieved spectacular results. But a second common theme we distill from the chapters as a whole is the system's continuation risks increasingly inefficient resource allocation, rising social problems, and magnified instability in the impending future. Different chapters assess the pros and cons of different policy options, but a common theme emerges throughout: if China's leaders aspire to guide their country into ranks of high income economies, looking beyond market socialism with Chinese characteristics appears inevitable. The most straightforward option is convergence toward the proven, albeit intermittently fallible, genuinely market-driven systems of the advanced industrial democracies. But another possibility is that, bolstered by the past decades' successes, China will continue forging a unique path forward. Having embraced Deng Xiaoping's call to "let a few people get rich first," China's next step is genuinely inscrutable.

References

Acemoglu, Daron, Philippe Aghion, and Fabrizio Zilibotti. 2006. "Distance to Frontier, Selection, and Economic Growth." *Journal of the European Economic Association* 4 (1): 37–74.

Aghion, Philippe, Costas Meghir, and Jérôme Vandenbussche. 2006. "Distance to Frontier, Growth, and the Composition of Human Capital." *Journal of Economic Growth* 11 (2): 97–127.

Allen, Franklin, and Douglas Gale. 2004. "Financial Intermediaries and Markets." *Econometrica* 72:1023–61.

———. 2007. *Understanding Financial Crises, Clarendon Lectures in Finance.* Oxford: Oxford University Press.

Allen, Franklin, Jun Qian, and Meijun Qian. 2008. "China's Financial System: Past, Present, and Future." In *The Transition That Worked: Origins, Mechanism, and Consequence of China's Long Boom,* edited by L. Brandt and T. Rawski, 506–68. Cambridge: Cambridge University Press.

Baumol, William J. 1990. "Entrepreneurship: Productive, Unproductive, and Destructive." *The Journal of Political Economy* 98:893–921.

Bertrand, Marianne, Francis Kramarz, Antoinette Schoar, and David Thesmar. 2010. "Politicians, Firms, and the Political Business Cycle." MIT Sloan School Working Paper.

Chamon, Marcos, Kai Liu, and Eswar Prasad. 2010. "Income Uncertainty and Household Savings in China." NBER Working Paper no. 16565. Cambridge, MA: National Bureau of Economic Research, December.

Chamon, Marcos, and Eswar Prasad. 2008. "Why Are Saving Rates of Urban Households in China Rising?" NBER Working Paper no. 14546. Cambridge, MA: National Bureau of Economic Research, December.

Coase, Ronald H. 1937. "The Nature of the Firm." *Economica* 4:386–405.

Deng, Yongheng, Randall Morck, Jing Wu, and Bernard Yeung. 2011. "Monetary and Fiscal Stimuli, Ownership Structure, and China's Housing Market." NBER Working Paper no. 16871. Cambridge, MA: National Bureau of Economic Research, March.

Easterly, William. 2006. *The White Man's Burden: Why the West's Efforts To Aid the Rest Have Done So Much Ill and So Little Good.* New York: Penguin.

Edwards, Sebastian. 2010. *Left Behind: Latin America and the False Promise of Populism.* Chicago: University of Chicago Press.

Fan, Joseph P. H., T. J. Wong, and Tianyu Zhang. 2007. "Politically Connected CEOs, Corporate Governance and Post-IPO Performance of China's Partially Privatized Firms." *Journal of Financial Economics* 84 (3): 330–57.

Fogel, Kathy, Randall Morck, and Bernard Yeung. 2008. "Big Business Stability and Economic Growth: Is What's Good for General Motors Good for America?" *Journal of Financial Economics* 89:83–108.

Freeman, Richard. 2006. "The Great Doubling: The Challenge of the New Global Labor Market." Harvard University Working Paper.

Fukuyama, Francis. 1992. *The End of History and the Last Man.* Toronto: Maxwell Macmillan.

———. 2011. *The Origins of Political Order: From Prehuman Times to the French Revolution.* New York: Farrar, Straus and Giroux.

Garnaut, Ross, Song Ligang, and Yao Yang. 2006. "Impact and Significance of State-Owned Enterprise Restructuring in China." *The China Journal* 55:35–63.

Gordon, Roger, and Wei Li. 1995. "The Change in Productivity of Chinese State Enterprises." *Journal of Productivity Analysis* 6 (1): 5–26.

Haber, Stephen. 2000. *Political Institutions and Economic Growth in Latin America: Essays in Policy, History, and Political Economy.* Stanford: Hoover Institution Press.

Hayek, Friedrich. 1941. *The Pure Theory of Capital.* Chicago: University of Chicago Press.

———. 1945. "The Use of Knowledge in Society." *American Economic Review* 35:519–30.

Heilbrunn, John. 2005. "Oil and Water? Elite Politicians and Corruption in France." *Comparative Politics* 37 (3): 277–96.

Hsieh, Chang-Tai, and Peter Klenow. 2009. "Misallocation and Manufacturing TFP in China and India." *Quarterly Journal of Economics* 124:1403–48.

Huang, Yasheng. 2008. *Capitalism with Chinese Characteristics.* New York: Cambridge University Press.

Jacques, Martin. 2009. *When China Rules the World: The Rise of the Middle Kingdom and the End of the Western World.* London: Penguin.

Jensen, Michael. 1986. "Agency Costs of Free Cash Flow, Corporate Finance, and Takeovers." *American Economic Review* 76 (2): 323–29.

Jin, Li, and Stewart C. Myers. 2006. "R2 around the World: New Theory and New Tests." *Journal of Financial Economics* 79:257–92.

Johnson, Simon, Rafael La Porta, Florencio Lopez-de-Silanes, and Andrei Shleifer. 2000. "Tunneling." *American Economic Review* 90 (2): 22–27.

Khanna, Tarun. 2008. *Billions of Entrepreneurs: How China and India Are Reshaping Their Future and Yours.* Cambridge, MA: Harvard Business School Press.

Knight, Frank. 1921. *Risk, Uncertainty and Profit.* Boston: Houghton Mifflin Company.

Kramarz, Francis, and David Thesmar. 2006. "Social Networks in the Boardroom." HEC Paris Working Paper.

Kuznets, Simon. 1955. "Economic Growth and Income Inequality." *American Economic Review* 45 (2): 1–28.

La Porta, Rafael, Florencio Lopez-de-Silanes, and Andrei Shleifer. 2002. "Government Ownership of Banks." *Journal of Finance* 57 (1): 265–301.

Landry, Pierre. 2008. *Decentralized Authoritarianism in China: The Communist Party's Control of Local Elites in the Post-Mao Era.* Cambridge: Cambridge University Press.

Lequiller, François, and Derek Blades. 2006. *Understanding National Accounts.* Paris: Organization for Economic Cooperation and Development (OECD).

Li, Hongbin, Lingsheng Meng, Qian Wang, and Li-An Zhou. 2008. "Political Connections, Financing and Firm Performance: Evidence from Chinese Private Firms." *Journal of Development Economics* 87 (2): 283–99.

Li, Hongbin, and Li-An Zhou. 2005. "Political Turnover & Economic Performance: The Disciplinary Role of Personnel Control in China." *Journal of Public Economics* 89 (9/10): 1743–62.

Li, Wei. 1997. "The Impact of Economic Reforms on the Performance of Chinese State-Owned Enterprises." *Journal of Political Economy* 105 (5): 1080–106.

Lü, Xiaobo. 2000. *Cadres and Corruption: The Organizational Involution of the Chinese Communist Party.* Stanford, CA: Stanford University Press.

Macdonald, James. 2003. *A Free Nation Deep in Debt: The Financial Roots of Democracy.* New York: Farrar, Straus and Giroux.

Macgregor, Richard. 2010. *The Party: The Secret World of China's Communist Rules.* New York: HarperCollins.

Maddison, Angus, and Harry X. Wu. 2008. "Measuring China's Economic Performance." *World Economics* 9 (2): 13–44.

Modigliani, Franco, and Richard Brumberg. 1954. "Utility Analysis and the Consumption Function: An Interpretation of Cross-Section Data." In *Post-Keynesian Economics,* edited by K. Kurihara, 388–436. New Brunswick: Rutgers University Press.

Morck, Randall. 2011. "Finance and Governance in Developing Economics." NBER Working Paper no. 16870. Cambridge, MA: National Bureau of Economic Research, March.

Morck, Randall, and Masao Nakamura. 2007. "Business Groups and the Big Push: Meiji Japan's Mass Privatization and Subsequent Growth." *Enterprise and Society* 8 (3): 543–601.

Morck, Randall, Daniel Wolfenzon, and Bernard Yeung. 2005. "Corporate Governance, Economic Entrenchment, and Growth." *Journal of Economic Literature* 43 (3): 655–720.

Morck, Randall, and Fan Yang. 2011. "The Shanxi Banks." In *Origins of Shareholder Advocacy,* edited by Jonathan Koppell, chapter 5. London: Palgrave Macmillan.

Morck, Randall, Bernard Yeung, and Wayne Yu. 2000. "The Information Content of Stock Markets: Why Do Emerging Markets Have Synchronous Stock Price Movements?" *Journal of Financial Economics* 58 (1): 215–60.

Murphy, Kevin, Andrei Shleifer, and Robert W. Vishny. 1989. "Industrialization and the Big Push." *Journal of Political Economy* 97 (5): 1003–26.

———. 1991. "The Allocation of Talent: Implications for Growth." *Quarterly Journal of Economics* 106 (2): 503–30.

Nee, Victor, and Sonja Opper. 2012. *Capitalism from Below: Markets and Institutional Change in China.* Harvard University Press, forthcoming.

North, Douglass. 1991. "Institutions." *Journal of Economic Perspectives* 5 (1): 97–112.

Olson, Mancur. 2000. *Power and Prosperity: Outgrowing Communist and Capitalist Dictatorships.* New York: Basic Books.

Prasad, Eswar. 2009. "Rebalancing Growth in Asia." NBER Working Paper no. 15169. Cambridge, MA: National Bureau of Economic Research, July.

Rajan, Raghuram, and Luigi Zingales. 1998. "Financial Dependence and Growth." *American Economic Review* 88 (3): 559–86.

Rosenstein-Rodan, Paul. 1943. "Problems of Industrialisation of Eastern and South-Eastern Europe." *Economic Journal* 53 (210/1): 202–11.

Schumpeter, Joseph. 1911. *Theorie der Wirtschaftlichen Entwicklung.* Leipzig: Duncker & Humblot.

Smith, Timothy. 2004. *France in Crisis: Welfare, Inequality, and Globalization since 1980.* Cambridge: Cambridge University Press.

Spence, Jonathan D. 1999. *The Search for Modern China.* New York: Norton.

Stigler, George. 1971. "Theory of Economic Regulation." *Bell Journal of Economics* 3 (1): 3–18.

Tiebout, Charles. 1956. "A Pure Theory of Local Expenditures." *Journal of Political Economy* 64:416–24.

Tobin, James. 1984. "On the Efficiency of the Financial System." *Lloyd's Bank Review* 153:14–15.

Veblen, Thorstein. 1921. *The Engineers and the Price System.* New York: Huebsch.

Wang, Xiaolu, and Wing Thye-Woo. 2011. "The Size and Distribution of Hidden Household Income in China." *Asian Economic Papers* 10 (1): 1–26.

Wei, Shang-Jin, and Xiaobo Zhang. 2011. "The Competitive Saving Motive: Evidence from Rising Sex Ratios and Savings Rates in China." *Journal of Political Economy* 119 (3): 511–64.

Wilson, James. 1989. *Bureaucracy: What Government Agencies Do and Why They Do It.* New York: Basic.

Wu, Harry. 2006. "The Chinese GDP Growth Rate Puzzle: How Fast Has the Chinese Economy Grown?" Hong Kong Polytechnic University Business School Working Paper.

Wurgler, Jeffrey. 2000. "Financial Markets and the Allocation of Capital." *Journal of Financial Economics* 58 (1–2): 187–214.

Xu, Chenggang. 2011. "The Fundamental Institutions of China's Reforms and Development." *Journal of Economic Literature* 49 (4): 1076–151.

Yang, Jisheng. 2008. *Tombstone: A Record of the Great Chinese Famine of the 1960s.* Hong Kong: Cosmos Books.

Yergin, Daniel, and Joseph Stanislaw. 1998. *The Commanding Heights: The Battle between Government and the Marketplace That Is Remaking the Modern World.* New York: Simon & Schuster.

Yu, Wei. 2009. "Party Control in China's Listed Firms." PhD diss. The Chinese University of Hong Kong.

I

Financial System and Its Governance

The Governance of China's Finance

Katharina Pistor

1.1 Introduction

This chapter discusses the governance of China's finances. It starts from two basic premises: first, that governance of finance can take multiple forms; and second, that the adoption of governance techniques that are common elsewhere does not necessarily imply that they will replace alternative modes of governance already in existence or designed to complement such techniques. Instead, adopting widely accepted governance techniques may serve to signal compliance but disguise the real allocation of control rights and their usage. Distinguishing between real and nominal governance requires closer inspection of governance regimes that transcends formal checklists, and instead probes more deeply into the configuration of power and influence and the channels through which such power is exercised.

This contribution suggests that China has largely mimicked formal governance regimes common in Western market economies. However, this regime remains largely incomplete as control rights that flow from equity positions are partitioned among different stakeholders. The chapter therefore explores an alternate mode of governing finance, namely human resource management (HRM), which uses control rights over the career path of top-level financial cadres. The importance of HRM for governing China's economy, including its financial system, is well understood within China. Outsiders,

Katharina Pistor is the Michael I. Sovern Professor of Law at Columbia Law School.

I would like to thank Hong Zhang for excellent research assistance and members of the NBER "Capitalizing China" project for comments and suggestions on an earlier version of this chapter. For acknowledgments, sources of research support, and disclosure of the author's material financial relationships, if any, please see http://www.nber.org/chapters/c12073.ack.

however, are more focused on governance structures that resemble those they are familiar with. Therefore, these are the primary addressees of this contribution. To document the extent of HRM in China's system of financial governance, this chapter makes use of a newly created database of current and previous top-level administrators and board members in key financial organizations to suggest that their career path through China's financial system is far from random; instead, financial cadres tend to be extensively groomed at different financial organizations within the state apparatus before they were appointed to financial intermediaries with greater formal autonomy, such as commercial banks. Based on secondary sources the chapter asserts that HRM is conducted by China's Communist Party (CCP) and that its reach and sophistication has increased rather than decreased over time. Indeed, one could argue that HRM has become a substitute to direct state control, which was still pervasive in China until the end of the 1990s, and a complement to the new rule-based formal mechanisms of control. The CCP's control over HR management intensified as the state apparatus loosened its direct control over the financial system, separated out different regulatory functions from the central bank's unitary system of control, and sold important stakes in formerly state-owned banks to nonstate, including foreign, investors. The HRM appears to work effectively for China's domestic system as a means for maintaining control over and stabilizing the financial system. Yet, it remains to be seen how effective it can be employed for governing China's exposure to global finance.

The chapter is organized as follows. Section 1.2 describes the formal changes in China's financial system over the past decade and asks whether the system of controls thus established has given rise to a coherent governance regime. Section 1.3 describes an alternate governance regime, one that relies less on formal mechanisms of control and instead uses controls over the careers of individuals who serve in the financial system, both in government agencies and in prominent financial intermediaries. It uses secondary sources to sketch the evolution of this system over the same period during which China introduced legal and regulatory means of governance. This evidence suggests that it would be wrong to assume that the withering away of direct state control of China's finances has set the country on a path toward convergence with standard formal governance regimes found in the West. Against this background section 1.4 presents data on patterns of China's human resource allocation within China's financial system. The data are comprised of information on 155 persons who occupy positions as top administrators at regulatory agencies, including China's central bank, as well as positions on the management or supervisory boards of major financial intermediaries. The chapter employs simple network analysis to show that most of these office holders either occupy important positions at other financial organizations concurrently or have held such positions prior to their current one. The pattern of affiliation that emerges from these personal ties differs from the pattern of hierarchical control rights that follows from the formal lines of authority. Network analysis reveals the centrality of organizations and individuals within China's HRM governance regime. However, our data also suggest that the number of people occupying management or supervisory board seats at major financial intermediaries relative to nonaffiliate board members is declining at intermediaries with more diversified ownership structures and greater exposure to global markets. This raises the question whether China will be able to rely on HRM as a key component for governing its financial system as more entities diversify globally—a topic that will be discussed in section 1.5. Section 1.6 places China's governance of finance in comparative perspective by drawing parallels, but also distinctions, to France and Japan. Section 1.7 concludes with some normative considerations about this particular regime of financial governance.

1.2   The Formalization of China's Financial System

China has been widely criticized for postponing reforms of its financial sector until well into the late 1990s—with some observers arguing that this failure might derail the success of China's economic reform project (Lardy 2002). However, over the past decade China has made major strides in overhauling its financial system. Today the financial sector's formal governance regime resembles in many aspects that found in developed Western market economies and can be described in conventional functional terms as follows: the Peoples' Bank of China (PBOC), China's central bank, is charged with monetary and exchange rate policies. Several new regulatory agencies were established, such as the China Banking Regulatory Commission (CBRC), which exercises oversight over China's banking sector; the China Securities Regulatory Commission (CSRC), which overseas stock exchanges and regulates the issuance and trading of securities on these changes; and the China Insurance Regulatory Commission (CIRC), which overseas the insurance sector. Formally, the PBOC and the three major regulators are subordinate to the State Council, the country's executive with the top officers at each of these entities having vice-ministerial status in China's bureaucratic hierarchy. As elsewhere, a single bank can simultaneously be subject to oversight by more than one regulatory agency: the PBOC window guidance policy, the CBRC for prudential supervision, and the CSRC's enforcement of securities regulations. China instituted these changes before the problems of a functional division of labor among different financial regulators became apparent in the context of the global crisis.[1] Notably, China had an intensive debate about whether carving out functional regulators from the unitary

---

1. For an overview of this debate and related reforms in the United Kingdom, but not the United States, see Schooner, Mandanis and Taylor (2003, 317).

structure of the PBOC was the right way to go[2] before CBRC was established in 2003, or whether it would be preferable to retain consolidated oversight and control over the financial system. In fact, PBOC has continued to be involved in key areas of banking supervision, not the least the preparation of BOC, CCB, and ICBC for their initial public offerings in 2005 and 2006 (ACFB 2007)—and presumably in other strategic decisions as well.

China has also begun an ownership transformation of the largest banks in the country, including three of the "big four" (ABC, BOC, CCB, and ICBC) as well as of other banks, such as the Bank of Communications (BComm), and China Development Bank (CDB). Cumulatively these banks control about 70 percent of China's bank assets (ACFB 2007). However, none of these banks have been fully transferred to private ownership. Table 1.1 details the stakes held by the five largest owners of those banks that are publicly traded and for which, therefore, ownership data are publicly available. Consistent with the capital structure of these banks, equity stakes are designated as A or H shares indicating whether they are traded on the Hong Kong Stock Exchange (H shares) or on one of the major domestic exchanges (A shares).

As can be seen, government ownership is fairly centralized in the hands of Central Hui Jin Investment Ltd. (hereinafter Hui Jin) and the Ministry of Finance (MoF) as the largest blockholders. Hui Jin and MoF are by no means the only state entities with substantial ownership stakes. Others include the National Council of the Social Social Security Fund (NCSSF), which holds as much as 15.3 percent in H shares in ICBC. Moreover, several state-owned enterprises hold sizable stakes in these companies.[3]

The role of more than one state or state-controlled entities as the dominant owner of China's banks is noteworthy, because their coexistence obfuscates the state's use of ownership as a means of controlling them. For wholly state-owned enterprises in the nonfinancial sector the new Law on State Owned Assets (SOA Law)[4] resolves the potential conflict among several state-controlled entities in the exercise of ownership rights, such as the election of management and supervisory board members by delegating this task to a single agent: the State-owned Asset Supervision and Administration Commission (SASAC). However, this law does not apply to financial companies. Instead, for the financial sector China has invented a new version of the famous separation of ownership and control first described by Berle and Means (1932); namely, the separation of the right to appoint the officers

2. See http://business.sohu.com/20090106/n261587587.shtml (in Chinese).

3. HKSCC does not represent another blockholder; the acronym stands for the Hong Kong Securities Clearing Company, which serves as a street name for other investors, each of which is likely to hold a much smaller stake than the combined shareholding of HKSCC indicated in the table.

4. The law was promulgated by the National People's Congress on October 28, 2008 and became effective on May 1, 2009.

Table 1.1 Ownership of China's largest banks

	Five largest shareholders by stake (% of all outstanding shares is given in parentheses)				
	1	2	3	4	5
Agricultural Bank of China Limited (as of January 2009 when ABC completed its reorganization and incorporated in form of stock company under the Company Law of the PRC)	Ministry of Finance 50.00	Hui Jin 50.00			
Bank of China Limited (H share Code 3988; A share Code 601988) (updated as of June 30, 2009)[a]	Hui Jin 67.53 (A shares)	HKSCC Nominees Limited 24.64 (H shares)	National Council for Social Security Fund PRC 3.30 (H shares)	Li Ka Shing[b] 1.21 (H shares)	Asian Development Bank 0.20 (H shares)
Bank of Communications Co., Ltd. (H share Code 3328; A share Code 601328) (updated as of June 30, 2009)[c]	Ministry of Finance 26.48 (6.12 H shares; 20.36 A shares)[d]	HKSCC Nominees Limited 21.91 (H shares)	HSBC 18.60 (H shares)	Capital Airports Holding Company SOE[e] 2.01 (A shares)	State Grid Asset Management Co. Limited SOE[e] 0.92 (A shares)
China Construction Bank Corporation (H share Code 939; A share Code 601939) (updated as of June 30, 2009)[f]	Hui Jin 57.08 (57.02% H and 0.06% A)[g]	HKSCC Nominees Limited 26.34 (H shares)	Bank of America 10.95[h] (H shares)	Baosteel Group[e] 1.28 (H shares)	Reca Investment Limited 0.34 (H shares)

(continued)

Table 1.1 (continued)

	Five largest shareholders by stake (% of all outstanding shares is given in parentheses)				
	1	2	3	4	5
Industrial and Commercial Bank of China Limited (H share Code 1398; A share Code 601398) (updated as of June 30, 2009)[i]	Hui Jin 35.4 (A shares, subject to selling restrictions)[j]	Ministry of Finance 35.3 (A shares, subject to selling restrictions)	HKSCC Nominees Limited 15.3 (H shares)	National Council for Social Security Fund PRC 4.2 (H shares)	Goldman Sachs 3.9 (H shares)

[a] The total number of outstanding shares is 253,839,162,009, of which the 76,020,251,269 shares are H shares, and 177,818,910,740 shares are A shares (listed at Shanghai Stock Exchange).

[b] Li Ka Shing is a famous HK billionaire, wealthy individual.

[c] The total number of outstanding shares is 48,994,383,703, of which the 23,064,468,136 shares are H shares, and 25,929,915,567 are A shares (listed at Shanghai Stock Exchange).

[d] Out of the 12,974,982,648 shares that MoF owns, all the 9,974,982,648 A shares are subject to selling restrictions.

[e] SOE denotes state-owned enterprise.

[f] The total number of outstanding shares is 233,689,084,000, of which the 224,689,084,000 are H shares, and 9,000,000,000 are A shares (listed at Shanghai Stock Exchange).

[g] In July 2009, Jianyin (Hui Jin's wholly owned subsidiary) transferred all of the H shares it originally owned to Hui Jin for free, and thus increased Hui Jin's shareholding percentage in CCB by 8.85 percent (i.e., 20,692,250,000 H shares subject to selling restrictions).

[h] Bank of America cannot sell those shares without CCB's written approval until August 29, 2011.

[i] The total number of authorized shares is 334,018,850,026, of which the 83,056,501,962 shares are H shares, and 250,962,348,064 are A shares (listed at Shanghai Stock Exchange).

[j] The "selling restrictions" refer to the restrictions imposed on the shareholders for reselling these shares on the market. These restrictions were imposed as part of the "share reform," which was launched in 2005 in China with the purpose of converting the nontradable state-owned shares in public companies into tradable shares, though subject to certain selling restrictions. Typically these restrictions impose certain lockup periods.

and board members of financial intermediaries from the economic costs and benefits associated with holding shares in such entities.

For purposes of illustration, take the example of Hui Jin, which next to the Ministry of Finance is the most important shareholder of China's dominant banks. Hui Jin was established in 2003 as a subsidiary of the State Administration for Foreign Exchange (SAFE), which in turn is an administrative agency subordinate to the PBOC. Hui Jin was authorized by the State Council—that is, by China's executive—to make "equity investments in major state-owned financial enterprises, and . . . , to the extent of its capital contribution, [to] exercise the rights and perform the obligations as an investor on behalf of the State in accordance with applicable laws."[5] In 2007, Hui Jin, which is organized as a limited liability company, became a wholly owned subsidiary of China Investment Corporation (CIC), China's newly established sovereign wealth fund. To this end, MoF issued special treasury bonds that were used to acquire Hui Jin from PBOC; subsequently Hui Jin was transferred to CIC for a price of US$70 billion; that is, almost one-third of CIC's initial capital of US$200 billion (Martin 2008). As the parent and sole shareholder of Hui Jin one would expect CIC to control the appointment of Hui Jin's management and supervisory board members. This, however, is not the case. Instead, Hui Jin's charter stipulates that the State Council exercises these rights[6]—irrespective of the fact that the State Council never held any shares in Hui Jin and CIC is now its parent.

This separation of control rights from ownership suggests that ownership is not conclusive in determining who actually exercises control rights over a state-owned entity. Indeed, even the contents of Hui Jin's charter is misleading in this regard, because ultimately the CCP appoints top officials to financial entities—including regulators, wholly and partially state-owned entities. The CCP's powers are not mentioned in Hui Jin's or any of the banks' charters; however, neither would it be appropriate to relegate them to "informal" means of control.[7] Within China the CCP continues to be recognized as an integral part of a dualistic power structure, with the state apparatus and the CCP forming two separate yet interlinked hierarchies that use different mechanisms of control (Naughton 2008). Whereas the state is associated with control rights exercised by way of ownership and administrative lines of control, the CCP controls the career paths of individuals in

---

5. See the statement on Hui Jin's web page available at www.huijin-inv.cn.

6. See excerpts from Hui Jin's articles of incorporation available at its website at http://www.huijin-inv.cn/hjen/governance/governance_2008.html?var1=Governance (last visited August 24, 2009).

7. A tradition has evolved in the new institutional economics literature to distinguish between formal and informal institutions depending on whether they are promulgated by the state or not. See North (1990). This distinction, however, can be misleading when applied to countries such as China with more complex power relations. For a critique of the formal-informality divide see Pistor (2006).

the party, the state, and in organizations that are critical to the party or the state (Huang 1996; Shih 2008).

1.3   China's Other Governance Regime: The CCP's Human Resource Management

A critical component of financial governance in China is the CCP's management of human resource. The CCP controls key positions in government, administration, and government-controlled sectors in the economy. This function has evolved over time and has been exercised via different channels. Critically, and perhaps counterintuitively, given China's economic rise and embrace of market mechanisms in many aspects of economic organization, it has not diminished in recent time. Indeed, the CCP's power of the financial sector by way of HRM seems to have increased arguably as a way of ensuring continued control over finance given its central role to economic, social, and political stability.

The role of the CCP in controlling key personnel is well established; in an attempt to bolster its legitimacy in China's evolving governance structure, the CCP has made some of its operations more transparent and has promulgated a set of "Regulations on Selection and Appointment of Party and Government Leading Cadres" (Bo 2004; Burns 1994). These regulations are not published, but are widely circulated among administrators and managers in government, and in practice they operate as binding rules. Neither the corporate law nor the charters of the major banks refer to these rules. Nonetheless, the CCP rules explicitly state that the CCP selects and appoints the chairman, vice-chairmen, president and vice presidents of the Bank of China and the equivalent positions at the other banks, as well as top management at CIC, China's sovereign wealth fund (established in 2007).

In order to understand the importance of CCP's HRM as a means of governing China's finance it is useful to analyze how the CCP's governance of human resources has coevolved with the formal changes in China's financial system just described. At the end of 1998 the basic governance structure of China's finances had not changed much from 1980 (Shih 2008). Consistent with the coexistence of state and party structures linked by the general oversight of the Standing Committee of the Politburo, state and party governance formed two partly overlapping vertical governance regimes: the State Council formally controlled the PBOC, which in turn controlled the four state banks; they in turn oversaw their own. There were no specialized regulators so that the PBOC acted as lender, regulator, and de facto owner in one. Parallel to this structure, the CCP imposed its own control mechanism in the form of Central Discipline and Inspection Commission (CDIC), which was subordinate to the Central Committee. It gained control over staffing the members of the disciplinary party committees found at each of the state-owned banks; local party committees exercised similar powers over local branches of the major banks. In addition to disciplinary supervision, the CCP appointed the PBOC's key management personnel and the PBOC in turn appointed the leadership at the major banks (Shih 2008).

This structure optimized centralized control of the CCP but did not easily accommodate a more differentiated division of labor among various functional regulators (such as the CBRC), which were established in China over the past decade; nor could it easily fit an ownership structure that included nonstate owners, including foreign investors. The latter was deemed important for China to comply with the opening of financial services under the General Agreement on Trade in Services (GATS), but also to impose greater financial discipline on the banks and expose them to foreign expertise (Allen 2005; Leigh and Podpiera 2006).

The East Asian financial crisis served as a wake-up call to those concerned with the governance of finance around the world, including politicians and party leaders in China. China was not directly affected by the crisis, because it had insulated itself from global markets by capital controls, tight exchange rate management, and a state-controlled financial system. Nonetheless, leaders in China quickly recognized the risk of financial destabilization to the Chinese economy and by implication, to the stability of the political regime,[8] and sought to address these concerns at the same time as they were embarking on reforming the financial system, which had seriously lagged behind institutional and governance reforms (Lardy 2002).

In response to these challenges, the CCP began to tighten its control over the financial sector (Heilmann 2005). The vehicle for this strategy was the Central Financial Work Commission (CFWC), a newly established body that was directly and exclusively answerable to the CCP's Central Committee. Wen Jiabao, vice-premier and Politburo member, served as its chairman. The changes implied that the CCP gained direct control over appointing and dismissing key personnel at China's four largest banks—powers that previously had been vested with the PBOC. Now, key personnel were nominated by the banks and approved by the CFWC (Shih 2008). In the words of Heilmann, who conducted numerous interviews in China to establish the role of the CFWC:

> After the establishment of the CFWC, the appointment procedures and authority relationships changed fundamentally. Thereafter, the CFWC, in cooperation with the financial institution and state regulatory body concerned, actively investigated, appraised and appointed financial cadres who were deemed loyal to the Party centre and professionally qualified to take leading positions. The headquarters of financial institutions still recommended persons to become senior managers. But they now had to submit and justify their choice to the CFWC for approval. The final deci-

8. The intimate connection between financial, economic, and political stability was forcefully demonstrated by the case of Indonesia during the East Asian financial crisis. It let to riots and brought down an autocratic regime under President Suharto.

sion rested with the CFWC. . . . Moreover, the CFWC installed vertical leadership authority by newly established full Party committees between the national and subnational management levels. (Heilmann 2005)

These powers did not make the CFWC a hands-on manager; its own rules prohibited it from taking up such a role. However, by appointing all members of the newly created supervisory boards of banks and other financial intermediaries that were corporatized at the time, the CFWC was able to place 200 members it had selected on sixteen newly established supervisory boards in 2000 alone (Heilmann 2005, 12).

The CFWC's control over human resources extended also to key regulators. Between 1998 and 2003 the CFWC controlled the appointment of senior executives across all key institutions in finance, including regulators, administrative agencies, and banks (see table 1.2).

The CFWC was disbanded in 2003 and its more regulatory functions were transferred to the newly created bank regulator, the CBRC—formally a spin-off from PBOC. However, its operation has left a decisive mark on the management of China's financial sector. First, CFWC was deeply involved in the establishment and staffing of CBRC and the new banking supervision law was prepared by it (Heilmann 2005). Indeed, of the CBRC's sixteen new departments within CBRC, only five were transferred from the PBOC, while eleven had previously been housed inside the CFWC (Heilmann 2005). Similarly, the newly appointed top officials at CBRC had all previously been members of CFWC.

More generally, the formal dissolution of CFWC—or perhaps rather its transformation into a regulatory body—did not put an end to party control over HRM in China's financial sector. Instead, CFWC's HRM functions were transferred to the CCP Central Organization Department (COD)—much to the critique of China's financial press.[9] The COD now exercises the power to appoint senior executives at China's national state supervisory organs (PBOC, CBRC, CSRC, CIRC) and ten national financial companies under central administration, including the big four national commercial banks, the three policy banks, Bank of Communications, Everbright Group and CITIC Group (formerly the China International Trust and Investment Corporation) (Heilmann 2005), and more recently CIC. Appointment powers for top cadres at the PBOC and the three functional regulators were delegated to CCP committees at these organizations. Moreover, the appointment of lower level appointees at these organizations' regional branch offices were transferred to corresponding local party committees (Heilmann 2005, 18). Interestingly, the administrative heads of the three regulatory agencies no longer combine the roles of party secretary and state or bureaucratic leader; instead a greater functional division was implemented, whereby the "number 1" at these agencies with the power to exercise overall strategic lead-

9. Heilmann quotes Caijing, China's leading financial paper, as bemoaning the lack of profound reform reflected in this decision. See Heilmann (2005, 17, fn. 59).

Table 1.2   CFWC's Human Resource Management (1998–2003)

National Financial Institutions, from vice-ministerial level (formally appointed by COD) down to the deputy bureau chief level	National commercial financial institutions with control over senior executives and supervisory board members	National commercial financial institutions with control over senior executives only
PBOC	BOC	Minsheng Bank
CSRC	CCB	Minsheng Securities
IRC	ICBC	Minsheng Life Insurance
	ABC	Merchants Bank
	CDB	Sci-Tech Securities
		Minzu Securities
	China Import Export Bank	Galaxy Securities
	4 AMC	Government Securities Depository Trust & Clearing Co.
	CITIC Group	Chung Mei Trust & Investment
	Everbright Group	
	Bank of Communications	
	People's Insurance	
	China Life Insurance	
	China Reinsurance	
	China Export & Credit Insurance	

Source: Heilmann (2005).

ership is now appointed by a CCP committee, but does not operate simultaneously as the representative of the party within the organization. Instead, this function is exercised by the "number 2" with the mandate to conduct human resource management (Naughton 2008). Rather than indicating a diminished role of the CCP at these entities, it can also be viewed as a sign for the increasing importance attributed by the party to HRM.

The continuing pervasive role of the CCP in China's financial system by way of controlling HRM should leave its marks on appointment patterns and promotions of key individuals. We will explore this in the following section, which introduces a new data set and brings to bear basic network analysis to explore the governance of China's finances.

1.4   Scale and Scope of the CCP's HRM: Empirical Evidence

This section presents empirical evidence on the scale and scope of the CCP's management of human resources over China's finances. To this end we have collected data on the key positions in management and supervision at China's major regulators and financial intermediaries. For each person who was identified as a current top-level administrator at a regulatory entity (PBOC, CBRC, CSRC, etc.), or as a member of either the management board or the supervisory board of a financial intermediary (BOC, CCB,

ICBC, ABC, etc.), we recorded his (and occasionally her) concurrent position at other entities as well as positions that person has held previously. These data were hand collected using information made available on the websites and annual reports of the organizations in question.[10] The database includes 155 people and a total of 41 entities or organizations with which they are or have been affiliated. Initially, we included thirteen entities in the analysis: PBOC, SAFE, CBRC, CSRC, CIC, Hui Jin, BOC, CCB, ICBC, ABC, Import Export Bank (IEB), BComm, and China Development Bank (CDB). We coded all top-level executives and board members at these entities and traced their current and previous ties to other entities throughout China's financial system. Indeed, we also included other important government positions, such as governor or vice-governor of a province. However, we did not include in our data set previous postings at multilateral institutions, such as the World Bank or the Asian Development Bank.

We use this database to establish the imprint of HRM on the governance of China's finances. As posited earlier, HRM can be regarded as an alternative governance regime to the formal control structure that China has established over the past decade. In order to establish the relation between formal control structures rooted in legally and administratively established lines of authority on one hand, and the scope of HRM within China's financial system on the other, we compare the governance structures of these two alternative regimes. Figure 1.1 depicts the governance regime that emerges from the analysis of formal lines of control; that is, ownership relations and lines of administrative or regulatory authority. It includes the largest owners of the banks listed in table 1.1 (except for HKSCC) as well as regulatory and supervisory authorities embedded in China's legal infrastructure.

The picture that emerges is a bifurcated governance structure headed by the State Council and divided into monetary and exchange rate policy represented by PBOC and SAFE on one hand (at the far right side of the figure) and financial intermediation, represented by banks and their regulators on the other. The central role of Hui Jin as a major owner in China's "big 4" is readily apparent. Contrast this picture with the one found in figure 1.2, which depicts the relations among the same entities, but this time the ties among entities are not determined by ownership or administrative lines of authority; instead, they depict interlocking positions held by senior executives or board members at two or more entities.

Unlike the first picture, the PBOC now takes a much more central role as a result of its many interlocking senior positions with the CCP Committees,[11] SAFE, CBRC, and CSRC, as well as CIC. Hui Jin remains a central

---

10. The full database names and affiliations, including explanations for the role of different organizations, is on file with the author.

11. Note that all top level officials at PBOC concurrently serve on PBOC's CCP Commission. In other words, the division of labor between strategic and human resource management described earlier is absent at the PBOC.

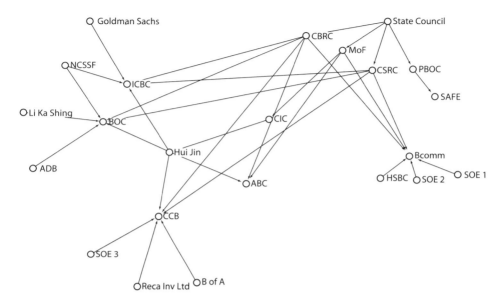

Fig. 1.1   Formal governance

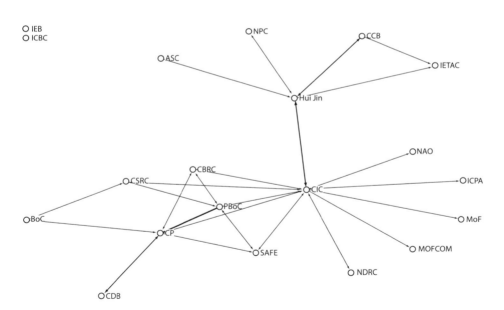

Fig. 1.2   HRM—Concurrent entity affiliations

player, less because of its ties to major banks—although it does have concurrent board seats at CCB—but instead, because members of its boards concurrently hold positions within the National People's Congress (NPC), the Accounting Society of China, as well as CIC, and indirectly (via interlocking board members at CCB) with China's International Economic Arbitration Commission.

In order to formally establish the relative importance of these various entities in the web of financial relations, we calculate the centrality of these different organizations based on *betweenness*. It measures the relation of a given actor to other actors in the system by calculating its position relative to other pairs of actors. The idea is that an actor that links multiple pairs of related actors confers power on that actor. The coefficient for betweenness increases with the number of geodesic paths to which it is linked; i.e. in our case the coefficient increases as a single entity is linked with each additional pair of organizations. According to this measure, CIC occupies the position of highest centrality for concurrent interlocking positions followed by the CCP.[12]

Figure 1.3 depicts the same affiliations, but this time we have included not only concurrent positions, but also the positions senior executives or board members had previously held at other entities within China's financial sector. The number of entities has increased and so has the complexity of the network. Visually it is apparent that CIC, Hui Jin, and the CCP, as well as the PBOC, occupy central positions within this network; in other words, each of them is linked to many other institutions by way of positions held by their top level financial cadres either concurrently or sequentially. However, the numerical analysis reveals that three of the "big 4" banks outperform CIC and PBOC on the centrality measure of betweenness[13]—even though CIC, the CCP, as well as the PBOC are close followers on this measure and outrank other state entities.[14] This suggests that they are more deeply embedded in the HRM governance regime as a result of previous appointments executive and supervisory board members at these entities have held than is apparent from analyzing only the current interlocking positions they occupy. It is also worth noting that whereas ICBC and IEB lack ties with other organizations in the financial system by way of current interlocking positions, many of their board members previously occupied such positions. Again, this suggests that they may in fact be less autonomous than their concurrent affiliations indicate.

Network analysis allows us not only to identify the centrality of different organizations in China's financial system, but also the centrality of individuals. The more positions a person occupies in a system, and the more other

12. The coefficient for CIC is 0.389 and for the CCP 0.283.
13. The coefficients for BOC, CCB, and ICBC are, respectively, 0.192, 0.252, and 0.244.
14. CIC 0.181, CCP 0.149, and PBOC 0.155.

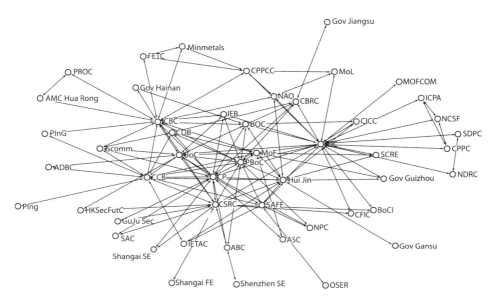

Fig. 1.3   HRM—Previous and concurrent entity affiliations

individuals are tied to it by holding positions at entities with which that individual is affiliated, the more powerful such a person is. Figure 1.4 reveals the relation among the 155 individuals in our database via organizations with which they are currently affiliated. The picture clearly insulates the people currently holding positions at ICBC and IEB from the rest of the financial cadres who maintain many ties with multiple entities throughout financial system by way of concurrent affiliation.

The measure we use to assert their centrality in this case is the degree of centrality, which measures how many ties a given node (here a financial cadre) has. In contrast to the betweenness measure used earlier, measuring centrality by degree is less concerned with how many dependency relations that individual intercepts. On this measure, three individuals, all affiliated with CIC, score the highest: Lou Jiwei, the chairman of CIC; Jin Liqun, the chairman of Hui Jin who also serves on CIC's board; and Cui Guangqin, also a concurrent board member of CIC and Hui Jin.[15] While perhaps not all personal ties should be given equal weight, because they do not necessarily confer the same level of influence in the governance of CIC, it is still remarkable how closely CIC is intertwined with other entities in China's financial system.

15. All three share the same score of 7.723. Note that for the purpose of this analysis we have excluded individuals that are only linked to ICBC or IEB as their score indicates relations to a much smaller network.

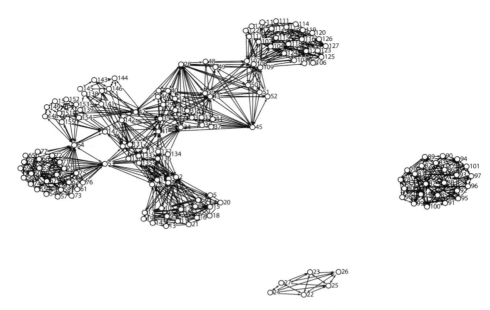

Fig. 1.4   Current personal affiliations

In practice, CIC portrays itself as an autonomous actor—an ordinary financial intermediary whose task it is to maximize financial returns on its assets without a political agenda or much explicit political interference. Yet, CIC has on its supervisory board representatives from virtually every important government entity within China's financial system and its executives previously served on important posts in other financial entities—including the PBOC, the MoF, and the CSRC.

Based on this analysis it seems fair to say that the 155 cadres currently occupying key positions in finance form a thick network, which links important entities and which comprises the core of China's governance regime for finance. The most striking result of this analysis is the contrast between the dense network relations depicted in figures 1.2 through 1.4 with the simple control structure in figure 1.1. While it may be too strong to suggest that personal ties substitute for formal control based on ownership ties, the former appear to dominate the latter. This is nowhere more apparent than in the role of the PBOC. Judging from the formal lines of control alone PBOC occupies a rather marginal place in China's financial system (see figure 1.1). However, based on the personal ties revealed in figures 1.2 and 1.3, there is little doubt that PBOC, or rather the financial cadres serving at PBOC, are central players within China's system of finance. Moreover, as in the early days of China's transition to a market economy, PBOC continues to operate as *the* link between state and party control over China's financial sector.

All of its leading cadres concurrently hold positions at PBOC's party committee and as such exercise HRM controls over key regulators within the system.

Yet our data also indicate that this system is not without vulnerabilities. As indicated in figures 1.2 and 1.4, some entities lack current interlocking ties with other organizations—most notably ICBC and IEB. The ICBC is particularly interesting, as it is traded on the Hong Kong and Shanghai stock exchanges and calls not only private investors, but also major foreign investors, such as Goldman Sachs, among its owners. This raises the question whether HRM as a governance regime can adapt China's increasing role in global finance.

1.5   China's Global Ambitions and the Future of HRM

The transformation of China's financial sector over the past ten years has gone hand in hand with its rapid expansion and its integration into the global financial system. The BOC, CCB, and ICBC, as well as Bank of Communications (BComm) were listed on Hong Kong's stock exchange and sold shares to foreign investors, including important strategic investors, as early as 2005 and 2007 (Pistor 2009a). The ABC followed suit in mid-2010.[16] While some of these foreign investors have shed or reduced their holdings in Chinese banks, mostly because they needed to raise fresh capital during the global financial crisis (Pistor 2009b), the bank's exposure to foreign investors has given them an opportunity to learn from other business models and adapt them to China's circumstances. Representatives of foreign banks served on the boards of China's commercial banks—albeit not in executive positions, giving them access to information on how the Chinese system of finance operates in practice, but also exposing other board members to the views of representatives of foreign financial intermediaries.

China's major banks have also become more active globally themselves. The BOC, which was carved out from the PBOC in 1984, took over the central bank's foreign currency portfolio at the time and has established branches and subsidiaries around the globe.[17] The CCB and ICBC have followed suit more recently and expanded their global operations. The ICBC has moved beyond opening representative or branch offices and has recently acquired a 20 percent stake in South Africa's Standard Bank in 2008. The

---

16. "Agricultural Revolution–Agricultural Bank's IP," *The Economist,* July 10, 2010, 69. Note that the key strategic investors for ABC were not private financial intermediaries from the West as in the case of the first three banks that went public, but instead were sovereign wealth funds (SWFs) from the Gulf states. This reflects the changing landscape of global finance. See Pistor (2009b) on the role of SWFs in the global financial system.

17. For details on BOC branches in different countries see http://www.BOC.cn/en/about BOC/.

two banks are now cooperating across the African continent in numerous ventures related to mining and natural resource exploration.[18] Last but not least, China established a new sovereign wealth fund in 2007. The CIC has made several widely reported foreign investments, including in the US private equity firm Blackstone and the investment bank Morgan Stanley (Pistor 2009b), and more recently in the natural resource sector.[19] In addition to CIC, the State Administration for Foreign Exchange (SAFE) and the National Security Fund (NSF) are engaging in foreign investments. In contrast to CIC, which has taken substantial minority stakes, SAFE and NSF seem to be taking smaller stakes and maintain a more diversified portfolio that includes both equity and debt securities.[20]

The involvement of foreign investors in China's state-controlled banks, the outward expansion of financial intermediaries, as well as the greater openness of China's financial system to foreign investments (including wholly owned banks and other financial intermediaries), raises questions about the viability of the described HRM governance regime as a long-term governance strategy.

A similar question can and should be asked about any governance regime, including those based on conventional formal mechanisms, such as ownership and regulatory controls. National regulators have only limited reach over their own banks with global operations and have had at best limited success in controlling foreign financial intermediaries operating on their shores. Nowhere has this been more apparent than in the recent global crisis. A good example is Iceland, which had allowed its bank Landsbanki to expand rapidly in foreign markets by using the interbank lending market for its liquidity needs and attracting foreign depositors with high interest rates in Internet retail operations primarily in the United Kingdom and the Netherlands (Turner 2009). When the interbank lending market froze, the Icelandic bank collapsed and Iceland was unable to cover deposit insurance for depositors in the United Kingdom. Legally, Iceland was responsible for insurance as well as lender of last resort functions of the Icelandic bank, because the UK operations were technically branch operations of the parent bank and as such under the jurisdiction of Iceland.[21] On the flip side, the United Kingdom had paid only scant attention to Icelandic's operations in the United Kingdom—after all, this was the responsibility of Iceland's

18. "ICBC cooperates with Standard Bank on 65 projects," *China Daily,* May 26, 2009, available at http://en.ce.cn/Industries/Financial-services.

19. For details on CIC's recent investments see http://www.swfinstitute.org/fund/cic.php.

20. See http://www.swfinstitute.org/fund/safe.php on SAFE. The National Council on Social Security Fund is only beginning to invest globally. See http://www.swfinstitute.org/fund/nssf.php.

21. For Iceland this followed not only from the Basel Concordat, but also from relevant EU legislation, as Iceland is a member of the EEA and as such subject to EU regulations and directives, which follow the Basel model in dividing responsibilities between home and host country regulators and lenders of last resort.

regulators. When that bank collapsed and amidst fears of another bank run,[22] the UK government stepped in to provide coverage and in return froze all assets of Iceland under an antiterrorism law. Similarly, regulators in Austria, Sweden, and other European countries witnessed their banking industry expand aggressively into Central and Eastern Europe (CEE). Again, these banking groups greatly contributed to a rapid credit expansion that proved unsustainable. Unlike the case of the Icelandic bank, the foreign operations usually took the form of wholly owned subsidiaries, which placed them under the jurisdiction of the host countries when it came to covering depositors and offering lender of last resort functions. Most of the CEE countries had tried to stem the flow of credit, but found this to be largely ineffective, because foreign parent banks quickly outmaneuvered them by switching to alternative channels for their continued credit expansion. As a result, most CEE saw themselves unable to rescue their own financial system and ended up seeking help from the International Monetary Fund (IMF) and other multilaterals (Pistor 2012). In short, neither the property rights regime of transnationally operating banking groups nor thirty years of international cooperation in developing common standards for banking supervision within the Bank for International Settlements (BIS) framework and the EU (which largely incorporated the BIS framework) have shielded countries that rely on those governance mechanisms from the prospects of financial collapse.

Similarly, both systems—the formal and the HRM governance regimes—have had their fair shares of rogue traders. For China, the wake up call that HRM might be insufficient for governing personnel located abroad came with the collapse of China Aviation Oil Company (CAO) on the Singapore Stock Exchange in December of 2004.[23] However, other governance regimes have experienced similar failures—one needs only to point to Barings or the more recent case of Société General.

Raising concerns about the vulnerability of HRM in the context of globalization is therefore not meant to benchmark this particular regime against an allegedly superior standard, but to detect the specific strengths and weaknesses of this regime in the global context.[24] China's HRM regime as described earlier is built around the notion that there is a centralized vetting of cadres for the financial sector not only when they first enter the system, but also as they advance through the system. For every major position at the central bank regulators (or financial intermediaries) the CCP or CCP committees at the PBOC or the CBRC vet and ultimately approve the relevant financial cadres. The PBOC also maintains its own training school from

22. The UK Bank Northern Rock failed in 2007 triggering the first bank run in the United Kingdom since 1866. See "The Run on the Rock," Report by the Treasury Committee of the UK House of Commons, January 24, 2008.
23. This case is explored in detail in Milhaupt and Pistor (2008, chapter 7, 125).
24. This approach is explained in greater detail in Milhaupt and Pistor (see note 23).

which people are recruited for important positions within the system.[25] As our data analysis suggests, a substantial number of persons in this universe have held other positions in finance before being appointed to the one they hold currently; moreover, they typically maintain direct and indirect ties to other entities where they served before or hold concurrent positions. The question then is, whether this system can adapt to the global operation of Chinese banks and/or the increase in job opportunities in China's expanding financial system, which includes an increasing number of entities that at least to our knowledge are not part of the CCP's HRM system.

In seeking answers to this question, this part of the chapter examines affiliations of members of management and supervisory boards of only those financial intermediaries that have substantial global operations. The purpose of this exercise is to analyze how deeply these entities are embedded in China's HRM system. This database includes 127 individuals at 18 entities. Twenty-four of the 127 individuals concurrently occupy another position within China's financial system, while the remaining 103 do not. Of those that are currently without interlocking positions, 54 have held positions at other financial organizations prior to their current position and 39 held positions at state entities in finance, such as the PBOC, SAFE, the CBRC, and so forth. The other fifteen individuals occupied positions at another bank—typically at a time when these banks were still an integral part of a state-controlled financial system. Still, this leaves forty-nine individuals without any current or previous affiliations—some of which are other representatives of foreign investors, others "independent" directors recruited, among others, from academic institutions in China.

As can be seen in figure 1.5, the density of current affiliations varies. As already noted, ICBC and IEB have no current affiliations. However, the number of current affiliates at other commercial banks with global operations, including BOC and CCB, is also strikingly low. In part this seems to be compensated by what one may want to call "strong" ties within China's HRM system. Thus, Xiao Gang, the CEO of BOC, is head of the CCP Commission at BOC, and thus closely tied to the party; but this is not the case for CCB's CEO, Guo Shuqing. Guo's future career may still be entirely dependent on the CCP's HRM system and that might suffice to ensure that his interests and the interests of the bank he heads are aligned with those of China's leaders. However, as CCB continues to expand globally, increasing tensions between global opportunities and concerns about China's internal stability may arise and, at least for an outside observer, it is difficult to determine how such a conflict might be resolved.

It may be too strong to assert that some banks with global operations

---

25. I am grateful to Professor Leonard K. Cheng at Hong Kong's University for Science and Technology for pointing this out.

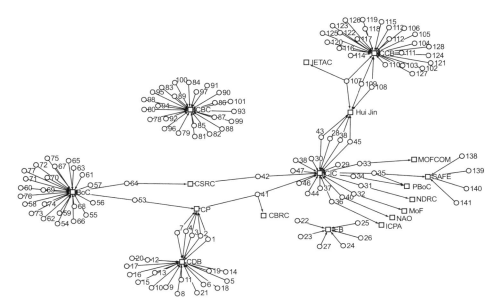

Fig. 1.5   HRM for global players

are "growing out"[26] of the HRM used to govern China's financial system. Nonetheless, the examples suggest that some entities have enjoyed greater leeway in recruiting from a pool of people with fewer ties to the broader network of China's financial cadres. Within China, this is a new experiment. There is little doubt that underperformance of these individuals too would be sanctioned were they to return to the state-controlled financial system. However, today they may well find job opportunities elsewhere. Nonetheless, as long as the flow of people the CCP can recruit into this system is sufficiently large, the fact that some will exit and find jobs in systems that maintain fewer controls over individuals may not lead to its demise. Of greater importance is the size of the financial system under the control of the CCP relative to those parts that escape its control. As mentioned, the CCP controls key positions only at China's largest banks. Today they still account for 70 percent of all bank assets (see ACFB 2007). However, smaller banks are no longer directly controlled by the state and the opening of China's financial system to new entrants, including greenfield establishments, may gradually change the financial landscape. Just as China's real economy has

---

26. This terminology is borrowed from Naughton's book *Growing out of the Plan* and the accompanying analysis, which suggests that China's path to economic success has been a gradual transformation of economic relations.

"grown out of the plan" (Naughton 1996), so too may the financial system grow out of CCP tutelage. This process, however, is only beginning. If anything, the global financial crisis has strengthened those who believe that a liberalized financial system poses a threat to China's economic success and its political foundations.

1.6 HRM in Comparative Perspective

China's governance of finance may be unique with respect to the central role the CCP plays in vetting cadres for key positions within the system. However, other countries also have a highly centralized elite structure that dominates the key echelons of power in politics, finance, and big business. A comparison of power elites in Britain and France reveals that in both countries elites are highly concentrated, but that the social processes by which elites are formed and the position they occupy on their path to power differ across systems (Maclean, Harvey, and Chia 2010). Maclean et al. identify the top power wielders in both countries by focusing on corporate executive and nonexecutive directorships. They allocate weights to positions in corporate hierarchies these directors hold (whether CEO, chairman of the board, etc.) for a sample of over one thousand agents in each system. They find that in France, 200 directors wield 63 percent of the combined power of the entire sample; and in Britain 54 percent (Maclean, Harvey, and Chia 2010, 336). The formation of this elite occurs primarily in the education system, especially in France. Ninety-five percent of the top 100 directors in France attended a Parisien *lycée* (high school) and virtually all attended one of France's elite schools (*grandes écoles*) for higher education, such as the École Poytechnique, the Institut d'Études Politiques de Paris, or the École Nationale d'Administration (ENA). Education at one of these institutions does not only open the path to top positions in state administration or politics, but also in the private sector. In Maclean's sample, 49 of the top 100 corporate directors in France began their career in government and advanced from there to one of the top positions in the private sector (Maclean, Harvey, and Chia 2010, 339). These findings are consistent with earlier findings that showed that a position at the French Treasury is a critical step in the career path of a future top level manager at one of France's financial institutions (Kadushin 1995). The Treasury is one of the most powerful agencies in France's political system and recruits the top graduates from the *grandes écoles* (Kadushin 1995, 210). Directorships and similar positions with the Treasury are term limited (five years). However, private sector financial institutions recruit their top corporate officers at the Treasury, offering them a multiple of their salaries.

The pattern of career advancement is thus not very different from China's. As suggested in this chapter, top corporate officers of China's largest banks typically served previously either at the PBOC or the Ministry of Finance at earlier stages in their career before advancing to their current position. Interestingly, this pattern of elite formation has not changed after France abandoned direct control over the corporate and financial sectors (Kadushin 1995). Existing literatures say little about whether this form of HRM has gained strength as the state has lost direct control over the corporate sector—a trend that is suggested by the CCP's strengthening of HRM since the late 1990s. At the very least, however, the experience of France confirms that state ownership is not needed for HRM, and that it survives changes of ownership as well as changes in government.

The aforementioned discussion could lead to the conclusion that HRM is more common in countries with a high level of state control over the economy, or in the language of the comparative capitalism literature, in "coordinated market economies" in contrast to "liberal market economies," as represented by the United Kingdom or the United States (Hall and Soskice 2001). In fact, Yoo and Lee suggest that elite networks are complementary to institutions of state dirigisme and associated low levels of social trust (Yoo and Lee 2009).

However, available evidence suggests that liberal market economies too are governed by elites. Thus, Maclean et al. find that in Britain over 88 percent of the top corporate directors attended elite framer schools, such as Eton, Winchester, or Harrow. While the level of higher education is much lower than in France, those with higher education tended to have gone to Oxbridge or Harvard (Maclean, Harvey, and Chia 2010). Moreover, 84 out of 100 corporate directors began their career in the private corporate sector and the remainder in law or similar professions, but not in government service. In the United States, linkages between the corporate and government sectors appear to be more prevalent. The importance of power networks that criss-cross government and business in the United States was first pointed to by Mills in 1956 (Mills 1956). Moreover, anecdotal evidence confirms that links between government and finance are strong, as suggested by the advancement of two former Goldman Sachs top managers to the position of US Treasury in two recent administrations: Paul Rubin in the Clinton administration, and Hank Paulson in the George W. Bush administration. Indeed, a more systematic analysis of elite structures for the 1990s reveals strong interlocks between the corporate, nonprofit, and state sectors in the United States (Moore et al. 2002). Using a newly created elite database, they show that many corporate directors link to nongovernmental organizations as well as to federal advisory bodies. Unlike China or France, however, the movement appears to be less from government into the private sector, but from the private sector into the government sector: "The most central (i.e., the best-connected) organizations in these interorganizational networks are also major corporations" (Moore et al. 2002, 740).

In sum, looking beyond the formal structures, such as ownership or regulatory oversight that are commonly used in economics and law to identify governance structures, serves as an eye opener not only in China, but equally in other countries. Elites are prominent in government and business, and in fact often link government and business. However, not all elites are formed in a similar manner and the dominance of government versus the private sector for elite formation differs across countries. Future research should focus on how these structures help shape the formal structures that govern finance—not only in China, but also in the West.

1.7   Concluding Remarks: HRM and Global Governance

This chapter has shown that governance of China's finances cannot be explained completely using conventional paradigms that rely on ownership and legal or regulatory controls alone. Instead, China's governance regime relies heavily on HRM. The regime evolved and strengthened during the transition from complete state control over finance, which lasted until the early 2000s, to a more diverse system that allows for more diverse ownership patterns, more players within China's domestic financial system, and greater opportunities for Chinese entities globally. Further diversification, in particular the greater job opportunities for financial cadres outside the CCP-controlled HRM system might undermine the logic of this regime; that is, control over future career prospects of financial cadres and the current governance regime needs to adapt to these ongoing changes. The possible direction of such changes can be gleaned from emerging patterns of governance employed by Chinese entities that operate globally. The relation between CIC with Blackstone and Morgan Stanley may serve as an example. The CIC holds over 10 percent in ownership stakes in both entities—in Blackstone, which is a limited partnership in the form of nonvoting "units," and in Morgan Stanley in the form of preferred stock as well as debt instruments. Yet in neither company does CIC hold board positions. While executive positions were excluded in the original investment agreements, CIC had the option to appoint representatives to the board of directors in both companies. The choice not to exercise these options could be interpreted to suggest that CIC has decided to operate as a purely passive investor. This, however, might not capture the whole story. As 10 percent owner and potential future funder, CIC undoubtedly has a voice with the management of these organizations. Moreover, CIC announced that Blackstone and Morgan Stanley have been chosen by CIC to manage hundreds of millions of dollars in new global investments. The Wall Street Journal captured this move with the headline "CIC turns to friends."[27] The move to strengthen personal ties even as financial gains were still outstanding suggests that CIC invested not only, and perhaps not primarily, in financial assets when it invested in these firms, but in relational bonds comprising of human capital. That investment appears

27. Carew and Strasburg (2009).

to be paying off handsomely for Blackstone and Morgan Stanley as they have gained money management opportunities for CIC's investments. It might also point the way toward a different form of HRM in the global context: one that does not rely primarily on controlling future careers, but access to future finance and markets. This would be akin to the world of international finance in the old days when family empires—from the Medici to the Rothchilds—dominated international finance.

References

ACFB. 2007. *Almanac of China's Finance and Banking.* Beijing.
Allen, Franklin. 2005. "Law, Finance, and Economic Growth in China." *Journal of Financial Economics* 77 (1): 57–116.
Berle, Adolf Augustus, and Gardiner Means. 1932. *The Modern Corporation and Private Property.* New York: Council for Research in the Social Sciences, Columbia University.
Bo, Zhiyue. 2004. "The Institutionalization of Elite Management in China." In *Holding China Together: Diversity and National Integration in the Post-Deng Era,* edited by B. J. Naughton and D. L. Yang, 70–100. Cambridge: Cambridge University Press.
Burns, John P. 1994. "Strengthening Central Ccp Control of Leadership Selection: The 1990 Nomenklatura." *The China Quarterly* 138:458–91.
Carew, Rick, and Jenny Strasburg. 2009. "CIC Turns to Friends: Blackstone and Morgan Stanley." July 31. Available from e.wsj.com/article/SB124896400764393841.html.
Hall, Peter A., and David Soskice, eds. 2001. *Varieties of Capitalism.* Oxford: Oxford University Press.
Heilmann, Sebastian. 2005. "Regulatory Innovation by Leninist Means: Communist Party Supervision in China's Financial Industry." *The China Quarterly* 181:1–21.
Huang, Yasheng. 1996. *Inflation and Investment Controls in China.* Cambridge: Cambridge University Press.
Kadushin, Charles. 1995. "Friendship Among the French Financial Elite." *American Sociological Review* 60 (2): 202–22.
Lardy, Nicholas R. 2002. *Integrating China into the Global Economy.* Washington, DC: Brookings Institutions Press.
Leigh, Lamin, and Richard Podpiera. 2006. "The Rise of Foreign Investment in China's Banks—Taking Stock." International Monetary Fund (IMF) Working Paper 2006(292).
Maclean, Mairi, Charles Harvey, and Robert Chia. 2010. "Dominant Corporate Agents and the Power Elite in France and Britain." *Organization Studies* 31 (3): 327–48.
Martin, Michael. 2008. "China's Sovereign Wealth Fund." Congressional Research Service (CRS) Report for Congress (RL34337).
Milhaupt, Curtis J., and Katharina Pistor. 2008. *Law and Capitalism: What Corporate Crises Reveal About Legal Systems and Economic Development around the World.* Chicago: University of Chicago Press.
Mills, Wright. 1956. *The Power Elite.* New York: Oxford University Press.
Moore, Gwen, Sarah Sobieraj, Allen J. Whitt, Olga Mayorova, and Daniel Beaulieu.

2002. "Elite Interlocks in Three U.S. Sectors: Nonprofit, Corporate, and Government." *Social Science Quarterly* 83 (3): 726–46.

Naughton, Barry. 1996. *Growing out of the Plan.* Cambridge: Cambridge University Press.

———. 2008. "A Political Economy of China's Economic Transition." In *China's Great Economic Transformation,* edited by L. Bradt and T. Rawski, 91–135. Cambridge: Cambridge University Press.

North, Douglass Cecil. 1990. *Institutions, Institutional Change, and Economic Performance.* Cambridge: Cambridge University Press.

Pistor, Katharina. 2006. "Comment: The Law and the Non-Law." *University of Michigan International Law Journal* 27 (3): 974–83.

———. 2009a. "Banking Reforms and Bank Bail Outs in the Chinese Mirror." Columbia Law and Economics Working Paper #354.

———. 2009b. "Global Network Finance." *Journal of Comparative Economics* 37:552–67.

———. 2012. "Into the Void: Governing Finance in Central and Eastern Europe." In *Economies in Transition: The Long-Run View,* edited by G. Roland, 134–52. Helsinki: Palgrave Macmillan for UNU-Wider.

Schooner, Heidi Mandanis, and Michael Taylor. 2003. "United Kingdom and United States Responses to the Regulatory Challenges of Modern Financial Markets." *Texas International Law Journal* 38:317.

Shih, Victor C. 2008. *Factions and Finance in China.* Cambridge: Cambridge University Press.

Turner, Lord Adair. 2009. *The Turner Review: A Regulatory Response to the Global Banking Crisis.* London: Financial Services Authority.

Yoo, Taeyoung, and Soo Hee Lee. 2009. "In Search of Social Capital in State-Activist Capitalism: Elite Networks in France and Korea." *Organization Studies* 30 (5): 529–47.

Comment   Zheng Song

This chapter is very useful for understanding how the financial system is governed in China. There is a widely held belief that the Chinese government (or the Communist Party of China) has firm control on Chinese financial markets. However, the underlying mechanism through which the Chinese government exercises its controls is far from clear. The problem becomes even more challenging as China has established formal ways of governing its financial sector (mimicking those in developed countries). So, more fundamentally, how can the Chinese government continue to maintain the direct state control given the substantial ownership changes over the past decade? This chapter looks at a data set covering a total of more than 150 top administrators or managers and concludes that human resource manage-

Zheng Song is assistant professor of economics at the University of Chicago Booth School of Business.

For acknowledgments, sources of research support, and disclosure of the author's material financial relationships, if any, please see http://www.nber.org/chapters/c12462.ack.

ment (HRM) has become an important substitute to the formal governance of finance in China. The approach of the chapter is innovative: checking whether those top office holders occupy important positions at other financial organizations concurrently or have held such positions prior to their current one. This reveals a close network of financial cadres whose career life is essentially supervised by the Chinese government (or more precisely, the Communist Party's Central Organization Department).

The evidence may also shed some light on the coexistence of the inefficient credit allocation and the efficient policy implementation that has puzzled many outsiders for a long time. On the one hand, financial imperfection in China and its efficiency losses have been well documented. For instance, the Chinese banks—mostly state owned—tend to offer much easier credit to state-owned enterprises (SOE). In a recent paper (Song, Storesletten, and Zilibotti 2011), we show that such asymmetric financing ability, interacted with the resource reallocation between the state and private sectors, may explain the rapid (inefficient) accumulation of foreign reserves in China. On the other hand, however, the Chinese financial system behaves in a remarkably efficient way to implement monetary stabilization policies. A well-known achievement is that in order to cool the potentially overheating economy, PBOC has been successfully sterilizing the foreign exchange market intervention with no major impacts on the domestic interest rate. Another example comes from the massive drop in new bank loans in December 2007, right after the Chinese government decided to tighten its monetary policy (see table 1C.1). Governance through HRM can easily explain both the inefficient credit allocation and the efficient policy implementation.

An important question is whether HRM is unique to China? First of all, the concept of HRM is not new. It is actually similar to the idea of "personnel controls" in the literature of economic transition. The government exercises its ultimate control over SOEs through personnel selection and dismissal, though some control rights are in hands of SOE managers (e.g., Qian 1996). Moreover, as mentioned in the chapter, some developed countries like France also feature elite concentrations. A similar pattern of career development can even be found in the United States, though the direction of the movement is different. Therefore, I am perfectly in line with a future research plan outlined in the chapter: "Future research should focus on how

Table 1C.1   New bank loans in December

	1 billion RMB
2006	214.4
2007	48.5
2008	764.5

Source: PBOC website.

these structures help shape the formal structures that govern finance—not only in China, but also in the West."

Although this chapter has explored very detailed individual data, some extra information can be potentially useful for addressing other interesting and related questions. For instance, a key issue is about the implementation of HRM. What if a bank CEO decides not to follow the Chinese government or the Communist Party? Can we reveal a reward/punishment scheme from the data? The existence of a personnel network is consistent with the hypothesis that the Chinese financial sector is governed through HRM, but it is not a direct test of the hypothesis.

Let me end with a remark about the future of HRM. The chapter points out an interesting feature of HRM: it can be compatible with the global markets and may even influence the future governance of the global financial system. However, I still want to take up two issues from other perspectives. First, given the fast development of the private financial sector in China, it would be increasingly difficult for the Chinese government to control the markets by exercising HRM within the state sector. Second, when appointing a bank COE, the Chinese government clearly faces a trade-off between her or his loyalty to the party and ability of profit maximization. Assuming that these two variables are uncorrelated (not a totally crazy assumption), a political economy model would predict a strengthening (relaxing) of HRM in periods when the government runs budget surpluses (deficits).

References

Qian, Yingyi. 1996. "Enterprise Reform in China: Agency Problems and Political Control." *Economics of Transition* 4 (2): 422–47.
Song, Zheng, Kjetil Storesletten, and Fabrizio Zilibotti. 2011. "Growing Like China." *American Economic Review* 101 (1): 196–233.

China's Financial System
Opportunities and Challenges

Franklin Allen, Jun "QJ" Qian, Chenying Zhang,
and Mengxin Zhao

2.1 Introduction

In this chapter we provide a comprehensive review of China's financial system and extensive comparisons with other countries. Almost every functioning financial system includes financial markets and intermediaries (e.g., a banking sector), but how these two standard financial sectors contribute to the entire financial system and economy differs significantly across different countries. In this regard, we discuss what has worked and what has not within the two sectors, and consider the effects of further development on the entire economy. We also examine a nonstandard financial sector, which operates outside the markets and banking sectors and consists of alternative financing channels, governance mechanisms, and institutions. Finally, we provide guidelines for future research on several unresolved issues, including how China's financial system can integrate into the world's markets and economy without being interrupted by damaging financial crises. Although there is no consensus regarding the prospects for China's future economic

Franklin Allen is the Nippon Life Professor of Finance and Economics at the Wharton School of the University of Pennsylvania and a research associate of the National Bureau of Economic Research. Jun "QJ" Qian is associate professor of finance at the Carroll School of Management, Boston College, and a research fellow at the Wharton Financial Institutions Center and the China Academy of Financial Research (CAFR). Chenying Zhang is a PhD candidate in finance at the Wharton School of the University of Pennsylvania. Mengxin Zhao is assistant professor in the Alberta School of Business of the University of Alberta.

We wish to thank Joseph Fan, Randall Morck, our discussant Chenggang Xu, and participants at the NBER's "Capitalizing China" Conference for helpful comments; Bibo Liu and Zhenrui Tang for excellent research assistance; Yingxue Cao and Lynn Yin for sharing data and information on China's real estate markets; and Boston College and the Wharton Financial Institutions Center for financial support. The authors are responsible for all the remaining errors. For acknowledgments, sources of research support, and disclosure of the authors' material financial relationships, if any, please see http://www.nber.org/chapters/c12071.ack.

growth, a prevailing view on China's financial system speculates that it is one of the weakest links in the economy and it will hamper future economic growth.

We draw four main conclusions about China's financial system and its future development. First, when we examine and compare China's banking system and financial markets with those of both developed and emerging countries, we find China's financial system has been dominated by a large banking system. Even with the entrance and growth of many domestic and foreign banks and financial institutions in recent years, China's banking system is still mainly controlled by the four largest state-owned banks. All of these "Big Four" banks have become publicly listed and traded companies in recent years, with the government being the largest shareholder and retaining control. This ownership structure has served these banks well in terms of avoiding major problems encountered by major financial institutions in developed countries that are at the center of the 2007 to 2009 global financial crisis. Moreover, the level of nonperforming loans (NPLs) over GDP has been steadily decreasing after reaching its peak during 2000 and 2001. Continuing improvement of the banking system, including further development of financial institutions outside the Big Four banks and extending more credit to productive firms and projects, can help stabilize China's financial system in the short run, given the uncertainties in the Chinese and global economies.

Our second conclusion concerns China's financial markets. Two domestic stock exchanges, the Shanghai Stock Exchange (SHSE hereafter) and Shenzhen Stock Exchange (SZSE) were established in 1990. Their scale and importance are not comparable to the banking sector; and they have not been effective in allocating resources in the economy, in that they remain speculative and driven by insider trading. In recent years the stock market has witnessed significant development. Going forward, financial markets are likely to play an increasingly significant role in the economy. We discuss several issues and potential problems related to increasing the size and scope and improving the efficiency of the stock and other financial markets.

Third, in an earlier paper, Allen, Qian and Qian (2005, AQQ hereafter) find that the most successful part of the financial system, in terms of supporting the growth of the overall economy, is not the banking sector or financial markets, but rather a sector of alternative financing channels, such as informal financial intermediaries, internal financing and trade credits, and coalitions of various forms among firms, investors, and local governments. Many of these financing channels rely on alternative governance mechanisms, such as competition in product and input markets, and trust, reputation, and relationships. Together this alternative financial sector has supported the growth of a "Hybrid Sector" with various types of ownership structures. Our definition of the Hybrid Sector includes all nonstate, nonlisted firms, including privately or individually owned firms, and firms that are partially owned by *local* governments (e.g., Township Village Enterprises, or TVEs).[1] The growth of the Hybrid Sector has been much higher than that of the State Sector (state-owned enterprises, or SOEs, and all firms where the central government has ultimate control) and the Listed Sector (publicly listed and traded firms with most of them converted from the State Sector). The Hybrid Sector contributes most of China's economic growth, and employs the majority of the labor force. The coexistence of the alternative financial sector with banks and markets can continue to fuel the growth of the Hybrid Sector.

Finally, a significant challenge for China's financial system is to avoid damaging financial crises that can severely disrupt the economy and social stability. These crises include traditional financial crises: a banking sector crisis stemming from an accumulation of NPLs and a sudden drop in banks' profits, or a crisis/crash resulting from speculative asset bubbles in the real estate market or stock market. There are also other types of financial crises, such as a "twin crisis" (simultaneous foreign exchange and banking/stock market crises) that struck many Asian economies in the late 1990s. Since its entrance to the World Trade Organization (WTO) in 2001, the integration of China's financial system and overall economy with the rest of the world has significantly sped up. This process introduces cheap foreign capital and technology, but large scale and sudden capital flows and foreign speculation increase the likelihood of a twin crisis. At the end of 2007, China's foreign currency reserves surpassed US$1.5 trillion, overtaking Japan to become the largest in the world; they increased to about US$3.2 trillion as of June 2011 with a large fraction invested in US dollar denominated assets such as T-bills (Treasury bills) and notes.[2] The rapid increase in China's foreign exchange reserves suggests that there is a large amount of speculative, "hot" money in China in anticipation of a continuing appreciation of the RMB, China's currency, relative to all other major currencies, especially the US dollar. Depending on how the government and the central bank handle the process of revaluation, especially when there is a large amount of capital outflow, there could be a classic currency crisis as the government and central bank try to defend the partial currency peg, which in turn may trigger a banking crisis if there are large withdrawals from banks.

The remaining sections are organized as follows. In section 2.2, we briefly review the history of China's financial system development, present aggregate evidence on China's financial system, and compare them to those

1. We include firms partially owned by local governments in the Hybrid Sector for two reasons. First, despite the ownership stake of local governments and the sometimes ambiguous ownership structure and property rights, the operation of these firms resembles more closely that of a for-profit, privately-owned firm than that of a state-owned firm. Second, the ownership stake of local governments in many of these firms has been privatized.

2. According to the US Treasury Department, China's holding of US treasury securities reached $ 1.17 trillion in July 2011. Morrison and Labonte (2008) estimate that around 70 percent of China's foreign reserves are invested in dollar denominated assets.

of developed and other developing countries. In section 2.3, we examine China's banking system and changes over time. In section 2.4, we briefly examine the growth and irregularities of financial markets, including the stock market, real estate market, and listed firms, and consider the effects of several initiatives to develop new markets and further develop existing markets, as well as changes in corporate governance among listed firms. In section 2.5, we examine the nonstandard financial sector, including alternative financial channels and governance mechanisms. Motivated by the success of this financial sector and firms in the Hybrid Sector, we also compare the advantages and disadvantages of using the law as the basis of finance and commerce. We then examine different types of financial crises and their potential effects on China's financial system in section 2.6. Finally, section 2.7 concludes the chapter. In terms of converting RMB into US dollars, we use the exchange rate of US$1 = RMB 8.28 (*yuan*) for transactions and events occurring before 2005, and the spot rate at the end of each year for those activities during and after 2005 (figure 2.18 provides a graph of the exchange rates between the US dollar and the RMB).

2.2   Overview of China's Financial System

2.2.1   A Brief Review of the History of China's Financial System

China's financial system was well developed before 1949.[3] One key finding in reviewing the history of this period, including the rise of Shanghai as one of the financial centers of Asia during the first half of the twentieth century, is that the development of China's commerce and financial system as a whole was by and large *outside* the formal legal system. For example, despite the entrance of Western-style courts in Shanghai and other major coastal cities in the early 1900s, most business-related disputes were resolved through mechanisms outside courts, including guilds (merchant coalitions), families, and local notables.[4] In section 2.5.3, we argue that modern equivalents of these nonlegal dispute-resolution and corporate governance mechanisms are behind the success of Hybrid Sector firms in the same areas in the 1980s and 1990s, and that these alternative mechanisms may be more responsive in adapting to changes in a fast-growing economy like China than the law and legal institutions.

After the foundation of the People's Republic of China in 1949, all of

---

3. For more descriptions of the pre-1949 history of China's financial system, see AQQ (2008); for more anecdotal evidence on China's financial system in the same period, see, for example, Kirby (1995) and Lee (1993).

4. See, for example, Chung (2005), for descriptions on family- and community-based mechanisms for contract enforcement. Looking at how disputes were resolved in and outside courts, Goetzmann and Köll (2005) conclude that the passing of China's first Company Law in 1904, which was intended to provide a better legal environment for business and commerce, did not lead to actual changes in corporate governance and better protection of (minority) shareholder rights.

the pre-1949 capitalist companies and institutions were nationalized by 1950. Between 1950 and 1978, China's financial system consisted of a single bank—the People's Bank of China (PBOC), a central government-owned and controlled bank under the Ministry of Finance, which served as both the central bank and a commercial bank, controlling about 93 percent of the total financial assets of the country and handling almost all financial transactions. With its main role to finance the physical production plans, the PBOC used both a "cash-plan" and a "credit-plan" to control the cash flows in consumer markets and transfer flows between branches.

The first main structural change began in 1978 and ended in 1984. By the end of 1979, the PBOC departed the Ministry and became a separate entity, while three state-owned banks took over some of its commercial banking businesses: the Bank of China[5] (BOC) was given the mandate to specialize in transactions related to foreign trade and investment; the People's Construction Bank of China (PCBC), originally formed in 1954, was set up to handle transactions related to fixed investment (especially in manufacturing); the Agriculture Bank of China (ABC) was set up (in 1979) to deal with all banking business in rural areas; and the PBOC was formally established as China's central bank and a two-tier banking system was formed. Finally, the fourth state-owned commercial bank, the Industrial and Commercial Bank of China (ICBC), was formed in 1984, and took over the rest of the commercial transactions of the PBOC.

For most of the 1980s, the development of the financial system can be characterized by the fast growth of financial intermediaries outside of the "Big Four" banks. Regional banks (partially owned by local governments) were formed in the Special Economic Zones in the coastal areas; in rural areas, a network of Rural Credit Cooperatives (RCCs; similar to credit unions in the United States) was set up under the supervision of the ABC, while Urban Credit Cooperatives (UCCs), counterparts of the RCCs in the urban areas, were also founded. Nonbank financial intermediaries, such as the Trust and Investment Corporations (TICs; operating in selected banking and nonbanking services with restrictions on both deposits and loans), emerged and proliferated in this period.

The most significant event for China's financial system in the 1990s was the inception and growth of China's stock market. Two domestic stock exchanges (SHSE and SZSE) were established in 1990 and grew very fast during most of the 1990s and in recent years in terms of the total market capitalization and trading volume. In parallel with the development of the stock market, the real estate market also went from nonexistent in the early 1990s to one that is currently comparable in size with the stock market.[6] Both

5. The BOC, among the oldest banks currently in operation, was originally established in 1912 as a private bank, and specialized in foreign currency-related transactions.
6. At the end of 2007, the total market capitalization of the two domestic exchanges (SHSE and SZSE) was around $1.8 trillion, whereas total investment in the real estate market was around $3.12 trillion.

the stock and real estate markets have experienced major corrections during the past decade, and are characterized by high volatilities and speculative short-term behaviors by many investors.

These patterns are in part due to the fact that the development of a supportive legal framework and institutions has been lagging behind that of the markets. For example, China's first bankruptcy law (governing state-owned enterprises, or SOEs) was passed in 1986 on a trial basis, but the formal Company Law did not become effective until the end of 1999. This version of the Company Law governs all corporations with limited liability, publicly listed and traded companies, and branches or divisions of foreign companies, as well as their organization structure, securities issuance and trading, accounting, bankruptcy, and mergers and acquisitions (for details see the website of China Securities Regulatory Commission [CSRC], http://www.csrc.gov.cn/). In August 2006, a new bankruptcy law was enacted, and it became effective June 1, 2007. We provide a brief analysis of the status and problems of the stock market and real estate market in section 2.4.

Following the Asian Financial Crisis in 1997, financial sector reform has focused on state-owned banks and especially the problem of NPLs (the China Banking Regulation Committee [CBRC] was also established to oversee the banking industry). We will further discuss this issue in section 2.3. China's entry into the WTO in December 2001 marked the beginning of a new era, as we continue to observe increasing competition from foreign financial institutions and more frequent and larger scale capital flows. While increasingly larger inflows of foreign capital and the presence of foreign institutions may continue to drive further growth of the financial system and economy, larger scale capital flows can also increase the likelihood of damaging financial crises. We will discuss these issues in sections 2.4 and 2.6.

A developed financial system is characterized by, among other factors, the substantial role played by institutional investors. In China, institutional investors began to emerge in the late 1990s: the first closed-end fund, in which investors cannot withdraw capital after initial investment, was set up in 1997, and the first open-end fund, in which investors can freely withdraw capital (subject to share redemption restrictions), was established in 2001. By November 2009, there were sixty-five fund companies managing 551 funds with 520 open-ended funds and the rest close-ended. The total net assets value (NAV) increased from RMB 11 billion (or US$1.3 billion) in 1998 to RMB 2.26 trillion (or $328 billion) in November 2009, which is still small compared to the assets within the banking sector. In 2003, a few Qualified Foreign Institutional Investors (QFII) entered China's asset management industry, and they have been operating through forming joint ventures with Chinese companies. On the other hand, China allowed Qualified Domestic Institutional Investors (QDII) to invest in overseas markets beginning in July 2006. At the end of 2008, the ten QDII funds had a total of $109.4 billion assets under management.

At the national level, the China Investment Corporation (CIC) was established in September 2007 with the intent of utilizing the accumulated foreign reserves for the benefit of the state and $207.91 billion foreign reserves were placed under management at the establishment. The CIC makes occasional announcements about its investment, but the overall transparency of its investment strategy is low. Since inception, CIC has made some aggressive investment decisions, including the well-publicized $3 billion (pre-IPO [initial public offering]) investment in private equity group Blackstone, and the $5 billion investment in Morgan Stanley (this took the form of mandatory convertible bonds that can be converted into almost 10 percent of the firm's equity).

Endowed with limited capital and given problems with the administration of the pension system, pension funds have not played a significant role in the stock or bond market.[7] With a fast aging population and the growth of households' disposable income, further development of a multipillar pension system, including individual accounts with employees' self-contributed (tax exempt) funds that can be directly invested in the financial markets, can lead to the development of both the financial system and the fiscal system as well as social stability. At the top of the pension fund system, China's National Social Security Fund (NSSF) was established in August 2002 and is administered by the National Council for Social Security Fund. This (sovereign) fund is mainly financed by capital and equity assets derived from the listing of state-owned companies, fiscal allocations from the central government, and other investment proceeds. It has recently shifted its core investment strategy of focusing on the domestic A-share and bond markets to a more diversified basket of assets, including investments in emerging markets and Europe. At the end of 2008, the fund had a total of $89.2 billion in assets; it grew to RMB 856.7 billion ($142.8 billion) at the end of 2010, according to the annual report of NSSF. Finally, there are very few hedge funds that implement "long-short" strategies, as short selling has been prohibited until recently.[8]

Figure 2.1 depicts the current structure of the entire financial system. In what follows we will describe and examine each of the major sectors of the financial system. In addition to the standard sectors of banking and intermediation and financial markets, we will document the importance of

7. While there is a nationwide, government-run pension system (financed mainly through taxes on employers and employees), the coverage ratio of the pension system varies significantly across regions and is particularly low in rural areas. Moreover, there is a very limited amount of capital in individual accounts and most of the capital has been invested in banks and government projects with low returns. See, for example, Feldstein (1999, 2003) and Feldstein and Liebman (2006), for more details on China's pension system.
8. Along with the introduction of an index future (for A shares) in April 2010, a trial program on short selling began for selected institutional investors (security companies; see, e.g., www.wsj .com, 3/31/2010). The impact of introducing these new programs and products on the financial market is yet to be seen.

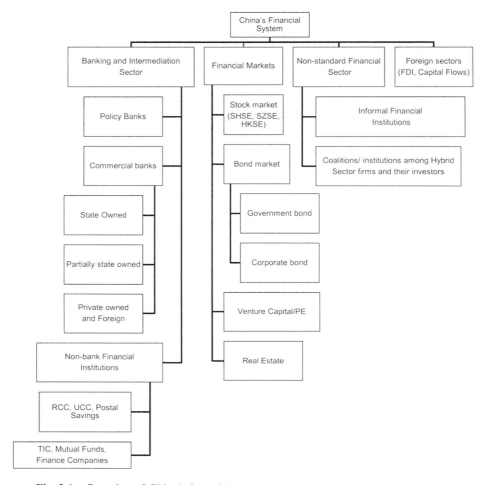

Fig. 2.1 Overview of China's financial system

the nonstandard financial sector. Due to space limitations, we do not cover China's "foreign sectors" in this chapter; for discussions on the history and the role of these sectors in supporting the growth of the economy, see, for example, Prasad and Wei (2007) for a review.

2.2.2 Size and Efficiency of the Financial System: Banks, Markets, and Alternative Finance

In table 2.1, we compare China's financial system to those of other major emerging economies, with measures for the size and efficiency of banks and markets taken from Levine (2002) and Demirgüç-Kunt and Levine (2001) and data from the World Bank Financial Database. We present average

Table 2.1   Comparing financial systems: Banks and markets (average 2001–2007)

Measures	Size of banks and markets				Structure indices: Markets vs. banks[a]				Financial development[b] (banking and market sectors)		
	Bank credit/GDP	NPL/total loans	Value traded/GDP	Market cap/GDP	Structure activity	Structure size	Structure efficiency	Structure regulatory	Finance activity	Finance size	Finance efficiency
China	1.16	0.16	0.62	0.64	−0.62	8.88	2.32	16	8.88	8.91	5.97
Argentina	0.14	0.10	0.04	0.48	−1.32	3.93	1.59	7	3.93	6.50	3.60
Brazil	0.34	0.04	0.19	0.53	−0.61	6.45	0.72	10	6.45	7.49	6.17
Egypt	0.52	0.21	0.19	0.60	−1.02	6.88	2.54	13	6.88	8.04	4.48
India	0.37	0.07	0.57	0.64	0.44	7.65	1.50	10	7.65	7.76	6.71
Indonesia	0.24	0.12	0.12	0.28	−0.69	5.66	1.23	n/a	5.66	6.51	4.60
Malaysia	1.15	0.12	0.43	1.45	−0.98	8.51	2.85	10	8.51	9.72	5.89
Mexico	0.18	0.03	0.06	0.26	−0.99	4.74	−0.26	12	4.74	6.11	5.38
Pakistan	0.26	0.14	0.72	0.28	1.01	7.55	1.36	10	7.55	6.61	6.26
Peru	0.21	0.08	0.03	0.44	−1.96	4.10	1.22	8	4.10	6.81	3.63
Philippines	0.34	0.15	0.07	0.47	−1.54	5.50	1.97	7	5.50	7.36	3.85
Russia	0.26	0.04	0.27	0.65	0.06	6.54	0.96	n/a	6.54	7.41	6.52
S. Africa	1.38	0.02	0.88	2.06	−0.45	9.40	1.43	8	9.40	10.25	8.38
Sri Lanka	0.31	0.15	0.03	0.18	−2.33	4.52	1.00	7	4.52	6.31	2.97
Thailand	1.02	0.11	0.50	0.63	−0.72	8.52	1.95	9	8.52	8.77	6.10
Turkey	0.20	0.10	0.39	0.28	0.67	6.65	1.05	12	6.65	6.32	5.93
Ave. for EMs	0.46	0.10	0.30	0.62	−0.70	6.44	1.41	9.46	6.44	7.46	5.36

Notes: This table compares the financial markets and banking sector of China with those of other large emerging economies. All the measures on the size and efficiency of banks and markets are based on Levine (2002) and Demirgüç-Kunt and Levine (2001), and data are from the World Bank Financial Database. We present the 2001–2007 average figures for all countries (except for "structure regulatory," which are based on 2005 figures). Average of other emerging economies are (simple) averages across other emerging economies excluding China.

[a]Structure indices measure whether a country's financial system is market- or bank-dominated; the higher the measure, the more the system is dominated by markets. Specifically, "structure activity" is equal to log(value traded/bank credit) and measures size of bank credit relative to trading volume of markets; "structure size" is equal to log(market cap/bank credit) and measures the size of markets relative to banks; "structure efficiency" is equal to log(market cap ratio × bank NPL ratio) and measures the relative efficiency of markets versus banks; finally, "structure regulatory" is the sum of the four categories in regulatory restriction, or the degree to which commercial banks are allowed to engage in security, firm operation, insurance, and real estate: (1) unrestricted; (2) permit to conduct through subsidiary; (3) full range not permitted in subsidiaries; and (4) strictly prohibited.

[b]Financial development variables measure the entire financial system (banking and market sectors combined), and the higher the measure, the larger or more efficient the financial system is. Specifically, "finance activity" is equal to log(total value traded ratio × bank private credit ratio), "finance size" is equal to log(market cap ratio × bank private credit ratio), and "finance efficiency" is equal to log(total value traded ratio/bank NPL ratio).

figures over the period 2001 to 2007 for each country as well as the average of all the other emerging economies (excluding China). We first compare the *size* of a country's banks and equity markets relative to that country's gross domestic product (GDP). In terms of total market capitalization, China's stock market, at 64 percent of its GDP over the period 2001 to 2007, is slightly larger than the 58 percent of GDP average of the other major emerging economies. "Value Traded" is perhaps a better measure of the actual size of the market than "market capitalization," because the latter includes nontradable shares or tradable shares that are rarely traded. In this regard, the size of China's stock market (62 percent of GDP) is significantly larger than the average of other emerging economies (with an average of 37 percent of GDP). Similarly, the size of China's banking system, in terms of total bank credit to nonstate sectors, is 116 percent of its GDP over 2001 to 2007, and considerably larger than the average of other major emerging economies (with an average of 65 percent of GDP). However, the majority of the bank credit goes to state-owned firms in China and only a small fraction goes to firms in the Hybrid Sector (more evidence of this is given later). In addition, NPLs account for a larger fraction of all the loans in China than the average of other emerging economies (16 percent vs. 10 percent), indicating that its banking sector still has scope to improve its efficiency.[9]

The next two columns of table 2.1 ("Structure indices") compare the relative importance of financial markets versus banks, with a lower score indicating that banks are more important relative to markets. China's score for "Structure size" (Log of the ratio of Market Capitalization/Total Bank Credit) is positive, suggesting that the size of total market capitalization is actually larger than that of bank credit, and the score is greater than the average of other emerging economies; its score for "Structure activity" (Log of the ratio of Float supply of market cap/Total Bank Credit) is negative, indicating that float supply fraction of the market cap is still smaller than bank credit, and it is similar to the average of other emerging economies. Taken together, these numbers suggest that the financial system of most emerging economies, including that of China, remains bank-dominated. In terms of "Structure efficiency" (Log of product [Market capitalization/ GDP] × [bank NPLs/bank total loans]), which denotes the relative efficiency of markets versus banks, China has a higher score than most other developing countries, suggesting that its banks are relatively less efficient than markets compared to other countries. "Structure regulatory" measures (based on 2005 data) the extent to which commercial banks are restricted to par-

9. Levine (2002) uses bank overhead cost/total assets to measure banking sector efficiency, and used this measure to construct the "Structure Efficiency" and "Finance Efficiency" measures. However, the World Bank Financial Database no longer reports the overhead cost/assets ratio; we replace this with NPLs/loans ratio as an alternative measure of efficiency and use this variable to define other efficiency measures in table 2.1.

ticipate in activities outside commercial lending, and China's score of 16 is higher than most other countries, suggesting that by law commercial banks in China face tight restrictions in operating in other areas.

We also compare the development of the financial system ("Financial development"), including both banks and markets (the last three columns of table 2.1). China's overall financial market size, in terms of both "Finance activity" (Log of product of [Float supply of market/GDP] × [Bank credit/GDP]) and "Finance size" (Log of product of [Market capitalization/GDP] + [Bank credit/GDP]), are larger than the averages of other emerging countries. In terms of "Finance efficiency" (Log of [Total floating supply/GDP]/[Bank NPLs Ratio]), China's measure is slightly higher than the average of other emerging countries. Based on the evidence from the past decade, we can conclude that China's banks and markets, or the formal sectors of the financial system, are as large as or larger than other major emerging economies (relative to its size of the economy). However, the banking sector does not lend much to the Hybrid Sector, which as we will see in section 2.5, is the dynamic part of the economy.

A related question to the size of banks and markets is where do most firms get the capital and funds? As shown in AQQ (2005, 2008), the four most important financing sources for all firms in China, in terms of firms' *fixed asset investments,* are (domestic) bank loans, firms' self-fundraising, the state budget, and foreign direct investment (FDI), with self-fundraising and bank loans carrying most of the weight. Self-fundraising, falling into the category of alternative finance (nonbank, nonmarket finance), includes proceeds from capital raised from *local* governments (beyond the state budget), communities and other investors, internal financing channels such as retained earnings, and all other funds raised domestically by the firms. The size of total self-fundraising of all firms has been growing at an average annual rate of 23.6 percent over the period of 1994 to 2009, and reached $2,213.2 billion at the end of 2009, compared to a total of $565.7 billion for domestic bank loans for the same year. It is important to point out that equity and bond issuance, which are included in self-fundraising (but fall into the category of formal external finance), apply only to the Listed Sector, and account for a small fraction of this category.

While the Listed Sector has been growing fast, SOEs are on a downward trend, as privatization of these firms is still in progress. Around 30 percent of publicly traded companies' funding comes from bank loans, and this ratio has been very stable. Around 45 percent of the Listed Sector's total funding comes from self-fundraising, including internal financing and proceeds from equity and bond issuance. Moreover, equity and bond sales, which rely on the use of external markets, only constitute a small fraction of total funds raised in comparison to internal financing and other forms of fundraising. Combined with the fact that self-fundraising is also the most important source of financing for the State Sector (45 percent to 65 percent), we can conclude that alternative channels of financing are important even for the State and Listed Sectors.

Not surprisingly, self-fundraising plays an even more important role for firms in the Hybrid Sector, accounting for close to 60 percent of total funds raised, while individually owned companies, a subset of the Hybrid Sector, rely on self-fundraising for 90 percent of total financing. Self-fundraising here includes all forms of internal finance, capital raised from family and friends of the founders and managers, and funds raised in the form of private equity and loans. Since firms in this sector operate in an environment with legal and financial mechanisms and regulations that are probably poorer than those available for firms in the State and Listed Sectors, financing sources may work differently from how they work in the State and Listed Sectors, and those in developed countries. In Allen et al. (2008, ACDQQ hereafter), the authors argue that alternative finance channels substitute for formal financing channels through banks and markets, and expand the capacity of financial systems in emerging countries such as China and India.

2.3   The Banking and Intermediation Sector

In this section, we examine the status of China's banking and intermediation sector. After reviewing aggregate evidence on bank deposits and loans, we analyze the size and time trend of NPLs. Finally, we review evidence on the growth of nonstate banks and financial intermediaries.

2.3.1   Aggregate Evidence on Bank Deposits and Loans

As in other Asian countries, China's household savings rates have been high throughout the reform era. Given the growth of the economy, the sharp increase in personal income, and limited investment opportunities, it is not surprising that total bank deposits from individuals have been growing fast since the mid-1980s. From figure 2.2, residents in metropolitan areas contribute the most to total deposits beginning in the late 1980s (roughly 50 percent), while deposits from enterprises (including firms from all three sectors) provide the second most important source. The role of deposits from government agencies and organizations (including nonprofit and for-profit organizations, not shown in the figure) has steadily decreased over time.

Table 2.2 compares total savings and bank deposits in China, Japan, South Korea, and India during the period 1997 to 2009. In terms of the ratio of Time and Savings Deposits/GDP, China maintains the highest or second-highest level (an average of over 90 percent in recent years), while Japan leads the group in terms of total amount. Looking at the breakdown of bank deposits, interest-bearing "savings deposits" are by far the most important form of deposits in China, providing a good source for bank

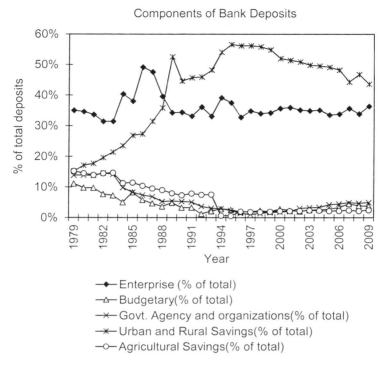

Fig. 2.2   Sources for bank deposits in China

loans and other forms of investment. Figure 2.3 compares total (nonstate) bank credit (over GDP) extended to Hybrid Sector firms in China, and privately-owned firms (including those publicly listed and traded) in Taiwan and South Korea. For South Korea, we also plot the bank credit ratios during its high economic growth period of the 1970s and 1980s (each year appearing on the horizontal axis indicates the time period for China, while a particular year *minus* 20 indicates the time period for South Korea). We can see that the scale and growth of China's "hybrid" bank credit during 1991 to 2009 are far below those (of private bank credit) of Taiwan and South Korea in the same period, but are similar to those of South Korea twenty years ago.

Table 2.3 breaks down China's bank loans by maturities, loan purposes, and borrower types during the period 1994 to 2009. While there has been a shift from short-term to long-term loans (first two columns), the majority of loans goes to SOEs in manufacturing industries ("Industrial loans" and "Commercial loans"). Most of the "Infrastructure/construction loans" (a small component of total loans) fund government-sponsored projects, while the size of "Agricultural loans" is much smaller. More importantly,

Table 2.2   Comparisons of total savings and deposits (in US$ billions)

	1998	1999	2000	2001	2002	2003	2004	2005	2006	2007	2008	2009
					China							
Demand deposits[a]	320	391	465	533	647	777	899	1,030	1,265	1,671	1,931	2,683
Savings deposits[b]	606	674	722	820	961	1,143	1,445	1,748	2,069	2,363	3,187	3,811
Time deposits[c]	100	114	136	171	199	253	307	410	676	878	1,205	1,661
Time and savings dep/GDP	68%	73%	72%	75%	80%	85%	91%	95%	101%	92%	100%	114%
					Japan							
Demand deposits[a]	1,793	2,259	2,073	1,838	2,567	3,523	3,795	3,541	3,523	3,683	4,560	—
Time, savings, and foreign currency deposits	7,921	8,997	8,059	5,351	5,383	5,416	5,448	4,642	4,536	4,778	6,160	—
Time and savings dep/GDP	181%	185%	184%	142%	131%	118%	114%	109%	106%	106%	110%	—
					South Korea							
Demand deposits[a]	18	22	23	27	36	38	46	54	67	66	50	63
Time, savings, and foreign currency deposits	185	251	289	315	383	410	467	485	546	543	471	574
Time and savings dep/GDP	46%	54%	61%	64%	63%	64%	58%	57%	56%	52%	58%	63%
					India							
Demand deposits[a]	24	28	31	32	35	44	60	71	89	114	96	119
Time, savings, and foreign currency deposits	140	161	175	198	235	277	333	368	460	647	653	800
Time and savings dep/GDP	34%	36%	39%	42%	46%	46%	46%	46%	49%	54%	59%	60%

Source: IMF and CEIC database.

[a]Demand deposits, balance of the accounts can be withdrawn on demand of customers (e.g., check writing).

[b]Savings deposits, interest-bearing accounts that can be withdrawn but cannot be used as money (e.g., no check writing).

[c]Time deposits, savings accounts, or CD with a fixed term.

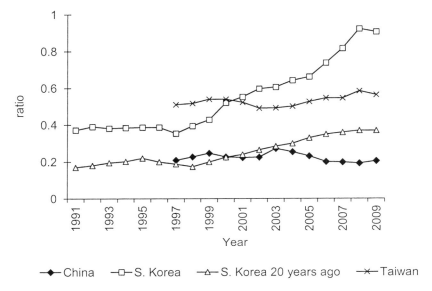

Fig. 2.3   Comparing total bank credit extended to private/hybrid sectors

the size of loans made to TVEs, privately- and collectively-owned firms, and joint ventures (last three columns), which all belong to the Hybrid Sector, is also much smaller. Consistent with the aggregate evidence from section 2.2 and our firm-level evidence later, we find that bank loans have been one of the important financing sources for Hybrid Sector firms, but the majority of the bank loans goes to the State and Listed Sectors. Researchers have argued that the imbalance between loans made to the State Sector and the Hybrid Sector reflects the government's policies of wealth transfer from the Hybrid Sector to the State Sector via state-owned banks (e.g., Brandt and Zhu 2000).

2.3.2   An Analysis of NPLs and Further Reform of the Banking Sector

China's banking sector is dominated by large state-owned banks, namely, the "Big Four" banks of ICBC, BOC, PCBC, and ABC. The dominance of the Big Four banks also implies that the degree of competition within the banking sector has been low. For example, Demirgüç-Kunt and Levine (2001) compare the five-bank concentration (share of the assets of the five largest banks in total banking assets), and find that China's concentration ratio of 91 percent at the end of 1997 (and for much of the 1990s) is one of the highest in the world. However, China's concentration ratio has been falling sharply since 1997 with the entrance of many nonstate banks and intermediaries.

The most significant problem for China's banking sector, and for the entire

Table 2.3   Breakdown of bank loans (end-of-year figures in RMB billions)

Year	Total loans	Short-term loans	Industrial loans	Commercial loans	Infrastructure construction loans	Agricultural loans	Loans to TVEs	Privately owned firms	Joint ventures and cooperative firms
1994	3,997.60	2,694.87	994.83	1,050.98	61.72	114.39	200.24	15.59	79.23
1995	5,054.41	3,337.20	1,177.47	1,283.71	79.93	154.48	251.49	19.62	99.91
1996	6,115.66	4,021.00	1,421.33	1,533.26	97.38	191.91	282.19	27.98	134.63
1997	7,491.41	5,541.83	1,652.66	1,835.66	159.11	331.46	503.58	38.67	189.10
1998	8,652.41	6,061.32	1,782.15	1,975.24	162.87	444.42	558.00	47.16	248.75
1999	9,373.43	6,388.76	1,794.89	1,989.09	147.69	479.24	616.13	57.91	298.58
2000	9,937.11	6,574.81	1,701.93	1,786.85	161.71	488.90	606.08	65.46	304.98
2001	11,231.47	6,732.72	1,863.67	1,856.34	209.96	571.15	641.30	91.80	326.35
2002	13,129.39	7,424.79	2,019.05	1,797.31	274.80	688.46	681.23	105.88	269.74
2003	15,899.62	8,366.12	2,275.60	1,799.44	300.21	841.14	766.16	146.16	256.94
2004	17,819.78	8,684.06	2,389.66	1,707.41	278.01	984.31	806.92	208.16	219.84
2005	19,469.04	8,744.92	2,251.67	1,644.76	298.37	1,152.99	790.18	218.08	197.53
2006	22,534.72	9,853.44	2,865.40	1,667.15	361.26	1,320.82	622.20	266.76	183.27
2007	26,169.09	11,447.79	3,362.33	1,783.33	374.19	1,542.93	711.26	350.77	206.91
2008	30,339.46	12,518.17	3,614.29	1,773.22	368.46	1,762.88	745.40	422.38	227.08
2009	39,968.48	14,661.13	3,876.92	1,948.33	364.68	2,162.25	902.90	712.10	218.03

Source: Statistical Yearbooks of China, CEIC database (1985–2009).

financial system during the last decade, was the amount of NPLs within state-owned banks, and in particular, among the Big Four banks. Reducing the amount of NPLs to normal levels was a high priority for China's financial system. We mainly rely on official sources for our analysis on NPLs, but we also speculate based on data from nongovernment sources, including case studies from particular regions or banks. Some of this data and speculations paint a much gloomier picture of the NPLs and China's state-owned banks than the official data suggests.

Comparing NPLs and Reducing NPLs in China

In panel A of Table 2.4, we compare NPLs in China, the United States, and other major Asian economies during 1998 to 2010 based on official figures. The NPLs are measured by their size (in US$ billion) and as a percentage of GDP in the same year (shown in parentheses). Notice that the official information on China's NPLs first became available in 1998, but the figures in 1998 and 1999 in table 2.4 probably significantly underestimate the actual size of NPLs; this also explains the jump in the size of China's NPLs from 1999 to 2000. China's NPLs are the highest in the group from 2000 to 2007, and as high as 20 percent to 22.5 percent of GDP (in 2000 and 2001). The cross-country comparison includes the period during which Asian countries recovered from the 1997 financial crisis (e.g., the size of NPLs in South Korea exceeded 12 percent of GDP in 1999 but it was reduced to below 3 percent two years later), and the period during which the Japanese banking system was disturbed by the prolonged NPL problem (the size of Japan's NPLs is the second-largest of the group throughout the period). However, the level of NPLs (over GDP) in China has shown a clear downward trend since the peak in 2000 and 2001, with the total amount of NPLs also falling during 2004 to 2010. In fact, with the banking sector in most developed countries struggling with the ongoing global financial crisis, China's banking sector has done quite well, with its total NPLs in 2010 ($68.1 billion) only one-seventh of that of the United States and the ratio of NPLs over GDP falling below that of the United States as well.

As bad as some of the NPL numbers in early years in panel A of table 2.4 appear, they may still significantly underestimate the amount of NPLs within China's banking system according to some critics. First, the official figures on outstanding NPLs (cumulated across all commercial banks in China) do not include the bad loans that have been transferred from banks to four state-owned asset management companies (AMCs) with the purpose of liquidating these bad loans. For example, if we add the NPLs held by the four AMCs (book value of RMB 866 billion, or $125.5 billion, shown in the last row of table 2.5) in the first quarter of 2006 to the mix of NPLs shown in panel A of table 2.4, the total amount of China's NPLs would increase by two-thirds. Furthermore, the classification of NPLs has been problematic in China. The Basle Committee for Bank Supervision classifies a loan

Table 2.4   **A comparison of nonperforming loans (NPLs) and government debt**

A. Size of NPLs: In US$ billion and as percentage of GDPs in the same year (in parentheses)

Year	China	United States	Japan	Korea	India	Indonesia	Taiwan
1997	—	66.9 (0.8%)	217.4 (5.1%)	16.2 (3.1%)	—	0.2 (0.1%)	19.6 (6.5%)
1998	20.5 (2.0%)	71.3 (0.8%)	489.7 (12.7%)	23.2 (6.7%)	12.7 (3.1%)	5.5 (5.2%)	21.8 (7.9%)
1999	105.1 (9.7%)	72.2 (0.8%)	547.6 (12.6%)	54.4 (12.2%)	14.0 (3.2%)	3.2 (3.8%)	27.2 (9.1%)
2000	269.3 (22.5%)	90.1 (0.9%)	515.4 (11.1%)	35.5 (6.9%)	12.9 (2.8%)	6.3 (2.7%)	33.2 (10.3%)
2001	265.3 (20.0%)	108.4 (1.1%)	640.1 (15.6%)	12.2 (2.5%)	13.2 (2.8%)	4.3 (1.7%)	37.9 (13.0%)
2002	188.4 (13.0%)	107.8 (1.0%)	552.5 (14.1%)	9.9 (1.8%)	14.8 (3.0%)	3.3 (2.0%)	30.7 (10.4%)
2003	181.2 (11.0%)	95.9 (1.0%)	480.1 (11.3%)	11.7 (1.9%)	14.6 (2.5%)	4.7 (1.5%)	23.1 (7.7%)
2004	207.4 (10.7%)	81.3 (0.9%)	334.8 (7.3%)	10.0 (1.5%)	14.4 (2.2%)	3.8 (2.1%)	26.4 (5.1%)
2005	164.2 (7.3%)	84.6 (0.7%)	183.3 (4.0%)	7.6 (1.0%)	13.4 (1.7%)	6.0 (1.5%)	11.2 (3.2%)
2006	157.4 (5.9%)	103.8 (0.8%)	157.8 (3.6%)	8.2 (0.9%)	11.2 (1.3%)	5.2 (1.4%)	11.3 (3.1%)
2007	166.8 (5.1%)	168.1 (1.2%)	148.6 (3.4%)	8.3 (0.8%)	13.6 (1.2%)	4.5 (1.0%)	10.0 (2.6%)
2008	80.6 (1.9%)	328.7 (2.3%)	190.8 (3.7%)	13.0 (1.4%)	15.4 (1.3%)	4.3 (0.8%)	9.0 (2.3%)
2009	72.6 (1.5%)	477.5 (3.3%)	188.5 (3.63%)	13.9 (1.5%)	18.2 (1.3%)	4.6 (1.0%)	6.7 (1.8%)
2010	68.1 (1.1%)	423.4 (2.9%)	208.7 (3.82%)	26.8 (2.6%)	20.7 (1.2%)	4.3 (0.6%)	3.8 (0.9%)

B. Outstanding government debt ($ billion)

Year	China Outstanding government bond	United States Total government debt	Japan Total government debt	Korea Outstanding treasury bonds	India Total public debt	Indonesia Outstanding government bond	Taiwan Outstanding government bond
1997	66.5	5,802.8	4,254.0	5.3	—	—	—
1998	93.8	5,788.8	4,858.0	14.4	178.4	—	—
1999	127.3	5,822.7	6,053.1	28.5	260.2	34.1	46.5
2000	165.1	5,612.7	6,209.8	32.7	232.4	45.1	45.5
2001	188.6	5,734.4	6,036.0	39.8	225.4	43.5	58.7
2002	233.5	6,169.4	6,321.3	45.2	250.2	42.1	77.7
2003	273.0	6,789.7	6,852.9	67.9	259.7	48.0	75.7
2004	311.3	7,335.6	7,446.6	107.0	299.6	44.7	85.2
2005	350.0	7,809.5	8,299.5	165.5	347.1	39.9	86.7

2006	364.6	8,451.4	7,587.1	216.7	375.2	45.7	85.8
2007	599.8	8,950.7	7,707.7	245.0	472.0	51.8	94.5
2008	701.6	9,985.8	8,966.2	217.8	496.4	52.8	90.4
2009	753.6	12,867.5	9,466.8	290.9	556.6	52.5	82.9
2010	805.3	14,551.8	11,284.9	364.0	643.6	68.4	102.0

C. (NPLs + Outstanding government debt)/GDP

Year							
1997	—	0.71 (0.54)	1.05 (0.40)	0.04	—	—	—
1998	0.11	0.67 (0.50)	1.39 (0.63)	0.11	0.46	—	—
1999	0.21	0.64 (0.45)	1.51 (0.64)	0.19	0.62	0.24	0.25
2000	0.36	0.58 (0.40)	1.45 (0.65)	0.13	0.53	0.31	0.24
2001	0.34	0.58 (0.39)	1.63 (0.83)	0.11	0.50	0.30	0.33
2002	0.29	0.60 (0.42)	1.76 (0.90)	0.10	0.54	0.23	0.37
2003	0.28	0.63 (0.45)	1.73 (0.86)	0.13	0.48	0.22	0.33
2004	0.27	0.63 (0.46)	1.70 (0.81)	0.17	0.47	0.19	0.32
2005	0.23	0.63 (0.47)	1.86 (0.84)	0.22	0.47	0.16	0.27
2006	0.20	0.65 (0.44)	1.78 (0.88)	0.24	0.44	0.14	0.26
2007	0.23	0.66 (0.45)	1.79 (0.89)	0.24	0.44	0.13	0.27
2008	0.18	0.72 (0.50)	1.78 (0.88)	0.25	0.42	0.11	0.25
2009	0.17	0.94 (0.46)	1.55 (1.15)	0.24	0.58	0.11	0.24
2010	0.21	1.01 (0.70)	1.94 (1.20)	0.33	0.45	0.10	0.25

Sources: Statistical Bureau of China, the People's Bank of China, Chinese Banking Regulatory Commission; Board of Governors of the Federal Reserve Bank, Statistical Abstracts of the United States; the Statistical Bureau of Japan; Ministry of Finance, Korea, the Bank of Korea, Korean Statistical Information System; IMF; World Bank; Bank Indonesia; Ministry of Finance, India; National Statistical Bureau of Taiwan, Bloomberg, Chinabond, and Taiwan financial supervisory commission.

Notes: This table compares total outstanding NPLs within the banking system, government debt, and the ratio of (NPLs + Government Debt)/GDP among China, the United States, and other major Asian countries for the period 1997–2010. Panel A presents the size of the NPLs, as measured by US$ billion and as the percentage of GDPs in the same year. The NPLs in the United States measure the outstanding "delinquency loan"; NPLs in Japan measure the "risk management loans" (or loans disclosed under the Financial Reconstructed Law and/or loans subject to self-assessment). In panel B, outstanding government debt is measured at the end of each year; for the United States and Japan, total government debt includes domestic and foreign debt. In panel C, the ratios for China include using the official NPL numbers and using doubled official NPLs (i.e., the ratios in the parentheses are [doubled NPLs + government debt]/GDP); the ratios in the parentheses for the United States and Japan are (net government debt + NPLs)/GDP, where net government debt is the difference between government borrowing (stock measure) and government lending (flow measure). All figures are converted into US dollars using the average exchange rate within the observation year.

as "doubtful" or bad when any *interest* payment is overdue by 180 days or more (in the United States it is 90 days); whereas in China, this step has not typically been taken until the *principal* payment is delayed beyond the loan maturity date or an extended due date, and in many cases, until the borrower has declared bankruptcy and/or has gone through liquidation. Qiu, Li, and Cai (2000) estimate that the ratio of loan interest paid to *state-owned* banks over loan interest owed is on average less than 50 percent in 1999, suggesting that the actual ratio of NPLs over total loans made can be higher than 50 percent in 1999. This piece of evidence, along with others, suggests that the amount of NPLs (and as a percentage of GDP) could be twice as large as the official figures reported in panel A of table 2.4.[10]

Since a large fraction of the NPLs among state-owned banks, and in particular, the Big Four banks, resulted from poor lending decisions made for SOEs, some of which were due to political or other noneconomic reasons, it can be argued that the natural party to bear the burden of reducing the NPLs is the government. This view of essentially treating NPLs as a fiscal problem implies that the ultimate source of eliminating NPLs lies in China's overall economic growth.[11] As long as the economy maintains its strong growth momentum so that tax receipts also increase, the government can always assume the remaining (and new) NPLs without significantly affecting the economy. In this regard, panel B of table 2.4 compares total outstanding government debt, and panel C presents a comparison of the ratio of (NPLs + Government Debt)/GDP across countries, with the sum of NPLs and government debt indicating the total burden of the government. Depending on data availability, total government debt is either measured by the sum of all types of domestic and foreign debt (the United States, Japan, and India), or by the level of outstanding government bonds (all other countries) in a given year.

Unlike the severity of its NPL problem in the early 2000s, the Chinese government has not issued a large amount of debt, with total outstanding government bonds growing from only 9 percent of GDP in 1998 to around 20 percent of GDP in 2010. By contrast, countries such as the United States and India have a large amount of government debt. Japan is the only country in the group that has a large amount of NPLs *and* government debt for most of the period. When we combine the results from panels A and B and compare the total government burden in panel C, we use two sets of ratios for the United States and Japan. In addition to using total outstanding

10. Consistent with this view, Lardy (1998) argues that, if using international standards on bad loans, the existing NPLs within China's state-owned banks as of the mid-1990s would make these banks' total net worth negative, so that the entire network of state banks would have been insolvent.

11. See, for example, Perkins and Rawski (2008) for a review and projections on the prospects of long-run economic growth and statistics in China.

government debt, we use ratios (in parentheses) based on the sum of *net* government debt and NPLs, where net government debt is the difference between government borrowing (a "stock" measure) and government lending (also a stock measure); not surprisingly, these ratios are much lower than using the gross figures.

From panel C, China's total government burden is in the middle of the pack: the ratios of total government burden over GDP (using the official NPL figures) are significantly lower than those in Japan, the United States, and India; are comparable with those of Taiwan and Korea; and are higher than Indonesia only. In recent years, even if we double the size of the official NPL figures, China's total government burden would not increase much as the total amount of NPLs is small relative to the size of GDPs. Based on these crude comparisons, going forward it seems that the NPLs should not be an arduous burden for the Chinese government (or the banking sector), while the same cannot be said for Japan and the United States. Caution is needed for this conclusion: first, new NPLs in China may grow much faster than other countries as the government's recent massive economic stimulus plan led to a significant increase in new loans made during 2008 and 2009, including many questionable loans to local governments;[12] and second, China's currently small government debt may experience a sharp increase in the near future given the need for higher fiscal spending in areas such as pension plans and other social welfare programs.

Recognizing the importance of and its responsibility in reducing NPLs in the Big Four banks, the Chinese government injected large amounts of foreign currency reserves (mostly in the form of US dollars, T-bills, Euros, and Yen) into these banks to improve their balance sheets in preparation for going public. This process began at the end of 2003, with the establishment of the Central Huijin Investment Company, through which the PBOC injected US$45 billion of reserves into the BOC and PCBC, while ICBC (the largest commercial bank in China and one of the largest in the world in terms of assets) received US$15 billion during the first half of 2005. In 2008, ABC received US$19 billion from Huijin in spite of the global financial crisis. All Big Four banks have since become publicly listed and traded on either the HKSE and/or the SHSE, including ABC (the last of the Big Four), which completed its IPO on July 15, 2010 (SHSE) and July 16 (HKSE).

However, the injection plan will not prevent new NPLs from originating in the banking system. In fact, it may create perverse "too big to fail" incentives

---

12. According to senior officials from the CBRC, Chinese banks are facing default risks on more than one-fifth of the RMB 7,700 billion ($1,135 billion) loans they have made to local governments across the country; most of these loans were used to fund regional infrastructure projects (*Financial Times,* 08/01/2010). In July 2011, Moody's estimated that local government loans can be as high as RMB 14.2 trillion, and the NPL ratio for Chinese banks could be 8 to 12 percent (*Reuters,* 07/05/2011).

for state-owned banks, in that if these banks believe that there will be a bail-out whenever they run into future financial distress, they have an incentive to take on risky, negative-NPV (net present value) projects. This moral hazard problem can thwart the government's efforts in keeping the NPLs in check, while similar problems occurred during and after the government bailouts in the S&L crisis in the United States in the 1980s (e.g., Kane 1989, 2003) and are among the most significant factors that caused the ongoing financial crisis. In this regard, a credible commitment from the government that the capital injection plan is a onetime measure to boost the capital adequacy of these banks, and that there will be no (similar) injection plans in the future can help alleviate the moral hazard problem.

Another measure taken by the Chinese government to reduce the NPLs is the establishment of four state-owned AMCs. As discussed earlier, the goal of the AMCs is to assume the NPLs (and offering debt-for-equity swaps to the banks[13]) accumulated in each of the Big Four banks and liquidate them. The liquidation process includes asset sales, tranching, securitization, and resale of loans to investors.[14] Table 2.5 shows that *cash* recovery on the bad loans processed by the AMCs ranges from 6.9 percent to 35 percent between 2001 and 2006 (first quarter),[15] while the asset recovery rates are slightly higher. A critical issue that affects the effectiveness of the liquidation process is the relationship among AMCs, banks, and distressed or bankrupt firms. Since both the AMCs and the banks are state-owned, it is not likely that the AMCs would force the banks to cut off (credit) ties with defaulted borrowers (SOEs or former SOEs) as a privately-owned bank would do. Thus, as the old NPLs are liquidated, new NPLs from the same borrowers continue to surface.

To summarize, NPLs have been considerably reduced in recent years. If the economy can maintain its current pace of growth, the government can always write off a large fraction of the rest (and newly accumulated) of the NPLs to avert any serious problems for China. Again, caution is in place for this optimistic outlook. One can argue that NPLs are bigger than the official statistics suggest to begin with, and that a substantial amount of new NPLs will continue to arise within state-owned banks. If the growth of the economy significantly slows down, while the accumulation of NPLs

13. One example is Cinda Asset Management Corporation, which was set up in April 1999 with a registered capital of RMB 10 billion provided by the Ministry of Finance. It took over RMB 220 billion NPLs from the China Construction Bank and funded its purchase via bond issues.

14. The sale of tranches of securitized NPLs to foreign investors began in 2002. The deal was struck between Huarong, one of the four AMCs, and a consortium of US investment banks led by Morgan Stanley (and including Lehman Brothers and Salomon Smith Barney) and was approved by the government in early 2003 (*Financial Times,* 05/2003).

15. The China Banking Regulatory Commission (CBRC), from which we obtained data (for 2004 to 2009), stopped reporting data on NPLs from AMCs.

Table 2.5   **Liquidation of NPLs by four asset management companies (RMB billion)**

	Book value of assets (accumulated)	Assets recovered	Cash recovered	Asset recovery rate (%)	Cash recovery rate (%)
			2001		
Hua Rong	23.21	12.54	7.55	54.00	32.50
Great Wall	53.11	6.30	3.69	11.90	6.90
Oriental	18.29	8.51	4.42	46.50	24.20
Xin Da	29.90	22.50	10.49	75.30	35.10
Total	124.51	49.86	26.15	40.00	21.00
			2002		
Hua Rong	32.04	11.43	10.20	35.70	31.80
Great Wall	45.48	7.94	5.47	17.50	12.00
Oriental	22.10	10.60	5.57	47.90	25.20
Xin Da	33.10	17.46	10.51	52.70	31.80
Total	132.73	47.43	31.75	35.70	23.90

	Accumulated disposal	Cash recovered	Disposal ratio (%)	Asset recovery ratio (%)	Cash recovery ratio (%)
			2004		
Hua Rong	209.54	41.34	59.77	25.29	19.73
Great Wall	209.91	21.57	61.91	14.43	10.27
Oriental	104.55	23.29	41.42	29.50	22.27
Xin Da	151.06	50.81	48.90	38.29	33.64
Total	675.06	137.00	53.96	25.48	20.29
			2005		
Hua Rong	243.38	54.39	69.17	26.92	22.35
Great Wall	263.39	27.35	77.88	12.90	10.39
Oriental	131.76	32.01	52.08	28.73	24.30
Xin Da	201.21	62.84	63.82	34.30	31.23
Total	839.75	176.60	66.74	24.58	21.03
			2006 (Q1)		
Hua Rong	246.80	54.66	70.11	26.50	22.15
Great Wall	270.78	27.83	80.11	12.70	10.28
Oriental	141.99	32.81	56.13	27.16	23.11
Xin Da	206.77	65.26	64.69	34.46	31.56
Total	866.34	180.56	68.61	24.20	20.84

Source: Almanac of China's Finance and Banking 2002–2005, and the reports of China Banking Regulatory Commission 2004–2009.

Notes: This table presents results on the liquidation of NPLs by four state-owned asset management companies in China during the period 2001 to the first quarter of 2006. These asset management companies were set up to specifically deal with NPLs accumulated in the Big Four state-owned banks. Accumulated disposal refers to the accumulated amount of cash and noncash assets recovered as well as loss incurred by the end of the reporting period. Disposal ratio = Accumulated disposal / Total NPLs purchased. Asset recover ratio = Total assets recovered / Accumulated disposal. Cash recovery ratio = Cash recovered / Accumulated disposal.

continues, the banking sector problems could lead to a financial crisis. This could spill over into other sectors of the economy and cause a slowdown in growth or a recession.

The Efficiency of State-Owned Banks

As discussed earlier, the size of NPLs in the banking sector critically depends on the efficiency of banks. We briefly discuss measures that have been taken to improve the efficiency of state-owned banks. First, state-owned banks have diversified and improved their loan structure by increasing consumer-related loans while being more active in risk management and monitoring of loans made to SOEs. For example, the ratio of consumer lending to total loans outstanding made from all banks increased from 1 percent in 1998 to 12 percent in 2008; by the third quarter of 2009, RMB 4.99 trillion (or $730.4 billion) of outstanding bank loans were extended to consumers. The size of housing mortgages, now the largest component (87 percent in the third quarter of 2009) of consumer credit, grew more than 200 times between 1997 and 2008, reaching a total of RMB 4.35 trillion ($637.2 billion), although the speed of growth has slowed down in 2011, according to the *China Quarterly Monetary Policy Report* of the PBOC. One problem with the massive expansion of consumer credit is that China lacks a national consumer-credit database to spot overstretching debtors, although a pilot system linking seven cities was set up in late 2004. The deficiency in the knowledge and training of credit risk and diligence of loan officers from state-owned banks is another significant factor in credit expansion, which can lead to high default rates and a large amount of new NPLs if the growth of the economy and personal income slows down.

Accompanying the rapidly expanding automobile industry, the other fast growing category of individual-based loans is automobile loans, most of which are made by state-owned banks. The total balance of all China's individual auto loans increased from RMB 400 million ($50 million) in 1998 to RMB 200 billion ($25 billion) at the end of 2003, and as much as 30 percent of all auto sales were financed by loans during this period (*Financial Times,* 05/25/2005). The growth in both auto sales and loans slowed down significantly since 2004, in part due to the high default rates. In 2008, outstanding auto loans decreased to RMB 158.3 billion ($23 billion). Only 8 percent of the auto sales were financed by loans during that year. Shanghai and Beijing have the largest number of car sales and loans. As many as 50 percent of debtors defaulted on their car loans in these cities. There are examples in which loan applications were approved based solely on the applicants' description of their personal income without any auditing (*Barron's,* 12/06/ 2004). However, the slowdown of the auto loan market was temporary and it quickly resumed its fast pace of growth, mainly driven by tremendous demand—China has recently overtaken the United States to become the largest auto market in the world. In aggregate auto loans amount to 10 to

20 percent of the total amount spent on autos. Most loans mature in three to five years.[16]

Second, the ongoing privatization process, including the listing of state-owned banks, is also an effective channel for enhancing efficiency. As state ownerships stakes shrink, these banks can focus more on for-profit goals, and, with more nonstate owners entering the mix, the strengthening of corporate governance to ensure profit-maximizing is the next step. Panel A of table 2.6 presents the performance of IPOs of the Big Four banks (ABC remains in the State Sector) and that of the Bank of Communications (BComm). A notable case is the IPO of ICBC (see Allen et al. 2012 for more details). Simultaneously carried out in the HKSE and SHSE on October 27, 2006, ICBC raised US$21.9 billion, making it the largest IPO (up to that date). The first day (and first week cumulative) return, measured by the net percentage return of the closing price on the first (fifth) trading day over offer price, was almost 15 percent, suggesting high demand for ICBC's H shares among (foreign) investors. In terms of ownership structure, the state, through various agencies, is by far the largest shareholder, where only 22 percent of the market cap is "free float" or tradable. The largest foreign shareholder is Goldman Sachs, with its 5.8 percent ownership stake negotiated before the IPO. The recent IPO of ABC also attracted a lot of attention. The total proceeds from its IPO from HKSE (July 16, 2010) and SHSE (July 15, 2010) reached $22.1 billion, overtaking the ICBC IPO as the world's largest IPO (*Associated Press*, 08/16/2010).[17] In particular, foreign investors, including institutional investors and wealthy families, contributed over 40 percent of the $12 billion raised from H shares (in the HKSE).[18] While the first-week stock performance in the two markets was not as impressive as that of ICBC, the fact that the IPO was carried out successfully during the recovery period following one of the worst global financial crises is evidence that investors from around the globe have confidence in ABC's role as a leading institution in the world.

The IPOs of the other three large state-owned banks were also successful in terms of total proceeds raised, and they all attracted significant foreign ownership at the IPO date as well. In fact, as shown in panel B of table 2.6, four of the ten largest banks in the world, measured in market capitalization

16. A few foreign lenders (e.g., GM and Ford) were approved to enter China's auto loan market by forming joint ventures with Chinese automakers (*Financial Times,* 05/27/2005).

17. From panel A, table 2.6, the total proceeds (in HK$ and RMB) of the ICBC IPO are actually larger than that of ABC's IPO, but given the appreciation of RMB over the period 2006 to 2010, the proceeds of the ABC IPO are slightly larger measured in US$.

18. Foreign institutional investors include Qatar Investment Authority ($2.8 billion), Kuwait Investment Authority ($800 million), Britain's Standard Chartered Bank ($500 million), Dutch bank Radobank Nederland ($250 million), Australia's Seven Group Holdings Ltd ($250 million), and Singapore's Temasek Holdings ($200 million); source: ABC's post-IPO news report. However, on a global basis, including shares that are distributed to various government agencies prior to the IPO, foreign investors only hold 4 percent of all of ABC's shares.

Table 2.6 Chinese banks' IPOs and comparison with other banks

A. Performance of Chinese banks' IPOs

	ICBC		BOC		PCBC	BComm	ABC[a]	
	HKSE (HK$)	SHSE (RMB)	HKSE (HK$)	SHSE (RMB)	HKSE (HK$)	HKSE (HK$)	HKSE (HK$)	SHSE (RMB)
IPO date	10/27/2006	10/27/2006	6/01/2006	7/05/2006	10/27/2005	6/23/2005	7/15/2010	7/16/2010
Offer price	3.07	3.12	2.95	3.08	2.35	2.50	3.20	2.68
Proceeds	124.95b	46.64b	82.86b	20.00b	59.94b	14.64b	93.80b	68.50b
First day return	14.66%	5.13%	14.41%	22.73%	0.00%	13.00%	2.20%	1.00%
First week return	16.94%	4.81%	19.49%	19.16%	-1.06%	13.00%	9.10%	1.90%
Foreign ownership	7.28%	—	14.40%	—	14.39%	18.33%	40.80%	—

B. Top 10 banks measured by market capitalization ($billion)

Rank	Bank name	HQ country	Market cap. $b (July 16, 2010)	Total return (%) YTD
1	IND & COMM BK	China	214.51	-20.14
2	CHINA CONST BANK	China	189.04	-1.99
3	HSBC HLDGS PLC	UK	166.51	-15.40
4	JPMORGAN CHASE	US	155.17	-6.06
5	BANK OF AMERICA	US	140.26	-7.06
6	WELLS FARGO & CO	US	136.71	-2.46
7	BANK OF CHINA	China	130.29	1.71
8	AGRICULTURAL BANK	China	128.60	0.40
9	CITIGROUP INC	US	113.00	17.82
10	BANCO SANTANDER	Spain	102.77	-21.87

C. Top 20 banks measured by total assets (July 2010; $trillion)

Rank	Bank name (HQ country)	HQ country	Total assets ($trillion)
1	BNP PARIBAS	France	2.95
2	ROYAL BANK SCOTLAN	UK	2.68
3	HSBC HLDGS PLC	UK	2.36
4	BANK OF AMERICA	US	2.36
5	DEUTSCHE BANK-RG	Germany	2.26
6	CREDIT AGRICOLE	France	2.23
7	BARCLAYS PLC	UK	2.23
8	MITSUBISHI UFJ F	Japan	2.18
9	JPMORGAN CHASE	US	2.01
10	CITIGROUP INC	US	1.94
11	IND & COMM BANK	China	1.73
12	MIZUHO FINANCIAL	Japan	1.67
13	LLOYDS BANKING	UK	1.66
14	BANCO SANTANDER	Spain	1.55
15	CHINA CONST BA-H	China	1.48
16	SOC GENERALE	France	1.47
17	SUMITOMO MITSUI	Japan	1.32
18	AGRICULTURAL BANK	China	1.30
19	UBS AG-REG	Switzerland	1.29
20	UNICREDIT SPA	Italy	1.28

Sources: IPO prospectuses submitted to SHSE and HKSE; SHSE and HKSE. *Bloomberg* (based on latest filings), July 15, 2010.

Notes: This table presents information on the IPOs of the Big Four banks and that of the Bank of Communications (BComm). BOC, ICBC and ABC were listed in both the HKSE (HK dollar) and SHSE (RMB), while PCBC and BComm only listed shares on the HKSE. First day (first week) return is percentage return of closing price of first day (fifth trading day) over offer price. Foreign ownership indicates size of ownership stakes of foreign institutions and investors at the date of IPOs.

[a] In US$, ABC raised $22.1 billion from its IPO, beating the record of $21.9 billion from ICBC's IPO. However, in terms of RMB, ICBC still holds the record of largest IPO since RMB has appreciated significantly since 2006.

as of July 2010, are Chinese banks, with ICBC leading the chart and the newly listed ABC making it into the chart too. In terms of (book) assets, ICBC is the eleventh-largest bank in the world (panel C); however, given the accounting problems of evaluating troubled assets related to subprime loans and sovereign debt in troubled Euro Zone countries, it is possible that ICBC's assets, with virtually no exposure to the US housing markets or European sovereign debt, could be one of the largest and highest quality in the world. Finally, Moody's current ratings on these publicly listed banks (on both deposits and loans) range from A to Baa (highest rating is Aaa); while S&P rates these banks' outstanding bonds between A and BBB (highest rating is AAA).

There are two imminent issues with the privatization process. The first is related to the structure of the banking sector, and in particular, whether more competition, including the entrance of more nonstate (domestic and foreign) banks and intermediaries, is good for improving the efficiency of both the Big Four banks and the entire sector.[19] Another issue is the government's dual role as regulator and as majority owner. These potentially conflicting roles can diminish the effectiveness of each of the two roles that the government intends to carry out. In section 2.4, we consider whether the ongoing process of floating nontradable government shares in many listed companies can be applied to the privatization process of many state-owned banks/institutions. Only after these banks are (majority) owned by nongovernment entities and individuals can they unconditionally implement all profit- and efficiency-enhancing measures. However, in light of what occurred in the developed countries, where excessive risk-taking and poor risk management and governance in a few large institutions essentially brought down the entire financial system, the current ownership structure of the largest Chinese banks, in which the government retains the majority control, can enhance the regulation of large financial institutions and help to prevent banking and financial crisis in China and other emerging economies.

Third, reforming the organization structure of banks and providing more incentives to banks and their employees can improve efficiency. For example, reforms taking place in the mid-1990s provided local banks with more autonomous power, and after the 1994 reforms, approved credit volume for specialized banks was based on a maximum ratio between loans and deposits instead of administrative quota, which provided those banks with greater flexibility to use within-bank transfers to adjust fund allocation.[20] The reforms also provide more profit incentives for managers. The evaluation criteria changed from adherence to the national credit plan to "a

19. For example, with a sample of both state- and non-state-owned banks, Berger, Hasan, and Zhou (2009) show that the addition of foreign ownership stakes into banks' ownership structure is associated with a significant improvement of bank efficiency.

20. These reforms did not liberalize interest rates; the PBOC continues to set the range (upper and lower bounds, or base rate and floating range) within which interest rates can be set; relending was also centralized by the PBOC.

combination of profits made by the bank branch, attention to cost control, investment in fixed capital of the branch, deposit increases, and reduction of overdue loans" (Park and Sehrt 2001, 619).

A critical aspect of the decentralization process is to provide individuals with more authority and responsibilities. According to a number of theories (e.g., Stein 2002), these changes improve the quality of "soft" information produced by banks, an essential part of the lending process. Under the old regime, decision making of the entire lending process was group-based and no individual loan officers were held responsible for poor decisions. Facing imminent pressure from competitors (including foreign banks) following China's entrance to WTO in 2001, many state-owned banks began implementing new lending policies in 2002. These new policies grant more authority to individuals in charge of different steps of making loans and monitoring borrowers and hold them responsible (ex post) for poor performance; decisions such as the final approval of loan contracts are left to a group of senior employees (through voting). Using detailed loan-level data from a large state-owned bank with branches throughout the country, Qian, Strahan, and Yang (2011) find that an internal risk assessment measure has a more pronounced effect, relative to publicly available information ("hard" information), on both pricing (interest rates) and nonpricing terms (loan size) of loan contracts after the reform and becomes a better predictor of loan outcomes. They also show that when the loan officer and the branch president who approves the loan contract work together for a longer period of time, the rating has an incrementally stronger effect on loan contracts. These results highlight how organizational structure and incentives can affect the production and quality of soft information. Better information, in turn, expands the supply of credit and improves (lending) outcomes.

One problem that hinders banks' efforts in improving efficiency is poor and inconsistent enforcement of bankruptcy laws and creditor protection. China's first bankruptcy law, passed in 1986, governed only SOEs and had little impact in practice. The new bankruptcy law, enacted in August 2006 and effective on June 1, 2007, applies to all enterprises except partnerships and sole proprietorships. In many aspects the new law resembles bankruptcy laws in developed countries. For example, it introduces the bankruptcy administrator, who manages the assets of the debtor after the court has accepted the bankruptcy filing. Moreover, the law states that these administrators should be independent professionals, such as those working for law or accounting firms. Despite all the legal procedures specified by the law, enforcement of the law remains weak and inconsistent. Many distressed and insolvent firms are kept afloat, and almost all the listed firms that file for bankruptcy end up with restructuring plans and these firms are rarely delisted.[21]

---

21. According to the National Development and Reform Commission, 67,000 small and midsized enterprises were shut down in the first half of 2008, but only 2,955 bankruptcy cases

A number of reasons can explain the weak enforcement of the bankruptcy law. There are regulations and circulars issued by the central government applicable to SOE bankruptcies that are de facto in priority over the law. A good example is Doctrine #10 of the State Council, which governs the bankruptcy process of SOEs in 111 pilot cities. This doctrine requires approval from secured/senior creditors (e.g., banks) before an enterprise can go through bankruptcy proceedings. In reality, however, the bankruptcy court also requires the consent of local government (Fan, Jun, and Ning 2008). Since local governments are usually responsible for the settlement of workers displaced by bankrupt firms, it is in their best interest to halt the bankruptcy filing until a satisfactory settlement plan is reached. As a result, mergers and acquisitions (M&As) with other firms are preferred to bankruptcy, and it has been documented that M&As have been indeed used extensively to resolve firms' distress (e.g., Kam et al. 2008), and many bankruptcy cases are postponed or avoided. In fact, when in distress, both the SOEs and local government give the greatest priority to employees; local government favors SOEs over banks since SOEs provide more employment opportunities. Furthermore, banks are often reluctant to push for bankruptcy since most of the distressed debt would be written off; the recovery rate for most bank loans is less than 10 percent (World Bank 2001). Taking the defaulted firm to court to recover loans or seize the firm's assets is a lengthy process and the chances of winning are slim; as a result, only a small number of lawsuits involving bankrupt firms reach the courts.

For insolvent SOEs, what triggers the bankruptcy procedure is not their financial status per se, but whether they can get preferential treatment from the government. The average number of bankruptcy cases placed on file (by courts) was 277 per year during 1989 to 1993. This then jumped to 5,900 per year between 1994 and 2003, after the Capital Structure Optimization Program for industrial SOEs was implemented in several pilot cities.[22] The number of cases fell after 2003, partly due to the central government's intention to maintain social stability by controlling the number of bankruptcies; the Supreme People's Court also ruled in 2002 that the courts would not process bankruptcy cases if the main intention were to escape debts. According to the surveys presented by Garnaut, Song, and Yao (2004), 90 percent of CEOs of the surveyed SOEs believe that bankruptcy is actually a feasible channel to evade bank debts. Because the government's program provides preferential treatments including debt write-offs, many SOEs would wait until they are covered by the program before filing for bankruptcy.

As the most senior creditors (secured debt), banks' willingness to lend

---

were filed nationwide for the same year. When a listed firm is in distress (with the "ST" flag), typically other (nonlisted) firms will invest in and restructure the ST firm to avoid delisting, since the "shell" of the distressed firm is valuable given the difficult and costly process of IPOs.

22. In China, a court must accept a case petition before deciding whether it should be declined or placed on file for investigation/prosecution; thus the number of cases accepted is always greater than the number of cases placed on file.

depends on their bargaining power and ability to seize collateralized assets upon default, and hence ineffective creditor protection not only increases potential losses from bad loans, it also reduces banks' incentive to investigate and monitor borrowers.[23] The favorable treatment SOEs enjoy during distress adversely change their incentives in investment and corporate governance; these effects can also spill over into banks' decisions to lend to nonstate firms and reduce the credit access of these firms. Therefore, *consistent* regulation guidelines in dealing with distress and bankruptcy by different types of firms, along with the government's commitment to leave the decision process to professionals and courts, can benefit the development of credit markets. On the other hand, we discuss evidence in the following that informal dispute resolution mechanisms outside the legal system based on reputation and relationships has been an effective substitute for Chinese firms and investors.

2.3.3   Growth of Nonstate Financial Intermediaries

The development of both nonstate banks and other (state and nonstate) financial institutions will allow China to have a stable and functioning banking system in the future. In addition to boosting the overall efficiency of the banking system, these financial institutions provide funding to support the growth of the Hybrid Sector.

First, we examine and compare China's insurance market to other Asian economies (South Korea, Taiwan, and Singapore). In terms of the ratio of total assets managed by insurance companies over GDP (figure 2.4), China's insurance market is significantly smaller than that of other economies. At the end of 2009 total assets managed are only about 10 percent of GDP, while this ratio for the other three economies is over 30 percent. It is clear that the insurance industry is also significantly smaller compared to China's banking industry, and property insurance is particularly underdeveloped due to the fact that the private real estate market was only recently established (in the past most housing was allocated by employers or the government). Despite the fast growth of insurance coverage and premium income, only 4 percent of the total population was covered by life insurance. Insurance premiums were only 3.2 percent of GDP in 2008, standing far behind the global average figure of over 7 percent; coverage ratios for property insurance are even lower (according to the reports by KPMG LLP). However, coverage ratios have been growing steadily at an average annual rate of 6 percent between 1998 and 2005 (*XinHua News*). In 2008 the insurance industry in China grew at the fastest pace (40 percent) since 2002. In the first quarter of 2010, China Insurance Regulatory Committee announced that

---

23. With a large sample of syndicated loans around the globe, Qian and Strahan (2007) show that strong creditor protection (in borrower countries) enhances loan availability as lenders are more willing to provide credit on favorable terms (e.g., longer maturities and lower interest rates).

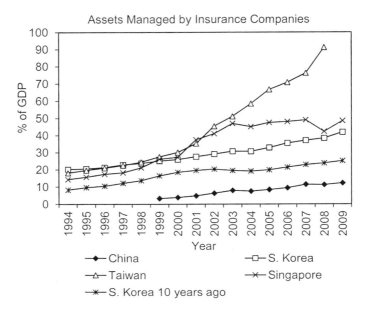

Fig. 2.4   A comparison of assets under management of insurance companies

China's insurance premiums totaled RMB 454.14 billion, representing an increase of 38.6 percent year on year.

Table 2.7 provides a (partial) breakdown of the different types of banks. During the period of 2001 to 2009, although the largest four or five banks (the fifth largest bank is Bank of Communications, also state-owned) dominate in every aspect of the banking sector, the role of other banks in the entire banking sector cannot be ignored. As of 2009, other banks (including foreign banks) and credit cooperatives' total assets compose over 70 percent of the largest five banks (the actual fraction is likely to be higher due to incomplete information on all types of deposit-taking institutions); similar comparisons can be made for total deposits and outstanding loans. In addition, these banks and institutions appear to have less NPLs than the largest state-owned banks. Table 2.8 provides evidence on the growth of nonbank intermediaries. Overall, the growth of these nonbank intermediaries has been impressive since the late 1990s. Among them, "other commercial banks" (many of them are state-owned), RCCs, and TICs hold the largest amount of assets; the size of foreign banks and mutual funds (not listed in the table) is minuscule, but these are likely to be the focus of development in the near future.[24] Finally, our coverage of nonbank financial institutions

---

24. Postal savings (deposit-taking institutions affiliated with local post offices) is another form of nonbank intermediation that is not reported in table 2.7 due to a lack of time series data. However, at the end of 2008, total deposits within the postal savings system exceeded RMB 2079 billion, or 9.5 percent of all deposits in China.

Table 2.7　　　　　State-owned and private banks in China (RMB billion)

Types of banks	Total assets	Total deposits	Outstanding loans	Profit[a]	NPL rate (%)
	2009				
Big five banks	40,089.0	29,506.5	20,151.7	400.1	1.8
Other commercial banks	17,465.0	15,041.5	9,606.6	—	—
1. Joint equity	11,785.0	10,548.7	6,707.4	92.5	1.0
2. City commercial banks	5,680.0	4,492.8	2,899.2	49.7	1.3
Foreign banks	1,349.2	668.8	727.1	6.5	0.9
Urban credit cooperatives	27.2	39.5	—	0.2	—
Rural credit cooperatives	5,492.5	4,742.1	5,421.3	22.8	—
	2008				
Big five banks	31,836.0	23,696.1	15,029.3	354.2	2.8
Other commercial banks	12,941.2	11,072.2	7,162.4	—	—
1. Joint equity	8,809.2	7,801.8	5,054.5	84.1	1.3
2. City commercial banks	4,132.0	3,270.4	2,107.9	40.8	2.3
Foreign banks	1,344.8	533.5	762.1	11.9	0.8
Urban credit cooperatives	80.4	76.2	—	0.62	—
Rural credit cooperatives	5,211.3	4,173.6	3,753.2	21.9	—
	2007				
Big five banks	28,007.0	20,067.7	13,850.9	246.6	8.05
Other commercial banks	10,589.9	9,023.3	5,684.4	—	—
1. Joint equity	7,249.4	6,432.0	4,001.9	56.4	2.15
2. City commercial banks	3,340.5	2,591.4	1,682.6	24.8	3.04
Foreign banks	1,252.5	390.0	700.0	6.1	0.46
Urban credit cooperatives	131.2	134.1	84.7	0.77	—
Rural credit cooperatives	4,343.4	3,534.9	3,256.1	19.3	—
	2006				
Big five banks	24,236.0	18,285.1	11,426.2	197.5	9.22
Other commercial banks	8,038.4	7512.8	5526.6	—	—
1. Joint equity	5,444.6	5,396.5	4,156.9	43.4	2.81
2. City commercial banks	2,593.8	2,116.2	1,369.7	18.1	4.78
Foreign banks	927.9	244.0	485.9	5.8	0.78
Urban credit cooperatives	183.1	157.9	100.7	1.0	—
Rural credit cooperatives	3,450.3	3,040.2	2,747.6	18.6	—
	2005				
Big five banks[b]	21,005.0	16,283.8	10,224.0	156.1	10.49
Other commercial banks	6,502.2	6,261.1	4,576.6	—	—
1. Joint equity	4,465.5	4,570.0	3,487.7	28.9	4.22
2. City commercial banks	2,036.7	1,691.2	1,088.9	12.1	7.73
Foreign banks	715.5	179.3	363.8	3.7	1.05
Urban credit cooperatives	203.3	181.3	113.1	0.9	—
Rural credit cooperatives	3,142.7	2,767.4	2,319.9	12.0	—
	2004				
Big four banks	16,932.1	14,412.3	10,086.1	45.9	15.57
Other commercial banks	4,697.2	4,059.9	2,885.9	50.7	4.93
1. Joint equity	—	—	—	17.6	5.01
2. City commercial banks	1,693.8	1,434.1	904.5	8.5	11.73
Foreign banks	515.9	126.4	255.8	18.8	1.34
Urban credit cooperatives	171.5	154.9	97.9	0.4	—
Rural credit cooperatives	3,101.3	2,734.8	1,974.8	9.65	—

(*continued*)

Table 2.7   (continued)

Types of banks	Total assets	Total deposits	Outstanding loans	Profit[a]	NPL rate (%)
	2003				
Big four banks	16,275.1	13,071.9	9,950.1	196.5	19.74
Other commercial banks	3,816.8	3,286.5	2,368.2	—	7.92
1. Joint equity	—	—	—	14.6	6.5
2. City commercial banks	1,465.4	1,174.7	774.4	5.4	14.94
Foreign banks	333.1	90.7	147.6	18.1	2.87
Urban credit cooperatives	148.7	127.1	85.6	0.01	—
Rural credit cooperatives	2,674.6	2,376.5	1,775.9	4.4	—
	2002				
Big four banks	14,450.0	11,840.0	8,460.0	71.0	26.1
Other commercial banks	4,160.0	3,390.0	2,290.0	—	—
1. Joint equity	2,990.0	—	—	—	9.5
2. City commercial banks	1,170.0	—	—	—	17.7
Foreign banks	324.2	—	154.0	15.2	—
Urban credit cooperatives	119.0	101.0	66.4	—	—
Rural credit cooperatives	—	1,987.0	1,393.0	—	—
	2001				
Big four banks	13,000.0	10,770.0	7,400.0	23.0	25.37
Other commercial banks	3,259.0	2,530.7	1,649.8	12.9	—
1. Joint equity	2,386.0	1,849.0	1,224.0	10.5	12.94
2. City commercial banks	873.0	681.7	425.8	2.4	—
Foreign banks	373.4	—	153.2	1.7	—
Urban credit cooperatives	128.7	107.1	72.5	2.6	—
Rural credit cooperatives	—	1,729.8	1,197.0	—	—

Sources: Almanac of China's Finance and Banking 2000–2008, CEIC database, Quarterly Monetary Report of PBC.

[a]It is before-tax profit up to 2006 and after-tax profit from 2006 to 2009.

[b]Big Four (stated-owned) banks refer to Bank of China, China Construction Bank, Industrial and Commercial Bank of China, and Agricultural Bank of China. Big Five banks are the Big Four banks and Bank of Communications.

excludes various forms of informal financial intermediaries, some of which are deemed illegal but overall provide a considerable amount of financing to firms in the Hybrid Sector.

2.4   Financial Markets

In this section, we examine China's financial markets, including both the stock and real estate markets, and the recent addition of venture capital and private equity markets as well as asset management industries. We also compare, at the aggregate level, how firms raise funds in China and in other emerging economies through external markets in order to determine if China's experience is unique. We then briefly review publicly traded

Table 2.8   Comparison of assets held by China's nonbank intermediaries (RMB billion)

Year	State-owned banks	RCCs	UCCs	Insurance companies	TICs	Nondeposit intermediaries	Other commercial banks	Foreign banks
1995	5,373.30	679.10	303.92	—	458.60	48.97	536.91	42.90
1996	6,582.70	870.66	374.78	—	563.70	82.02	769.98	55.30
1997	7,914.40	1,012.20	498.94	—	636.40	100.42	948.61	75.80
1998	8,860.90	1,143.11	560.63	—	802.50	120.97	1,128.18	118.40
1999	9,970.60	1,239.24	630.15	260.40	907.50	137.08	1,376.89	191.40
2000	10,793.70	1,393.06	678.49	337.40	975.90	160.82	1,828.26	379.20
2001	11,188.20	1,610.80	780.02	459.10	1,088.30	223.67	2,255.70	341.80
2002	13,549.60	2,205.21	119.23	649.40	1,544.10	408.10	2,997.72	317.90
2003	16,275.10	2,674.62	148.72	912.30	—	495.58	3,816.80	331.10
2004	16,932.10	3,103.30	171.50	1,185.40	—	—	4,697.20	515.90
2005	21,005.00	3,142.70	203.30	1,529.60	—	—	6,502.20	715.50
2006	24,230.00	3,450.30	183.10	1,973.10	—	—	8,038.40	927.90
2007	28,007.00	4,343.40	131.20	2,900.40	—	—	10,589.90	1,252.50
2008	31,836.00	5,211.30	80.40	3,341.80	—	—	12,941.20	1,344.80
2009	40,089.00	5,492.50	27.20	4,063.50	—	—	17,465.00	1,349.20

Source: Aggregate Statistics from the People's Bank of China (China's Central Bank) and CEIC, 2000–2009.
Note: This table compares total assets held by banks and nonbank intermediaries during the period 1995–2009.

companies' financing and investment decisions. Finally, we discuss the further development of financial markets as well as corporate governance and the performance of listed firms.

2.4.1   Overview of Stock Markets

After the inception of China's domestic stock exchanges, the SHSE and SZSE, in 1990, they initially grew quickly. The high growth rates continued through most of the 1990s, and the market reached a peak by the end of 2000. As shown in figure 2.5, the momentum of the market (indicated by the SSE Index) then reversed during the next five years as it went through a major correction with half of the market capitalization lost. Most of the losses were recovered by the end of 2006, and the market reached new heights during 2007. However, following a string of negative news worldwide (culminating with the subprime loans-led global crisis) and domestically (including high levels of inflation), the market lost three-quarters of its value by the end of 2008. During the first half of 2009, with the impact of the massive stimulus package and rebounding from a trough, China's stock market bounced back and recovered about one-third of the losses in 2008. However, the stock market dipped again in the first half of 2010, partly due to the concern that the government is taking measures to cool down the fast growing housing market. Figure 2.5 compares the performance of some of the major stock exchanges around the world, as measured by the "buy-and-hold" return in the period of December 1992 and December 2010 (gross

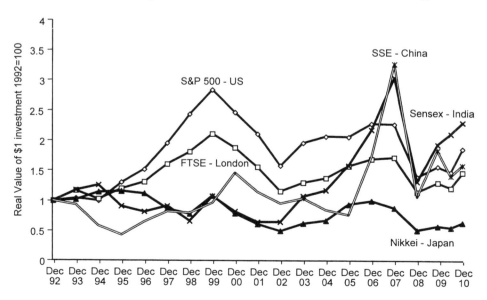

Fig. 2.5   A comparison of performance of major stock indexes (buy-and-hold returns of \$1 between Dec. 1992 and Dec. 2010)

Table 2.9   **A comparison of the largest stock markets in the world (January 1–
December 31, 2010)**

Rank	Stock exchange	Total market cap (US$ million)	Concentration (%)	Turnover velocity (%)
1	NYSE Euronext (US)	13,394,081.8	57.0	130.2
2	NASDAQ OMX	3,889,369.9	71.9	340.4
3	Tokyo SE Group	3,827,774.2	60.1	109.6
4	London SE Group	3,613,064.0	82.3	76.1
5	NYSE Euronext (Europe)	2,930,072.4	68.9	76.5
6	Shanghai SE	2,716,470.2	55.8	178.5
7	Hong Kong Exchanges	2,711,316.2	69.4	62.2
8	TSX Group	2,170,432.7	79.5	74.1
9	Bombay SE	1,631,829.5	87.7	18.1
10	National Stock Exchange India	1,596,625.3	69.6	57.3
11	BM&FBOVESPA	1,545,565.7	64.2	64.7
12	Australian Securities Exchange	1,454,490.6	79.4	82.3
13	Deutsche Börse	1,429,719.1	78.4	119.3
14	Shenzhen SE	1,311,370.1	31.2	344.3
15	SIX Swiss Exchange	1,229,356.5	65.6	73.5
16	BME Spanish Exchanges	1,171,625.0	n/a	117.2
17	Korea Exchange	1,091,911.5	75.7	176.3
18	NASDAQ OMX Nordic Exchange	1,042,153.7	69.7	79.7
19	MICEX	949,148.9	64.3	52.8
20	Johannesburg SE	925,007.2	35.0	33.3

Notes: All figures are from http//:www.world-exchanges.org, the website of the international organization of stock exchanges. Concentration is the fraction of total turnover of an exchange within a year
coming from the turnover of the companies with the largest market cap (top 5 percent). Turnover velocity is the total turnover of domestic stocks for the year expressed as a percentage of the total market
capitalization.

return at December 2010 with $1 invested in each of the valued-weighted
stock indexes at the end of 1992). We plot inflation-adjusted real returns.
Over this period, the performance of the value-weighted SHSE index (the
calculation for the SZSE is very similar) is below that of the SENSEX
(India), which has the best performance among the group, and that of S&P
(United States), but better than FTSE (London) and the Nikkei Index, the
worst among the group.

As table 2.9 indicates, at the end of 2010, the SHSE was ranked the sixth-
largest market in the world in terms of market capitalization, while the SZSE
was ranked the fourteenth. The Hong Kong Stock Exchange (HKSE), where
selected firms from Mainland China have been listed and traded, is ranked
the seventh-largest in the world. Needless to say, the Chinese financial markets will play an increasingly important role in world financial markets.
Also from table 2.9, "Concentration" is the fraction of total turnover of an
exchange within a year coming from the turnover of the companies with the
largest market cap (top 5 percent), and SHSE (55.8 percent) is in line with
that of other large exchanges, indicating that trading is concentrated among

large-cap stocks. "Turnover velocity" is the (annual) total turnover for all the listed firms expressed as a percentage of the total market capitalization, and the figures for SZSE and SHSZ are the highest among the largest exchanges, suggesting that there is a large amount of speculative trading, especially among small- and medium-cap stocks (as these are more easily manipulated than large-cap stocks) in the Chinese markets.

There are two other markets established to complement the two main exchanges. First, a fully electronically operated market ("*Er Ban Shi Chang*" or "Second-tier Market," similar to the NASDAQ) for Small and Medium Enterprises (SMEs) was opened in June 2004. It was designed to lower the entry barriers for SME firms, especially newly established firms in the high-tech industries. By the end of February 2007, there were 119 firms listed in this market. Second, a third-tier market ("*San Ban Shi Chang,*" or "Third-tier Market,") was established to deal primarily with delisting firms and other over-the-counter (OTC) transactions. Since 2001, some publicly listed firms on both SHSE and SZSE that do not meet the listing standards have been delisted and the trading of their shares shifted to this market. On October 23, 2009, China launched a NASDAQ-style Growth Enterprises Market (GEM, or "Chuang Ye Ban") with twenty-eight companies, mainly from hi-tech, electronic, and pharmaceutical industries. The main purpose of GEM is to provide financing for small and medium-sized private enterprises. The first ten firms seeking to list on the GEM drew a combined RMB 784 billion in subscriptions in September 2009, while the second and third sets had eighteen firms, including *Huayi Brothers Media,* China's largest privately-owned film company. As of October 2011, no index is available for the GEM but most of the listed stocks have outperformed the indexes of the two main exchanges. By April 2010, the number of listed firms on the GEM reached 200.

There is abundant evidence showing that China's stock markets are not efficient in that prices and investors' behavior are not necessarily driven by fundamental values of listed firms. For example, Morck, Yeung, and Yu (2000) find that stock prices are more "synchronous" (stock prices move up and down together) in emerging countries (including China) than in developed countries. They attribute this phenomenon to poor minority investor protection and imperfect regulation of markets in emerging markets. In addition, there have been numerous lawsuits against insider trading and manipulation (see, e.g., AQQ 2008 for more details). In many cases, unlike Enron and other well-known companies in developed markets stricken by corporate scandals, managers and other insiders from the Chinese companies did not use any sophisticated accounting and finance maneuvers to hide their losses (even by China's standards). These cases reveal that the inefficiencies in the Chinese stock markets can be (partially) attributed to poor and ineffective regulation. In the following, we discuss issues related to regulation, market efficiency, and the further development of China's financial markets.

2.4.2   Overview of Bond Markets

Table 2.10 provides information on China's bond markets. The government bond market had an annual growth rate of 25.3 percent during the period 1990 to 2009 in terms of newly issued bonds, while total outstanding bonds reached RMB 4,976.8 billion (or $721.3 billion) at the end of 2008.[25] The second-largest component of the bond market is called "policy financial bonds" (total outstanding amount RMB 3,668.6 billion, or $531.7 billion, at the end of 2008). These bonds are issued by "policy banks," which operate under the supervision of the Ministry of Finance, and the proceeds of bond issuance are invested in government-run projects and industries such as infrastructure construction (similar to municipal bonds in the United States). Compared to government-issued bonds, the size of the corporate bond market is small. In terms of the amount of outstanding bonds at the end of 2008, the corporate bond market is less than one-fourth of the size of the government bond market. However, the growth of the corporate bond market has picked up pace in the past few years and this trend is likely to continue in the near future.

The small size of the bond market, especially the corporate bond market, relative to the stock market, is common among Asian countries. Allen, Qian, and Qian (2008) compare different components (bank loans to the private sectors or the Hybrid Sector of China, stock market capitalization, public/government and private/corporate bond markets) of the financial markets around the world at the end of 2003. Compared to Europe and the United States, they find that the size of both the government (public) and corporate (private) bond markets is smaller in Asia, excluding Japan (i.e., Hong Kong, South Korea, Malaysia, Taiwan, Singapore, Indonesia, Philippines, and Thailand); even in Japan, the size of the corporate bond market is much smaller compared with its government bond market. They also find that the size of all four components of China's financial markets are small relative to that of other regions and countries, including bank loans made to the Hybrid Sector (private sector) in China (other countries). Moreover, the most underdeveloped component of China's financial markets is the corporate bond market (labeled "private" bond market).

There are a number of reasons for the underdevelopment in bond markets in China and other parts of Asia (see, e.g., Herring and Chatusripitak 2000). Lack of sound accounting/auditing systems and high-quality bond-rating agencies is a factor.[26] Given low creditor protection and court inefficiency

25. On July 26, 2007, Moody's raised the rating on China's government bonds to A1 from A2 and kept it unchanged up to now. In November 2009 it raised China's sovereign rating outlook from stable to positive. These ratings are better or comparable than Moody's ratings on government bonds from most emerging economies.

26. *Dagong Global Credit Ratings,* a leading Chinese credit ratings agency, recently released its first sovereign ratings report, in which the Chinese and German sovereign debt received higher ratings (AA+ and a stable outlook) than those of the United States, the United Kingdom, and Japan (AA or lower ratings and a negative outlook; *Bloomberg,* 7/14/2010).

Table 2.10   China's bond markets: 1990–2009 (amount in RMB billion)

Year	Treasury bonds Amount issued	Treasury bonds Redemption amount	Treasury bonds Balance	Policy financial bonds Amount issued	Policy financial bonds Redemption amount	Policy financial bonds Balance	Corporate bonds Amounts issued	Corporate bonds Redemption amounts	Corporate bonds Balance
1990	19.72	7.62	89.03	6.44	5.01	8.49	12.40	7.73	19.54
1991	28.13	11.16	106.00	6.69	3.37	11.81	24.90	11.43	33.11
1992	46.08	23.81	128.27	5.50	3.00	14.31	68.37	19.28	82.20
1993	38.13	12.33	154.07	0.00	3.43	10.88	23.58	25.55	80.24
1994	113.76	39.19	228.64	0.00	1.35	9.53	16.18	28.20	68.21
1995	151.09	49.70	330.03	—	—	170.85	30.08	33.63	64.66
1996	184.78	78.66	436.14	105.56	25.45	250.96	26.89	31.78	59.77
1997	241.18	126.43	550.89	143.15	31.23	362.88	25.52	21.98	52.10
1998	380.88	206.09	776.57	195.02	32.04	512.11	15.00	10.53	67.69
1999	401.50	123.87	1,054.20	180.09	47.32	644.75	15.82	5.65	77.86
2000	465.70	152.50	1,367.40	164.50	70.92	738.33	8.30	0.00	86.16
2001	488.40	228.60	1,561.80	259.00	143.88	853.45	14.70	0.00	100.86
2002	593.43	226.12	1,933.60	307.50	155.57	1,005.41	32.50	0.00	133.36
2003	628.01	275.58	2,260.36	456.14	250.53	1,165.00	35.80	0.00	169.16
2004	692.39	374.99	2,577.76	414.80	177.87	1,401.93	32.70	0.00	201.86
2005	704.20	404.55	2,877.40	585.17	205.30	1,781.80	204.65	3.70	401.81
2006	888.33	620.86	3,144.87	898.00	379.00	2,300.80	393.83	167.24	553.29
2007	2,313.91	584.68	4,874.10	1,109.02	413.36	2,992.68	505.85	288.09	768.33
2008	855.82	753.14	4,976.78	1,082.30	406.38	3,668.60	843.54	327.78	1,285.06
2009	1,792.70	707.15		1,167.80	—		1,662.90	440.00	—
Yearly growth	25.3%	24.4%	25.0%	29.7%	27.7%	40.1%	25.5%	22.3%	26.2%

Source: Aggregate Statistics from the People's Bank of China (China's Central Bank) 2000–2009 and the Statistical Yearbook of China 2000–2009.

Notes: This table presents the development of China's bond markets. "Policy financial bonds" are issued by "policy banks," which belong to the Treasury Department, and the proceeds of bond issuance are invested in government-run projects and industries such as infrastructure construction (similar to municipal bonds in the United States) (in China and most other emerging economies) the recovery rates for bond-holders during default are low, which in turn leads to underinvestment in the market (by domestic and foreign investors). Lack of a well-constructed yield curve is another factor in China, given the small size of the publicly traded Treasury bond market and lack of historical prices. The situation is improving, however, as the terms of China's Treasury bonds now range from one month to thirty years. In December 2009, China's first fifty-year government bond made its trading debut simultaneously in the interbank market and the stock exchange bond market, extending the bond yield curve even further. The deficiencies in the term structure of interest rates have hampered the development of derivatives markets that enable firms and investors to manage risk, as well as the effectiveness of the government's macroeconomic policies. Therefore, further development of China's bond markets, along with its legal system and related institutions, can help the advancement of other markets and the overall financial system.

2.4.3   Evidence on the Listed Sector

In this section, we briefly examine publicly listed and traded companies in China. It is worthwhile to first clarify whether firms from the Hybrid Sector can become listed and publicly traded. Regulations and laws (the 1986 trial version of the bankruptcy law and the 1999 version of the Company Law) did not prohibit the listing of Hybrid Sector firms, and selected firms from the Hybrid Sector did enter the Listed Sector through an IPO or acquisition of a listed firm from the inception of SHSE and SZSE. However, the accessibility of equity markets for these firms has been much lower than for former SOEs in practice due to the enforcement of the listing standards and process. As a result, AQQ (2005) find that 80 percent of their sample of more than 1,100 listed firms are converted from former SOEs. In recent years, the government has attempted to change the composition of listed firms by relaxing regulations toward Hybrid Sector firms, including the establishment of the recently opened GEM.

Until the recent share reform, which is discussed further in the following, listed firms in China issued both tradable and nontradable shares (table 2.11). The nontradable shares were either held by the government or by other state-owned legal entities (i.e., other listed or nonlisted firms or organizations). Table 2.12 shows that, as of the end of 2009, nontradable shares constituted around half of all shares (53 percent, column [2]) and the majority of tradable shares were A shares. Among the tradable shares, class A and B shares are listed and traded in either the SHSE or SZSE, while class A (B) shares are issued to and traded by Chinese investors (foreign investors, including those from Taiwan and Hong Kong and QFIIs). While the two share classes issued by the same firm are identical in terms of shareholder rights (e.g., voting and dividend), B shares were traded at a significant discount relative to A shares and are traded less frequently than

Table 2.11   **Types of common stock issued in China**

Tradable?		Definition
No (Private block transfer possible)	State-owned shares[a] (G shares after recent reform and tradable)	Shares that are controlled by the central government during the process when firms are converted into a limited liability corporation but before listing. These shares are either managed and represented by the Bureau of National Assets Management or held by other state-owned companies, both of which also appoint firms' board members. After reforms announced in 2005 and implemented in 2006–2007, state shares became G shares and are tradable.
	Entrepreneur's shares	Shares reserved for firms' founders during the same process described above; different from shares that founders can purchase and sell in the markets.
	Foreign owners	Shares owned by foreign industrial investors during the same process.
	Legal entity holders	Shares sold to legal identities (such as other companies, listed or nonlisted) during the same process.
	Employee shares	Shares sold to firm's employees during the same process.
Yes (Newly issued shares)	A shares	Shares issued by Chinese companies that are listed and traded in the Shanghai or Shenzhen Stock Exchange; most of these shares are sold to and held by Chinese (citizen) investors.
	B shares	Shares issued by Chinese companies that are listed and traded in the Shanghai or Shenzhen Stock Exchange; these shares are sold to and held by foreign investors; starting in 2001 Chinese investors can also trade these shares.
	H shares	Shares issued by selected Chinese companies listed and traded in the Hong Kong Stock Exchange; these shares can only be traded on the HK Exchange but can be held by anyone.

[a]There are subcategories under this definition.

A shares.[27] The "B share discount" has been reduced significantly since the CSRC allowed Chinese citizens to invest and trade B shares (with foreign currency accounts) in 2001. In addition, class H shares, issued by selected "Red Chip" Chinese companies, are listed and traded on the HKSE. Finally,

27. Explanations of the B share discount include: (1) foreign investors face higher information asymmetry than domestic investors; (2) lower B share prices compensate for the lack of liquidity (due to low trading volume); and (3) the A share premium reflects a speculative bubble component among domestic investors. See, for example, Chan, Menkveld, and Yang (2008) and Mei, Scheinkman, and Xiong (2003) for more details.

Table 2.12   Tradable versus nontradable shares for China's listed companies

Year	Shanghai SE: State/total shares	Nontradable/ total shares[a]	Tradable/ total shares	A/total shares	A/tradable shares[b]
1992	0.41	0.69	0.31	0.16	0.52
1993	0.49	0.72	0.28	0.16	0.57
1994	0.43	0.67	0.33	0.21	0.64
1995	0.39	0.64	0.36	0.21	0.60
1996	0.35	0.65	0.35	0.22	0.62
1997	0.32	0.65	0.35	0.23	0.66
1998	0.34	0.66	0.34	0.24	0.71
1999	0.43	0.65	0.35	0.26	0.75
2000	0.44	0.64	0.36	0.28	0.80
2001	0.50	0.64	0.36	0.29	0.80
2002	0.52	0.65	0.35	0.26	0.74
2003	0.57	0.64	0.35	0.27	0.76
2004	0.58	0.64	0.36	0.28	0.77
2005	0.57	0.62	0.38	0.30	0.78
2006	0.36	0.65	0.35	0.27	0.81
2007	0.37	0.69	0.31	0.28	0.90
2008	0.47	0.58	0.42	0.37	0.91
2009	0.49	0.53	0.47	0.50	0.98

Sources: China Security Regulation Committee Reports (2000–2006), CEIC database, and http://www.csrc.gov.cn.

[a]Nontradable shares include "state-owned" and "shares owned by legal entities." This column is calculated as "(Nontradable in Shanghai SE + Nontradable in Shenzhen SE)/(Market cap in Shanghai SE + Market cap in Shenzhen SE)."

[b]Tradable shares include A, B, and H shares.

there are N shares and S shares for firms listed in the United States and Singapore but that operate in China (we omit discussions on these shares since they are not listed on the domestic exchanges). After the share reforms discussed in section 2.4.7, government shares became G shares and are tradable.

We next describe standard corporate governance mechanisms in the Listed Sector. First, according to the (2005) Company Law, listed firms in China have a two-tier board structure: the Board of Directors (five to nineteen members) and the Board of Supervisors (at least three members), with supervisors ranking above directors. The main duty of the Board of Supervisors is to monitor firms' operations as well as top managers and directors; it consists of representatives of shareholders and employees, with the rest either officials chosen from government branches or executives from the parent companies; directors and top managers of the firms cannot hold positions as supervisors. The company has the discretion to decide the number of representatives of employees on the Board of Supervisors, but representatives of employees must account for at least one-third of the board. The Board of Directors serves similar duties as its counterparts in the United States, including appointing and firing CEOs. According to the "one-share, one-vote" scheme adopted by firms in the Listed Sector, shareholders including the state and legal person shareholders (that typically own the majority of shares) appoint the board members. Specifically, the chairman (one person) and vice-chairman (one or two) of the board are elected by all directors (majority votes); at the approval of the board, the CEO and other top managers can become members of the board. The CSRC requires at least one-third (and a minimum of two people) of the board to be independent.

Since the law does not specify that every member of the board must be elected by shareholders during general shareholder meetings, in practice some directors are nominated and appointed by the firms' parent companies and the nomination process is usually kept secret, in particular for former SOEs. Since not all members of either board are elected by shareholders, a major problem with the board structure is the appointment of and contracting with the CEOs. Based on firm-level compensation data (available since 1998 due to disclosure requirements), Fung, Firth, and Rui (2003) and Kato and Long (2004) find that no listed firms grant stock options to CEOs or board members. The situation is somewhat different now. Among overseas listed SOEs, barriers to exercising stock options have been overcome, and some senior executives have been granted stock options (examples include the former chairman of China National Offshore Oil Corporation [CNOOC] Wei Liucheng and Bank of China-Hong Kong former chairman Liu Mingkang) and received substantial rewards (*Caijing Magazine,* 2008). However, the cash-based compensation level for CEOs is still much lower than their counterparts in developed countries, and the consumption of perks, such as company cars, is prevalent.

Second, the existing ownership structure, characterized by the large amount of nontradable shares including cross-holdings of shares among listed companies and institutions, makes it difficult for value-increasing M&As. According to the *China Venture Source,* there were 2,656 M&A deals involving listed firms in 2010 totaling US$169.6 billion, a small fraction of the total market capitalization. In many deals, a Hybrid Sector firm (nonlisted) acquires a listed firm that is converted from an SOE, but the large amount of nontradable shares held by the state remain intact after the transaction.[28] Such an acquisition can be the means through which low quality, nonlisted companies bypass listing standards and access financial markets (e.g., Du, Rui, and Wong 2008).

---

28. If we include the cross-border M&As and transactions between parent companies and subsidiaries, the total amount increases to US $47 billion in 2000, $14 billion in 2001, $29 billion in 2002, and $24 billion in the first three quarters of 2003. Sixty-eight percent of all M&A deals (66 percent in terms of dollar deal amount) are initiated by Hybrid Sector firms, while former SOEs and foreign firms initiate 29 percent and 3 percent of the rest, respectively (27 percent and 7 percent in deal amount). The M&As are most active in coastal regions, and in industries such as machinery, information technology, retail, and gas and oil.

Third, one factor contributing to the occurrence of corporate scandals is the lack of institutional investors (including nondepository financial intermediaries) as they are a very recent addition to the set of financial institutions in China. Professional investors would perhaps not be so easily taken in by simple deceptions. Another factor is that the enforcement of laws is questionable due to the lack of legal professionals and institutions.

Fourth, the government plays the dual roles of regulator and blockholder for many listed firms, including banks and financial services companies. The main role of the CSRC (counterpart of the Securities and Exchange Commission [SEC] in the United States) is to monitor and regulate stock exchanges and listed companies. The government exercises its shareholder control rights in listed firms through the Bureau of National Assets Management, which holds large fractions of nontradable shares, or other SOEs (with their holdings of nontradable shares). However, since the senior managers of the bureau are government officials, it is doubtful that they will pursue their fiduciary role as controlling shareholders diligently, since their compensation is probably not incentive-based; even if their compensation was tied to performance, they may lack the expertise to make the correct strategic decisions. Moreover, the government's dual roles can lead to conflicting goals (maximizing profits as shareholder versus maximizing social welfare as regulator or social planner) in dealing with listed firms, which in turn weaken the effectiveness of both of its roles.[29] There are cases in which the government, aiming to achieve certain social goals, influenced the markets through state-owned institutional investors (e.g., asset management companies) but created unintended adverse effects. Based on a sample of 625 firms with 28 percent of the CEOs being ex- or current government bureaucrats, Fan, Wong, and Zhang (2007) find that the three-year post-IPO average stock returns of the sample underperform the market by 20 percent, and the underperformance of firms with such politically-connected CEOs exceeds those without politically-connected CEOs by almost 30 percent. Firms with politically-connected CEOs are also more likely to appoint other bureaucrats (but not personnel) with relevant professions to boards of directors.

Overall, internal and external governance for the Listed Sector is weak, and further development of governance mechanisms is likely in this sector going forward. In section 2.4.7 we further discuss this issue.

2.4.4   Real Estate Market

Like other economic sectors, China's real estate market has long been operating under the "dual tracks" of both central planning and market-oriented systems. Prior to 1998, government control was dominant, with the

---

29. See Pistor (chapter 1, this volume) for a description of the complicated relationships among various regulatory agencies and the central government branches, and how these relationships affect the decision-making process of regulations and enforcement.

market only playing a secondary role, and mortgages were not designated for retail customers and households. Chinese citizens working for the government and government-owned companies and organizations could purchase properties at prices significantly below market prices, with the subsidies coming from their employers. The reform policies introduced in 1998 aimed to end the distribution of properties by employers and establish new housing finance and market systems. Provinces and autonomous regions have established programs to sell properties (e.g., apartments in urban areas) to individuals instead of allocating residency as part of the employment benefits.

Since 1998 the residential housing reform and the development of individual mortgages, along with rising household income and demand for quality housing, had stimulated the fast growth of the real estate market. Figure 2.6 shows the total real estate investments and their funding sources over time. Total investment increased from RMB 321 billion in 1996, 12 percent of the national fixed assets investments, to RMB 4.8 trillion in 2010 and 20 percent of the national fixed assets investment. Most of the investment funds have come from domestic sources. Not surprisingly, bank loans are the most important source of real estate financing. China's continuing economic growth, especially in private sectors, urbanization and industrialization, limited land supply, increasing foreign direct investments and institutional investments, will further enhance the liquidity and long-term prospects of China's real estate assets.

As the real estate sector gained more weight in the economy, its impact on other industries, especially the financial and banking industries, increased considerably. With the expansion of the real estate market, banks and other financial institutions lent more to keep up with the demand for financing. When the fast expansion, in part fueled by the inflows of speculative capital and agency problems in investment, could not be sustained, increased demand led to hikes in property prices and real estate bubbles surfaced. The bursting of such bubbles can lead to painful consequences in the entire economy.

The real estate prices in major cities have risen sharply in recent years, and whether these fast growing prices are bubbles and how to cool down the markets are among the most closely watched and hotly debated issues in China. We provide some simple analysis here; for a more thorough and careful analysis see, for example, Wu, Gyourko, and Deng (2011). Figure 2.7 shows the trends of total housing space developed versus total space sold over the period 2002 to 2009 for the entire nation, and figure 2.8 compares the growth rates of total housing space developed versus total space sold; actual space is normalized so that both charts begin at 100 in 2002; hence the vertical axis measures growth rates. We can see that while total space developed and total space sold (for both residential and nonresidential properties) grew at similar rates over the period (figure 2.8), the gap between total space developed and sold—a proxy for the inventory of housing supply in

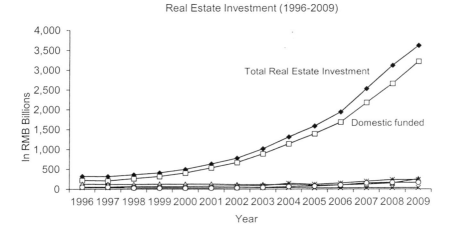

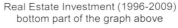

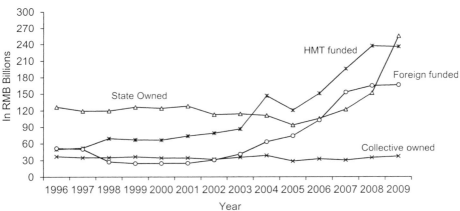

Fig. 2.6   Total real estate investments and their sources (1996–2009)

Note: Bottom part of the figure in the top panel is enlarged and plotted in the bottom panel, which presents the funding sources of real estate investment over the period of 1996–2009.

the markets—widened from around 0.6 billion square meters in 2002 to 2.2 billion square meters in 2009.

In figures 2.9 through 2.13 we plot and compare growth rates of average housing prices and disposable household income, over the period 2002 to 2009, for the nation and the four major cities: Beijing, Shanghai, Shenzhen, and Guangzhou. Once again, actual housing prices (RMB per square meter) and disposable income are normalized so that both charts begin at 100 in 2002; hence the vertical axis measures growth rates and all the figures

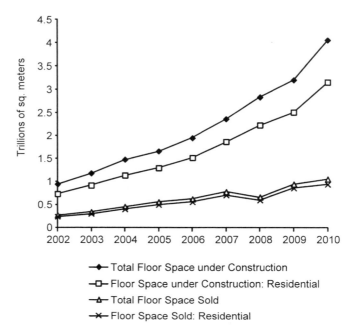

Fig. 2.7   Total floor space (developed versus sold) in China
Source: CEIC.

Normalized chart, 2002=100

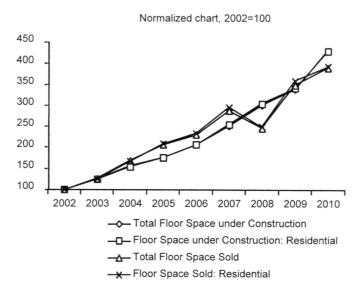

Fig. 2.8   Growth rates in total floor space (developed versus sold) in China
Source: CEIC.

Fig. 2.9 Comparing the growth of national housing prices and disposable household income

Source: CEIC (also source for figs. 2.10 through 2.13).

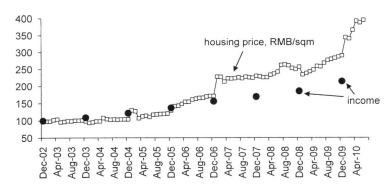

Fig. 2.10 Growth of housing prices and disposable household income in Beijing

Fig. 2.11 Growth of housing prices and disposable household income in Shanghai

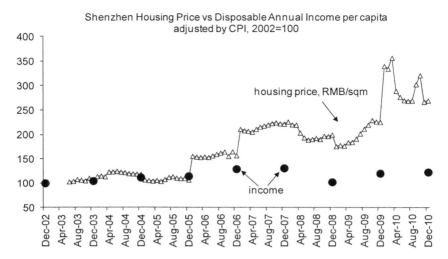

Fig. 2.12   Growth of housing prices and disposable household income in Shenzhen

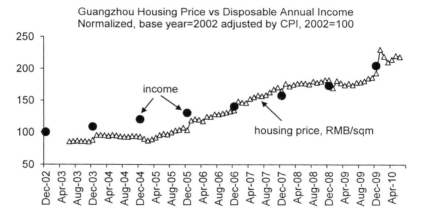

Fig. 2.13   Growth of housing prices and disposable household income in Guangzhou

for prices and income are inflation adjusted. Steady growth of disposable income in line with rising housing prices can help sustain the growth of the housing markets, and hence considerable and increasing gaps in the growth rates reflect potential bubbles in the housing markets. Based on the figures it appears that while at the national level and in the city of Guangzhou there are no signs of bubbles, the opposite can be said for the large regional markets in Beijing, Shanghai, and Shenzhen, where housing prices have been rising at much higher paces than those of real disposable income in recent years. Shenzhen presents the most worrisome case, where despite fast-rising housing prices fueled by the inflow of speculative capital, real household income actually declined in 2008 and 2009 (from 2007 levels), perhaps (partially) due to the adverse effects of the global financial crisis on the exporting sectors, which rely mainly on migrant workers from other regions.

We would like to emphasize again that our results are based on simple measures; however, analyses from Wu, Gyourko, and Deng (2011), who use more sophisticated metrics and regressions controlling for other factors that may affect housing prices, yield similar results that there may well be bubbles in the regional markets of Beijing, Shanghai, and Shenzhen. There is some evidence that speculative foreign capital (the "hot money") flowing into China is partially responsible for the accelerated rise in real estate markets (e.g., Chu and Sing 2004; Guo and Huang 2010). Given the rising status of the Chinese economy and its currency, coupled with the weakening of the US economy (and other developed countries), and the dollar and near-zero interest rates in most developed countries, the inflow of "hot money" into China's real estate markets (and other sectors) may continue.

The government has been taking aggressive measures to control property prices. Since 2004, it has issued new policies in order to suppress speculative activities; another policy measure to control the growth of the real estate market is through the PBOC's required reserve deposit ratio. In 2010 and 2011, in response to the fast rising housing prices, the government has announced a series of interventions including: (a) increased equity down payment shares from 20 percent to 30 percent for first homes of more than 90 square meters in size; (b) increased equity down payment shares from 40 percent to 50 percent for second homes; (c) general discouragement of the use of any leverage on third homes or by external buyers (i.e., those not living in the market of the intended purchase); (d) new rules to prevent developers from hoarding housing units; (e) preparation of the introduction of a local property tax, with possible pilot implementations in Chongqing, a large city in the southwestern region that is under direct control of the central government, within the next one to two years; and (f) direct administrative orders on how much land and units of buildings can be developed.[30] Among these measures, the proposed property tax may play a significant role in cooling down the markets, because it would raise the cost of carry on speculative investments in owner-occupied housing.

Despite the government's macroprudential policies in recent years and the newly announced measures and strong signals in recent months, the impact of these measures on the housing markets seems to be limited. One reason, as stipulated by many observers, is that since various government agencies and officials have played a major role in developing "commercial properties" it is not in their best interest to see major market corrections. The evidence

---

30. For more details, see "Gazette of Executive Meeting of the State Council," December 14, 2009; and "Circular of the State Council on Resolutely Containing the Precipitous Rise of Housing Prices in Some Cities" (Decree No. [2010] 10), April 17, 2010, and Wu, Gyourko, and Deng (2011).

in Wu, Gyourko, and Deng (2011) provides some support of this view. They find that much of the increase in housing prices is occurring in land values. Using land auctions data from Beijing, they also find SOEs controlled by the central government paid 27 percent more than other bidders for an otherwise equivalent land parcel. Since many vested government officials have a lot to lose following a crash in the real estate markets, it is argued that the new measures, including the proposed property taxes, will not be effectively enforced; such a belief can also explain why speculative capital continues to enter the housing markets.

Given the experiences of many other countries in the recent and previous financial crises, the government's efforts in controlling the rise of housing markets in the aforementioned regions, and preventing this spreading to other regions of the country can augment its other efforts in stabilizing the economy and alleviating social tensions. In section 2.6 we further examine how the inflow of speculative capital and subsequent outflow can create bubbles in the markets and then the bursting of the bubbles can spread to other sectors of the economy.

2.4.5   Private Equity/Venture Capital and the Funding of New Industries

Allen and Gale (1999, 2000a) have suggested that stock market-based economies, such as the United Kingdom in the nineteenth century and the United States in the twentieth century, have been more successful in developing *new* industries than intermediary-based economies such as Germany and Japan. They argue that markets are better than banks for funding new industries, because evaluation of these industries based on experience is difficult, and there is wide diversity of opinion. Stock market-based economies such as the United States and United Kingdom also tend to have well-developed systems for the acquisition and distribution of information, so the cost of information to investors is low. Markets then work well because investors can gather information at low costs and those that anticipate high profits can provide the finance to the firms operating in the new industries.

A key part of this process is the private equity/venture capital sector (see, e.g., Kortum and Lerner 2000). Venture capitalists are able to raise large amounts of funds in the United States because of the prospect that successful firms will be able to undertake an IPO. With data from twenty-one countries, Jeng and Wells (2000) find that venture capital is less important in other countries, while the existence of an active IPO market is the critical determinant of the importance of venture capital in a country. This is consistent with the finding of Black and Gilson (1998) in a comparison of the United States and Germany, that the primary reason venture capital is relatively successful in the United States is the active IPO market that exists there.

These facts imply that the development of active venture capital and private equity markets can increase the financing for China's new industries. What is unusual about China (perhaps along with India) is that it currently has the ability to develop both traditional industries, such as manufacturing, and in the near future new, high-tech industries, such as aerospace, computer software, semiconductors, and biogenetics. This is different from the experience of South Korea and Taiwan in the 1970s and that of most other emerging economies in the 1990s, as all these other countries focused on developing manufacturing industries first. In terms of developing traditional industries (e.g., Korea and Taiwan in the 1970s), China has already followed suit in first introducing advanced (relative to domestic companies) but not the most advanced technologies from developed countries, and "nationalizing" these technologies within designated companies before moving toward the more advanced technologies. Allen and Gale (1999, 2000a) argue that banks are better than financial markets for funding mature industries because there is wide agreement on how they are best managed, so the delegation of the investment decision to a bank works well. This delegation process, and the economies of scale in information acquisition through delegation, makes bank-based systems more efficient in terms of financing the growth in these industries. Therefore, the banking system can contribute more in supporting the growth and development of these industries than markets.

2.4.6   Asset Management Industries

The mutual fund industry in China has gone through three stages of development. The first stage is between 1992, when China's first fund (*LiuBo*) was established, and 1997, when the first version of the mutual fund regulation was drafted and passed by the CSRC. The *LiuBo* Fund was a closed-end fund with NAV RMB 100 million RMB ($12.5 million) and began to trade on the SHSE in 1993. While the industry experienced fast growth in the few years after 1992, lack of regulation and problems associated with fund trading hampered the further development of the industry. The first open-end fund was established in September, 2001 (*Hua An Chuangxin*), following the announcement of the proposal for open-end fund investment by the CSRC, a milestone for China's mutual fund industry.

Figure 2.14 shows the development of the mutual fund industry in China. With only a handful of funds in 1998, China now has sixty-five fund companies managing 551 different funds as of November 2009. The total net assets value increased from RMB 11 billion (or $1.3 billion) in 1998 to about RMB 2.26 trillion (or $328 billion) in November 2009 (this figure was much higher in the second half of 2007 before the markets went south). In 2001, the NAV of all funds was about 0.8 percent of GDP and 1.19 percent of total national savings; these figures rose to 6.16 percent of GDP and 8.58 percent of total savings in 2008. The growth of open-end funds contributed to most of the growth in the industry. As of November 2009, 520 funds are

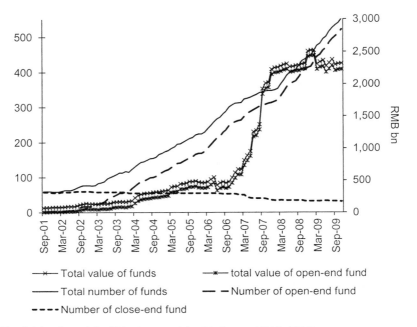

Fig. 2.14   Growth in China's mutual fund industry (1998–2009)

open-ended and 31 are close-ended, with 96 percent of the total fund value managed by open-end funds. The most popular investment style is actively managed (domestic) equity, with only a few index funds and ETFs (exchange traded funds).

Many mutual fund companies are owned by securities and other financial services companies. Like their counterparts in the United States, management fees are the major source of income for fund companies, accounting for about 80 percent of total income. Administration fees account for 9 percent of total income, and the rest of the income comes from investment and other incomes. More than half of the fund managers have a master-level or higher academic degree, and the majority of them are thirty-six to forty-five years old. Investment capital from institutional investors is about the same as that from individual investors in 2005, but in 2006 individual investors account for 70 percent of the total mutual fund investment. Among the twenty-three newly launched funds in the first half of 2009, individual investors account for 75.8 percent.

The first fund managed by a qualified foreign institutional investor (QFII) was set up in 2002. The State Administration of Foreign Exchange (SAFE) is the government agent that regulates the QFII funds. The QFII Act allows foreign investors to invest in Chinese securities, with the intention of introducing sophisticated foreign investors to the Chinese market with the hope that their presence will improve market efficiency. In addition, with the exercise of their shareholder rights, their presence can also help improve corporate governance of the Listed Sector. However, the original QFII rules imposed restrictions on foreign investors, such as a capital lock-up period of one to three years limiting capital withdrawal (and leaving China) and other operating restrictions. In August 2006, CSRC revised QFII rules to promote more participation from foreign investors. Under the new rules, there has been a significant increase in applications from foreign investors for QFII quotas.

Most of the institutions in the first group of QFII applicants were securities companies and investment banks, with other financial services companies such as insurance companies and pension fund companies also on the list. By the end of July 2006, China had approved a total of $7.495 billion foreign investment capital (quota) from forty-five QFIIs, or three-quarters of the then-ceiling of $10 billion capital inflow through QFIIs. In December 2007, the investment quota/ceiling tripled, from $10 billion to $30 billion. In September 2009, draft rules were issued by SAFE to increase the upward limit of investment for an individual QFII institution to $1 billion from the previous $800 million. Some analysts believe that the move to increase the QFII quota was also intended to prepare for the large amount of floating of nontradable shares. If the holders of the newly floated shares rush to sell, QFII funds can be a stabilizing source of the market. As of August 2011, there were a total of 116 approved QFIIs operating in China, of which 103 were investment funds. The approved investment quotas reached $20.69 billion.

The approval of qualified domestic institutional investors (QDII) to invest in overseas markets came after QFII, in July 2006. The QDII funds invest in stocks, bonds, real estate investment trusts, and other mainstream financial products in markets such as New York, London, Tokyo, and Hong Kong. Similarly to the QFII scheme, it is a transitional arrangement that provides limited opportunities for domestic investors to access foreign markets at a stage in which a country/territory's currency is not freely convertible and capital flows are restricted. As of early 2008, ten fund companies had obtained the approval to launch QDII. The total number of QDII funds reached seventy-five in July 2009. By April 2011, QDIIs had approved investment quotas of $72.67 billion. Given the recent turmoil in the global financial markets, the performance of the QDII funds has been less than stellar. Going forward, the probable continuing appreciation of the RMB against major international currencies including the dollar is a major concern for QDII investors.

China's asset management industry is expected to continue its growth in the near future. In the United States, mutual funds became the largest group of financial intermediaries in financial markets in 1999, holding 29 percent of all financial assets. By contrast, mutual funds in China only held around

8.1 percent of all financial assets at the end of 2009. The further growth of the economy and continuing reform of the pension system will generate both demand and supply of capital for the industry. If the trend of opening up domestic markets to foreign investors continues, there will be a greater inflow of QFIIs.

2.4.7   Further Changes in Financial Markets

As we have documented, the financial markets in China do not currently play nearly as important a role as banks. Going forward, further improvements in the operation of China's financial markets can help to promote the development of high-technology industries as discussed in section 2.4.5. In addition, developing new financial products and markets can enhance the risk management capabilities of China's financial institutions and firms. Finally, deep and efficient markets can provide an alternative to banks for raising large amounts of capital.

In recent years the performance of the stock markets has been volatile. This is somewhat surprising given the robust performance of the real economy. We attribute this (relatively) poor performance to a number of factors including the following:

1. Limited self-regulation and formal regulation.
2. The large overhang of shares owned by government entities.
3. The lack of listed firms originating in the Hybrid Sector.
4. The lack of trained professionals.
5. The lack of institutional investors.
6. Limited financial markets and products.

Efforts have been made to address some of these weaknesses. However, some of these are problems that can only be tackled over the long run. We discuss each in turn.

Regulations

There are two ways in which markets are regulated in practice and each has advantages and disadvantages: first, market forces and self-regulation, and second, government regulation.

A good example of regulation through market forces and self-regulation is provided by the capital markets in the United Kingdom in the nineteenth and early twentieth centuries (Michie 1987). The role of government regulation and intervention was minimal. Despite this, the markets did extremely well and London became the financial capital of the world. Many firms and countries from all over the world raised large amounts of funds. Reputation and trust were an important factor in the smooth operation of these markets. For example, Franks, Mayer, and Rossi (2003) compare the early twentieth century capital markets with those in the mid-twentieth century. Despite extensive changes in the laws protecting minority shareholders, there was very little change in the ways in which the market operated. The authors attribute this to the importance of trust.

We argue later that China's Hybrid Sector is another example of a situation where market forces are effective. Formal regulation and legal protections do not play much of a role and yet financing and governance mechanisms are quite effective. In this case, as we shall see, it appears that competition as well as reputation and trust work well.

In contrast, the examples of fraud and other problems of manipulation and the inefficiency of markets pointed to in section 2.4.1 suggest that in China's formal financial markets these alternative mechanisms do not work well. Although such mechanisms may develop in the long run as in the nineteenth and early twentieth century United Kingdom, or in the short run, formal government regulation of the type introduced in the United States in the 1930s and subsequently as a response to the stock market collapse that started in 1929 and the following Great Depression, may allow Chinese markets to function better. There is evidence from many countries that this type of formal regulation is effective. For example, based on a study of securities laws with the focus on the public issuance of new equity in forty-nine countries (China is not included) La Porta, Lopez-de-Silanes, and Shleifer (2006, LLS hereafter) find that disclosure and liability rules help to promote stock market development.

Sale of Government Shares in Listed Firms

One of the major problems Chinese stock markets have faced in recent years has been caused by the large amount of shares in listed companies owned by the government and government entities shown in table 2.12. The Chinese government attempted sales of state shares of selected firms in 1999 and 2001, but halted the process both times after share prices plunged and investors grew panicky about the value of the entire market. This overhang created great uncertainty about the quantity of shares that would come onto the market going forward. This uncertainty was probably in part responsible for the stagnation of share prices between 2002 and 2005 despite the very high levels of growth in the economy.

In 2005 the government announced a plan of "fully floating" state shares. Under the plan, the remaining state shares among listed firms were converted to G shares. The CSRC outlined the format for compensating existing shareholders and also imposed lockups and restrictions on the amount of G shares that could be sold immediately after they became tradable. More specifically, the plan stipulated that G shares were not to be traded or transferred within twelve months after the implementation of the share structure reform. Shareholders owning more than 5 percent of the original nontradable shares can only trade less than 5 percent of the total shares outstanding within one year and less than 10 percent within two years. These restrictions of G share sales were intended to reduce the downward pressure on the stock price, maintain market stability, and protect the interests of public investors. The details of the "fully floating plan" for a firm, including the number of G shares to be granted to each class A shareholder and the time window (e.g., one to three years) of G shares to become fully floating, had to be approved by two-thirds of class A shareholders of the firm.

Share reforms began with a pilot program with only four companies participating in April 2005. By the end of 2006, 96 percent of all the listed companies had completed share reforms; by the end of 2007, there were only a few companies that had not reached an agreement with their shareholders on the terms of the reform.[31] As documented in table 2.12, as of September 2009, for the first time tradable shares accounted for more than half of the stock market, suggesting that the floating of nontradable shares is progressing.

Another fact worth mentioning is that for the firms that go public (IPOs) after the share reform, not all of their stocks are immediately floated to the market. Lock-up periods may still apply to large shareholders who obtained the shares before the IPO. For example, in the case of ABC's recent IPO, the majority of A shares (87.6 percent) have already been distributed to various agencies of the government before the IPO. In fact, only 25.5 billion A shares (8.6 percent of total outstanding A shares) were issued in the IPO. Those shares held by the government have a lock-up for three years. However, they are technically A (not G) shares. Thus no compensation will be paid when those shares become freely tradable.

The Listing of Firms from the Hybrid Sector

One of the major problems of the stock exchanges is that most of the firms listed are former SOEs. Relatively few are firms from the more dynamic Hybrid Sector. Reforming listing requirements and procedures to make it advantageous for dynamic and successful companies to become listed on the exchanges can enhance the overall quality of the Listed Sector. The establishment of the recently opened "GEM" provides an example in this regard.

The Training of More Professionals

This step will allow an improvement in the enforcement of laws and contracts. An independent and efficient judicial system requires a sufficient supply of qualified legal professionals. The Ministry of Justice of China states that there are 143,000 lawyers and 12,428 law firms as of 2007. Two

31. Hwang, Zhang, and Zhu (2006) document that share reform increases turnover, especially for firms with low liquidity prior to the reform, and reduces speculative trading. Although share prices drop significantly on the day of share supply increases, shareholder wealth increases by 15 percent overall. Beltratti and Bortolotti (2006) document an 8 percent abnormal return around the date of share reform announcement. Liao and Liu (2008) show that market reactions to share reforms are positively associated with the quality of the listed firms (as measured by firm disclosure), providing evidence of improved market efficiency.

hundred and six out of China's 2,000 counties still do not have lawyers. Lawyers represent only 10 to 25 percent of all clients in civil and business cases, and even in criminal prosecutions, lawyers represent defendants in only half of the cases. Among the approximately five million business enterprises in China, only 4 percent of them currently have regular legal advisers. Moreover, only one-fifth of all lawyers in China have law degrees, and even a lower fraction of judges have formally studied law at a university or college. As mentioned before, a similar situation exists for auditors and accounting professionals.

Institutional Investors

In most developed stock markets institutional investors—such as insurance companies, pension funds, mutual funds, and hedge funds—play an important role. They employ well-trained professionals who are able to evaluate companies well. This causes markets to have a higher degree of efficiency than if they are dominated by individual investors. In addition, there can be advantages in terms of corporate governance if institutional investors actively participate in the monitoring of firms' managers and are directly involved in firms' decision-making process as blockholders of stocks. For example, in the United States, pension funds such as CALPERS have become the symbol of shareholder activism that strengthens corporate governance, while in Japan and Germany, financial intermediaries serve similar purposes. For China, the efficiency of China's stock markets as well as corporate governance of listed firms can be improved by further entry of domestic financial intermediaries that can act as institutional investors. With their large-scale capital and expertise in all relevant areas of business, financial intermediaries can provide a level of stability and professionalism that is sorely lacking in China's financial markets.

Currently institutional investors such as insurance companies, mutual funds, and pension funds are relatively small in terms of assets held given their early stage of development. However, they are expanding dramatically. Among policies that can further encourage the development of such intermediaries are those that provide tax advantages to various types of products such as life insurance and pension-related savings and investments.

A Greater Range of Financial Products and Markets

A larger amount of financial products allow investors to form diversified portfolios with more than just stocks. First, as discussed earlier, corporate bond markets, along with better enforcement of bankruptcy laws and bond rating agencies, provide an alternative class of assets to stocks. Second, the introduction of more derivative securities such as forwards, futures, and options on commodities (already in place and trading) as well as on other securities, enlarges the risk management toolbox of investors and firms. In fact, China has launched an index future on April 16, 2010, tracking the

Shanghai-based *Hushen 300,* the index of 300 Shanghai- and Shenzhen-listed class A shares. On the first day four contacts were traded. Of the 2,200 index future accounts opened as of May 4, 2010, 95 percent of them were individuals, and the rest were institutional investors. The proportion of institutional investors is expected to rise in the future, since the index future is targeted mainly toward more sophisticated investors for hedging purposes. The launch of this long awaited index future is a major step in the reform of capital markets in China and introduces a new tool for risk management. Along with the index future, margin trading and short selling of shares were also permitted in April.

Third, the expansion of their coverage and products (e.g., in property and auto insurance as well as life and medical insurance) by insurance companies, and the introduction and development of asset-backed securities and other structured finance products by financial services companies, can further diversify the supply of financial products.

2.5   The Nonstandard Financial Sector and Evidence on Hybrid Sector Firms

In this section we study how the nonstandard financial sector supports firms in the Hybrid Sector to raise funds and to grow from start-ups to successful industry leaders. We also examine the alternative governance mechanisms employed by investors and firms that can substitute for formal corporate governance mechanisms. Due to data limitations, much of this evidence is by necessity anecdotal or by survey.[32]

We first compare the Hybrid Sector with the State and Listed Sectors to highlight the importance of its status in the entire economy in section 2.5.1. Second, we consider survey evidence in section 2.5.2. Finally, section 2.5.3 provides discussions and comparisons of alternative financing channels and governance mechanisms that support the growth of the Hybrid Sector versus formal financing channels (through banks and markets) and governance mechanisms (laws and courts).

2.5.1   Comparison of Hybrid Sector versus State and Listed Sectors

Figure 2.15 compares the level and growth of *industrial output* produced in the State and Listed Sectors combined versus that of the Hybrid Sector from 1998 to 2009.[33] The output from the Hybrid Sector has been steadily

32. All firms, including Hybrid Sector firms, must disclose accounting and financial information to the local Bureau of Commerce and Industry, and most of the reports are audited. However, these data are then aggregated into the Statistical Yearbook without any firm-level publications.

33. The National Bureau of Statistics (NBS) of China revised its total industrial output statistics in the 2000 yearbook without any explicit explanations. The outputs in previous years (i.e., 1997) were significantly revised down compared to the 1998 yearbook. To be consistent and avoid confusion, we only use data from the NBS after 1998.

Industrial Output by Sectors (above Designated Size)

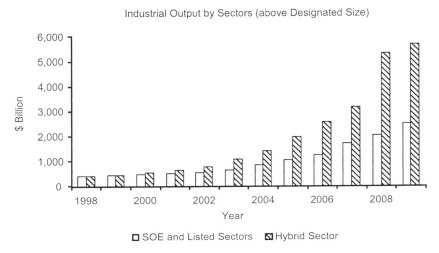

Fig. 2.15   **Comparing the sectors—Industrial output**
Source: Chinese Statistical Yearbook (2000–2009).
Notes: In this figure we plot total "industrial output" for State (SOEs) and Listed (publicly listed and traded firms) Sectors combined and for the Hybrid Sector (all the rest of the firms) during 2000 to 2008.

increasing during this period and exceeded that of the other two sectors in 1998. The total output in 2009 is almost $5,700 billion for the Hybrid Sector, while it is around $2,500 billion in the State and Listed Sectors combined.[34] The Hybrid Sector grew at an annual rate of over 23 percent between 1998 and 2009, while the State and Listed Sectors combined grew at around 15 percent during the same period.[35] In addition, the growth rates for investment in fixed assets of these sectors are comparable (*China Statistics Yearbooks;* AQQ 2005), which implies that the Hybrid Sector is more productive than the State and Listed Sectors. In fact, with large samples of firms (from sources) with various ownership structures, Liu (2007) and Dollar and Wei (2007) both find that the returns to capital are much higher in

34. Due to data limitations, our calculations underestimate the output of the State and Listed Sectors. We use the output produced by SOEs and listed firms in which the state has at least a 50 percent ownership stake as the total output for these sectors, but this calculation excludes output from listed firms that are *not* majority owned by the state; the output for the Hybrid Sector is the difference between the total output and the total for the other two sectors. However, as mentioned earlier, only around 20 percent of all listed firms do not have the state as the largest owner, hence the total output of these firms is not likely to change our overall conclusion on the dominance of the Hybrid Sector over the other two sectors.

35. There is an ongoing process of privatizing SOEs. Potentially this may bias the growth rate of the Hybrid Sector higher, as there are firms shifting from the State Sector to the Hybrid Sector. However, the overwhelming majority of SOEs became Listed Sector firms (the main channel through which SOEs were partially privatized prior to 2004), thus this process is unlikely to change the validity of the previous results.

nonstate sectors than the State Sector, and that a capital reallocation from state to private sectors will generate more growth in the economy. Fan, Rui, and Zhao (2006) and Li, Yue, and Zhao (2007) find that state-owned firms in China have a much easier access to the debt market and accordingly higher leverage than nonstate firms. One reason for the differences is that due to government protection (for economic and social/political reasons), the costs for bankruptcy and financial distress are much lower for state-owned firms. These firms also have easier access to bank loans, especially credit extended by state-owned banks.

All of the just mentioned facts make the growth of the Hybrid Sector even more impressive. Not surprisingly, there has been a fundamental change among the State, Listed, and Hybrid Sectors in terms of their contribution to the entire economy: the State Sector contributed more than two-thirds of China's GDP in 1980 and (nonagricultural) privately-owned firms, a type of Hybrid Sector firm, were negligible, but in 2009 the State Sector only contributed 30 percent of the GDP (*China Statistical Yearbook, 1998–2010*). The trend of the Hybrid Sector replacing the State Sector is likely to continue in the near future.

Figure 2.16 presents the number and growth of nonagricultural employees in the three sectors. The Hybrid Sector is a much more significant source for employment opportunities than the State and Listed Sectors. Over the period from 1990 to 2010, the Hybrid Sector employs an average of over 77 percent of all nonagricultural workers; the TVEs (part of the Hybrid Sector)

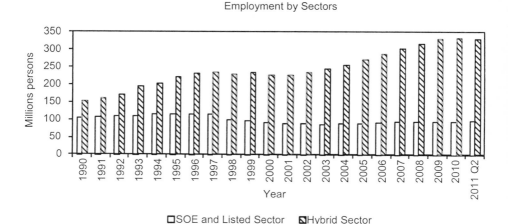

Employment by Sectors

Fig. 2.16   Comparing the sectors—Employment
Source: Chinese Statistical Yearbook and CEIC database.

Notes: In this figure we plot total number of workers employed by the State (SOEs) and Listed (publicly listed and traded firms) Sectors combined and by the Hybrid Sector (all the rest of the firms) during 1990 to 2008.

have been the most important employers providing (nonagricultural) jobs for residents in the rural areas, while (nonagricultural) privately-owned firms employ more than 40 percent of the workforce in the urban areas. Moreover, the number of employees working in the Hybrid Sector has been growing at 1.5 percent over this period, while the labor force in the State and Listed Sectors has been shrinking.[36] These patterns are particularly relevant for China, given its vast population and potential problem of unemployment.

2.5.2   Survey Evidence

Much of the information concerning the Hybrid Sector comes from surveys. We focus on evidence in AQQ (2005) and Cull and Xu (2005). The most significant findings of these surveys regarding financing channels are the following. First, during the start-up stage, funds from founders' families and friends are an essential source of financing. Banks can also play an important role. Second, internal financing, in the form of retained earnings, is also important. During their growth period financing from private credit agencies (PCAs) instead of banks, as well as trade credits, are key channels for firms in AQQ's sample. As documented by Tsai (2002), PCAs take on many forms, from shareholding cooperative enterprises run by professional money brokers, lenders, and middlemen, to credit associations operated by a group of entrepreneurs (raising money from group members and from outsiders to fund firms; *zijin huzushe*), from pawn shops to underground private money houses.

As far as corporate governance is concerned, when asked about what type of losses concern them the most if the firm failed, every firm's founders/executives (100 percent) included in the AQQ study said reputation loss is a major concern, while only 60 percent of them said economic losses are of major concern. Competition also appears to be an important factor ensuring firms are well run.

Cull and Xu (2005) find that firms in most regions and cities rely on courts to resolve less than 10 percent of business-related disputes (the highest percentage is 20 percent), with a higher reliance on courts in coastal and more developed areas. One reason that firms go to courts to resolve a dispute is because the courts are authoritative so that the dispute will be resolved even though the resolution may not be fair (e.g., Clarke, Murrell, and Whiting 2008).

2.5.3   Discussion on How the Nonstandard Financial Sector Works

In this subsection we first discuss mechanisms within the nonstandard financial sector in supporting the growth of the Hybrid Sector. We then

---

36. Our calculations of the total number of workers employed by the Hybrid Sector actually underestimate the actual workforce in the sector, because the *Chinese Statistical Yearbooks* do not provide employment data for all types of firms (by ownership structure), especially small firms, in the Hybrid Sector.

compare these alternative institutions that operate outside the legal system with the law and legal institutions that have been widely regarded as the basis for conducting finance and commerce. There are two aspects to alternative financing channels in the Hybrid Sector. The first is the way in which investment is financed. The second is corporate governance. We consider each in turn.

Once a firm is established and doing well, internal finance can provide the funds necessary for growth. Allen, Qian, and Qian (2005) find that about 60 percent of the funds raised by the Hybrid Sector are generated internally. Of course, internal finance is fine once a firm is established but this raises the issue of how firms in the Hybrid Sector acquire their "seed" capital, perhaps the most crucial financing during a firm's life cycle. Allen, Qian, and Qian present evidence on the importance of alternative and informal channels, including funds from family and friends and loans from private (unofficial) credit agencies (see also Tsai 2002). There is also evidence that financing through illegal channels, such as smuggling, bribery, insider trading and speculations during early stages of the development of financial markets and real estate market, and other underground or unofficial businesses can also play a critical role in the accumulation of seed capital.

Perhaps the most significant corporate governance mechanism is competition in product and input markets, which has worked well in both developed and developing countries (e.g., McMillan 1995, 1997; Allen and Gale 2000b). What we see from the success of Hybrid Sector firms in WenZhou and other surveyed firms recounted in AQQ, suggest that it is only those firms that have the strongest comparative advantage in an industry (of the area) that survived and thrived. A relevant factor for competition in an industry is entry barriers for new firms, as lower entry barriers foster competition. Djankov et al. (2002, DLLS hereafter) examine entry barriers across eighty-five countries, and find that countries with heavier (lighter) regulation of entry have higher government corruption (more democratic and limited governments) and larger unofficial economies. With much lower barriers to entry compared to other countries with similar (low) per capita GDP, China is once again an "outlier" in the DLLS sample given that China is one of the least democratic countries, and such countries tend to have high barriers to entry. Survey evidence from AQQ (2005) reveals that there exist nonstandard methods to remove entry barriers in China, which can reconcile these seemingly contradictory facts.

Another mechanism is reputation, trust, and relationships. Greif (1989, 1993) argues that certain traders' organizations in the eleventh century were able to overcome problems of asymmetric information and the lack of legal and contract enforcement mechanisms because they had developed institutions based on reputation, implicit contractual relations, and coalitions. Certain aspects of the growth of these institutions resemble what worked to promote commerce and the financial system in China prior to 1949 (e.g.,

Kirby 1995) and the operation of the nonstandard financial sector today (AQQ 2005), in terms of how firms raise funds and contract with investors and business partners. In addition, Greif (1993) and Stulz and Williamson (2003) point out the importance of cultural and religious beliefs for the development of institutions, legal origins, and investor protections.

The aforementioned factors are of particular relevance and importance to China's development of institutions. Without a dominant religion, some argue that the most important force in shaping China's social values and institutions is the set of beliefs first developed and formalized by *Kongzi* (Confucius). This set of beliefs clearly defines family and social orders, which are very different from Western beliefs on how legal codes are formulated. Using the World Values Survey conducted in the early 1990s, La Porta et al. (1997, LLSV hereafter) find that China has one of the highest levels of social trust among a group of forty developed and developing countries.[37] We interpret high social trust in China as being influenced by Confucian beliefs. Throughout this chapter and AQQ (2005, 2008) we have presented evidence that reputation and relationships make many financing channels and governance mechanisms work in China's Hybrid Sector.

There are other effective corporate governance mechanisms. First, Burkart, Panunzi, and Shleifer (2003) link the degree of separation of ownership and control to different legal environments, and show that *family-run* firms will emerge as the dominant form of ownership structure in countries with weak minority shareholder protections, whereas professionally managed firms are the optimal form in countries with strong protection. Survey evidence on the Hybrid Sector in AQQ and empirical results on the Listed Sector, along with evidence in Claessens, Djankov, and Lang (2000) and Claessens et al. (2002) and ACDQQ (2008), suggests that family firms are a norm in China and other Asian countries, and these firms have performed well. Second, Allen and Gale (2000a) show that, if cooperation among different suppliers of inputs is necessary and all suppliers benefit from the firm doing well, then a good equilibrium with no external governance is possible, as internal, mutual monitoring can ensure the optimal outcome. Allen, Qian, and Qian (2005) and ACDQQ (2008) present evidence on the importance of trade credits as a form of financing for firms in the Hybrid Sector. Cooperation and mutual monitoring can ensure payments (as long as funds are available) among business partners despite the lack of external monitoring and contract enforcement. The importance of trade credits is also found in other emerging economies (e.g., ACDQQ 2012 on India) as well as in developed countries (Burkart, Elligensen, and Giannetti 2011 on the United States).

It is worth mentioning how entrepreneurs and investors alleviate and

---

37. Interestingly, the same survey, used in LLSV (1997), finds that Chinese citizens have a low tendency to participate in civil activities. However, our evidence shows that, with effective alternative mechanisms in place, citizens in the developed regions of China have a strong incentive to participate in business/economic activities.

overcome problems associated with government corruption. According to proponents of institutional development (e.g., Rajan and Zingales 2003b; Acemoglu and Johnson 2005), poor institutions, weak government, and powerful elites can severely hinder China's long-run economic growth. However, our evidence shows that corruption has not prevented a high rate of growth for China's firms, in particular, firms in the Hybrid Sector, where legal protection is perhaps weaker and problems of corruption worse compared to firms in the State and Listed Sectors.

A potentially effective solution for corruption is competition among local governments/bureaucrats from different regions within the same country. Entrepreneurs can move from region to region to find the most supportive government officials for their private firms, which in turn motivates officials to lend "helping hands" rather than "grabbing hands" in the provision of public goods or services (e.g., granting of licenses to start-up firms), or else there will be an outflow of profitable private businesses from the region (Allen and Qian 2009). This remedy is typically available in a large country with diverse regions like China. Complementing this view, Xu (2011) reviews China's unique institutional foundation of "regionally decentralized authoritarian system," in which the subnational governments have considerable autonomous power over regional economic decisions and at the same time remain under the control of the central government. Under this structure, local governments play a major role in supporting TVEs, allocating bank credits to firms, and choosing good firms to get listed. This system alleviates the information problem that regulators face, and creates incentives for subnational governors through personnel control and regional competition. Xu argues that this governance structure is responsible for the spectacular economic growth of China, despite weak enforcement of formal laws.

To summarize, the extraordinary economic performance of China in recent decades, especially that of the Hybrid Sector, raises questions about the conventional wisdom of using the legal system as the basis of commerce. Most observers would characterize the economic performance in China and India as "successful *despite* the lack of Western-style institutions," and the failure to adopt Western institutions will be one of the main factors to halt the long-run economic growth. By contrast, Allen and Qian (2010) argue that China's economy has been successful *because of* this lack of Western-style institutions—in that conducting business outside the legal system in fast-growing economies such as China can actually be superior to using the law as the basis for finance and commerce.

Focusing on dispute resolution and contract enforcement mechanisms based on the law and courts versus alternative mechanisms operating outside the legal system, Allen and Qian (2010) argue that despite many well-known advantages, there are disadvantages in using legal institutions. First, recent research on political economy factors, and in particular, work by Rajan and

Zingales (2003a, 2003b) shows that rent-seeking behaviors by vested interest groups can turn legal institutions into barriers to changes. We expect these problems to be much more severe in developing countries and the costs of building good institutions can be enormous.[38] One way to solve this problem is *not* to use the law as the basis for commerce but instead to use alternative mechanisms *outside* the legal system. Evidence presented in this chapter and other related work on China and other emerging economies (e.g., ACDQQ 2012 on India) suggests that these alternative mechanisms can be quite effective.

Second, in democracies there can be a lengthy political process before significant changes can be approved (by the majority of the population and/or legislature), and the people in charge of revising the law (e.g., politicians and judges) may lack the expertise of business transactions and have limited capacity (time and effort) to examine the proposed changes.[39] In the context of a fast-growing economy with frequent changes such as China, Allen and Qian (2010) show that there is an additional advantage of using alternative institutions because this type of system can adapt and change much more quickly than when the law is used. In particular, competition can ensure the most efficient mechanism prevails and this process does not require persuading the legislature and the electorate to revise the law when circumstances change.

To conclude, we argue that while legal institutions, along with formal financing channels, are an integral part of developed economies' institutions, alternative mechanisms and financing channels play a much more prominent role in emerging economies, and can be superior to legal mechanisms in supporting business transactions in certain industries or entire economies. Therefore, the development of alternative dispute resolution and contract enforcement mechanisms alongside the development of legal and other formal institutions can promote a broader base of economic growth that is also more sustainable in emerging economies. The coexistence of

38. A frequently talked about and controversial topic is intellectual property rights, including patents and copyrights. The practice of enforcing intellectual property rights by courts is much more vigilant and prevalent in developed countries than in developing countries such as China. An extensive literature in economics has found mixed evidence on the relationship between patent/copyright protection and the pace of innovations. While exclusive property rights provide strong incentives for innovations and do lead to more innovations in a few industries such as chemicals and pharmaceuticals, excessive protection deters competition, which is another important factor in spurring innovations.

39. A good example is the US payment system. At the beginning of the twenty-first century the United States had a nineteenth century system: checks had to be physically transported from where they were deposited to a central operations center, then to the clearer and then back to the banks they were drawn on. Despite repeated calls for changes from the banks and businesses, the US Congress did not act on this simple yet costly problem until after September 11, 2001. After the terrorist attack all commercial flights were grounded for several days, completely halting the check-clearing process. The Check Clearing for the 21st Century Act was signed in October 2003, allowing electronic images to be a substitute for the original checks, and thus the clearing process is no longer dependent on the mail and transportation system.

and competition between alternative and legal mechanisms can also exert positive impact on the development of legal institutions, so that they are less likely to be captured by interest groups and become more efficient in adapting to changes.

2.6 Financial Crises

Financial crises often accompany the development of a financial system. Conventional wisdom says that financial crises are bad. Often they are very bad, as they disrupt production and lower social welfare, as in the Great Depression in the United States. Hoggarth, Reis, and Saporta (2002) carefully measure the costs of a wide range of recent financial crises and find that these costs are on average roughly 15 to 20 percent of GDP. It is these large costs that make policymakers so averse to financial crises.

It is worthwhile to point out, however, that financial crises may be welfare improving for an economy. One possible example is the late-nineteenth-century United States, which experienced many crises but at the same time had a high long-run growth rate. In fact, Ranciere, Tornell, and Westermann (2003) report an empirical observation that countries which have experienced occasional crises have grown, on average, faster than countries without crises. They develop an endogenous growth model and show theoretically that an economy may be able to attain higher growth when firms are encouraged by a limited bailout policy to take more credit risk in the form of currency mismatch, even though the country may experience occasional crises (see Allen and Oura [2004] for a review of the growth and crises literature, Allen and Gale [2004a] who show that crises can be optimal, and Allen and Gale [2007] for a review of the crises literature).

In this section, we consider financial crises in China. Given China's current situation with limited currency mismatches any crisis that occurs is likely to be a classic banking, currency, or twin crisis. It is perhaps more likely to be of the damaging type that disrupts the economy and social stability than of the more benign type that aids growth. The desirability of preventing crises thus needs to be taken into account when considering reforms of China's financial system. First, we examine how China can prevent traditional financial crises, including a banking sector crisis and a stock market or real estate crisis/crash. We then discuss the impact of different types of financial crises, such as the "twin crises" (simultaneous foreign exchange and banking/stock market crises) that occurred in many Asian economies in the late 1990s, on China.

2.6.1 Banking Crises and Market Crashes

Among traditional financial crises, banking panics, arising from the banks' lack of liquid assets to meet total withdrawal demands (anticipated and unanticipated), were often particularly disruptive. Over time one of the most critical roles of central banks came to be the elimination of banking panics and the maintenance of financial stability. To a large degree central banks in different countries performed well in this regard in the period following World War II. However, in recent years, banking crises are often preceded by abnormal price rises ("bubbles") in the real estate and/or stock markets. At some point the bubble bursts and assets markets collapse. In many cases banks and other intermediaries are overexposed to the equity and real estate markets, and following the collapse of asset markets a banking crisis ensues. Allen and Gale (2000c) provide a theory of bubbles and crises based on the existence of an agency problem. Many investors in real estate and stock markets obtain their investment funds from external sources. If the providers of the funds are unable to observe the characteristics of the investment, and because of the investors' limited liability, there is a classic risk-shifting problem (Jensen and Meckling 1976). Risk shifting increases the return to risky assets and causes investors to bid up asset prices above their fundamental values. A crucial determinant for asset prices is the amount of credit that is provided for speculative investment. Financial liberalization, by expanding the volume of credit, can interact with the agency problem and lead to a bubble in asset prices.

As discussed in section 2.3, if NPLs continue to accumulate and/or if growth slows significantly then there may be a banking crisis in China. This may involve withdrawal of funds from banks. However, given the government's strong position regarding the low level of debt (table 2.4), it is feasible for the government to prevent this situation from getting out of control. Since the real estate markets in Shanghai and Shenzhen (largest volume and most developed) and other major cities have already experienced bubbles and crashes (see *China Industry Report,* http://www.cei.gov.cn, http://house.focus.cn and Cao and Liao [2008] for more details), it is quite possible that similar episodes in the future could cause a banking crisis that will be more damaging to the real economy. With booming real estate markets, there will be more speculative money poured into properties with a large amount coming from banks. The agency problem in real estate lending and investment mentioned earlier worsens this problem. If the real estate market falls significantly within a short period of time, defaults on bank loans could be large enough to trigger a banking panic and crisis. The size of the stock market during the first decade of its existence was small relative to the banking sector and the overall economy, and hence a crash in the market could hardly put a dent in the real economy. However, given the quick growth of the stock market (as shown in table 2.9) and the fact that large and small investors may borrow (from banks) to finance their investment, especially during a bubble period, a future market crash could have much more serious consequences. Overall, a banking crisis triggered by crashes in the real estate and/or stock markets represents the most serious risk of a financial crisis in China.

Having said that, we also want to point out that the Chinese government has maintained strong control over the big banks through their (nontradable) shareholdings. While government control may have a negative effect in more developed countries in terms of efficiency, it may be beneficial in countries with less developed financial markets. In particular, the government can help to control the risk-taking behaviors of the banks by regulations and direct interventions as a shareholder. Moreover, in the case of a crisis, the government has the ability to speed up the recovery and maintain the stability of the market by loan expansion if it has control over major banks. In fact, the Chinese banking sector and financial markets were not affected much by the 2007 to 2009 global financial crisis. Though we recognized earlier in the chapter that government's dual roles as regulator and as majority owner can be problematic, this can also be beneficial both in terms of preventing and coping with a crisis.

2.6.2   Capital Account Liberalization, Sterilization, Twin Crises, and Contagion

After the collapse of the Bretton Woods system in the early 1970s, a different breed of financial crisis emerged. Lindgren, Garcia, and Saal (1996) found that three-quarters of the International Monetary Fund's (IMF's) member countries suffered some form of banking crisis between 1980 and 1996, and their study did not include the subsequent Asian financial crisis in 1997. In many of these crises, banking panics in the traditional sense were avoided either by central bank intervention or by explicit or implicit government guarantees. But as Kaminsky and Reinhart (1999) find, the advent of financial liberalization in many economies in the 1980s, in which free capital in- and out-flows and the entrance and competition from foreign investors and financial institutions follow in the home country, has often led to "twin" banking and currency crises. Common precursors to these crises were financial liberalization, significant credit expansion, subsequent stock market crashes, and banking crises. In emerging markets this is often then accompanied by an exchange rate crisis as governments choose between lowering interest rates to ease the banking crises or raising them to defend the home currency. Finally, a significant fall in output occurs and the economies enter recessions.

Liberalization of the Capital Account and Financial Sector

Capital account liberation can attract more foreign capital, but large-scale and sudden capital flows and foreign speculation significantly increase the likelihood of a twin crisis. The first key question is, when and to what extent does a country open its capital account and financial sector to foreign capital and foreign financial institutions? With a model of endogenous financial intermediation, Alessandria and Qian (2005) demonstrate that an efficient financial sector prior to liberalization is neither necessary nor sufficient for a successful financial liberalization. Applying these ideas to China, even though the overall efficiency of China's banking sector (especially state-owned banks) is still low compared to international standards, banks can have a stronger incentive to limit the moral hazard concerning borrowers' choices of investment projects through monitoring and designing of loan contracts (e.g., adjusting interest rates and/or maturities) following a capital account liberalization. Therefore, the efficiency of the banking sector improves and the liberalization can generate a large welfare increase, since it leads to both a larger scale of investment *and* a better composition of investment projects. This is more likely to occur with low interest rates in international markets (so that cost of capital for domestic banks is also low). A financial sector liberalization, which allows foreign financial institutions to enter China's lending markets, can further improve welfare as more competition provides stronger incentives for all banks to further discourage moral hazard in investment.

Sterilization of Foreign Currency Reserves

China has experienced a large increase in its foreign exchange reserves since 2001, due to a continuous inflow of capital and the commitment to maintain a fixed rate against the US dollar initially and then a crawling peg exchange rate regime after 2005. Figure 2.17 plots the exchange rate of RMB against the US dollar. The RMB kept appreciating against the US dollar until mid-2008, when the exchange rate stayed flat again at around 6.83 RMB/US$. It resumed the path of appreciation in June 2010 and the exchange rate further dropped to 6.5 RMB/US$ by April 2011. Figure 2.18 plots monthly foreign reserves as shown on the balance sheet of the PBOC; a clear trend emerges as the reserves increased rapidly since 2003.[40] On the balance of payments side, the current account surplus grew from $37 billion in 1997 to $305.4 billion in 2010; net export grew from 2.5 percent of GDP in 2004 to 8 percent of GDP in 2008 and then dropped to 3.1 percent in 2010 due to a decrease in net exports. The capital account was mostly positive during the period 1995 to 2009, implying a net capital inflow. The current account surplus has come mainly from trade surpluses, while the capital account surplus mainly comes from FDI. It has long been recognized that a large stock of foreign reserves has both pros and cons. Abundant foreign reserves enable a country to maintain a stable exchange rate and to meet its foreign debt obligations. It can also be used to cushion the sudden shocks on a country's current and capital accounts. However, an increase in foreign exchange reserves leads to an accumulation of foreign assets, a component of the monetary base. Thus an increase in foreign reserves, ceteris paribus

---

40. The PBOC has made use of its foreign reserves in ways other than investing in low-risk assets such as long-term government bonds. As discussed before, some foreign reserves were used to recapitalize the large state-owned financial institutions.

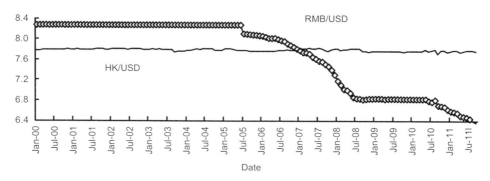

Fig. 2.17   Trends of exchange rates (US$, RMB, and HK$)

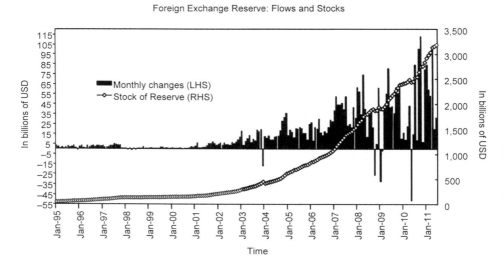

Fig. 2.18   China's foreign exchange reserves

causes monetary expansion and puts inflationary pressures on the economy, resulting in an appreciation of the real exchange rate. This experience is not unique for China. Many East Asian countries have experienced similar problems induced by large (private) capital inflows starting in the late 1980s.

To offset the expansionary effect of the increasing foreign reserves, the central bank can sterilize the foreign assets by taking opposite actions with domestic assets, or implement other contractionary monetary policies. In China's case, the major sterilization tools are open market operations (OMO) and raising required reserve ratios. These two methods affect the liability side of the central bank's balance sheet in a similar way. Generally the cost of sterilization using required reserves is lower than open market operations, since the central bank pays minimal interest on required and excess reserves. The OMOs in China mainly include central bank bill issuance and short-term repurchase operations (repos, usually within ninety-one days). Since February 2003, the central bank has engaged in two or more OMOs each week. The total PBOC bonds outstanding as percentage of foreign reserves has been increasing consistently from 2000 to 2010, implying an increasing trend in sterilization.[41]

Moreover, China has been gradually raising the required reserve ratios since the third quarter of 2003, corresponding to an increase in foreign reserves inflows. The required reserve ratio rose from 6 percent to 21.5 percent in June 2011, an historical high. Since Chinese commercial banks tend to maintain a high excess reserve ratio due to a lack of alternative investment channels, the PBOC has decreased the interest rate on excess reserves from 1.62 percent in 2003 to 0.72 percent in 2008 to discourage the hoarding of excess reserves. To make sterilization effective, China also has to impose tight capital controls. As the famous "trilemma" implicates, with a fixed exchange rate and free capital flows, the sterilization process will be immediately offset by further capital inflows. Though it has been documented that capital controls in China are somewhat porous (Prasad and Wei 2007), it is still widely believed that China has successfully sterilized at least some of its rising foreign reserves (e.g., Goodfriend and Prasad 2007; Ouyang, Rajan, and Willett 2007; He et al. 2005). Moreover, due to a combination of rapid increases in foreign reserves and low interest rates on domestic bonds, the PBOC's income from foreign reserve investment is likely to exceed the sterilization cost stemming from central bank bill issuance and high required reserve ratios, enabling China to carry out sterilization to a large extent. Nevertheless, possible appreciation of the RMB may have a profound negative impact on the PBOC's income from foreign reserves in domestic currency terms.

Currency Crisis and Banking Crisis (a Twin Crisis)

A currency crisis that may trigger a banking crisis is a possibility. The rapid increase in foreign exchange reserves in recent years suggests there is a lot of speculative money in China in anticipation of an RMB revaluation. If there is a significant future revaluation or if after some time it becomes clear there will not be one then much of this money may be withdrawn. What happens then will depend on how the government and central bank respond. If they allow the currency to float so they do not use up the exchange reserves

---

41. There are also nonmarket tools such as transferring the deposits from the commercial banking system to the central bank. In recent years, the PBOC also started making foreign exchange swaps with big commercial banks as a tool for controlling liquidity.

then any falls in the value of the RMB may occur quickly and this may limit further outflows. If they try to limit the exchange rate movement then there may be a classic currency crisis. This in turn may trigger a banking crisis if there are large withdrawals from banks as a result. Quickly adopting a full float can help to avoid a twin crisis, and thus reduce the overall economic costs of the currency crisis.[42]

Financial Contagion

Another phenomenon that has been present in many recent crises (e.g., the 1997 Asian crisis) is that financial crises are contagious. A small shock that initially affects only a particular region or sector can spread by contagion within the banking system or asset markets to the rest of the financial sector, then to the entire economy and possibly other economies. Contagion can occur in a number of ways. In the Chinese context with tight capital control and where financial markets are relatively unimportant it is most likely they will occur either from contractually interconnected financial institutions or large asset price movements that cause spillovers to financial institutions.

Allen and Gale (2000d) focus on the channel of contagion that arises from the overlapping claims that different regions or sectors of the banking system have on one another through interbank markets. When one region suffers a banking crisis, the other regions suffer a loss because their claims on the troubled region fall in value. If this spillover effect is strong enough, it can cause a crisis in the adjacent regions, and a contagion can occur that brings down the entire financial system. Allen and Gale (2004b) show how large price falls can come about as a result of forced liquidations when there is a limited supply of liquidity in the market. Cifuentes, Ferrucci, and Shin (2005) show that contagion is likely to be particularly severe when these two factors interact.

Given China's current financial system, what is the likelihood of financial contagion caused by contractual interlinkages as in the interbank market or because of a meltdown in asset prices if there are forced sales? China's interbank market grew very quickly since its inception in 1981; in fact, the growth of this market was so fast, with the participation of many unregulated financial institutions and with large amounts of flows of funds through this market to fixed asset investment, that it exacerbated high inflation in the late 1980s. Since then the government and PBOC increased their regulation by limiting participation of nonbank financial institutions and by imposing restrictions on interest rate movements. In 1996 a nationwide, uniform

---

42. Chang and Velasco (2001) develop a model of twin crises based on the Diamond and Dybvig (1983) model of bank runs. Money enters agents' utility function, and the central bank controls the ratio of currency to consumption. In some regimes, there exists both a "good" equilibrium in which early (late) consumers receive the proceeds from short-term (long-term) assets, and a "bad" equilibrium in which everybody believes a crisis will occur and these beliefs are self-fulfilling. If the bad equilibrium occurs, there is a twin crisis.

Table 2.13   Trading volume of national interbank market (RMB billion)

Maturity	Overnight	7 days	20 days	30 days	60 days	90 days	120 days
2001	103.88	560.69	93.35	35.28	9.40	4.73	0.87
2002	201.52	852.34	100.35	29.17	10.78	4.76	11.81
2003	641.89	1,456.31	56.60	44.11	10.14	10.18	2.81
2004	283.34	1,041.41	30.67	18.93	9.20	5.84	2.57
2005	223.03	896.26	60.42	29.91	7.51	14.09	1.54
2006	635.21	1,290.43	38.13	19.11	12.03	5.22	1.41
2007	8,030.47	2,178.01	50.16	34.16	27.94	31.80	13.34
2008	10,651.36	3,500.47	110.71	113.55	44.52	66.61	18.50
2009	16,166.60	2,134.79	102.15	204.84	53.80	71.00	62.30
2010	24,486.20	2,426.90	65.01	161.30	46.61	134.02	19.75

Source: The People's Bank of China (2001–2010).

system of interbank markets was set up. It contains two connected levels: the primary network, which includes the largest PBOC branches, large commercial banks, and a few large nonbank financial institutions; and the secondary network that includes many banks and nonbank institutions and their local branches (see *China Interbank Market Annual Reports* for more details). Table 2.13 documents the growth of the interbank market during 2001 to 2010: while the trading volume of long maturity contracts (twenty days or longer) is low, the volume of short-term contracts (overnight and week-long) has been high (reaching RMB 10 trillion to 20 trillion, or $1.5 billion to $2.9 billion). Therefore, the increasing interlinkages can potentially create a contagion if a crisis develops in one area or sector.

With regard to a meltdown of asset prices, this can happen because of a limited supply of liquidity if there is a rapid liquidation of assets. It seems unlikely that this can occur and cause a serious problem in China's securities markets. A more serious threat is real estate markets if there are bankruptcies and forced selling. This could potentially interact with bank interlinkages and cause a systemic problem. As mentioned before, a crash in real estate and/or stock markets could quite possibly be the cause of a financial crisis in China.

2.7   Summary and Concluding Remarks

One of the most frequently asked questions about China's financial system is whether it will stimulate or hamper its economic growth. Our answer to this question, based on examining the history and current status of the financial system and comparing them to those of other countries, is in four parts. First, the large banking sector dominated by state-owned banks has played a much more important role in funding the growth of many types of firms than financial markets. While the problem of NPLs has been under control in recent years, continuing the improvement of the efficiency of major banks toward international standards will allow growth to continue. Second, the stock market has been growing fast since 1990, but has played a relatively limited role in supporting the growth of the economy. However, with rapid growth that is likely to be sustained in the near future the role of the financial markets in the economy will become increasingly more significant.

If we can summarize that the role of the banking sector and financial markets has been that they have done enough *not* to slow down the growth of the economy, our third conclusion is that alternative financing channels have had great success in supporting the growth of the Hybrid Sector, which contributes most of the economic growth compared to the State and Listed Sectors. The nonstandard financial sector relies on alternative financing channels including internal finance, and on alternative governance mechanisms, such as those based on trust, reputation, and relationships, and competition in output and input markets to support the growth of the Hybrid Sector. It is possible that these alternative institutions are superior to Western-style legal institutions in supporting a fast-growing economy such as China's.

We conclude by pointing out that economic stability is crucial for the continuing development of the Chinese economy, and the stability of the financial system relates to economic stability in three dimensions. The continuing effort by banks to reduce NPLs and improve efficiency can help to avoid a banking crisis, while the efforts to improve the regulatory environment surrounding the financial markets (including governance and accounting standards) can help to prevent a crash/crisis in the stock and/or real estate markets. If China further opens the capital account, there will be a large inflow of foreign capital, but large scale capital flows and speculations also bring the risk of a twin crisis (foreign exchange and banking/stock market crisis), which severely damaged emerging economies in Asia in 1997.

References

Acemoglu, Daron, and Simon Johnson. 2005. "Unbundling Institutions." *Journal of Political Economy* 113:949–95.
Alessandria, George, and Jun Qian. 2005. "Endogenous Financial Intermediation and Real Effects of Capital Account Liberalization." *Journal of International Economics* 67:97–128.
Allen, Franklin, Rajesh Chakrabarti, Sankar De, Jun Qian, and Meijun Qian. 2008. "The Financial System Capacities of China and India." Working Paper. Wharton School, University of Pennsylvania.
———. 2012. "Financing Firms in India." *Journal of Financial Intermeditation,* 21:409–45.

Allen, Franklin, and Douglas Gale. 1999. "Diversity of Opinion and Financing of New Technologies." *Journal of Financial Intermediation* 8:68–89.

———. 2000a. "Bubbles and Crises." *Economic Journal* 110:236–55.

———. 2000b. *Comparing Financial Systems.* Cambridge, MA: MIT Press.

———. 2000c. "Corporate Governance and Competition." In *Corporate Governance: Theoretical and Empirical Perspectives,* edited by Xavier Vives, 23–94. London: Cambridge University Press.

———. 2000d. "Financial Contagion." *Journal of Political Economy* 108:1–33.

———. 2004a. "Financial Fragility, Liquidity and Asset Prices." *Journal of the European Economic Association* 2:1015–48.

———. 2004b. "Financial Intermediaries and Markets." *Econometrica* 72:1023–61.

———. 2007. *Understanding Financial Crises.* Clarendon Lectures in Finance. Oxford and New York: Oxford University Press.

Allen, Franklin, and Hiroko Oura. 2004. "Sustained Economic Growth and the Financial System." *Monetary and Economic Studies, Bank of Japan* 22 (S-1): 95–119.

Allen, Franklin, and Jun Qian. 2009. "Corruption and Competition." Working Paper. University of Pennsylvania.

———. 2010. "Comparing Legal and Alternative Institutions in Commerce." *Global Perspectives on the Rule of Law,* edited by James J. Heckman, Robert L. Nelson, and Lee Cabatingnan. Routledge-Cavendish.

Allen, Franklin, Jun Qian, and Meijun Qian. 2005. "Law, Finance, and Economic Growth in China." *Journal of Financial Economics* 77:57–116.

———. 2008. "China's Financial System: Past, Present, and Future." In *China's Great Economic Transformation,* edited by L. Brandt and T. Rawski, 506–68. New York: Cambridge University Press.

Allen, Franklin, Jun Qian, Chenyu Shan, and Mengxin Zhao, 2012. "The IPO of Industrial and Commercial Bank of China and the 'Chinese Model' of Privatizing Large Financial Institutions." *European Journal of Finance,* forthcoming.

Beltratti, Andrea, and Bernardo Bortolotti. 2006. "The Nontradable Share Reform in the Chinese Stock Market." Working Paper 2006.131. Fondazione Eni Enrico Mattei.

Berger, Allen, Iftekhar Hasan, and Mingming Zhou, 2009. "Bank Ownership and Efficiency in China: What Will Happen in the World's Largest Nation?" *Journal of Banking and Finance* 33 (1): 113–30.

Black, Bernard S., and Ronald J. Gilson. 1998. "Venture Capital and the Structure of Capital Markets: Bank versus Stock Markets." *Journal of Financial Economics* 47:243–77.

Brandt, Loren, and Xiaodong Zhu. 2000. "Redistribution in a Decentralized Economy: Growth and Inflation in China under Reform." *Journal of Political Economy* 108:422–39.

Burkart, Mike, Tore Elligensen, and Mariassunta Giannetti. 2011. "What You Sell Is What You Lend? Explaining Trade Credits Contracts." *Review of Financial Studies* 24:1261–98.

Burkart, Mike, Fausto Panunzi, and Andrei Shleifer. 2003. "Family Firms." *Journal of Finance* 58:2167–201.

Cao and Liao. 2008. "An International Comparison of Real Estate Prices" (in Chinese). *Price Theory and Practice (Jia Ge Li Lun Yu Shi Jian)*: 2:56–57.

Chan, Kalok, Albert Menkveld, and Zhishu Yang. 2008. "Information Asymmetry and Asset Prices: Evidence from the China Foreign Share Discount." *Journal of Finance* 63 (1):159–96.

Chang, Roberto, and Andres Velasco. 2001. "A Model of Financial Crises in Emerging Markets." *Quarterly Journal of Economics* 116:489–518.

Chu, Yongqiang, and Tien Foo Sing. 2004. "Inflation Hedging Characteristics of the Chinese Real Estate Market." *Journal of Real Estate Portfolio Management* 10:145–54.

Chung, Stephanie Po-yin. 2005. "Changes and Continuities. Evolution of a Chinese Family Business (1876–2004)." *Asia Europe Journal* 3 (2): 259–68.

Cifuentes, Rodrigo, Gianluigi Ferrucci, and Hyun Song Shin. 2005. "Liquidity Risk and Contagion." *Journal of the European Economic Association* 3:556–66.

Claessens, Stijn, Simeon Djankov, Joseph Fan, and Larry Lang. 2002. "Expropriation of Minority Shareholders in East Asia." *Journal of Finance* 57:2741–71.

Claessens, Stijn, Simeon Djankov, and Larry Lang. 2000. "The Separation of Ownership and Control in East Asian Corporations." *Journal of Financial Economics* 58:81–112.

Clarke, Donald, Peter Murrell, and Susan Whiting. 2008. "The Role of Law in China's Economic Development." In *China's Great Economic Transformation,* edited by L. Brandt and T. Rawski, 375–428. New York: Cambridge University Press.

Cull, Robert, and Colin Xu. 2005. "Institutions, Ownership, and Finance: The Determinants of Reinvestments of Profit among Chinese Firms." *Journal of Financial Economics* 77:117–46.

Demirgüç-Kunt, Asli, and Ross Levine. 2001. *Financial Structure and Economic Growth: Cross-Country Comparisons of Banks, Markets, and Development.* Cambridge, MA: MIT Press.

Diamond, Douglas, and Philip Dybvig. 1983. "Bank Runs, Deposit Insurance, and Liquidity." *Journal of Political Economy* 91:401–19.

Djankov, Simeon, Rafael La Porta, Florencio Lopez-de-Silanes, and Andrei Shleifer. 2002. "The Regulation of Entry." *Quarterly Journal of Economics* 117:1–37.

Dollar, David, and Shang-jin Wei. 2007. "Das (Wasted) Kapital: Firm Ownership and Investment Efficiency in China." Working Paper. International Monetary Fund (IMF).

Du, Julan, Oliver Rui, and Sonia Wong. 2008. "Financing Motivated Takeovers: The Case of China." Working Paper. Chinese University of Hong Kong.

Fan, Joseph, Jun Huang, and Ning Zhu. 2008. "Distress without Bankruptcy: An Emerging Market Perspective." Working Paper. Chinese University of Hong Kong. http://papers.ssrn.com/sol3/papers.cfm?abstract_id=1102859.

Fan, Joseph, Oliver Rui, and Mengxin Zhao. 2006. "Rent Seeking and Corporate Finance: Evidence from Corruption." Working Paper. Chinese University of Hong Kong.

Fan, Joseph, T. J. Wong, and Tianyu Zhang. 2007. "Politically-Connected CEOs, Corporate Governance and Post-IPO Performance of China's Partially Privatized Firms." *Journal of Financial Economics* 84 (2): 330–57.

Feldstein, Martin. 1999. "Social Security Pension Reform in China." *China Economic Review* 10:99–107.

———. 2003. "Banking, Budgets, and Pensions: Some Priorities for Chinese Policy." Speech presented at the China Development Forum 2003. http://www.nber.org/feldstein/chinaforum5.pdf.

Feldstein, Martin, and Jeffrey Liebman. 2006. "Realizing the Potential of China's Social Security Pension System." In *Public Finance in China: Reform and Growth for a Harmonious Society,* edited by Jiwei Lou and Shuilin Wang, 309–13. Washington, DC: World Bank.

Franks, Julian, Colin Mayer, and Stefano Rossi. 2003. "Ownership: Evolution and Regulation." Working Paper. London Business School.

Fung, Peter, Michael Firth, and Oliver Rui. 2003. "Corporate Governance and CEO Compensation in China." Working Paper. Chinese University of Hong Kong.

Garnaut, Ross, Ligang Song, and Yang Yao. 2004. "SOE Restructuring in China." Stanford Center for International Development Working Paper No. 204.

Goetzmann, William, and Elisabeth Köll. 2005. "The History of Corporate Ownership in China: State Patronage, Company Legislation, and the Issue of Control." In *A History of Corporate Governance around the World: Family Business Groups to Professional Managers,* edited by Randall K. Morck, 65–148. Chicago: University of Chicago Press.

Goodfriend Marvin, and Eswar Prasad. 2007. "A Framework for Independent Monetary Policy in China." *Economic Studies* 53 (1): 2–41.

Greif, Avner. 1989. "Reputation and Coalitions in Medieval Trade: Evidence on the Maghribi Traders." *Journal of Economic History* 49:857–82.

———. 1993. "Contract Enforceability and Economic Institutions in Early Trade: The Maghribi Traders' Coalition." *American Economic Review* 83:525–48.

Guo, Feng, and Ying Sophie Huang. 2010. "Does 'Hot Money' Drive China's Real Estate and Stock Markets?" *International Review of Economics and Finance* 19:452–66.

He, Doug, Carmen Chu, Chang Shu, and Amy Wong. 2005. "Monetary Management in Mainland China in the Face of Large Capital Inflows." Research Memorandum No. 07/2005, Hong Kong Monetary Authority.

Herring, Richard, and N. Chatusripitak. 2000. "The Case of the Missing Market: The Bond Market and Why It Matters for Financial Development." Working Paper. Wharton Financial Institutions Center.

Hoggarth, Glenn, Ricardo Reis, and Victoria Saporta. 2002. "Costs of Banking System Instability: Some Empirical Evidence." *Journal of Banking and Finance* 26:825–55.

Hwang, Chuan-Yang, Shaojun Zhang, and Yanjian Zhu. 2006. "Float Liquidity, Speculation, and Stock Prices: Evidence from the Share Structure Reform in China." Working Paper. Nanyang Technological University.

Jeng, Leslie, and Philippe Wells. 2000. "The Determinants of Venture Capital Funding: Evidence across Countries." *Journal of Corporate Finance* 6:241–89.

Jensen, Michael, and William Meckling. 1976. "Theory of the Firm: Managerial Behavior, Agency Costs, and Ownership Structure." *Journal of Financial Economics* 3:305–60.

Kam, Amy, David Citron, and Gulnur Muradoglu. 2008. "Distress and Restructuring in China: Does Ownership Matter?" *China Economic Review* 1:567–79.

Kaminsky, Graciela, and Carmen Reinhart. 1999. "The Twin Crises: The Causes of Banking and Balance-of-Payments Problems." *American Economic Review* 89:473–500.

Kane, Edward. 1989. *The S&L Mess: How Did It Happen?* Washington, DC: The Urban Institute Press.

———. 2003. "What Economic Principles Should Policymakers in Other Countries Have Learned from the S&L Mess?" *Business Economics* 38:21–30.

Kato, Takao, and Cheryl Long. 2004. "Executive Compensation and Corporate Governance in China." William Davidson Institute Working Paper No. 690.

Kirby, William. 1995. "China Unincorporated: Company Law and Business Enterprise in Twentieth-Century China." *Journal of Asian Studies* 54:43–63.

Kortum, Samuel, and Josh Lerner. 2000. "Assessing the Contribution of Venture Capital on Innovation." *RAND Journal of Economics* 31:674–92.

La Porta, Rafael, Florencio Lopez-de-Silanes, and Andrei Shleifer. 2006. "What Works in Securities Laws?" *Journal of Finance* 61:1–32.

La Porta, Rafael, Florencio Lopez-de-Silanes, Andrei Shleifer, and Robert Vishny. 1997. "Trust in Large Organizations." *American Economic Review* (proceedings issue) 87:333–38.

Lardy, Nicholas R. 1998. *China's Unfinished Economic Revolution.* Washington, DC: Brookings Institution Press.

Lee, Tahirih V. 1993. "Risky Business: Courts, Culture, and the Marketplace." *University of Miami Law Review* 47:1335–414.

Levine, Ross. 2002. "Bank-Based or Market-Based Financial Systems: Which is Better?" *Journal of Financial Intermediation* 11:1–30.

Li, Kai, Heng Yue, and Longkai Zhao. 2007. "Ownership, Institutions, and Capital Structure: Evidence from Non-Listed Chinese Firms." Working Paper. University of British Columbia.

Liao, Li, and Bibo Liu. 2008. "Moral Hazard, Information Disclosure and Market Efficiency: Evidence from China's Share Reform." Working Paper. Tsinghua University.

Lindgren, Carl-Johan, Gillian Garcia, and Matthew Saal. 1996. *Bank Soundness and Macroeconomic Policy.* Washington, DC: International Monetary Fund.

Liu, Qiao. 2007. "Institutions, Financial Development, and Corporate Investment: Evidence from an Implied Return on Capital in China." Working Paper. University of Hong Kong.

McMillan, John. 1995. "China's Nonconformist Reform." In *Economic Transition in Eastern Europe and Russia: Realities of Reform,* edited by Edward Lazear, 419–33. Stanford: Hoover Institution Press.

———. 1997. "Markets in Transition." In *Advances in Economics and Econometrics,* vol. 2, edited by David M. Kreps and Kenneth F. Wallis, 210–39. Cambridge: Cambridge University Press.

Mei, Jianping, Jose Scheinkman, and Wei Xiong. 2003. "Speculative Trading and Stock Prices: An Analysis of Chinese A-B Share Premia." Working Paper. Princeton University.

Michie, R. 1987. *The London and New York Stock Exchanges 1850–1914.* London: Allen & Unwin.

Morck, Randall, Bernard Yeung, and Wayne Yu. 2000. "The Information Content of Stock Markets: Why Do Emerging Markets Have Synchronous Stock Price Movement?" *Journal of Financial Economics* 58:215–60.

Morrison, Wayne, and Marc Labonte. 2008. "CRS Report for Congress: China's Holding of US Securities: Implications for the US Economy." *Congressional Research Service.*

Ouyang, Alice, Ramkishen Rajan, and Thomas Willett. 2007. "China As a Reserve Sink: The Evidence from Offset and Sterilization Coefficients." Hong Kong Institute for Monetary Research.

Park, Albert, and Kaja Sehrt. 2001. "Tests of Financial Intermediation and Banking Reform in China." *Journal of Comparative Economics* 29:608–44.

Perkins, Dwight, and Thomas Rawski. 2008. "Forecasting China's Economic Growth to 2025." In *China's Great Economic Transformation,* edited by Loren Brandt and Thomas Rawski, 829–86. New York: Cambridge University Press.

Prasad, Eswar, and Shang-Jin Wei. 2007. "The Chinese Approach to Capital Flows: Patterns and Possible Explanations." In *Capital Controls and Capital Flows in Emerging Economies: Policies, Practices, and Consequences,* edited by Sebastian Edwards, 421–80. Chicago: University of Chicago Press.

Qian, Jun, and Philip Strahan. 2007. "How Laws and Institutions Shape Financial Contracts: The Case of Bank Loans." *Journal of Finance* 62:2803–34.

Qian, Jun, Philip Strahan, and Zhishu Yang. 2011. "The Impact of Incentives and

Communication Costs on Information Production: Evidence from Bank Lending." Working Paper. Boston College.

Qiu, Yuemin, Bing Li, and Youcai Cai. 2000. "Losses of State-Owned Commercial Banks: Reasons and Policy Response." *Jingji gongzuozhe xuexi ziliao* [Study Materials for Economic Workers], no. 44.

Rajan, Raghuram, and Luigi Zingales. 2003a. "The Great Reversals: The Politics of Financial Development in the Twentieth Century." *Journal of Financial Economics* 69:5–50.

———. 2003b. *Saving Capitalism from Capitalists: Unleashing the Power of Financial Markets to Create Wealth and Spread Opportunity.* New York: Random House.

Ranciere, Romain, Aaron Tornell, and Frank Westermann. 2003. "Crises and Growth: A Re-evaluation." NBER Working Paper no. 10073. Cambridge, MA: National Bureau of Economic Research, November.

Stein, Jeremy. 2002. "Information Production and Capital Allocation: Decentralized vs. Hierarchical Firms." *Journal of Finance* 57:1891–921.

Stulz, René, and Rohan Williamson. 2003. "Culture, Openness, and Finance." *Journal of Financial Economics* 70:261–300.

Tsai, Kellee. 2002. *Back-Alley Banking.* Ithaca: Cornell University Press.

Xu, Chenggang. 2011. "The Institutional Foundations of China's Reforms and Development." *Journal of Economic Literature,* 49:1076–1151.

World Bank. 2001. "Bankruptcy of State Enterprises in China—A Case and Agenda for Reforming the Insolvency System." Working Paper no. 33267.

Wu, Jing, Joseph Gyourko, and Yongsheng Deng. 2011. "Evaluating Conditions in Major Chinese Housing Markets." *Regional Science and Urban Economics,* forthcoming.

Comment   Chenggang Xu

This chapter provides an excellent overview of China's financial system from a cross-country comparative perspective. It is very insightful and informative that I have learned a lot from this chapter. But my job is to provide critical comments, which are in the following.

One of the most distinctive features of Chinese economy and China's financial system is regional heterogeneity and importance of regional governments. Although this can be quite consistent with the arguments made by the chapter, this is its weak point. National aggregate or average figures miss the feature. At the national level, the Chinese economy is larger than the whole of Latin America (China's total GDP is \$3.4 trillion vs. Latin America GDP of \$2.4 trillion, 2007). However, China's regional heterogeneity in development and so forth is a lot larger than that of Latin America. The per

Chenggang Xu is the Quoin Professor in Economic Development at the University of Hong Kong and the World Class University visiting professor at Seoul National University (WCU-SNU).

For acknowledgments, sources of research support, and disclosure of the author's material financial relationships, if any, please see http://www.nber.org/chapters/c12460.ack.

capita GDP in China's richest region, Shanghai, is 9.6 times of that of the poorest region, Guizhou. As a comparison, the per capita GDP of Chile, the richest country in Latin America, is 7.3 times of Bolivia, the poorest country in Latin America. Most Latin American countries are about the average size of a Chinese prefecture. At that level, the regional disparity in China will be ten times higher than in Latin America.

This chapter is almost silent on the basic governance structure of China's financial system. The Chinese economy is featured by centralized personnel control and decentralized regional operations (Xu 2011). Although China's banking and financial markets are more centralized than other sectors, they still share the same basic feature. The central-local games determine the operation of the financial system. These games deeply affect the finance of most projects. Subnational governments' influences were prevalent and are not negligible in lending decisions of local branches of major banks; and they are important players of financial market regulation.

A central theme of this chapter is to find out whether China's financial system "will stimulate or hamper its economic growth." But the question is yet to be addressed by systematic empirical evidence. Concerning the formal financial sector, by using nationwide firm-level census data and provincial bank lending data, Demetriades et al. (2008) find huge regional variations in regional financial development, measured by total loans to private sector over GDP ratio. They find everything else being equal, firms located in provinces with better financial development have significantly higher total factor productivity (TFP) growth rates and vice versa. And in general, China's banking system contributes to Chinese firms' TFP growth. This discovery is consistent with the market performance of the major Chinese commercial banks. But one has to be very careful on these observations since these are based on an upside of the cycle in the Chinese real sector since the year 1999. During this period of time, the interest rate has been very low. What will happen in the downside of the cycle when the interest rate goes up substantially is yet to be known.

Concerning the informal sector, intrigued by the township-village enterprise (TVE) development, major alternative mechanisms beyond the formal legal system have been discussed since long ago (e.g., Weitzman and Xu 1994). There are huge cross region variations in culture and on the level of trust in doing business that some distinctive local business culture (without formal law) can be traced back to one thousand years ago; that is, the Song Dynasty. These coincide well with local TVE development in the 1980s and the 1990s, and also coincide well with today's development of hundreds of town-based world factories (i.e., local industrial cluster developments [Xu 2011]). Here, the key point is that alternative mechanisms are local and most Chinese towns are not well developed. Thus, it could be misleading to speak of China as one phenomenon.

When discussing financial crisis, the chapter ignores an important fact: China is the only major economy which has largely escaped from the 1997

East Asia and the 2008 global financial crises. This luck is not accidental and is worth exploring. A key mechanism for escaping from the 1997 crisis is the capital account control. In addition to this, another key mechanism that allowed China to escape from the 2008 crisis is that asset-backed securities have never been allowed to be originated or to be traded in China. Should China keep controlling capital account? Should China keep banning financial innovations? These are critically important issues for China's forthcoming financial reforms.

The chapter points out the importance of venture capital (VC). However, it does not discuss the extraordinary development of China's VC sector and the serious problems the sector faces. Since the late 1990s, with a rapid development in VC, China has become the second-most active economy in the world in attracting VCs (after the United States). China has the second-largest VC investment in the world since 2008; in that year, the VC investment in China is equivalent to the 1994 level of the United States; China's VC/GDP ratio is about half of that of the United States; and 62 percent of VC investments are in high-tech sectors. Nevertheless, the VC sector development in China faces serious institutional problems. About two-thirds of VC investments in China are from foreign VCs, mostly from the United States. Although they face no serious governance problems, the foreign VCs are not allowed to raise funds in China, whereas the Chinese domestic VCs face much worse institutional constraints in determining their corporate governance structure (Guo 2009).

My last comment is about the claim of the chapter that "[t]he role of deposits from government agencies and organizations has steadily decreased over time." However, many research papers and reports by the World Bank and the Chinese government document the opposite: that the share of government and enterprise deposits in total deposits has increased, and the share of household in total deposits has decreased (e.g., Bai 2009). In fact, this has been a major concern for Chinese policymakers and there are many policy debates regarding how to deal with this trend.

References

Bai, Chong-en. 2009. "Chinese National Income Distribution and Economic Growth Pattern: Facts, Reasons and Policies." "(国民收入分配格局与经济增长模式: 事实、原因和对策)." Working Paper. Tsinghua University.

Demetriades, Panicos O., Jun Du, Sourafel Girma, and Chenggang Xu. 2008. "Does the Chinese Banking System Promote the Growth of Firms?" World Economy and Finance Research Programme Working Paper No. 0036.

Guo, Di. 2009. "Do Institutions Matter? An Empirical Examination on VCs' Project Screening in China." Working Paper. University of Hong Kong.

Weitzman, M. L., and C. Xu. 1994. "Chinese Township Village Enterprises As Vaguely Defined Cooperatives." *Journal of Comparative Economics* 18 (2): 121–45.

Xu, C. 2011. "The Fundamental Institutions of China's Reforms and Development." *Journal of Economic Literature* 49 (4): 1076–1151.

II

Governance of Stock Markets

3

Assessing China's Top-Down Securities Markets

William T. Allen and Han Shen

It is widely observed that, despite its remarkable economic progress over the last thirty years, the economy of China continues to require substantial development of its legal and financial infrastructure. In that connection, this essay seeks to assess an important part of that infrastructure: the securities markets of China. We assess those markets, both in terms of their size and composition and in terms of their economic function and importance to the Chinese economy. In doing so, we also review and assess the regulatory regime within which these markets function and the corporate governance mechanisms that operate upon the firms that are listed on the Chinese stock exchanges. For reasons of space, we do not review the history of the evolution of these markets (see Green 2003; Tan 2006), the corporatization program that created the firms that, for the most part, make up the listed firms on the two mainland exchanges (Aharony, Lee, and Wong 2000) or, except briefly, the original share segmentation system that restricted ownership of shares.

The Shanghai and Shenzhen Stock Exchanges represent an effort initiated

William T. Allen is director of the New York University Center for Law and Business, and professor of law on the law faculty and professor of business in the department of finance at the Stern School of Business, New York University. Han Shen is an associate at Davis Polk & Wardwell LLP.

The authors wish to thank the editors of this volume, Justice Jack B. Jacobs of the Delaware Supreme Court, and Ms. Huang, Jie, NYU LL. M. 2005, for their very helpful comments on earlier drafts of this chapter and Ms. Gao, Yi, NYU LL. M. 2009, and Ms. Wei, Quiju, NYU LL. M. 2010, for their research assistance. The authors are responsible for the errors or omissions that remain. For acknowledgments, sources of research support, and disclosure of the authors' material financial relationships, if any, please see http://www.nber.org/chapters /c12072.ack.

in the early 1990s to centralize and develop securities trading in modern China. Since that time those exchanges have grown rapidly in terms of listings, trading, products, and regulatory structures. They remain, however, a work in progress. While quite large by some measures, these markets do not yet play a very important role in the finance of the Chinese economy. The finance of the Chinese economy continues to be dominated, on large scale projects, primarily by bank finance and direct and indirect government support and, on entrepreneurial finance level, primarily by foreign direct investment and a range of less formal arrangements including friends and family, trade credit, business alliances and, importantly, local government support (Allen, Qian, and Qian 2005; Allen et al. 2013). The securities markets serve as a secondary source of finance to the Chinese economy. Access to the securities markets in China has been tightly controlled by the state and these markets have largely played the role of a supplemental source of finance for large state-owned enterprises (SOEs). The resulting markets are comparatively small in terms of the size of the general economy. Prices of securities traded on them are volatile and do not appear to price securities very well. Because prices on these markets do not appear to be efficiently set and because, as we show, the governance standards of the legal system they incorporate are ineffective, the market's prices do not provide either a positive signaling function or a disciplinary function for the corporate management of listed firms. Finally, because they have not yet evolved developed futures markets or a large capacity to create derivative securities, the Chinese securities markets do not yet provide adequate opportunities for the management of financial risks. For all of these reasons, the Chinese securities markets do not presently appear to deliver to the Chinese economy the principle allocative or disciplinary functions that a developed securities markets can provide.

If these markets do not provide the fundamental economic benefits that securities markets can provide, one may ask, why do they exist and grow? In this essay, we suggest that they flourish because they provide valuable benefits both to investors and to the Chinese state. Even without substantial legal system protection from exploitation, these markets do provide investors a way to participate in the rapid growth of Chinese economy. In addition, these markets provide the following significant benefits to the country and its leadership: (a) they provide a mechanism through which foreign capital can flow to support the SOEs that comprise the largest part of the firms listed on the mainland exchanges; (b) they provide a channel through which can flow a limited amount of investment from the very large reservoir of domestic savings in order to do the same thing; (c) they serve as means to induce improvements in the management and governance of listed SOEs; (d) they provide to the leadership a possible option for future expansion of the role of private sector in financing enterprise, including both the existing state sector and the entrepreneurial sector of the economy; and finally (e) they provide in some measures the noneconomic satisfaction of locating a globally important center of finance on mainland China.

Thus, despite the limited economic importance of Chinese securities markets to the nation's economy at the moment, they continue to command both international investors' interest and the support of the country's leadership. The leadership has demonstrated its continuing commitment to building out the infrastructure that might allow Chinese securities markets to play a greater role in the future in its extended effort to restructure the Chinese share segmentation system (see section 3.1.1) and in facilitating the continued development of instruments of modern finance (see section 3.1.4). The following essay aims to assist readers who are interested in thinking about the future of these markets.

In section 3.1 we provide a descriptive report on the current state of the Chinese securities markets, discussing their place in the national system of finance, their current size and scope, their interesting relationship to the Hong Kong securities market, and the gradual development of new tools of securities investing in China. In section 3.2 we discuss the current regulatory environment of these markets, focusing on the structure and operation of the Chinese Securities Regulatory Commission (CSRC), which has a powerful role in controlling these markets, access to listing shares on them, and supervision of all the institutional actors on them. In section 3.3 we discuss the corporate governance of listed firms, including both the formal or legal system of corporate governance and, more importantly, the role of the Chinese Communist Party in the internal affairs of listed companies. In section 3.4 we conclude with observations concerning the fundamental contradiction between the Chinese securities markets' top-down design and control on the one hand and, on the other hand, their possible effectiveness in efficient capital allocation, in risk management and as a tool of discipline. We discuss the factors that may someday weigh on the perceived need of the leadership to address this contradiction.

3.1   The Characteristics of the Chinese Securities Markets Today

The Chinese securities markets constitute an impressive accomplishment. The technological, legal, and human infrastructure supporting these markets has been created from almost nothing two decades ago. While they remain a work in progress, that progress has been remarkable.

In assessing these markets, we begin by placing them in context of the formal system that finances business activities in China today. China's system of formal finance is essentially a bank-centered system primarily dominated by its four largest state-owned banks. China's economy has a substantially higher ratio of bank credit to GDP (1.27 at the close of 2009 according to the National Bureau of Statistic of China), than even the German, bank-centered system of finance (.99). Securities markets by comparison, while large by some measures, are small in economic terms. Moreover, when assessing the reported size of these markets, it is important to understand that what actually trades on the mainland exchanges (and in fact what, until quite recently was legally tradable on them) is in almost all cases a very small percent of the outstanding shares (see e.g., the analysis of the holdings of the shares in the Industrial and Commercial Bank of China (ICBC), China's largest bank, reported in section 1.3).

Expressed in terms of proportion of financial assets rather than percentage of GDP, data for 2006, confirms the relatively undeveloped state of the mainland securities markets. According to CSRC data for that year, the total value of securities in the PRC (equities and bonds, including treasury bonds) constituted just 22 percent of total financial assets, while in the United States, United Kingdom, Japan, and Korea those percentages were far higher (82 percent, 71 percent, 62 percent, and 75 percent, respectively) (CSRC Report, 2008, 237). Data compiled by McKinsey & Company for year 2008 reported in figure 3.1 is consistent with this view. China appears on this data to have a substantially higher proportion of financial assets in bank deposits than any other region. Moreover, this figure most probably exaggerates the importance of securities markets in China by using market capitalization data without adjusting for the very thin float of listed firms, which we discuss later.

As we noted, an accurate understanding of the scale and scope of the Chinese securities markets must consider the ongoing effects of the now reformed share segmentation system that until recently limited the number of shares of each listed SOE that could be traded on an exchange. Therefore, we begin our discussion of the markets with a brief description of that reform. Those familiar with the well-known share segmentation system and its now largely completed reform may safely move directly to section 3.1.2.

3.1.1   Background: The Share Segmentation System and Its Reform

Among the signal marks of the program of liberalization that was initiated in 1978 under the leadership of Deng Xiaoping was its pragmatism and gradualism. Among the steps taken to ensure that corportization of certain state sector production facilities could be safely tried, while not engendering unforeseen complication, was the adoption of a plan strictly to limit the potential nonstate ownership of shares of the corporations that were to be formed from state and province production facilities. Thus newly incorporated enterprises carved from state assets in the 1990s were authorized by the State Council to issue shares pursuant to an elaborate share segmentation plan.

Under the share segmentation scheme that governed the listing of shares on securities exchanges, a majority of shares of SOEs (which from the begin-

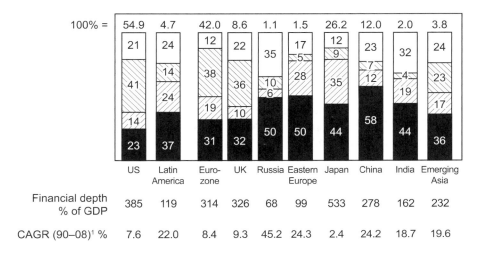

Fig. 3.1   Financial assets by region, 2008 ($ trillion, %)
Source: McKinsey Global Institute Global Financial Stock database.
Note: Some numbers do not sum due to rounding.
[1]Compound annual growth rate using 2008 exchange rates.

ning and today constitute most of the companies listed on the exchanges) would be nontradable and held by institutions that were directly or indirectly controlled by the government. The minority of shares that were to be tradable were themselves broken down into A shares and B shares on both Shanghai Stock Exchange and Shenzhen Stock Exchange. The A shares constitute the vast majority of shares traded on these exchanges, are traded in renminbi on the Shanghai or Shenzhen stock exchanges, and originally could be purchased only by Chinese nationals or institutions. The B shares are traded on the same exchanges but were listed in US dollars in Shanghai and Hong Kong dollars in Shenzhen; they could be purchased originally only by foreign nationals or institutions (now they can be purchased by Chinese nationals as well).[1] In addition to A and B shares, some larger Chinese firms, seeking access to foreign capital, have received (from the CSRC)

1. The B share prices traded at prices below the same shares trading in A shares. But when Chinese nationals were given access to the B share market, the arbitration then eliminated the price differences.

permission to list on foreign exchanges. Stocks traded on these exchanges are denominated H shares (Hong Kong Stock Exchange), N shares (New York Stock Exchange [NYSE]), L shares (London Stock Exchange [LSE]), and S shares (Singapore Exchange) and carry the same voting and cash flow rights as A shares.

Importantly, in addition to the segmentation of shares into A and B shares, Chinese shares were distinguished by the nature of the holder. Shares could be either (1) pre-IPO (initial public offering) shares issued in connection with the "corporitization" of the assets to (a) instrumentalities of the state—such as a Ministry, the State-owned Assets Supervision and Administration Commission (SASAC), or provincial or municipal governments—or (b) to certain legal persons (principally the parent of the listed SOE, which itself will generally be controlled by a provincial or municipal body); or (2) shares issued in or after the IPO to Chinese nationals or institutions (for example, the Qualified Foreign Institutional Investors, or QFIIs). At least prior to the recent reform described below, the pre-IPO shares issued to state or municipal entities or to SOE management as part of the IPO process were generally classified as "C shares" and were not tradable on the exchange. Nontradable shares (NTSs) could only be transferred to legal persons (including in recent years foreign strategic investors) in private placements with the prior approval of both SASAC and the CSRC.

Prior to the completion of share segmentation reform, significantly, with respect to every listed SOE—and most of the firms listed on the Shanghai Stock Exchange are SOEs, recent estimates varying between 70 percent and 80 percent (Chen, Firth, and Xu 2009)—NTSs significantly outnumbered the proportion of shares that are tradable. According to CSRC data, for example, at the end of 2004, there were 714.9 billion shares outstanding of all listed Chinese companies, of which 454.3 billion or 64 percent were nontradable. Thus, a fact of fundamental importance is that the trading market on the Chinese securities exchanges has represented only minority interests. Generally for most listed firms control exists in one or more state affiliated firms or entities. For a relatively small minority of listed firms control exists in an individual, family, or small group.

The nontradability of control blocks has been deemed undesirable and the CSRC attempted for several years to reform this structure. After several failed attempts to do so, the CSRC has now largely completed its program in which most NTSs have been converted to shares that may be traded on the exchanges. The state-owned shares are now legally capable of being gradually floated to the open market according to relevant rules.[2]

---

2. Article 27 of "The Administrative Measure of Share Segmentation Reform of Listed Companies" issued by the CSRC in September 2005 requires that (1) the NTSs cannot be publicly traded or transferred within twelve months after the implementation of the reform proposal of NTSs adopted by the listed company; (2) with regards to these NTSs shareholders who own more than 5 percent shares of a listed company, after the expiration of the above required

However, the completion of the share segmentation reform raises a new series of economically interesting questions. Will the state in fact dissolve its control blocks through secondary market sales of formerly NTSs? If so, the control of which firms will be put on the market and when? It seems highly unlikely that the state will allow control over key elements of the economy (e.g., finance, transportation, energy, communications, and natural resources) to pass into the market. And with respect to less vital SOEs, the state may raise capital by sale of state-owned shares while retaining blocks of 20 to 25 percent, which ordinarily would be deemed sufficient to thwart a market based change in corporate control.

Thus while the completion of the NTSs reform removes a formidable impediment to the development of an effective securities market, it remains to be seen if, when, and with respect to which firms the reform will be operationalized.

3.1.2   Growth in Market for Large Company (SOEs) Shares

The Chinese stock exchanges are now quite large. By close of June 2010, the Shanghai and Shenzhen Stock Exchanges together listed 1,891 companies. The majority listed companies were SOEs.[3] Using the market capitalization metric, with its weaknesses, the two mainland Chinese exchanges would have together constituted the fourth-largest exchange in the world at the close of June 2010. At that time, the total market capitalization of both markets equaled US$2,877.6 trillion, about one-quarter of the size of the NYSE. While in the context of the Chinese securities markets, market capitalization figures may mislead as much as inform, still the numbers are impressive. Daily trading volume on both markets averaged US$33.4 billion as of April 30, 2010.[4] Again, measured in total market capitalization, the comparative growth rates of these exchanges and their volatility appears remarkable. Comparative data for the periods of 2006 through 2009 are set forth in table 3.1.

In recent years, the mainland exchanges have been active sites for raising new capital. Indeed, according to data collected by the World Federation

---

twelve-month period, they are not allowed to sell more than 5 percent of shares converted from NTSs on a stock exchange within twelve months and are not allowed to sell more than 10 percent of shares converted from NTSs within twenty-four months.

3. As of 2000, Tam (2002) put the number at 90 percent Liu and Sun (2003) put the number at 84 percent. See Clarke (2008). One study looked at the period of 1999 to 2004, consisting of 6,113 samples, and it concluded that the state directly and indirectly acted as major controlling shareholder at 79.7 percent of firms. See Chen, Firth, and Xu (2009). As of the end of 2007, it appeared that 65 percent of these listing were SOEs (and essentially all of the largest firms). In 2006 there were fourteen new listings on the Shanghai Exchange, all of which were SOEs.

4. The Shanghai Stock Exchange Composite Index, which has a base (1991) value of 100, started 2006 at less than 1,500. It peaked at 6,124.0 in October 2007 and then began to decline steeply. It dipped below 2,000 in late 2008 and then began to recover. By early 2010 it stood at slightly more than 3,000 and then it dropped to around 2,300 by the end of June 2010.

Table 3.1   **Global stock market capitalizations and percent changes**

Stock exchange	Stock market capitalization (US$ in millions)				Percent changes		
	2009	2008	2007	2006	2009 vs. 2008	2008 vs. 2007	2007 vs. 2006
NYSE	11,837,793.30	9,208,934.10	15,650,832.50	15,421,167.90	↑28.5%	↓41.2%	↑1.5%
Nasdaq	3,239,492.44	2,396,344.30	4,013,650.30	3,865,003.60	↑35.2	↓40.3	↑3.8
London SE	2,796,444.32	1,868,064.80	3,851,705.90	3,794,310.30	↑49.7	↓51.5	↑1.5
Hong Kong SE	2,305,142.79	1,328,768.50	265,416.1	1,714,953.30	↑73.5	↓49.9	↑54.8
Shanghai SE	2,704,778.45	1,425,354.00	3,694,348.00	917,507.50	↑**89.8**	↓**61.4**	↑**302.7**
Shenzhen SE	868,373.99	353,430.00	784,518.60	227,947.30	↑**145.7**	↓**54.9**	↑**244.2**
Singapore SE	481,246.70	264,974.40	539,176.60	384,286.40	↑81.6	↓50.9	↑40.3
Korea SE	834,596.47	470,797.30	1,122,606.30	834,404.30	↑77.3	↓58.1	↑34.5
Bombay SE	1,306,520.21	647,204.80	1,819,100.50	818,878.60	↑101.9%	↓64.4%	↑122.1%

Source: World Federation of Exchanges.

Table 3.2   Market capitalization of newly listed shares (US$ in millions)

	2004	2005	2006	2007	2008	2009
Shanghai SE	14,438	3,140	223,322	1,576,732	92,118	99,924
Shenzhen SE	8,536	1,634	23,691	74,655	38,769	71,450
Hongkong SE	37,347	98,292	102,941	155,199	28,767	95,235
NYSE	118,944	135,719	192,412	244,515	207,612	64,810
LSE	52,468	322,269	131,137	144,674	77,560	24,437
Tokyo SE	87,832	110,399	81,982	35,969	40,106	18,062

Source: World Federation of Exchanges.

Table 3.3   Market concentration, percentages of total market capitization
                      represented by largest ten firms

	2004 (%)	2005 (%)	2006 (%)	2007 (%)	2008 (%)	2009 (%)
NYSE	19.6	16.4	16.1	19.3	20.1	15.7
London SE	40.2	40.9	37.1	38.2	46.3	41.3
Shanghai SE	29.0	32.6	56.6	51.6	49.0	41.2
Tokyo SE	18.1	18.1	20.1	18.5	18.3	17.6

Source: World Federal of Exchanges.

of Exchanges, the Shanghai Stock Exchange raised more capital during the period of 2006 to 2009 than any other global market (see table 3.2).

3.1.3   Concentration, Liquidity, and Pricing Efficiency of the Shanghai Stock Exchange

The largest SOEs dominate trading on the Shanghai Stock Exchange. Of more than 800 listed firms as of June 2010, the ten largest firms represent 39.5 percent of the exchange's total market capitalization. The two largest listed firms, PetroChina Company Limited ("PetroChina") and Industrial and Commercial Bank of China ("ICBC"), together account for approximately 20 percent of the market capitalization of the entire exchange as of June 2010.[5] The Shanghai Stock Exchange is substantially more concentrated than either the New York Stock Exchange or the Tokyo Exchange, but about the same as the London Stock Exchange (see table 3.3) in 2009.

As we suggested earlier, market capitization figures of the Chinese exchanges must be interpreted carefully because of the large blocks of untraded (albeit now legally tradable) shares in virtually every listed firm.

5. The equity market cap of PetroChina and ICBC accounted for 11.93 percent and 7.33 percent, respectively, of the market capitalization of the entire Shanghai Stock Exchange as of June 30, 2010 (Shanghai Stock Exchange Statistics).

Table 3.4   **Top five shareholders of ICBC as of June 30, 2010**

Name of shareholder	Nature of shareholder	Type of shares	Total number of shares held	Shareholding percentage (%)
Central Huijin Investment Limited[a]	State-owned	A shares	118,316,816,139	35.4
Ministry of Finance of the PRC	State-owned	A shares	118,006,174,032	35.3
HKSCC Nominees Limited[b]	Foreign corporation	H shares	68,577,667,687	20.5
The Goldman Sachs Group, Inc.	Foreign corporation	H shares	13,180,811,324	3.9
American Express Company	Foreign corporation	H shares	638,061,117	0.2

[a]Central Huijin Investment Limited is a wholly owned subsidiary of China Investment Corporation, the Chinese state sovereign investment company.

[b]Most retail and institutional investors hold their shares through a bank, broker, or custodian who in turn hold them in an account with the Central Clearing and Automated Settlement System (CCASS) operated by Hong Kong Securities Clearing Co., Ltd. (HKSCC), a subsidiary of HKEx. HKSCC Nominees Ltd., a subsidiary of HKSCC, is the registered shareholder of listed companies and acts as nominee for the account holders of CCASS. The total number of shares held by HKSCC also included H shares held by PRC National Council for Social Security Fund.

Consider, for example, the share ownership structure of ICBC, the second-largest market cap listing on the Shanghai Stock Exchange. In October 2006, ICBC, the state-owned bank, simultaneously listed and distributed a minority block of its shares on the Shanghai Stock Exchange and the Hong Kong Stock Exchange, in what proved at the time to be the world's largest IPO, generating approximately US$21.9 billion in proceeds.

As of June 30, 2010, ICBC had more than 334 billion shares outstanding; 24.87 percent of its outstanding shares were H shares listed and traded on the Hong Kong Stock Exchange. The remainder of its shares, following the completion of share segmentation reform were A shares technically tradable on the Shanghai Stock Exchange. But how much of this equity was actually public floated and controlled by nonstate affiliate entities? Table 3.4 sets forth shareholding of the top five shareholders of ICBC as of June 30, 2010.[6]

From the table, we conclude the *publicly owned* ICBC shares tradable on the Shanghai Stock Exchange constitute less than 4.3 percent of ICBC A shares (since most of the 75.13 percent of ICBC shares that could in theory be traded on the Shanghai Stock Exchange are actually held by Central Huijin Investment Limited or the Ministry of Finance). One must look to the Hong Kong Stock Exchange to find more substantial private investment

6. Shareholding percentage of each of top 6–10 ICBC shareholders was 0.1 percent.

in ICBC shares.[7] There we find listed ICBC H shares constitute 24.87 percent of all outstanding ICBC shares. One obvious conclusion from these figures is that in the case of ICBC, the Hong Kong Stock Exchange has been much more important than Shanghai as a source of new capital. Specifically, more than six times the capital raised by ICBC from investors on the Shanghai Exchange was raised by it on the Hong Kong Stock Exchange.

The ICBC's share trading structure is not unique among the largest SOEs. The proportion of shares not controlled by state-affiliated entities of the largest firms on the Shanghai Stock Exchange is typically quite small. For example, as of June 30, 2010, 67.53 percent of the A shares of Bank of China were owned by Central Huijin Investment Ltd. and less than 2.35 percent A shares were publicly floated and controlled by domestic non-state-owned entities or individuals.[8]

Notably, the same cash flow rights usually command a somewhat higher price on the Shanghai Stock Exchange than on the Hong Kong Stock Exchange. This mainland premium is chiefly due, we believe, to impediments to low cost arbitrage between mainland markets and the Hong Kong market and to the huge demand for investment that the high personal or family savings rate in China generates. The Hang Seng China A-H Premium Index, launched on July 9, 2007, tracks the average price difference between A shares and H shares for the largest and most liquid China enterprises with both A-share and H-share listings. The Hang Seng China A-H Premium Index reached a high at 208 in January 2008, meaning A shares are trading at an average premium of 108 percent above H shares and the index for the first half of 2010 was generally between 100 to 120 percent. Greater opportunities for arbitrage between these markets will, of course, reduce or eliminate this difference.

The upshot of the fact that the trading markets in Shanghai are relatively thin and are more highly concentrated than most developed markets and that Chinese investors have highly restricted alternative investment opportunities, is that there is a good reason to suppose that the prices reflected on the mainland markets are not a good signal of fundamental value of the shares or the firms listed on the exchange. In fact, Chinese stock markets are frequently described as highly volatile; price movements are notably synchronous (e.g., Morck, Yeung, and Yu 2000; Xie, Dai, and Xu 2003) and when market prices are compared to prices at which control transactions occur it has been found that the control of a listed firm is traded by private

---

7. Chinese companies form a substantial part of the market capitalization of the Hong Kong Stock Exchange. As reported by the Hong Kong Stock Exchange, by the end of June 30, 2010, the market capitalization of China-related stocks on its main board reached 48.54 percent of the market capitalization.

8. As of June 30, 2010, 70 percent of the issued shares of Bank of China were A shares. 67.53 percent of the A shares of Bank of China were owned by Central Huijin Investment Ltd., and China Southern Power Grid Co., Ltd., Aluminum Corporation of China, and Shenhua Group Corporation Limited each held 0.04 percent.

contract on average at almost a 20 percent *discount* to market price (Tuan et al. 2007). The reasonable conclusion is that traded prices are likely not a good signal of fundamental firm value.

3.1.4   Product Innovation: Short Sales, Margin Sales, and Indexed Futures

The securities markets in China have yet to develop a range of investment tools that are used elsewhere for investor risk management and which tend to reduce market volatility. These tools include short selling, margin buying, and equity futures contracts. In recent years, however, steps have been going forward to carefully introduce these investment techniques. In 2007, the State Council, after long study, approved regulations formally permitting trade in financial futures and options. The Chinese Financial Futures Exchange (CFFEx) was then formed under the authority of the CSRC. The CFFEx spent the following years building an electronic platform for futures trading and a comprehensive set of procedures to facilitate trading by brokers and discourage retail participation in a possible futures market.[9] It was not until January 2010, however, that the State Council approved a trial period for the introduction of these investment tools.

Caution was also reflected in the introduction of short sales of equities and margin trading in January 2010. Regulatory restrictions have been designed to control the effects of these innovations. For example, only selected securities firms will be authorized to execute short sales or margin sales and they must use their own capital and shares to effect these transactions. Thus, it is expected that no market in borrowed shares for the purpose of short sales will develop for the present at least. These restrictions will limit the use of these techniques and should be seen as an attempt to introduce these techniques in a guarded way.

The inability to sell shares short or to buy or sell futures in securities has starkly limited the ability of Chinese institutional investors to hedge financial risk and has likely contributed to excessive market volatility of the Chinese markets. No doubt the financial market turbulence during the period 2008 to 2009 made that period seem an inauspicious time in which to implement these desirable securities market innovations. It is a sign both of the confidence of the leadership in the Chinese economy and their serious desire to build out the Chinese securities markets as large modern securities markets, that these changes were kick-started again in January 2010.

3.1.5   Institutional Investors

Retail investors dominated China's stock markets from their inception.

---

9. Thus draft regulations established a minimum 10 percent margin requirement and a price for a single contract, at current price levels of the Shanghai-Shenzhen 300 Index (January 2010) of approximately RMB 100,000.

This fact has doubtlessly contributed to the relative price volatility of these markets. The dominance of retail investors, however, has gradually eroded in China, as QFIIs and domestic institutional investors, such as insurance companies, a variety of managed investment funds, and the national social security fund have grown in importance. In fact, by the end of 2008, the CSRC could report that institutional investors had for the first time became the dominant force in the market, by holding 54.6 percent of market capitalization of all tradable shares in the domestic markets.[10] By comparison, we note that institutional investors have been reported to represent 70 percent of the Hong Kong Stock Exchange and 80 percent of the New York Stock Exchange.

The participation of QFIIs in the two mainland exchanges, however, remains quite limited. These foreign institutional investors would no doubt be interested in channeling increasing amounts of foreign investment into the Chinese securities markets. But their ability to do so is limited. Following the initiation of the QFII program in 2003, qualifying institutions were permitted to invest in the A share and the government bond markets. According to the State Administration of Foreign Exchange, as of June 30, 2010, there were eighty-eight QFIIs approved in China, with an approved investment amount of US$17.1 billion.[11] As a percentage of market capitalization of trading volumes in the A share market, this quota represents only about 2.5 percent of former "A shares" and of course a much smaller proportion of postmarket reform potential market capitalization.

A Chinese institutional investor deserving mention in this connection is the National Council for Social Security Funds (NSSF), established in 2000. The NSSF is responsible for the investment of funds to support a future retirement system. The investment fund it manages comes from central government budget allocations, from investment returns it can earn, and from liquidation of state-owned shares in SOEs. That is, in order to help fund future pension system needs, the Chinese government has required that in connection with any share sale by one of 131 SOEs, that the NSSF be funded with 10 percent of the proceeds of such sales up to the limit of the state's holding in the company. At the end of 2009, NSSF managed total assets of RMB 562.4 billion.

3.1.6   Market Access for "Private" Firms: The SME Board and the GEM Board

To a large extent, the growth of the Chinese economy is attributable not to the SOEs that dominate the Shanghai Stock Exchange, but to private

---

10. See CSRC 2008 Annual Report available from http://www.csrc.gov.cn/pub/newsite/zjhjs /zjhnb/200906/P020090630327035004673.pdf, at 19.

11. See data from State Administration of Foreign Exchange, available from http://www.safe .gov.cn/model_safe/glxx/glxx_detail.jsp?ID=120700000000000000.

and hybrid firms; that is, those firms with private as well as local government involvement (as lenders, minority owners, or business partners).
But formal sources of finance—either bank loans or securities markets—
are difficult for private firms in China (Shen et al. 2009). These firms have
largely, but not completely, been excluded by the CSRC from listing on
the stock exchanges. While there are about 570 private companies listed
on the two Chinese stock exchanges, representing 34.8 percent of the
total number of all listed companies, those firms represent only 12.2 percent of the market capitalization (Shanghai Stock Exchange, August 10,
2009).

Private firms have tended not to be approved for listing by the CSRC
for a variety of reasons. First, of course, is the fact that the fundamental
mission of the securities markets, at least for the first fifteen years of their
existence, has been to support SOEs with additional capital. Especially in
the first years of the exchanges, allocation of listings were heavily influenced
by the capital needs of inefficient provincial level SOEs. Second, the CSRC
deems itself charged to protect investors from excessively risky companies.
Thus an unwillingness to approve listings for private firms may, in part,
reflect a belief that these firms will on average be more risky than existing
state-affiliated enterprises. Third, these smaller more entrepreneurial enterprises may lack political patrons, which in a system (and a culture) that is
inevitably affected by political and personal networks, may be a significant
disadvantage. Finally, the underrepresentation of small and growing private
firms may in part reflect an ideological bias against "private" wealth building. Whatever the source of the bias, given the fact that, as a class, private
or hybrid firms represent the greatest prospect for substantial economic
growth, the failure of the securities markets to provide finance to this seg-
ment must be deemed as a substantial current weakness. The leadership has
recognized this fact and approved substantial steps to address it. The CSRC
has two initiatives in that respect. In 2004, a Small and Medium Enterprises
Board (the "SME Board") was opened in Shenzhen Stock Exchange and
more recently a Growth Enterprise Board ("GEB Board") was opened on
the same exchange.

The SME Board has met with some success. Private enterprises have a very
significant presence on the SME Board. They are said to represent approximately 76 percent of listed companies as of October 2005 (Zhang 2005). By
June 2010, 437 firms had listed shares on this board. Moreover, reportedly
the annual average revenue growth rate of these firms was 30 percent and
growth rate of net profit was reportedly 18.5 percent.[12] However, in many
respects the listing standards for the SME Board are similar to those of the
bigger boards. The SME Board requires companies to have a minimum
RMB 30 million of accumulated net profits in the three recent years prior

---

12. *China Global Times,* March 25, 2010. http://china.globaltimes.cn/editor-picks/2009-05
/432813.html

to listing. This rather importantly limits its utility to smaller entrepreneurial firms.

The CSRC's second, more recent and more substantial step to try to begin to afford better access to capital markets to nonstate enterprises was reflected in the first IPO in October 2009 on the new GEB Board, also sometimes referred to as "ChiNext," of the Shenzhen Stock Exchange. This board has been designed to function much as the NASDAQ market does in the United States, providing public capital to entrepreneurial, especially high-tech firms. One aspect of this initiative is to provide a potential exit channel for venture capital funded enterprises, thus further encouraging the development of a PRC venture capital business. Access to the GEB Board will be overseen by a special review committee, which will presumably be professionally familiar with the special character of entrepreneurial and venture financed firms. The standards for listing on the GEB Board are lower than those of the SME Board: a minimum RMB 10 million in retained earnings.[13] Nevertheless, in contrast to similar markets in other countries, companies that apply for the listing on the GEB Board must already be profitable, a test that neither Amazon nor Ebay, for example, would have been able to satisfy. Thus, even these innovative small company boards may reflect a strong regulatory bias against more risky enterprises. This bias may be appropriate in a system with a weak information environment, but it does limit the benefits that entrepreneurial activity can provide.

The first batch of twenty-eight selected firms for listing on the GEB Board went public on October 30, 2009 to warm market acceptance.[14] As of June 2010, ninety companies were listed on the GEB Board.

3.1.7   The Absence of a Substantial Market for Commercial Bonds

From the perspective of more highly developed financial markets, a notable feature of the Chinese securities markets, is the practical absence of a market for commercial bonds and indeed a very small bond market even when government bonds are included.

For example, at the close of 2006, the PRC bond market was reported to equal just 35.3 percent of China's GDP. Comparable international bond market numbers demonstrate the undeveloped nature of the Chinese bond market: Japan (201.0 percent), the United States (188.5 percent), United Kingdom (140.5 percent), Korea (125.1 percent), and Germany (69.0 percent) (CSRC Report, 245). The existing bond market is heavily dominated by treasury bonds and financial institutions bonds. Huang and Zhu report that there are primarily four types of bonds in the domestic Chinese bond

---

13. See C. Guan and S. Li, Preliminary Comparison between ChiNext and SME, http://www.chinalawandpractice.com/Article/2351745/Channel/9846/Preliminary-comparison-between-ChiNext-and-SME.html.

14. According to Caijing (October 26, 2009), a total of 188 companies applied to list on the GEB and about 70 percent of the applicants are from the electronics, new materials, alternative energy, biomedicine, and other emerging sectors.

markets: Treasury bonds (they estimate at RMB 2,149 billion in late 2006), central bank notes (RMB 2,931 billion), financial bonds (RMB 2.097 billion), and commercial bonds (RMB 170 billion). Thus the bond market supplies only a tiny portion of the capital available to nonfinancial firms. The CSRC gives somewhat different estimates but the proportions are about the same. It estimates treasury bonds at 53.3 percent of the market and bonds of government-owned financial institutions at 37 percent at the end of 2007 (CSRC Report, 246). The CSRC reports that only 4.2 percent of the small PRC bond market represents what it classifies as "corporate bonds," and most of that amount represents the small short-term commercial paper market at 3.7 percent. Reportedly, only .05 percent of the bond market represents bonds issued by listed companies. When coupled with the very limited ability to hedge equity investments through derivative or futures trading, one can see the job of insurance company investment managers as very challenging in China.

China's lack of a substantial bond market does not make it an outlier among developing nations, however. As figure 3.1 shows, India and Russia both have small bond markets. But neither of these countries has developed their economy or the formal institutions of capital markets as consistently as has China. Therefore, one is entitled to wonder why this aspect of capital market development has not made more progress in China? A possible answer might involve a desire to protect the large state-owned banks from bond or money market competition. Should a substantial bond market be available for long- or short-term debt, presumably the strongest credits would tend to migrate there, leaving weaker creditors for the subsidized banking system.[15] In addition, bank lending may appear to the leadership to be superior to a commercial bond market because bank lending is arguably more easily susceptible to influence by government officials than would be a bond market—both with respect to allocating capital in the first place and with respect to controlling the consequences of a default.

3.2   The Regulatory Environment: The CSRC

Prior to 1992, China's infant securities markets had been lightly regulated by local governments and the local branch offices of the People's Bank of China (the PBOC). Following the establishment of the Shanghai and Shenzhen Stock Exchanges in 1990 and 1991, respectively, the State Council,

15. Something rather like this happened in US banking following the great growth in the US commercial paper market starting in the late the 1960s. Strong credits such as General Electric, Ford, GMAC, and other leading firms of the period migrated from bank-revolving credit lines to commercial paper markets to satisfy much of their working capital needs (Johnston 1968; Handal 1972). Indeed, the decline in commercial lending that followed over an extended period would appear to be one of the business drivers for the evolution of the "originate to securitize" model of banking that ultimately played an important role in the financial crisis of 2008.

in order to consolidate the complex, multilayered, and fragmented institutional framework for securities trading, in fall of 1992 formed the Securities Committee of the State Counsel (the SCSC) and the CSRC, as the SCSC's executive arm. These new entities were charged to create a centralized supervisory framework for securities issuance and trading in China.

3.2.1 CSRC's Dual Mandate: Advance State Policy While Also Protecting Investors

As an executive arm of State Council, the CSRC has a primary obligation to advance state policy and programs. These state aims importantly include successful implementation of the state corporitization program, the development of the securities markets, and the modernization of management of corporatized state-owned firms. In connection with its effort to supervise and guide the development of modern securities markets, the CSRC has adopted approaches that in some respects appear to have been influenced by the structure and policies of the US Securities and Exchange Commission (SEC). In other respects, however, the CSRC's mission and the nature of the PRC governmental structure requires quite different treatment of problems than that of western securities regulators.

As set forth in the PRC (People's Republic of China) Securities Law of 2006, the CSRC's functions are broad indeed. They are to

1. formulate relevant rules and regulations to supervise and administer the securities markets and exercise the power of examination or verification;[16]

2. supervise and administer the issuance, offering, trading, registration, custody, and settlement of securities (including granting or withholding permission to issuers to distribute shares);

3. supervise and administer securities activities of securities issuers, listed companies, securities firms, securities investment funds, securities trading service institutions, stock exchanges, and securities registration and clearing institutions;

4. formulate the standards for securities practice qualification and code of conduct and carry on the supervision and implementation;

5. supervise and examine information disclosure relating to securities issuance, offering, and trading;

6. offer guidance for and supervise activities of securities industries associations;

---

16. Under the CSRC's direct supervision, the Shanghai Stock Exchange and the Shenzhen Stock Exchange are the major SROs in China. The CSRC holds the power to appoint and remove major officers of the exchanges. The stock exchanges themselves are not empowered with formal investigative and sanction authorities over frauds on the market; the CSRC is. But the CSRC's enforcement capacity is still restrained and the SROs may offer considerable depth and expertise regarding market operations and practices.

7. investigate and punish violations of any securities laws and administrative rules; and

8. perform any other functions and duties in accordance with law or administrative rules.

The CSRC is widely regarded as one of China's most highly professional regulatory bodies. It has been an active and effective participant in guiding market development, improving market transparency, and in encouraging the development of modern management techniques.[17] Perhaps its role differs from that of the SEC most fundamentally in that, as an executive arm of the State Council, it has assumed the power to control access to the securities markets by all potential issuers of shares. Thus it acts as a gatekeeper to public finance available both in the initial public offerings and the secondary issuance markets. We turn to this aspect of CSRC functioning first and then to its disclosure policy and enforcement activities. We discuss the CSRC's role in modernization of management later, when we discuss corporate governance of listed firms.

3.2.2   Access to Listing: The Merits-Based Regulatory Approach

CSRC as Gatekeeper

In its role of overseeing the development of the Chinese securities markets, the CSRC seeks to advance state interests by limiting the number of new listing and number of shares to be issued in any period, and by selecting those applicants for initial public offerings or secondary issuances on the PRC securities exchanges. In doing so, it exercises merits-based discretionary judgment.[18]

A number of considerations affect this selection process. In the earliest phase of the process of corporatization and issuance of shares in China, decisions concerning which companies would be permitted to sell listed shares were heavily influenced by local politics. In this period, listing opportunities were allocated among provincial governments on a quota basis. The allocation of this opportunity to local firms was made by local governments, which would be reviewed by the CSRC, who would give final approval. Provincial governments tended to allot these allowances so as to raise money for the SOEs that were the most significant local employers and were most in need of capital. Thus, as it happened, underperforming SOEs were disproportionately selected for listing at the expense of more dynamic entrepreneurial companies (Tan 2006). During this period approximately

17. See CSRC Report (2008) for a comprehensive review of its activities.
18. Article 12, Provisional Administrative Measures of Stock Issuance and Trading (1993); Article 10, the PRC Securities Law of 2006.

Table 3.5   PORC review results (2004–2007)

Year	Number of applications	Number of approved applications	Number of rejected applications	Rejection rate (%)
2007	354	298	55	15.5
2006	181	159	22	13.8
2005	16	9	6	37.5
2004	177	119	58	32.8

Source: Shenzhen Stock Exchange (2008).

949 SOEs were listed on the domestic stock exchanges while only 30 private firms were permitted access to the securities markets (Zhang 2002).

This allocation system was modified in 1998 and abandoned in 2001. Currently, in determining whether to permit access to listing the CSRC deploys a process in which a committee—the Public Offering Review Committee (the Committee or the PORC) makes a recommendation respecting access to listing. The PORC is comprised of a minority of CSRC officials and a majority of outside experts in law, accountancy, and financial markets. The decisions of PORC may consider all relevant considerations, including the issuer's qualifications, use of proceeds, legitimacy of business operation, competitive strength, assets' quality, profit generating ability, independence, information disclosure, and corporate governance.[19] Table 3.5 sets forth the review results of companies seeking to issue shares from 2004 to 2007.

Looking more closely at rejections for the year 2007, one notes that of the fifty-five rejected applications, thirty-eight were for initial public offerings and seventeen were requests for secondary offerings. Among those rejected applications, sixteen were stated as being primarily due to PORC's view of risky or impracticable plans for use of proceeds; fourteen rejections were primarily due to perceived overreliance on business with the controlling shareholders or major clients and the lack of competitiveness or independence; eleven rejections were primarily due to poor accounting practices, such as inconsistent accounting policies, noncompliance in revenue recognition, insufficient provisions and significant contingency issues; eight rejections were primarily due to the failure to meet qualification requirements such as material changes of management in the reporting period; and four rejections were primarily due to insufficient or false information disclosure.

Thus, formally, the CSRC system for allocating listings appears to be moving away from political allocations toward economic merits-based listing

19. The CSRC also has set up a review committee for mergers & acquisitions and restructuring activities of listed companies in 2008 and a review committee for initial public offering on the Growth Enterprise Board in Shenzhen.

decisions. There can be little doubt, however, that both political and policy-based factors continue to have a large impact on these decisions. First, while geographical allocations to various provinces was formally abandoned in 2001 in favor of an independent merits-based approach, a 2004 study found that the 2003 geographical distribution of IPO fund allocations was not significantly different than the distribution in year 2000 (Chen, Fan, and Wong 2004). Secondly, the number of new listings itself during any period is subject to macro-level policy considerations. Thus, the CSRC may reduce or even eliminate for a time the number of IPOs authorized without regard to the investment quality of any pending applicant for listing. For example, in order to accommodate the nontradable shares reform, all IPO activities were held in abeyance from October 2004 to January 2005 and from July 2005 to May 2006. Also in reaction to the worldwide financial crisis of 2008, in an effort to slow the descent of prices on the Shanghai and Shenzhen Stock Exchanges, all CSRC work on new IPOs quietly came to a halt in mid-September 2008 until late June 2009.

Finally, while recent changes in the IPO listing process clearly appear to represent improvements (if one assumes that the system of access should allow investors access to those firms that have the highest risk adjusted future value) the improved system still leaves substantial room for inefficient allocations both because of human judgment error in being able to distinguish "good" bets from bad ones and from the possibility for corruption that gatekeeper systems inevitably invite.

IPO Pricing

In addition to access itself, the CSRC has a role in the setting of IPO prices. The CSRC once set bounds on IPO offering prices by a formula in which average firm earnings over the last three years were multiplied by a floor rate (usually 15) and a ceiling rate (usually 20). Within the resulting range underwriters and issuers set an offering price. But unsurprisingly, the setting of such prices, as well as access to the exchange listing itself, has been found to be affected by what might be termed "connections." Based on a study of 423 PRC IPOs during period 1994 to 1999, Francis, Hasan, and Sun (2009) find that, on various measures of political connectedness (e.g., corporate directors who are retired high-level officials), "connected" firms were more likely to receive a higher than median P/E (price-to-earnings) ratio in the price setting process and thus an authority for a higher range of issuance prices.

But not all firms are well connected; for most firms the setting of offering prices tends to be on the low side. This, of course, is true in Western securities markets too. Underwriters want happy investors and even issuers want share prices to rise initially to some extent. Thus it is common to observe average price increases following an IPO. But the degree of underpricing on the Shanghai Stock exchange appears substantially greater than observed in the Western markets. Xiu and Chang (2008) found that in China, the degree of IPO underpricing measured by the first-day return is higher than 100 percent, which is larger than almost all the documented IPO initial returns in other countries. See also Tan (2006).

Perhaps responding to this apparent large systematic IPO underpricing, at the close of 2004, the CSRC began to experiment with the introduction of a price inquiry mechanism and book-building process, which would seek to move toward an IPO price more reflective of market sentiment. In accordance with these initiatives, IPO issuers, after receiving CSRC's green light for share issuance, must initially inquire about appropriate IPO prices from at least twenty institutional investors (more if the issuance is planned at 400 million shares or more). Presumably the range of P/E ratios that the CSRC will use setting IPO price ranges in specific cases will take these opinions into account.[20]

Mandatory Information Disclosure

The quality of information availability is of course a foundational condition for relatively efficient price fixing on securities (or other) markets. Chinese statutory law mandates that issuers accurately disclose all material information and prohibits any material false statement or omission.[21] Disclosure obligations are periodic and continuous.[22] To be effective, a disclosure regime requires that the quality of information disclosed is good (truthful, timely and material) and that when it is not that some sanctions be enforced. Despite these legal requirements, however, the credibility of information disclosed by Chinese listed companies is regarded as doubtful by investors and scholars (e.g., Aharony, Lee, and Wong 2000).

There are some efforts to improve the quality of information available. A 2008 study by Shanghai Stock Exchange found that disclosure violations represented approximately 78 percent of all violations punished by CSRC and two stock exchanges for the period of 1996 to 2007 (Shanghai Stock Exchange 2008). An earlier Shenzhen Stock Exchange study covering the period 1993 to 2001 found that material omission and misrepresentation were the two top categories of violations (Shenzhen Stock Exchange 2002). They represented 69.7 percent and 13.3 percent, respectively, of the 218 violations discovered during that period. The absolute number of violations disciplined does not, however, seem large (see section 3.2.3 regarding enforcement).

20. With the introduction of this system, it was found that some institutional investors "conspired" with underwriters during the initial consultation process to drive up initial offering prices, but thereafter withdrawing from the process to allow retail investors to invest at what the CSRC concludes may be artificially high prices. The Chinese regulators are now considering new measures to build up a more reliable IPO pricing process.

21. Article 62, the PRC Securities Law of 2006.

22. Periodic reports include annual reports, interim reports, and quarterly reports. Ad hoc reports are primarily related to material events disclosure.

Would a Disclosure-Based IPO System
Be Feasible for China and Beneficial?

For the reasons mentioned earlier (i.e., human bias or error in price fixing, the possibility of both political influence and personal corruption), a system of full disclosure and market-based offering prices would no doubt be the policy recommendation of most Western law and finance experts. But it should be acknowledged that a merits-based securities regulatory system may offer benefits in a society in which financial information is not yet of high quality, retail investors' sophistication is not high and market prices appear to be relatively inefficiently set. These conditions appear to obtain in China currently.

Thus, while the CSRC has announced an intention to move toward a disclosure-based system, as Hong Kong, Malaysia, and Singapore are doing, until there is greater respect for the integrity of financial statements, and greater evidence that prices are fixed in an efficient secondary market,[23] we can expect movement toward a disclosure-based system to be unhurried.

3.2.3   Enforcement

It is a commonplace for legal scholars to note the critical role of enforcement in effective securities regulation (e.g., Coffee 2007). The difference between law as written on a page and law as implemented by active agents and courts can be great.

Securities law enforcement is one of the CSRC's major regulatory functions.[24] Prescribed market misconduct includes: illegal stock offerings, material misrepresentation and omission in connection with the offer or sale of securities, insider trading, market manipulation and professional (securities firm/accounting firm/law firm) misconduct in connection with the offer or sale of securities.[25] Among the recurring matters that give rise to enforcement activities of the CSRC are disclosure violations and also securities firm misconducts such as misappropriation of client funds and market manipulation. Authorized penalties against public companies or securities firms include disgorgement, fines,[26] revocations of business licenses, orders

---

23. We assert that the (relative) efficiency of secondary market prices is a condition for the optimal deployment of a disclosure-based system because the overall character of price setting is what allows the IPO market to estimate value of new issues reasonably well.

24. See Article 180 of PRC Securities Law of 2006. There is some controversy among Chinese academic commentators whether the CSRC as an institutional unit of the State Council (*shiye danwei*) not an administrative department of the State Council, is authorized under the Constitution to make rather than apply rules. See Clarke (2008), citing Zhou, Zheng, and Hui (1998).

25. See "Interim Provisions on the Management of the Issuing and Trading of Stocks," issued by the State Council, effective April 22, 1993; The PRC Securities Law of 2006, Standing Committee of the National People's Congress, effective January 1, 2006; The Regulation on the Administration of Futures Trading, State Council, effective April 15, 2007.

26. The amount ranges from RMB 100,000 (US\$14,622 equivalent) to RMB 600,000 (US\$87,732 equivalent), 1 to 5 percent of or 1 to 5 times of illegal proceeds.

of business suspension and internal correction, and warnings or censure. Fines,[27] an up-to a lifelong bar from the industry, and warnings are available against individuals, including directors and senior management in listed companies.

While it is empowered, it is difficult to say that the CSRC is as an effective enforcement body.[28] For the most part, CSRC's enforcement activities are limited and its penalties are mild. While the number of CSRC enforcement actions has grown as the markets have grown, the number of such actions does not seem large. In the early years, fewer than fifteen cases were investigated and adjudicated annually. In recent years, the number of administrative prosecutions has increased to more than forty. These numbers, however, are small. It is suggestive, but little more than that, given the differences in the scale of US financial markets, but in 2008 for example, it was reported that the SEC brought 671 enforcement actions (SEC 2008). In 2007, the SEC filed 656 enforcement actions (SEC 2007). In 2006, the total had dropped by about 9 percent to 574 enforcement actions compared to the prior year (SEC 2006).[29] There are grounds to believe that in China powerful SOEs are treated lightly by the CSRC; despite making up a small portion of listed companies in China's securities markets, private companies are more often sanctioned than SOEs.[30] But it is possible, of course, that the private firms may be less law abiding.

In all events, the result in most CSRC enforcement cases in which a listed company is accused of wrongdoing is censure; fines are quite rare (Firth et al. 2005). Yet Donald Clarke wisely notes that where senior officers of SOEs are state officials, as may be the case in many large SOEs, a censure may be an effective remedy because it is likely to have serious career effects (Clarke 2008).

In recent years private actions by misled investors have been permitted. Enforcement of securities private litigation in the PRC courts is a recent phenomenon. The PRC courts have faced a problem similar to that of the CSRC: they need to provide access to investors claiming fraud often in connection with SOE's issuance of shares, while at the same time considering the interests of state in front of massive private securities litigations.[31]

---

27. The amount ranges from RMB 30,000 (US$4,386 equivalent) to RMB 100,000 (US$14,622 equivalent).

28. It is suggestive that in a study of all voluntary tender offers, Tuan et al. (2007) found that an investor following a long arbitrage strategy on the date of announcement would not profit. The authors infer that information concerning the offers had fully been absorbed into prices before the announcement and that insider trading was the likely technique.

29. In 2005, the SEC filed 629 enforcement actions. See SEC (2005).

30. Liebman and Milhaupt (2008) posit that private firms may be less politically connected than state-owned firms, but they may also tend to have weaker governance.

31. As a supplement to CSRC enforcement, since 2002 CSRC enforcement has been augmented by possible private actions for misrepresentation. See *Notice on Accepting Cases Regarding Civil Tort Disputes Arising from Securities Market Misrepresentations, Supreme*

3.3   Listed Companies: Corporate Governance with Chinese Characteristics

It is generally thought that one of the institutional preconditions for the evolution of an efficient securities market is the existence of reasonable protections for investors against both the risks of ex post exploitation of their investment and of management incompetence. A potential source of such protections is the system of corporate governance. By "corporate governance" we mean that set of authoritative rules or practices that define how and by whom power over the internal affairs of a business corporation is distributed, exercised, and disciplined. Of course, even countries with successful securities markets differ in the way in which and extent to which this protection is provided. But the Chinese securities markets remind us that what is important is the assurance, not its source. That is, it is not essential that such protections come from a legal system, although the legal system is the formal source of such protection in "rule of law" systems. What is important is that investors perceive in a system a reliable set of practices that offers reasonable protections against ex post investor exploitation or management incompetence.

3.3.1   Realism and the Governance of Internal Affairs in Chinese Corporations

Across the world, the topic of corporate governance receives attention from scholars, regulators, and investors. China is not different; both its scholars[32] and lawmakers (e.g., State Counsel 2004) appear deeply interested in this topic. The CSRC (e.g., CSRC 2003) and the two stock exchanges have addressed the topic of advisable corporate governance structures for listed companies. In this discussion, the very special features of "corporate governance with Chinese characteristics" are not always emphasized. Therefore, we begin our discussion by identifying the most significant aspects of these special characteristics.

Court of People's Republic of China, effective January 15, 2002. In 2003, the Supreme Peoples Court indicated to lower courts that they could accept such actions if but only if the CSRC had imposed a sanction on the party defendant. According to a recent news article, by the end of 2008, approximately 10,000 investors brought suits against more than 20 public companies for claimed damages, totaling about RMB 800 million to 900 million (US$117.0 million to US$131.6 million equivalent). Most cases were settled and about 90 percent of the plaintiffs were compensated. See http://finance.ifeng.com/stock/zqyw/20090401/499677.shtml. Additionally, in 2006, for the first time, the PRC Securities Law of 2006 established legal basis regarding civil liability for insider trading cases (Shen 2008).

32. See, for example, Li, Naughton, and Hovey (2008); Allen, Qian, and Qian (2005); and Clarke (2008) for relevant scholarship.

Government and Party Involvement with Internal Firm Governance

With its legal system of "corporatized" joint stock companies, shareholder voting, takeover regulation, and derivative lawsuits, China appears formally to be sufficiently similar to European or other western "rule of law" societies to justify discussing its economic control systems in these terms. As we discuss in this part, however, to treat these legal structures as representing the principal supports in the actual system of Chinese corporate governance would be a mistake. Chinese corporate governance is fundamentally different from that in the west. For Chinese listed firms, the formal system of board of directors, share-voting at meetings, of tender offers and of derivative law suits is of little importance in the actual system of power delegation, monitoring or discipline. Rather, actual control over important internal affairs in Chinese listed firms is usually in the hands of a control structures operated by the Chinese Communist Party ("CCP"). That system operates through several avenues. In the largest firms it is operated through a combination of Ministry supervision and CCP Central Committee action. For other listed firms, whether SOEs or "private" firms, that control operates through local, party designated committees that function in each large firm[33] (Wei Yu 2009), as well as through the operation of local government bureaucracies (Fan and Huang 2010).

The firm-based party committee is an important structure in this regard. This committee, which will be headed by a party secretary who will often sit on the company's supervisory board, will influence the voting of state-controlled shares, will nominate both "independent" directors and insiders, and will have significant influence in designating or dismissing the CEO. As quoted by Howson (2009) from a 2006 interview in *Caijing Magazine,* Mr. Jiang Chaoliang, the CEO of China Bank of Communications, discussed the role of the party in the operation of the bank as follows:

> What does the party committee govern? First, it is in charge of overseeing strategy. The government has a 65% [share interest in] Bank of Communications, and as the controlling shareholder, it has the power to propose strategic arrangements for the future development of the bank.

---

33. Concerning party activities, Article 17 of the Company Law of 1993 stated that the activities of the local party committees of the CCP in a firm shall be carried out in accordance with the constitution of the CCP. Article 19 of the 2005 revised Company Law provides that "the organizations of CCP shall be established in companies in accordance with the constitution of the CCP so as to carry out their activities." and it further adds "The companies shall provide party organization with conditions necessary to carry out their activities." Article 31 of the constitution of the CCP assigns the implementation function of higher party decisions to local party committees within firms, while Section 7 assigns the right to supervise party cadres and any other personnel explicitly to local party committees. In effect, this provision gives local party committees a supervisory and monitoring role in shareholding firms (Chang and Wong 2004).

Second, [the Party Committee] oversees human resources. . . . The Party Committee recommends to the Board of Directors, senior management candidates with the Board of Directors making the final decision. Third, the Party Committee oversees corporate social responsibility such as lawfully paying taxes, operating the business in accordance with law, and not being lawless and chaotic. If the nation implements macroeconomic measures, [the Bank] must abide by these measures [and by implication it is the Party Committee that sees that it does]. (Hu, Cheng, and Fu 2006, 40–41)

Under the Constitution of the Chinese Communist Party (CCP) local party committees are charged to "supervise the members of CCP in the firm" and "implement higher party policy" (Article 31). The Constitution also provides that they "shall not be in charge of business operations of the firm" (Article 32). Nevertheless, as we noted earlier, a member of the party committee usually sits on the board and it is not rare for the party secretary to serve as board chair. Chang and Wong (2004) found that in their large sample, in 16.4 percent of firms the party secretary served also as a senior officer of the company.

In the largest firms, the governance role of the party is formally directed from the central organs of the party. In December 2008, the Organization Department of the Communist Party of China (CPC) Central Committee and SASAC issued a notice that key positions in fifty-three major SOEs must be appointed by the Organization Department of CPC Central Committee. The list of affected SOEs included, among others, ICBC (Industrial and Commercial Bank of China), China Construction Bank, Bank of China, China Life Insurance Co., China National Overseas Oil Company, China Telecom, China Oil & Foodstuff Co., and China Coal Co., Ltd. Key position generally include Chairman of Party Committee, Chairman of Board of Directors, and President or CEO of SOEs. In smaller enterprises the province-level CCP designates local party committees.

Thus, while the process by which senior officers are designated, paid, and promoted or disciplined is formally a corporate process, in reality it is dominated by party processes. Presumably the designation of officers is based on a blend of considerations, including both competence in administration and on political reliability or connections. Relations between party committees in legal person shareholders and those in listed firms is an internal party matter that occurs behind a veil. Sometimes, apparently, the party committee of a parent company may not appoint a committee in the subsidiary, but itself function directly in that capacity (Wei Yu 2009).

In fact, as the quotation of Jiang Chaoliang suggests, in China's listed SOE firms the formal board of directors has tended to play a secondary and formal role, with the party committee directing matters (through the board or otherwise) that it deems important. It is reported that the party exercises its influence primarily on questions of strategy and personnel, going much deeper into the organization than simply designating the CEO (Wong, Opper, and Hu 2004). While they exercise great influence or control over corporate processes, party committees owe no fiduciary duties to public shareholders. Each party committee fits into the CCP governance structure that establishes appointment, goal setting, reporting, and disciplinary structures (Howson 2009; Wei Yu 2009; and Pistor 2013).

Finally, with respect to smaller listed firms, the multidimensional involvement of local bureaucracies, which has been studied by Fan, Wong, and Zhang (2007) and Gordon and Li (2013), radically reduces the scope of areas over which even effective instruments of shareholder-centered corporate governance could operate.

Does the State (Party) Governance Role Help or Hurt Public Shareholders?

The conventional scholarly view of this degree of political control of the internal affairs of a business corporation is that it will tend to be inefficient, diverting corporate resources away from activities designed to maximize market returns toward the achievement of political objectives, including unnecessary employment (e.g., Blanchard and Aghion 1996; Hellman and Schankerman 2000). The policy implication of this view is unambiguous: reductions in political control should be associated with more efficient firms. Some studies find this effect in China for SOEs (presence of party secretary associated with poorer operating performance and lower labor productivity) (Wei Yu 2009).

Other scholars, however, deploying the same theoretical framework, have seen the question of CCP's role in the corporate governance of Chinese listed firms in a more subtle way. They point out that while party committees certainly may involve the potential inefficiency of diversion of resources, or of excessive local employment, these committees may also have other positive effects from the point of view of the firm. They may assist management in securing limited resources (such as land, finance, or possibly IPO allocations) and may limit both managerial agency costs and controlling shareholder expropriation (Che and Qian 1996). Moreover, the incentives of bureaucratic actors in China are to some extent aligned with long-term investors' interests, in that it is understood that a key metric in bureaucratic promotion is growth in GDP in the province or region. On this more textured view, the systemic effects of party committees or of local government actors on the efficiency of listed firms presents a difficult empirical question. The studies done—based largely on accounting measures—are inconclusive; they suggest that for their sample as a whole party committees add value in constraining agency costs of management but are associated with inefficient levels of employment (Chang and Wang 2004).

Alongside its system of direct and indirect Communist Party control, China has developed the legal infrastructure of liberal corporate governance. We turn now to a discussion of this formal system. We suggest that the legal system represents a supplemental system that has two main purposes: it offers some assurance to foreign investors and may help in the modernization of management of listed SOEs. In the following sections of this part, we discuss the current status of formal governance system. In section 3.3.2 we discuss the command and control type of governance that originates chiefly in the CSRC. In section 3.3.3 we discuss formal legal governance rights of investors, which will look familiar to those familiar with Western corporate governance mechanisms.

3.3.2   Top-Down Corporate Governance in China: The CSRC Governance Role

In addition to other aspects of CCP direct and indirect corporate governance power, the CSRC exercises significant authority with respect to the establishment of certain governance standards and practices for listed firms.

The Code of Corporate Governance for Listed Companies

In 2001, the CSRC issued its *Code of Corporate Governance for Listed Companies.*[34] In this code the CSRC, in ninety-five numbered paragraphs, establishes standards for corporate governance. They include three paragraphs on Related Party Transactions (12–14), seven paragraphs on Behavior Rules for Controlling Shareholders (15–21), six paragraphs (22–27) on the Independence of the Listed Company, and three paragraphs on Disclosure of Controlling Shareholder's Interests (92–94). These rules of corporate governance plausibly seem directed toward protecting holders of state (formerly) NTS (and public shareholder incidentally) by forcing disclosure by legal person shareholders.

In addition, the CSRC establishes rules for board procedure (44–48), for specialized committees of the board (52–58), and for Performance Assessments and Incentive and Disciplinary Systems (69–72). These rules seem directed to instructing management (and controlling shareholders of legal person shares) about best management practices.

In fact, agencies of the state with large economic interests in residual earnings of listed SOEs would not be dependent on regulatory or judicial remedies in responding to mismanagement self-dealing or even for poor corporate governance practices. If SASAC, as the body holding the residential state interest in many publicly listed SOEs (or the Ministry of Finance in the case of the largest banks) or other agencies, learn of mismanagement, they can and presumably are expected to act through government or Communist Party channels for redress or discipline. Thus, a plausible explanation of the

---

34. English translation of this Code is available from http://www.csrc.gov.cn/n575458 /n4001948/n4002030/4062964.html.

2001 CSRC Corporate Governance standards is that in it, the CSRC in effect provides such state agencies with expert guidance or standards respecting the topics it covers. Simultaneously, these standards and practices may serve to induce listed SOEs (and other listed firms coincidentally) to adopt more transparent and modern management and governance practices.

Goals of CSRC's Formal Governance Activities

More fully, we suggest that in promulgating the Corporate Governance Code or other governance-type regulations the CSRC seeks to advance three main aims. First, the promulgation of sensible governance standards and practices will offer some assurance to foreign institutional investors on the Hong Kong or New York exchanges that investment in the large PRC SOEs listed on those exchanges constitutes an investment in a sensibly governed, modern commercial enterprise. Currently, as we indicated previously, Hong Kong appears to be more important for raising capital for such firms than Shanghai and those shares enjoy special class voting rights.

The second reason we suppose that CSRC engages in serious corporate governance activity, even though public shareholders have virtually no ability to enforce such standards (as we see later), involves the apparent aim of the leadership to construct the infrastructure for a modern securities market—including statutory shareholder rights, fiduciary obligations, and the modern standards of corporate governance—as an option for future finance of SOEs. The Share Segmentation Reform was an elaborate, time-consuming effort to make it possible to sell to public investors more of the state's share interest in large, listed SOEs. That effort must have been motivated by a desire to sell more stock to Chinese and (to some extent) overseas institutional investors. Time will tell to what extent these sales will occur and with respect to which firms. But, as with foreign investors in Hong Kong (as well as other overseas markets), it is reasonable to expect that Chinese investors, especially institutional investors, will at that time be more likely to make further investments in SOEs at not-excessively discounted prices, if those firms appear to be governed by structures and "rights" consistent with those pertaining in other markets.

The third, and we suggest the most important, reason that it makes sense for the leadership to authorize the CSRC to promulgate (and care about) corporate governance practices, even though shareholders have virtually no way to enforce such standards, is that these standards may also be thought of as attempts to modernize management practices of SOEs and to coordinate CCP governance of firms. Modernization of management of its state sector is important to China and the modern SOEs constitute a vital part of that sector. Listing standards on the exchanges and regulatory requirements by the CSRC can be seen both as a way to control undesirable management practices (such as self-dealing transactions) that hurt the state as a shareholder (and incidentally hurt public shareholders) and as a way to encourage the development of better management techniques, such as better financial reporting or incentive compensation programs.[35] The CSRC as a specialist organization will obviously be more knowledgeable than decentralized party committees in establishing such things as transparent accounting standards or responsible management practices, in which the state and the party have an interest.

3.3.3.   The Limited Role of "Internal" Corporate Governance in Chinese Securities Markets

We turn now to the formal legal system of investors' rights that appear in many respects similar to shareholders' rights in the United States or other Western systems. We structure this discussion of the formal aspects of Chinese corporate governance around three primary investor governance mechanisms: the investors' rights to vote and to sell shares, thus facilitating a change in control and to sue.

Public Shareholders' Right to Vote

Turning first to the right to vote, we note that while all shares listed on Chinese securities exchanges carry one vote, voting rights with respect to PRC listed firms must be understood in the shadow of the fact that, in essentially all cases, block holders hold controlling blocks of shares. In SOEs, the controller is typically state affiliated; in the 20 percent or so of listed firms that are not SOEs, the controller is an individual, family, or affiliated groups of investors. Thus, at first glance one would conclude that for public investors, corporate voting is almost wholly immaterial. This, while largely true, may not be entirely so.

Since one aim of the corporitization and listing process has been the attraction of capital—and as we show earlier, predominately foreign capital—to listed firms, it was seen as prudent, if not essential, to offer certain limited protections to foreign investors against the risk that a simple majority vote of shares could alter the character of their investment once it was made. This protection was offered through a mandatory class voting right for H shares (and other overseas' listing shares, if any) for the approval of transactions or charter amendments that would constitute an abrogation or variation in the rights of the H shares (or other overseas' listed shares, if any).[36] The mandatory provisions identify the various types of corporate actions (identified in footnote below) that require a class vote of H shares

35. See CSRC, *Guidelines for Equity-based Compensation* (2005, No. 151) (restricted stock and options as compensation limited to 10 percent of outstanding shares).
36. *Mandatory Provisions for Articles of Association of Companies to Be Listed Overseas* were issued in 1994 jointly by the Securities Commission of the State Council (then the parent organization to the CSRC) and the State Economic System Restructuring Commission.

(or other overseas' listed shares, if any) to be implemented.[37] The voting rule to determine such class votes is set at two-thirds of the issued and outstanding H shares (or other overseas' listed shares, if any). The class vote right can offer substantial protection to foreign investors in covered matters.

There exists another share voting protection of some significance that relates to related party transactions. Under "Guidelines for Articles of Association of Listed Companies" first issued by the CSRC in 1997 and revised in 2006, the authorization of any related party transactions that requires a shareholder vote requires that only disinterested shareholders vote. In practice, listed companies have adopted this provision in their articles of association. Not all related party transactions do require a shareholder vote, however. According to the Listing Rules of the Shanghai Stock Exchange, a shareholder's vote is required in three cases: if the transaction is approved by fewer than three "independent" directors or the transaction is large (greater than 5 percent of net assets and in excess of RMB 30 million) or there is a guarantee issued by the company to a related party.

Shareholder voting might in the future become more important in Chinese corporate governance, now that share segmentation reform is largely completed. But it remains to be seen whether and when some firms will in fact distribute their formerly nontradable shares to the public and how many shares will be distributed in this way. Certainly these holders will have a substantial economic incentive to sell at market prices if, as has been the case in the past, the market prices are higher than the private market prices.

If and when control of some listed firms does become available in the securities markets, a number of very important corporate governance issues will be faced. Some of these are mentioned in the following in connection

37. Art. 80 of chapter 9 of the Mandatory Provisions provides the following situations that shall be considered as a variation or abrogation of the rights of a certain class of shareholders: (1) the increase or reduction of the number of shares of that class of shares or the increase or reduction of the number of shares in another class which carry the same or more right to vote, right of distribution, or other privileges; (2) the conversion of all or part of the shares of that class to another class, or the conversion of all or part of the shares of another class into the shares of that class or the granting of such right of conversion; (3) the cancellation or reduction of the rights of that class of shares to receive dividends declared or accrued; (4) the reduction or cancellation of the preferential rights of that class of shares to receive dividends or to receive distribution of assets upon the liquidation of the Company; (5) the increase, cancellation, or reduction of the share conversion rights, options rights, voting rights, rights of transfer, preemptive rights, and rights to acquire the securities of the Company of that class of shares; (6) the cancellation or reduction of the rights of that class of shares to receive payment payable by the Company in a particular currency; (7) to create a new class of shares that enjoys the same or more voting rights, distribution rights, or other privileges than those enjoyed by that class of shares; (8) to restrict or increase the restriction on the transfer or ownership of that class of shares; (9) the granting of subscription rights or conversion rights in respect of that class or another class of shares; (10) the increase of the rights and privileges of another class of shares; (11) the reorganization of the Company as a result of which different classes of shareholders assume obligations otherwise than in proportion; and (12) the amendment or abrogation of the provisions in this chapter 9.

with tender offers for control, but others will relate directly to shareholder voting. Given the high cost of any shareholder-initiated proxy contest, the most significant of these issues will be whether and on what terms shareholders might have access to the company's proxy statement, which has been a contentious issue in the United States for some time, and whether successful proxy contestants can get reimbursement for some or all of the costs of the contest and under what circumstances.

Public Shareholders' Inability to Participate in Disciplinary Tender Offers

In systems in which control over listed companies is in the market ("Contestable Control Systems"), the mechanism of hostile changes in corporate control has been treated both by scholars of law and of finance, as well as governance activists as the ultimate market corrective for inefficiency of management (Easterbrook and Fischel 1991; Bebchuk 1987). The theory is well-known. The evolution of a disciplinary "market for corporate control" is often seen as a potentiality that can be useful in systems in which securities markets play a major financing role. But as neat as the theory of a market for corporate control appears to be, there are substantial grounds to believe that the types of costs and imperfections that affect the efficiency of securities markets generally (e.g., principally information problems, agent's incentive misalignment problems, and systematic limitations of human rationality) coupled with recurring periodic excess system liquidity, render this market far from perfect (e.g., Schleifer and Summers 1988; Lipton 1997). Thus, in the United States there has long been a debate concerning how "free" the market for corporate control should be. There are, of course, numerous techniques open to any legal system for moderating the market for corporate control when it is permitted to exist: approval of "takeovers" by substantive regulatory agencies where there is a strong public interest in the industry;[38] enactment of "constituency" statutes or regulations that give non-shareholder constituencies a legally cognizable interest in such transactions (Allen, Kraakman, and Subramanian 2012); authorization of "poison pill" securities which give boards of directors certain powers to defend against unwanted takeovers (Kahan and Rock 2002); and less powerful company law devices, such as staggered election of the board of directors (Bebchuk, Coates, and Subramanian 2002; Bebchuk and Cohen 2005). China need not address these secondary issues relating to a market in corporate control at this time because, while tender offers for control are legally possible, in fact there is virtually no market for corporate control.[39] "Takeovers" play no disciplinary role in China today.

---

38. Thus most systems require governmental preapproval of changes in corporate control of major financial institutions.

39. In an apparent effort to aid public shareholders, the CSRC issued "Measures for the Administration of the Takeovers of Listed Companies" in 2002 and revised in 2006, which for the first time contemplated public tender offers for shares of listed companies in China.

Some "change in control" transactions do occasionally occur in China, but they are in the form of contracts in which an acquirer contracts with the holders of some or all formerly nontradable shares for transfer of controlling block of stock. The state—that is both CSRC and often SASAC—must consent to such a transfer of control where state-controlled shares are involved. When these transfers involve listed companies, under CSRC regulations, the buyer is required to extend a tender offer to all public shares *at a price no less than that paid in the control transfer.*[40] (Such a rule is called a mandatory bid rule and is common in the European Union and under some state law systems in the United States.) While the beneficial effect of mandatory bid rules is controversial (Easterbrook and Fischel 1989), what is notable is that in China such tender offers, when they occur, are merely formal and have no economic effect at all.

Professors Tuan, Zhang, Hsu and Zhang located just twenty-four instances of tender offers for shares of listed firms in China between June 2003 and December 2006 (Tuan et al. 2007). Of these, seventeen tender offers were "mandatory" in character and offered a price *below* the market price for the traded A shares! That is, in these cases, the price per share paid for the control block was below market price for the traded shares! Thus the public tender offer required by the CSRC mandatory bid rule could be and was made at a below-market price. The authors report that on average the discount from market price offered was 19.6 percent. Unsurprisingly, none of these offers closed. We might call these tender offers "phantom tender offers," because they have the formal look of a tender offer, but have no economic substance. The remaining seven cases of tender offers were cash tender offers. All of these bids were in the petroleum and chemicals sector and all were initiated either by Petro China or by Sinopec, the giant SOEs in the petroleum business.

More interesting than the question of why do buyers of control offer a price below market—having acquired control, they apparently saw no advantage in buying out the public shares—is the question, why do the original holders of control agree to sell at substantial discount to market price? A standard answer, grounded in a belief in the fundamental efficiency of stock markets, would be that very large blocks often trade at a discount due to market illiquidity. An alternative possible account of this phenomena would posit that the market price for noncontrolling A shares is recognized by both buyers and sellers of control to be irrationally high on the Shanghai or Shenzhen Stock Exchanges, at least part of the time. That is, there may at times be a bubble premium reflected in the market that more informed and rational buyers are unwilling to pay.

40. More specifically, whenever a holder acquires 30 percent or more of the traded shares of a listed company, the mandatory bid rules require a tender offer to the public shareholders at a price no less than a price set by a multifactor test (Huang 2008). See Article 24 of Measures of Administration of Takeovers of Listed Companies.

In all events, we observe that, even though the legal technology to govern tender offers has been well developed by the CSRC (Huang 2008), at least for the present, tender offers for corporate control play little role in Chinese corporate governance. The CSRC's formal takeover regulation appears to be another example of the development of a future option available to the leadership. Whether disciplinary takeovers in fact will be observed in the future in China will depend on two factors. First, will control of (some) listed firms actually become available on the market (i.e., will state-affiliated holders sell control of SOEs into the market?) and second, should this occur, will the leadership permit the management of listed firms to be determined by a market for corporate control processes? That, of course, appears to be unlikely now or in the intermediate future. The more likely role for takeover regulation is to offer some modest protection to minority shareholders as control blocks are in the future shifted as part of industry consolidations or other restructurings. Moreover, given the likely inefficiency of the pricing of shares on the mainland exchanges, even if shareholdings were such as to make hostile takeovers feasible, there is doubt that they would serve useful public purpose at this time.

3.3.4   Chinese Courts and Shareholders' Right to Sue

The Institutional Contributions That Courts Can Provide

While administrative agencies such as CSRC can act as powerful instruments in structuring and operating a system of market regulation, courts could supplement such activity in useful ways. Courts can give force and effect to abstract statements of law by determining contested facts and declaring and enforcing rights and duties of managers, shareholders, or directors in those factual contexts. Among the institutional advantages of courts are the following: (a) well-functioning courts offer a professional commitment to make decisions only in accordance with preexisting law and to be unaffected by other matters; (b) they have expertise in the content of preexisting law and in accepted professional techniques of interpretation of it; (c) they make decisions grounded in the facts of a particular case, which are determined in an unbiased manner; and (d) they often or usually provide written justification for their results. In a judicial system in which courts function in this way, citizens know after a litigation has been determined that they have been heard by a disinterested judge with expertise who has ruled according to law. In this way, well-functioning courts can provide a form of satisfaction even to parties who lose their disputes. The reliable provision of these services can ex ante facilitate investment and, more broadly, contracting among strangers.

As an arbiter of disputes between shareholders and those controlling the management of the firm, courts could serve a corporate governance function either at the instance of government actors (e.g., administrative agencies) or at the instance of shareholders directly. In fact, since the 2006 amendment of the Company Law, Chinese courts have been authorized to adjudicate claims of director wrongdoing in so-called "derivative" lawsuits—that is, a suit brought by a shareholder in the name and for the benefit of the corporation itself.[41] Such suits are brought against the corporate directors or officers who are alleged to have violated their duty and injured the company in some way.

Derivative lawsuits can be subject to abuse, but they can serve as an important constraint on corrupt behavior. Generally, these suits can be useful even if directors are not frequently required to pay damages for wrongs in such lawsuits. In the United States, most such suits are settled through the payment of a relatively small payment from an insurance underwriter. Nevertheless, such suits are useful to investors because, ex ante, directors adjust their behavior knowing that in certain types of transactions they face a high probability that their conduct will be subject to derivative litigation and thus close judicial review. Thus the existence of this type of lawsuit and the legal infrastructure that permits them to be brought, can serve an important chilling effect on violations of the corporate directors' fiduciary duties.

"Fiduciary Duties" and Shareholder Suits in China

Formally, the corporate board of directors, under Chinese company law and that of most Western countries, holds power over corporate managers; it is responsible for overseeing the operation of the company. If those individuals wrongfully injure the corporation, under most systems they can be held responsible and in some jurisdictions, including China, they may be held liable for such harm in a suit brought by shareholders on behalf of the corporation itself. Most such suits would charge a violation of a general duty to try in good faith to undertake transactions only in an effort to advance corporate purposes. Such a duty is generally characterized as the fiduciary duty of loyalty. As part of the early corporatization movement, the first modern PRC Company Law of 1994 did expressly state that officers and directors of companies formed under its authority[42] shall be liable for damage caused to the company by their violation of law, administrative regulation, or the company's articles of association.[43] It did not mention any concept similar to the open-ended fiduciary duty of loyalty and, more importantly, did not authorize shareholders to initiate any action upon an

---

41. For a full description of derivative suit, see Allen, Kraakman, and Subramanian (2012, chapter 10).

42. For example, Articles 59, 60, and 61, the PRC Company Law of 1994.

43. See Article 63, the PRC Company Law of 1994.

allegation of such unauthorized conduct nor was it interpreted by courts to do so.

Nevertheless, some PRC courts did from time to time signal receptivity to the idea of a shareholder suing on the corporation's behalf to redress injury caused by an alleged violation of law.[44] In 1997, a court in Fuijian Province upheld the right of a minority shareholder (in a joint venture corporation) to sue on the corporation's behalf on a debt where the majority of the board were related to the debtor, and had refused to do so. The courts said:

> If the infringement suffered by the shareholders is to the right of the company, then the shareholders should first present a written application to the organ of power of the company requesting that the company take action. . . . Where the company does not take any action, the shareholder may in its stead bring a lawsuit." (Clarke 2008, citing Xie and Chen 2001)

This is a clear statement of the derivative theory, and its articulation by a Chinese provincial court in 1997 evidences the strong appeal of the logic of the form of action. Nevertheless, other provincial courts during this period rejected the theory (Shen 2008; Deng 2005).[45]

In its Corporate Governance Code, the CSRC endorsed the concept of the derivative lawsuit when, it stated that:

> Shareholders shall have the right to protect their interests and rights through civil litigation or other legal means in accordance with law and administrative regulations. In the event the resolutions of the shareholders' meeting or the resolutions of the board of directors are in breach of laws or administrative regulations, or infringe shareholders' legal interests or rights, the shareholders shall have the right to initiate litigation. (CSRC 2003)

But it is not free from doubt that the CSRC intended to try to advance derivative lawsuits by this provision. This translation of the language of Article 4 of the Corporate Governance Code appears on the CSRC website. Some scholars, however, translate the provisions as giving shareholders only the right to demand the company initiate lawsuits (Clarke 2008).

Derivative Suits and Shareholder Problems of Collective Action

Despite the shadowy legitimacy of shareholder derivative suits prior to the 2005 revision of the Company Law, the legitimacy of the shareholders'

44. An early example, dealing with a foreign joint venture involving the Zhangjiagang Fiber Company in which the Supreme People's Court allowed a Chinese joint venture partner to sue on behalf of the joint venture when the managing partner had refused to do so, allegedly because it had inappropriate motivations. See Deng (2005).

45. San Jiu Pharmaceutical Company, where the Shenzhen Basic Level People's Court rejected a derivative suit unless unanimous shareholder action was taken (an obviously impossible precondition to such suits). See Deng (2005).

derivative suits in China was made clear in Article 152 of the PRC Company Law of 2005. That enactment specifically acknowledged corporate directors owe fiduciary duties of loyalty and care (Art. 146) and also authorized derivative suits by shareholders. The preconditions to such suits are as follows: first, plaintiffs must represent more than 1 percent of the shares of the company for more than 180 consecutive days, alone or jointly. Second, demand to sue must be made upon the board of directors and suit may be filed only after thirty days following such a demand. The latter prerequisite is designed to allow the corporate board an opportunity to study the matter and take action with respect to it. It is a conventional precondition to such suits in the United States. The first requirement appears to be an attempt to limit so-called "strike suits" brought by persons with insignificant equity investment merely for the purpose of extracting a nuisance settlement. It may, however, serve as an impediment to meritorious claims also.

It is early to judge whether this new statutory authorization may in time provide a remedy that is useful to shareholders, but there is, in the short term, little hope for a strong investor protection tool at present, with respect to listed companies. The problem stems from the fact that investors who buy shares on securities markets generally face severe collective action disabilities caused by their small proportionate interest in the firm. There appears to be little willingness to innovate a solution to the collective action problem that potential shareholder plaintiffs would face. For the holder of a relatively small proportion of total shares, the costs of suit would be prohibitive, even if the claim to be litigated seemed quite strong, unless there were a mechanism to allow these costs to be shared among all other shares. Yet neither the statutory law nor judicial innovation recognizes a way to impose this cost sharing.

Thus, the few derivative cases that are found in modern Chinese law tend to be cases involving joint ventures in a corporate form. In those cases, the representative plaintiff necessarily owns a large proportionate share of the firm (and potential damages). This may provide sufficient economic incentive for him to bear the costs of bringing such a suit. Where the investor's stake is proportionately small, however, unless there is a way to force the sharing of his costs, such an investor will not sue, even if the violation is clear. But neither the PRC Company Law, nor the few courts who have discussed derivative suits, have suggested that costs of this litigation, including attorney's fees, might be awarded to a successful derivative plaintiff. Therefore, it is not to be expected that shareholders who acquire shares on the exchange will undertake to fund such litigation, where they own only a minor percentage of the company's securities.

Thus despite the fact that formally Chinese law has adopted the investor-initiated derivative suit, at this time courts are not in fact a realistic source of constraint on management misbehavior in Chinese listed companies.

3.4   The Future of China's "Top-Down" Securities Markets

3.4.1   Assessing Chinese Security Market Growth

The creation in less than twenty years of the complex technological, financial, and legal infrastructure necessary to operate the two mainland securities exchanges is unquestionably a great achievement. With these exchanges, and the corporatization effort that is their premise, the people of China have created one of the essential working parts of a world-class economy. They have successfully organized the former state and provincial production facilities into individual firms in which professional managers can direct activities with an eye to market-oriented production. They have created embryonic corporate governance structures and a structure of legal rights and duties that might be used to create more highly elaborated investor-based corporate governance protections in the future. They have created a means for the corporatized firms to access domestic household savings and world global investment pools. They have created the option to institute some forms of stock or stock price related incentive compensation for professional senior managers. And they have made initiating some forms of capital markets-based disciplinary methods (such as takeovers) a policy option for the future, as well.

Nevertheless, in their present state these markets represent more potential value to China than realized value. They are not economically highly important yet. While the equity markets have grown rapidly in terms of market capitalization and in terms of listings, when compared to the securities markets in more developed financial systems, they appear as quite small relative to the Chinese economy. They lack deep liquidity and are excessively volatile; there is good evidence that they do not price equities very efficiently. An economically significant market for nongovernmental bonds has not yet arisen in China and is important. Financial risk management has been severely limited, in part because hedging opportunities are constricted by a prohibition, now to be eased, on borrowing shares. Futures markets for securities are in their infancy. Quite significantly, the public markets continue to offer little assistance in funding growth in the important nongovernmental sector of the economy. And by most accounts there is significant level of managerial and other forms of corruption and virtually little investor corporate governance remedies available.

3.4.2   Future Development Steps

A more important role for securities markets could include, most importantly: (a) broader access to the securities markets for the purpose of raising capital for the entrepreneurial sector of the economy; (b) the development of a substantial commercial bond market open to all corporate borrowers of requisite credit standing; (c) the development of an array of financial instruments capable of hedging of financial risk, which is now beginning; (d) the gradual floatation into the market of a majority of outstanding voting stock in a significant number of former SOEs; and possibly, (e) the development of public shareholder protective institutions of corporate governance, as discussed before, including development of the infrastructure necessary for proxy voting, tender offers and shareholder law suits. Consistent with policy on the country's currency, a more developed PRC securities market might also involve: (f) easier access for foreign investors to Chinese markets and securities; and (g) easier access for domestic investors to foreign shares through the Hong Kong or Shanghai Stock Exchanges. Were the leadership to permit and direct this further development of the securities markets, we would expect those markets to more effectively provide to the Chinese economy the three great benefits of fully developed securities markets: (relatively) efficient capital allocation, flexible financial risk management, and useful techniques of financial market discipline of ineffective corporate management.

Expansion of the use of securities markets would have distinct economic or development advantages for China, but it would raise two related issues. First, more significant securities markets would heighten political issues of Communist Party control that economic liberalization generally and securities markets particularly have raised from the beginning of reform. A market allocation of capital and market discipline of managers, if they are to be effective, would entail reduction in the ability of Communist Party committees to direct economic development, to appoint senior managers of firms, and to direct operational outcomes on the firm level. While in the event of such liberalization, the sovereign power of the government could redirect its control to external tax and regulation of business to some extent, such a system would inevitably have less direct and immediate control over listed firms than the present system offers. Thus, these are effects that are unlikely to be eagerly embraced in the near future. Secondly, and more abstractly, fundamental growth in the securities markets (meaning a change in their structural limitations) raises the question: To what extent does or should China wish to expose its economy to the types of gyrations which the financial crisis of 2008 and 2009 has shown, again, that capital markets including securities markets are capable? The claim of some in the United States that its system, dominated by financial markets of ever greater complexity and shorter average holding periods, has become unduly short-term oriented, is often dismissed by academic commentators. But it is unlikely that the near collapse of the US financial system in the fall of 2008 leaves its model of finance in quite the same position as a role model. China's quick bounce-back from the global financial crisis of 2008 and 2009, on the other hand, leaves its leadership or elements among its leadership in a position to question the value of such capital market liberalization.

Almost certainly the leadership will feel its way in assessing the risks and benefits of further expansion of the economic role that securities markets play in the Chinese economy. We do, however, have least two telling bits of evidence of an intention to foster further development of the Chinese securities markets. First, despite its occurring before the global financial crisis, the elaborate effort of the Chinese government to remove the NTS designation (briefly outlined in this chapter) provides strong evidence that the leadership recently intended for the securities markets to have the capacity to grow into more powerful instrumentalities of finance. Second, more recently, the 2010 approval of futures trading and short selling innovations confirm that intent is unchanged.

Of course, it is very unlikely that the leadership will, for the foreseeable future, allow the most significant components of the economy—the large banks and insurance companies, natural resource companies, the national transport infrastructure and the telecom industries, for example—to be subject to the risk of investor "interference" that might potentially occur if a majority of voting shares of these firms were traded in the markets. But, we assume, that in the next period of development (whenever that may occur) the leadership will direct that a majority of the shares of at least some SOEs in nonstrategic sectors of the Chinese economy be moved from government control into nongovernment, including market control. Thus, we expect certain firms in consumer electronics and soft goods, textiles, footwear, recreation and leisure, home supplies and repair materials, health, beauty, and hygiene products, and various other nonstrategic products or activities to increase the proportion of their shares that trade on securities markets. Furthermore, we expect that CSRC continuing current efforts to open the securities market to smaller entrepreneurial enterprises will meet with some success and we will in the future observe greater use of securities markets by private entrepreneurial or foreign firms. Even these steps, however, will take time.

3.4.3   The Secondary Role of Legal Infrastructure in Chinese Securities Markets

Continued growth in Chinese securities markets, however, is not dependent on improvements in the legal infrastructure of those markets. While the attractiveness of those markets to investors would be increased by, for example, the improvement in quality of financial disclosure, the reduction in insider trading, or improvements in corporate governance generally, such changes are not essential presently. Chinese securities markets will continue to attract domestic and international investors without improvement in corporate governance protections for the immediate and indefinite future.

Even substantial levels of investor exploitation by managers or by controlling shareholders—for example, insider trading, self-dealing transactions, or other forms of corruption—need not prevent the development of a large or growing securities market.

What is essential for these markets to continue to grow is only that the perceived expected risk-adjusted returns available to investors, net of the expected cost of exploitation, is attractive when compared to all alternative opportunities to invest funds. Therefore, so long as the net returns expected to be generated on Chinese securities markets exceed risk-adjusted expected returns offered by alternative investment opportunities, Chinese securities markets will continue to attract investors. It is the growth of the Chinese economy, not the improvement of Chinese corporate governance, that is the primary driver of the growth in the Chinese securities markets. While there has been some controversy about just how accurate the reported growth rates for China have been, there is no doubt that real growth rates over the period 1990 to 2008 have been very high.[46] Indeed, some informed views see this growth rate continuing for a substantial period (Fogel 2006).

3.4.4 Are Investor-Initiated Protections and More Efficient Securities Markets Likely in Modern China?

The fact that we can expect the Chinese securities markets to continue to be highly attractive to international investors, even if we expect no improvement in legal infrastructure of those markets, does not mean improvement in corporate governance and other public investor protections is unimportant for China. The logic is compelling that, holding all other factors constant, an improvement in the range of financial products available in the securities markets, in access to listing and in the quality of disclosure together with a reduction in the amount of investor exploitation, would reduce the costs at which capital would be committed to investment in China and improve the efficiency with which capital would be allocated among potential users. Regardless of the period in which elevated growth rates can continue, experience teaches that, in time, these growth rates will reduce. When that occurs, the marginal improvement in costs of capital that investor protective governance can yield systemically will become relatively more important.

As one looks to that future, one can imagine the leadership of the country considering steps to try to make investment in China more attractive both

---

46. While officially reported statistics on Chinese GDP growth rates have been controversial, see Thurow, Zhou, and Wang (2003) (using data on electricity consumption to cast doubt on reliable of official GDP growth rate numbers). Official government sources reported the average real growth of GDP over the period 1999 to the close of 2008 was 14.4 percent per year. See *China Statistical Yearbook* (2008).

to international capital and, more importantly, to domestic savers. Obvious first steps would be improvements in transparency, in reducing corruption and management inefficiency. The first instinct will presumably be China's traditional top-down style response—that is, an increase in CCP campaigns to encourage right conduct and diligence. Should such campaigns fail, as one might expect, then we would expect the second top-down response: greater or more effective party discipline or official prosecution of corruption. But there are reasons to think even that technique would, alone, be ineffective. Public officials or party secretaries are likely to have either poorer quality information concerning breaches of fiduciary duty (or subpar managerial performance) or weaker incentives to take corrective action than investors, whose financial interests are adversely affected by managerial conduct. Therefore, at some point in time the leadership of the country will experience increased pressure to improve the whole range of practices concerning internal corporate affairs. When this does occur the leadership will face again some recurring issues: how much can decentralized, shareholder-initiated mechanisms be trusted; how much can "rule of law" institutions, such as shareholder voice and independent courts or free access to listing by all who meet objective criteria, be made consistent with China's culture and existing political institutions?

Can fostering better disclosure, less administratively controlled access to finance, and greater privately-initiated governance mechanisms be consistent with the leadership role of the CCP in China's one-party state? There seems to be no reason in logic why it cannot. Control over law creation, taxation, and law enforcement (not to mention appointment and pay of the judiciary) provides sufficient levers to allow the leadership effectively to guide the direction and speed of economic growth without losing that degree of control necessary to safeguard those values that the leadership holds most sacred. Yet change always does entail unforeseen risks. Much of the magnificent success that has occurred in the development of the Chinese economy over the last thirty years, despite being increasingly guided by free market prices, has occurred on a top-down, controlled model of development.[47] Movement toward a more decentralized "bottom-up" mode of change, marked in the securities regulation area by high quality disclosure, investor empowerment to change underperforming management teams, and court adjudication under a rule of law approach, can be expected to be unwelcomed. Empowered investors would act through voting shares, or selling shares into tender offers or by initiating suit against

47. It is claimed by Professor Yasheng Huang that much growth at the beginning of liberalization appears to have been resulted from the spontaneous action of farmers and rural residence when simply allowed access to land and ability to contract (Huang 2007, 2008). But certainly with respect to the SOEs and the stock markets post-1990, the whole story is one of designed top-down development.

insiders or other controllers of the firms in which they make investments. These means of action, however, involve instrumentalities (boards, courts, shareholder meetings) that, in a bottom-up development regime, would not formally be a part of or agents of the Chinese Communist Party. Thus, it is reasonable to expect that substantial reform of the corporate governance of firms listed on Chinese securities markets will not occur until there is a pressing developmental reason for the leadership to force such change. Certainly those pressures are not sufficient at this time to occasion real change.

The existing limitations of the Chinese securities markets can be expected to be remedied over time—and the securities markets can be expected to play a more productive role in the Chinese economy—if, but only if, the leadership of the country wants Chinese securities markets to assume a more important role. This conclusion reflects the fundamental nature of these markets. Unlike securities markets in New York, London, or Amsterdam, the Chinese markets were designed and created by government principally to serve government purposes. Like their existence, their future depends upon the judgments to be made by the country's political leadership. Trying to predict choices those leaders may make is fraught with risk of miscalculation. It seems certain that even absent improvement in the practical ability of equity investors to protect their own economic interests, Chinese securities markets will for a period continue to grow as the PRC economy grows. Thus these markets will continue to satisfy the limited economic role that they have thus far been permitted to play. But they will not serve the larger important economic functions of efficient capital allocation, nor the useful role of signaling, incenting, or disciplining corporate management. But Rome, we have often been reminded, was not built in a day; nor have the great Redwood trees of California reached their enormous size and beauty in just sixty years.

References

Aharony, J. J. Lee, and T. J. Wong. 2000. "Financial Packaging of IPO Firms in China." *Journal of Accounting Research* 38:103–26.

Allen, Franklin, Jun Qian, and Meijun Qian. 2005. "Law, Finance and Economic Growth in China." *Journal of Financial Economics* 77:57–116.

Allen, William T., Reinier Kraakman, and Guhan Subramanian. 2012. *Commentaries and Cases on Law of Business Organization,* 4th ed. Wolters Klur Law & Business Publishers.

Agrawal, Ashwini K. 2009. "The Impact of Investor Protection Laws on Corporate Policy: Evidence from the Blue Sky Laws." http://pages.stern.nyu.edu/~sternfin/aagrawal/public_html/blue_sky.pdf.

Bebchuk, Lucian. 1987. "The Pressure to Tender: An Analysis and a Proposed Remedy." *Delaware Journal of Corporate Law* 12:911–49.

Bebchuk, Lucian A., John C. Coates IV, and Guhan Subramanian. 2002. "The Powerful Antitakeover Force of Staggered Boards: Further Findings and a Reply to Symposium Participants." *Stanford Law Review* 55:885–917.

Bebchuk, Lucian, and Alma Cohen. 2005. "The Costs of Entrenched Boards." *Journal of Financial Economics* 78:409–33.

Blanchard, O., and P. Aghion. 1996. "On Insider Privatization." *European Economic Review* 40:759–66.

Caijing Magazine. 2009. "188 Companies Apply to Liston GEM." October 26. http://english.caijing.com.cn/2009-10-26/110294620.html.

Chang, E., and S. Wong. 2004. "Political Control and Performance in China's Listed Firms." *Journal of Comparative Economics* 32 (4): 617–36.

Che, Jiahua, and Yingyi Qian. 1996. "Insecure Property Rights and Government Ownership of Firms." http://papers.ssrn.com/sol3/papers.cfm?abstract_id=5201.

Chen, Dong-Hua, Joseph P. H. Fan, and T. J. Wong. 2004. "The Board Structure, Government Influence, and the Performance of Listed Companies in China."

Chen, Gongmeng, Michael Firth, and Liping Xu. 2009. "Does the Type of Ownership Control Matter? Evidence from China's Listed Companies." *Journal of Banking and Finance* 33: (1): 171–81.

Chinese Securities Regulatory Commission (CSRC). 2003. *Principles of Corporate Governance for Listed Companies.* http://www.csrc.gov.cn.

———. 2005. *Guidelines for Equity-Based Compensation.*

———. 2008. *China Capital Markets Development Report.* China Financial Publishing House.

Clarke, Donald C. 2008. "The Ecology of Corporate Governance in China." George Washington Law School Working Paper. http://ssrn.com/abstract=1245803.

Coffee, John C., Jr. 2007. "Law and the Market: The Impact of Enforcement." Columbia Law and Economics Working Paper No. 304. March 7. http://ssrn.com/abstract=967482.

Deng, Jiong. 2005. "Building an Investor-Friendly Shareholder Derivative Lawsuit System in China." *Harvard International Law Review* 46:347, 365, n. 108.

Easterbrook, Frank, and Daniel Fischel. 1989. "The Corporate Contract." *Columbia Law Review* 89 (7): 1416–48.

———. 1991. *The Economic Structure of Corporate Law.* Cambridge, MA: Harvard University Press.

Fan, Joseph P. H., T. J. Wong, and Tianyu Zhang. 2007. "Politically Connected CEOs, Corporate Governance and Post-IPO Performance of China's Partially Privitized Firms." *Journal of Financial Economics* 84:330–57.

Francis, Bill B., Iftekhar Hasan, and Xian Sun. 2009. "Political Connections and the Process of Going Public: Evidence from China." *Journal of International Money and Finance* 28 (4): 696–719.

Firth, Michael, Gong-meng Chen, Daniel Ning Gao, and Oliver M. Rui. 2005. "Is China's Securities Regulatory Agency a Toothless Tiger? Evidence from Enforcement Actions." January. http://ssrn.com/abstract=711107.

Fogel, Robert W. 2006. "Why China is Likely to Achieve its Growth Objectives." NBER Working Paper no. 12122. Cambridge, MA: National Bureau of Economic Research, March.

Gordon, Roger H., and Wei Li. 2013. "Provincial and Local Governments in China: Fiscal Institutions and Government Behavior." In *Capitalizing China*, edited by Joseph P. H. Fan and Randall Morck, 337–69. Chicago: University of Chicago Press.

Green, Stephen. 2003. "Better than a Casino: Some Good News from the Front Lines of China's Capital Market Reform." China Project Working Paper. http://papers.ssrn.com/sol3/papers.cfm?abstract_id=431200.

Handal, Kenneth. 1972. "The Commercial Paper Market and the Securities Laws." *University of Chicago Law Review* 39:362–402.

Hellman, Joel, and Mark Schankerman. 2000. "Intervention Corruption and Capture: The Nexus between Enterprises and the State." *Economics of Transition* 8:545–76.

Howson, Nickolas. 2009. "China's Restructured Commercial Banks: Nomenclature Accountability Serving Corporate Governance Reform?" In *China's Emerging Financial Markets,* edited by Martha Avery, Min Zhu, and Jinqing Cai, 123–64. Singapore: John Wiley & Sons.

Hu, Runfeng, Zhe Cheng, and Tao Fu. 2006. "Zhonghang Shenqiu Zhibang Zai Bao Piaoju An [Another Bank of China Shenqiu Branch Receipts Case Explodes]." *Caijing Magazine* 161:40–41.

Huang, Hui. 2008. "The New Takeover Regulation in China: Evolution and Enhancement." *The International Lawyer* 42:153.

Huang, Yasheng. 2007. "The Rural Roots of China's Miracle." *Financial Times,* October 21. http://www.ftchinese.com/story.php?lang=en&storyid=001014907.

———. 2008. *Capitalism with Chinese Characteristics.* Cambridge: Cambridge University Press,

Johnston, Robert. 1968. "The Rebirth of Commercial Paper." *Monthly Review Federal Reserve Bank of San Francisco:* 137–42.

Kahan, Marcel, and Edward B. Rock. 2002. "How I Learned to Stop Worrying and Love the Pill: Adaptive Responses to Takeover Law." *University of Chicago Law Review* 69 (3): 871–915.

Li, Larry, Tony Naughton, and Martin Hovey. 2008. "A Review of Corporate Governance in China." http://ssrn.com/abstract=1233070.

Liebman, Benjamin, and Curtis Milhaupt. 2008. "Reputational Sanctions in China's Securities Market." *Columbia Law Review* 108: 929, 958.

Lipton, Martin. 1997. "Poison Pill Update." *M&A Law* Jul./Aug., 3.

Morck, Randall, Bernard Yeung, and Wayne Yu. 2000. "The Information Content of Stock Markets: Why Do Emerging Markets Have Synchronous Stock Price Movements." *Journal of Finance and Economy* 58: 215.

McKinsey Global Institute. 2006. *Putting China's Capital to Work: The Value of Financial System Reform.* May. http://www.mckinsey.com/mgi/publications/china_capital/index.asp, at 62.

———. 2009. *Global Capital Markets: Entering a New Era.* September. http://www.mckinsey.com/locations/swiss/news_publications/pdf/Global_Capital_Markets_Sept_2009.pdf, at 27.

Pistor, Katharina. 2013. "The Governance of China's Finance." In *Capitalizing China,* edited by Joseph P. H. Fan and Randall Morck, 35–60. Chicago: University of Chicago Press.

Shleifer, A., and L. Summers. 1988. "Breach of Trust in Hostile Takeovers." In *Corporate Takeovers: Causes and Consequences,* edited by A. Auerbach, 33–68. Chicago: University of Chicago Press.

Shanghai Stock Exchange. *Zhongguo Gongsi Zhili Baogao (2008): Shangshi Gongsi Toumingdu yu Xinxi Pilu (2008 PRC Corporate Governance Report: Transparency of Listed Companies and Information Disclosure).* http://www.sse.com.cn/cs/zhs/xxfw/research/special/special20081120.pdf.

Shanghai Stock Exchange. Monthly Statistic Report. http://www.sse.com.cn/sseportal/ps/zhs/yjcb/sztjyb.shtml.

Shen, Han. 2008. "A Comparative Study of Insider Trading Regulation Enforcement in the U.S. and China." *Journal of Business and Securities Law* 9:41–74.

Shen, Yan, Minggao Shen, Zhong Xu, and Ying Bai. 2009. "Bank Size and Small- and Medium-sized Enterprise (SME) Lending: Evidence from China." *World Development* 37: 800.

Shenzhen Stock Exchange. 2002. *Zhongwai Xinxi Pilu Zhidu Ji Shiji Xiaoguo Bijiao Yanjiu (Comparative Study of the Information Disclosure System and Effects).* http://www.cninfo.com.cn/finalpage/2002-04-23/590499.PDF.

Shenzhen Stock Exchange. 2008. "Key Issues relating to the Review of Public Offering Applications and An Analysis of Rejected Applications." http://www.szse.cn /main/images/2008/11/10/20081110152952164.pdf.

Tam, Kit. 2002. "Ethical Issues in the Evolution of Corporate Governance in China." *Journal of Business Ethics* 37: 305, 307.

Tan, Wentao. 2006. "History of China's Stock Markets." In *China's Financial Markets: An Insider's Guide to How the Markets Work,* edited by Salih N. Neftci and Michelle Yuan Menager-Xu, 215–36. Burlington, MA: Academic Press.

Thurow, Lester, Ning Zhou, and Yunshi Wang. 2003. "The PRC's Real Economic Growth Rate." www.oes.org/pdf/presentations/lesterthurow/pdf.

Tuan, Jason, JinXin Zhang, Jason Hsu, and Qiusheng Zhang. 2007. *Merger Arbitrage Profitability in China.* http://www.ssrn.com/abstract=992650.

US Securities and Exchange Commission (SEC). 2005. *Annual Report of US Securities and Exchange Commission,* 7. http://www.sec.gov/about/secpar/secpar2005 .pdf#sec1.

———. 2006. *Annual Report of US Securities and Exchange Commission,* 8. http:// www.sec.gov/about/secpar/secpar2006.pdf#sec1.

———. 2007. *Annual Report of US Securities and Exchange Commission,* 25. http:// www.sec.gov/about/secpar/secpar2007.pdf#sec1.

———. 2008. *Annual Report of US Securities and Exchange Commission,* 12. http:// www.sec.gov/about/secpar/secpar2008.pdf#sec1.

Wei Yu. 2009. "Party Control in China's Listed Firms." http://ssrn.com/abstract =1326205.

Wong, S. M. L., S. Opper, and R. Hu. 2004. "Shareholder Structure, Depoliticalization, and Firm Performance: Lessons from China's Listed Firms." *Economics of Transition* 12:29–66.

World Federation of Exchanges (WFE). 2009. *Annual Report and Statistics 2007.* Accessed April 1, 2009. http://www.world-exchanges.org/files/file/2007%20WFE %20Annual%20Report.pdf, at 74.

Xie, Baishan, Xuelai Dai, and Lan Xu. 2003. "Comparative Study of US and Chinese Securities Markets." In *International Comparison of Securities Markets 3–4,* edited by Baisan Xie, 535–50. Beijing: Tsinghua University Press.

Xie, Zhihong, and Mingtian Chen. 2001. "Guhong Paisheng Susong Zai Sikao [Rethinking Shareholder Derivative Suits]." *Fuijian ZhengFa Guanli Ganbu Xueyuan Xue bao [Journal of the Fuijian Politcal-Leghal Administrative Cadre Institute* 4: 24.

Xiu Shi-yu, and Liu Chang. 2008. "The Degree of IPO Underpricing in China." *Journal of Modern Accounting and Auditing* 4 (4): 32–36.

Zhang, Wenkui. 2002. "The Role of China's Securities Market in SOE Reform and Private Sector Development." http://www.tcf.or.jp/data/20020307-08_Wengkui _Zhang.pdf.

Zhang Yujun. 2005. "Developing the SME Board and Encourage the Growth of SMEs." http://www.sme.gov.cn/web/assembly/action/browsePage.do?channel ID=1129097785944&contentID=1130306361557.

Zhou, Weimin, Zhongguo Zheng, and Jian Hui. 1998. "A Critique of the Shortcomings of the CSRC's Temporary Rules on Prohibiting Entry to the Securities Market." *FaXue* [Legal Science] 4:60–61.

Comment   Qiao Liu

The current chapter by William T. Allen and Han Shen (henceforth AS) assesses the Chinese securities markets from aspects that are of central concern in developing these markets: the positioning of securities markets in the national system of finance, their size and scope, their evolution pattern, the regulatory environment, and the corporate governance of the Chinese listed firms. Allen and Shen carefully document and discuss at length several key characteristics of the Chinese securities markets, including the share segmentation system, the state sector centric market design, concentrated ownership structures, low level of liquidity and poor pricing efficiency, limited market access for the private sector, the contradictory mandates of the CSRC (China Securities Regulatory Commission, the watchdog of the Chinese capital markets), and the control-based corporate governance mechanisms used by the listed firms. Allen and Shen characterize the Chinese securities markets as top-down markets designed by the government to ensure the state purposes. As such, these markets deem to be politically driven and cannot exert significant economic effects on the Chinese economy. The authors also conclude that the further development of China's securities markets hinges on whether the Chinese government is willing to give up the control over these markets and allow them to serve basic economic roles rather than the state purposes.

This chapter offers many structured details to illustrate the top-down nature of the Chinese securities markets. Such illustrations contribute to the understanding of the approaches used by the Chinese government to develop capital markets and assist interested readers, especially those with little knowledge about China, to understand the working of the Chinese securities markets.

I have two principal concerns about the thesis of this chapter. First, as I will show later, I believe that top-down is an oversimplified characterization of the Chinese securities markets. Second, AS overemphasize the state sector in their analysis and fail to consider the quick surge of the private sector.

Qiao Liu is professor of finance and of economics at Guanghua School of Management, Peking University.

For acknowledgments, sources of research support, and disclosure of the author's material financial relationships, if any, please see http://www.nber.org/chapters/c12461.ack.

This missing link, as I will show, is arguably a more important shaper of the future of the Chinese securities markets.

Top-Down Meets Bottom-Up

Although I agree with AS on all the facts provided in their chapter, I believe that top-down is an oversimplified characterization. Several more fundamental institutional factors shape the Chinese securities markets. Some of them are top-down, and some are bottom-up.

Allen and Shen correctly point out that the purposes of developing the securities markets in China are twofold: one is to find alternative financing sources for the state sector, and the other is to improve the state sector's governance and efficiency. However, together with this top-down consideration, several other factors are also in a full play to shape the Chinese securities markets. These factors include a weak legal system and law enforcement, strong ties between politics and business, poorly developed financial intermediation that leaves the general public with fewer investment vehicles and hence fosters their enthusiasm about the securities markets, and the retail investors' dominated investor base. In such an institutional context, the Chinese government naturally chose an "administrative governance" approach to actively control the securities markets. The regulatory authorities, especially the CSRC, also have to take balancing acts between control and growth, instead of acts solely for the purpose of control.

The top-down nature of the Chinese securities markets is therefore a reflection of these driving forces. More fundamental institutional factors lie underneath the control approach used in the Chinese markets. This understanding yields a very different policy implication—the further development of the Chinese securities markets, to a great extent, depends on the overall intuitional improvement rather than the government's willingness to give up their control.

Take the following as one example: many conclusions in AS result from their analysis of the share segmentation system, which has its root traced back to the specific Chinese institutional background. Without improving overall institutions, even a complete reform of the share segmentation system, which as a matter of fact is under way, cannot solve problems in China's capital markets.

The State Sector versus the Private Sector

Allen and Shen's characterization of the Chinese securities markets as top-down is largely due to the focus of their analysis on the state-controlled listed firms in China, which used to account for more than 90 percent of China's listed firms. However, the structure of the Chinese stock markets is changing significantly over time—more and more listed firms are now controlled by families or groups of individuals with concerted actions. Table

3C.1, which is modified from a table in Liu, Zheng, and Zhu (2010), shows that from 2001 to 2008, the faction of the privately-controlled listed firm increased from 12.2 to 35.8 percent. If this trend continues, the private firms very likely will account for more than 50 percent of China's listed firms by 2015. Notably, the quick surge of the private sector in the Chinese stock markets was not planned by the government. It is largely driven by the market mechanisms and the changes in the institutional environment.

Since the private firms are now playing an increasingly important role in the Chinese markets, an assessment of the Chinese securities markets should factor them into the analysis. Firms controlled by individuals or families differ from the state-controlled listed firms in many ways. As shown in table

Table 3C.1   **Corporate ownership structures of the Chinese listed firms by ownership types of the ultimate controllers**

	2001	2002	2003	2004	2005	2006	2007	2008	Total
Central state-controlled listed firms									
No. of firms	199	210	230	232	239	244	264	280	1,898
Layer	3.734	3.757	3.774	3.819	3.887	3.898	3.939	4.000	3.860
Control rights	0.484	0.489	0.476	0.472	0.461	0.431	0.434	0.435	0.458
Ownership	0.432	0.435	0.416	0.410	0.400	0.374	0.377	0.377	0.400
OC	0.883	0.871	0.852	0.846	0.850	0.859	0.861	0.855	0.859
Control rights–Ownership wedge	0.052	0.054	0.060	0.062	0.060	0.058	0.057	0.059	0.058
Local state-controlled listed firms									
No. of firms	660	662	640	644	619	571	568	569	4,933
Layer	3.136	3.160	3.211	3.244	3.278	3.317	3.347	3.404	3.257
Control rights	0.483	0.483	0.479	0.473	0.458	0.416	0.416	0.422	0.455
Ownership	0.463	0.459	0.451	0.441	0.424	0.380	0.378	0.381	0.424
OC	0.955	0.945	0.934	0.926	0.918	0.908	0.900	0.898	0.924
Control rights–Ownership wedge	0.020	0.024	0.028	0.032	0.034	0.036	0.038	0.040	0.031
Privately-controlled listed firms									
No. of firms	129	178	237	317	332	377	435	474	2,479
Layer	3.698	3.753	3.654	3.546	3.593	3.531	3.421	3.344	3.522
Control rights	0.355	0.341	0.347	0.353	0.346	0.343	0.360	0.370	0.354
Ownership	0.212	0.196	0.216	0.225	0.219	0.225	0.256	0.267	0.234
OC	0.579	0.567	0.603	0.623	0.621	0.642	0.699	0.709	0.647
Control rights–Ownership wedge	0.142	0.144	0.132	0.128	0.127	0.118	0.104	0.103	0.120

Notes: The table is modified from table 3 in Liu, Zheng, and Zhu (2010). It reports the means of variables measuring the extent of corporate pyramids by the ownership types of the ultimate controllers over 2001 to 2008. The sample includes all listed firms, with the ultimate owners controlling at least 20 percent of voting rights. The sample accounts for more than 93 percent of the universe of the Chinese listed firms. "Layer" is the number of intermediate layers between the ultimate controller and the listed firm. "OC" is the ratio of ownership rights to control rights. "Wedge" is defined as control rights minus ownership rights.

3.1, a comparison of the ownership structures of the privately-controlled and the state-controlled listed firms shows that (a) both the private owners and the state owners build extensive pyramidal structures, and the ones built by the private owners tend to be more extensive; (b) the evolution trajectories for the privately-controlled and the state-controlled pyramids are divergent in China from 2001 to 2008—while the privately-controlled pyramids become streamlined over time (measured by an increasing OC and a decreasing Wedge), the local state-controlled pyramids get more extensive over time.

This dichotomy shows that the private and state owners in China respond to the changing economic and institutional conditions in different ways. Fan, Wong, and Zhang (2010) find that quality of institutions affects the extent of the local state-controlled pyramids. Specifically, the local states tend to build more extensive pyramidal structures in the listed firms when they are subject to a greater degree of market and legal discipline. They also find that the extent of local state-controlled pyramids is positively correlated with firm performance because corporate pyramids allow the ultimate government owners to transfer decision rights to professional managers, and effectively separate firm management from political interferences. Liu, Zheng, and Zhu (2010) further point out that the quality of institutions affects the privately-controlled pyramids in an exactly opposite way. The private owners build more extensive corporate pyramids when they are subject to a lesser degree of market and legal discipline and more political discretion; the extent of pyramidal structures is negatively correlated with the performance of the private firms.

The dichotomy just discussed thus highlights the importance of distinguishing the private ownership and the state ownership in understanding the Chinese listed firms and the Chinese capital markets. A more complete assessment of the Chinese capital markets should consider these differences.

Concluding Remarks

Allen and Shen depict the Chinese securities markets as some sort of caged creature designed by the Chinese government to serve the state purposes. This depiction is largely true for these markets in their early development stages. However, this creature has already grown bigger than the cage. The changes in the institutional environment and the surge of the private sector have greatly changed the nature of the Chinese securities markets. The top-down forces driven by the government are meeting with the bottom-up forces driven by the market system. Mapping out such interactions and understanding their dynamics are the key to assess the Chinese securities markets and understand their future developments.

References

Fan J., T. J. Wong, and T. Zhang. 2010. "Institutions and Organizational Structure: The Case of State-Owned Corporate Pyramids." Working Paper. Chinese University of Hong Kong.

Liu, Q., Y. Zheng, and Y. Zhu. 2010. "The Evolution and Consequence of the Chinese Pyramids." Working Paper. University of Hong Kong.

4

Institutions and Information Environment of Chinese Listed Firms

Joseph D. Piotroski and T. J. Wong

The objective of this chapter is to describe the financial reporting practices and information environment of Chinese listed firms, to document the influence that local and national institutions have on reporting incentives and the resultant information environment in China, and to discuss how actual and potential changes in China's institutional and regulatory environment are expected to impact the country's information environment.

Following the framework outlined in Bushman, Piotroski, and Smith (2004), we define corporate transparency as the widespread availability of firm-specific information to those market participants outside the publicly-traded firm. At the country-level, we recognize that corporate transparency is the output of a multifaceted system whose components collectively produce, gather, validate, and disseminate information to market participants outside the firm. This output is generated by country, regional, and firm-level information mechanisms that fall under three broad headings: (1) the corporate reporting regime, which includes the quality of the firm's financial reports and the underlying audit function; (2) the intensity of private information acquisition activities, which includes the depth and breadth of

Joseph D. Piotroski is associate professor of accounting at the Graduate School of Business, Stanford University. T. J. Wong is dean of CUHK Business School and a professor of accountancy at the Chinese University of Hong Kong.

This chapter has benefited from the comments of Joseph Fan and Randall Morck (editors), Li Jin (discussant), Bernard Yeung, and participants at the NBER "Capitalizing China" conference held at the Chinese University of Hong Kong in December 2009. Professor Piotroski acknowledges the financial support of Stanford University's Graduate School of Business. Professor Piotroski was the John A. Gunn and Cynthia Fry Gunn Faculty Scholar for 2010–2011. Professor Wong acknowledges the support of the Institute of Economics and Finance and the Center for Institutions and Governance of the Chinese University of Hong Kong. For acknowledgments, sources of research support, and disclosure of the authors' material financial relationships, if any, please see http://www.nber.org/chapters/c12076.ack.

analyst and institutional investor activity; and (3) the strength of dissemination mechanisms, including the role of media and freedom of the press. This framework allows us to systematically document China's information environment and forms the basis for assessing the expected informational consequences of various institutional and market reforms in China. Given our background as accountants, specific attention is paid to the impact of the financial reporting system and audit function on the information environment in China.

It is well-established that the widespread availability of information is a key determinant of the efficiency of resource allocation decisions and growth in an economy. For example, at the heart of most theories about financial development is the key role that financial markets play in the reduction of information and transaction costs in an economy. Similarly, greater transparency and stricter disclosure standards have the capability of strengthening corporate governance by improving monitoring and limiting the consumption of private benefits by controlling shareholders, resulting in better asset management and investment decisions (e.g., Rajan and Zingales 2003; Stulz 1999; Doidge 2004; Doidge, Karolyi, and Stulz 2004). Consistent with these arguments, countries with strong information environments have been shown to garner significant benefits in terms of greater economic development, lower costs of capital, better functioning capital markets, greater foreign investor interest, and higher valuations. As such, greater corporate transparency has the potential to help developing economies such as China.

In spite of the developmental benefits arising from transparency, financial reporting practices and the resultant information environment are not exogenously determined; instead, reporting practices are the outcome of competing incentives for and against transparency. Given the concentrated ownership structures, weak legal systems, highly politicized institutional arrangements, rent-seeking behavior, and corruption that characterize many developing economies, the benefits from opacity frequently outweigh the market and contracting-based benefits of transparency. As a result, many emerging economies, including China, suffer from opaque information environments and weak corporate transparency.

In the case of China, great strides have been taken in the last decade in an attempt to improve corporate governance, accountability and transparency at both the state and firm level. Regulations mandating convergence toward IFRS (International Financial Reporting Standards), the use of IAAS (International Auditing and Assurance Standards), the presence of independent directors and limits on insider trading activity, along with broad government disclosure reforms and significant anticorruption programs, have been implemented with the goal of improving the investing environment in China. Yet despite these recent institutional and regulatory improvements, China's financial markets continue to be plagued by weak information systems and, as a result, low-quality financial information.

The objective of this chapter is to provide a deeper understanding of China's information environment and the impact that the underlying institutional structure has on the financial reporting practices and information environment of publicly listed firms in China. Section 4.1 provides an overview of the information environment in China vis-à-vis other developed and developing economies. Section 4.2 describes the influence of China's legal, political, financial, and regulatory institutions on financial reporting incentives and the resultant information environment. Section 4.3 describes the state of information acquisition and dissemination activities in China. Section 4.4 concludes by outlining the expected impact of current and future institutional changes on the information environment of China's listed firms.

4.1   Information Environment of China's Listed Firms

The suppression of bad news remains an unedifying habit that dies hard on the Mainland.
—*South China Morning Post, June 2007*

Even in a China that is more capitalist than ever, the instinctive official response to bad news is to suppress it with all the force available to the nominally communist state.
—*Financial Times, July 2007*

Local politicians suppressed a company report about tainted milk powder until the completion of the Olympic Games to avoid "creating a negative influence on society."
—*The People's Daily, October 2008*

The influence of the State and politicians on China's information environment is a well-documented, publicized, and vigorously discussed topic both within and outside China. Although much has changed since the start of Deng Xiaopeng's economic reforms and his famous "southern excursion," information remains a powerful tool in the hands of China's local politicians and leaders. Currently, cultural and political incentives exist in China that prevents the widespread dissemination of unbiased information in a timely basis. The incentives for opacity span across a wide range of settings and topics, from environmental and health issues (e.g., tainted milk scandal, SARS and Bird Flu outbreaks) to government policy and actions (e.g., events of June 4, 1989) to demographic and economic data (e.g., growth data during the Asian Financial Crisis).

Given the rapid growth and increasing importance of China's capital markets, the natural question is whether the incentives for opacity extend to the financial markets and affect the reporting practices of Chinese listed firms. Investors, especially foreign investors, have a demand for timely, unbiased financial information to assess the risks, payoffs, and value of listed entities and other investment opportunities in the country. The demand for transparency also arises for stewardship purposes; credible financial reporting facilitates monitoring by both controlling and minority shareholders and allows for more efficient contracting arrangements, potentially resulting in better corporate governance practices and improved decision making at the firm level. Reporting firms have an incentive to supply this information to reap these benefits and to minimize the adverse pricing and resource allocation consequences arising from information asymmetry and illiquidity.

Despite these market-based and contracting-based incentives for transparency, there exist countervailing political, legal, and cultural incentives for opacity in China. Factors shaping these incentives include the desire to minimize political costs associated with the reporting bad outcomes, the need to hide expropriation and/or rent-seeking behavior, the importance of relationship-based contracting and social connections, and the effects of institutional arrangements that attenuate demand for information and high-quality audits (e.g., weak protection of property rights, concentrated ownership, limited contracting role for accounting). As a result of these countervailing pressures, China's capital markets are frequently ranked as one of the least transparent of the world's large economies.

The following sections present descriptive evidence on the quality of the information environment of Chinese listed firms using survey data and cross-country empirical evidence on the behavior of stock prices and financial reporting practices.

4.1.1 Standards and Regulations

On the basis of regulations and standards alone, the information environment for China's listed firms should be strong. As noted in the China Securities Regulatory Commission's (CRSC) 2008 annual report, one of the primary objectives of the commission is to "give priority to protecting the legitimate rights and interests of investors . . . and maintaining the principles of an 'open, fair and just' market." At the heart of these objectives is a need for greater corporate transparency to increase the ability of investors, stakeholders, and the State to monitor the activities of listed firms. To that end, the CSRC has adopted US and European-style regulations and standards that promote transparency and strong corporate governance practices.

In terms of disclosure requirements, current CSRC regulations and the exchange rules of the Shanghai and Shenzhen Stock Exchanges require all listed Chinese firms to make periodic disclosures of the company's business activities and financial performance.[1] These rules and regulations require all listed firms to provide an "annual report" within four months of the end of

---

1. Disclosure rules for Chinese listed firms can be found in chapter 3, section 3 of the Securities Law of the People's Republic of China (as amended August 29, 2004) and chapter VI of the Rules Governing the Listing of Stocks on the Shanghai Stock Exchange.

each fiscal year, an "interim report" within two months following the end of the first half of each fiscal year, and "quarterly reports" within one month following the end of the first three and nine months of a given fiscal year. All annual reports are required to be audited by a qualified CPA firm. Quarterly reports are exempt from an audit requirement, while interim reports require an audit if the company plans to distribute profits, transfer reserves into share capital, or use the reserve to offset losses in the next half of the fiscal year. For accountability purposes, the directors and senior officers of the company are required to sign their opinion of consent or dissent to each periodic report, and if the financial report of the listed company is issued a modified opinion, directors are required to provide a specific explanation and express a specific opinion on the matter to which the modified audit opinion relates.

In addition to these periodic reporting requirements, listed firms are also required to file "ad hoc" reports when a "major event" occurs that is not yet known to investors and may considerably affect the price at which the firm's securities are traded. All reports and announcements are required to be published in the media outlet(s) specified by the relevant department of the State, as well as filed with the relevant stock exchange and the CSRC. Finally, all reports and announcements are required to be "truthful, accurate and complete; they may not contain any falsehoods, misleading statements or major omissions." Together, these reporting requirements should produce timely and accurate disclosures about corporate activities, operating performance, and the firm's financial conditional.

The CSRC has also implemented a series of regulations specifically designed to improve the quality of financial reporting and auditing practices of publicly-traded Chinese firms. The most noteworthy action in this area was the harmonization of Chinese accounting standards with International Financial Reporting Standards (2006) and, ultimately, the issuance of regulations mandating that listed firms comply with IFRS (effective January 1, 2007). Additionally, the CSRC has recently implemented new auditing standards and stricter auditor guidelines (effective January 1, 2007); these new rules follow the earlier adoption of International Auditing Standards in 1994. Together, these regulatory actions have the potential to improve the quality of the published financial reports through the convergence of Chinese practices with high-quality, globally-accepted standards and practices.

Finally, outside the direct realm of financial reporting, the CSRC has issued regulations to improve corporate governance and to reduce the incentives for directors and managers to withhold information from capital market participants. These regulations include stricter requirements for independent board membership, limitations on insider trading activity, penalties for activities that manipulate stock markets, and greater personal liability for the managers, supervisors, and directors of the listed firm for losses arising from "falsehoods, misleading statements or major omissions." The

Chinese government has also introduced numerous ordinances and reforms designed to promote greater transparency and accountability within government and to counter political corruption. These actions have the potential to improve the investing environment in China, and should have a spillover effect on the information environment of listed firms by removing, or at least attenuating, some of the institutional frictions and costs that impede firm-level disclosure practices and inhibit the information acquisition and dissemination activities of market participants.

Unfortunately, it is possible that these reporting standards and regulations simply amount to "window dressing," adopted to ameliorate the concerns of foreign and domestic investors without producing any meaningful change in the information environment or governance practices (e.g., Berkowitz, Pistor, and Richard 2003; Allen and Shen 2011). Absent a commensurate increase in enforcement activities, existing institutional arrangements and cultural factors have the potential to erode the efficacy of these standards and regulations in practice. Ultimately, any assessment of China's information environment should be evaluated on the basis of practices and outcomes, not standards and regulations alone. The following sections outline this evidence.

4.1.2   Evidence from the Behavior of Stock Prices

Through the price formation process, market prices aggregate all available information. The accuracy and efficiency of these prices is influenced by numerous factors, including the disclosure practices of the listed firms, the acquisition and processing activities of information intermediaries, the effectiveness of information dissemination mechanisms, and the expected costs and benefits of arbitrage. As such, the behavior of stock prices represents one means of assessing the information environment of Chinese listed companies.

In an efficient market, stock prices react instantaneously and completely to new information; firm-level residual returns display minimal cross-sectional correlation, no serial correlation, and approximate a log normal distribution. In markets with a limited flow of firm-specific information or significant trading frictions, stock returns will not take on these characteristics. Specifically, a limited supply of firm-specific information is expected to produce firm-level stock returns that are highly synchronized with general market movements (e.g., Roll 1988; Morck, Yeung, and Yu 2000; Durnev et al. 2003), while the systematic suppression of bad news will produce a stock return distribution that is significantly left skewed and subject to a greater frequency of stock return crashes (Jin and Myers 2006; Chen, Hong, and Stein 2001). Finally, the presence of market frictions, the absence of arbitrageurs and the activities of noise traders can result in a delayed reaction to new information, yielding serial correlated returns and momentum effects (Jegadeesh and Titman 1993; Chan, Jegadeesh, and Lakonishok 1996). Stock prices on China's exchanges exhibit all of these characteristics.

First, China's stock prices exhibit high levels of comovement. In their seminal study on stock return synchronicity, Morck, Yeung, and Yu (2000) measure the average comovement of weekly returns for securities traded on the local exchanges of forty countries during 1995. Measured as both (a) the fraction of security prices moving together in an average week and (b) as the average R^2 of firm-level regressions of firm-level returns on local and US market indices, stock return synchronicity is designed to inversely measure the amount of firm-specific information being impounded into firm-level stock prices (see Roll 1998). Essentially, the synchronization of stock returns in a given market are expected to increase (decrease) in the absence (presence) of new firm-specific information.

Morck, Young, and Yu (2000) find that, on average, 57.9 percent of US stock prices move together in a given week, and market returns can be explained for approximately 2.1 percent of variation in firm-level returns. These percentages are the lowest of all surveyed countries, consistent with strong information and regulatory environment that characterizes US markets. In contrast, Morck, Young, and Yu (2000) find that nearly 80 percent of Chinese stocks move together in an average week, and market returns explain approximately 45.3 percent of the variation in weekly firm-level returns.[2] These statistics highlight the significant differences that exist in both the information and regulatory environments of the mature US market versus the developing Chinese market.

More striking, however, is the behavior of stock prices in China relative to the complete sample of developed and developing countries. Out of forty countries examined, China ranked second in terms of stock return synchronicity using both measures. This compares very unfavorably to the fraction of comovement in weekly returns documented in other large economies (e.g., UK = 63.1 percent; Germany = 61.1 percent; Japan = 66.6 percent), in other large emerging economies (e.g., Brazil = 64.7 percent; India = 69.5 percent), and in Hong Kong (67.8 percent).[3] Similarly, over the longer period 1991 to 2000, Jin and Myers (2006) find that Chinese firms displayed the highest level of stock return synchronicity out of the forty countries included in their study. Together, the evidence suggests that one of the defining characteristics of the Chinese stock market—highly synchronized stock price movements—is likely an artifact of the country's weak information environment.

Second, current research suggests that Chinese stocks are more crash prone than the global average. As discussed in Chen, Hong, and Stein (2001), a failure to release negative information in a timely manner will ultimately

2. Gul, Kim, and Qiu (2010) find, over the period 1996 to 2003, that daily market and industry returns explain approximately 45.4 percent of the variation in daily firm-level returns. Moreover, as discussed in section 4.3, the level of stock return synchronicity observed is a function of the firm's ownership structure and audit quality.

3. Of the countries included in the study, only Poland exhibited greater stock return synchronicity during the sample period (82.9 percent).

produce a larger subsequent price reaction when the information reaches the market. Consistent with large stock price crashes being driven by previously suppressed news, Jin and Myers (2006) show that the skewness of negative returns is inversely related to the level of disclosure in an economy. Although Jin and Myers do not specifically examine Chinese data, Piotroski, Wong, and Zhang (2011) show that the negative skewness in daily excess returns in China is significantly greater than the global average documented in Jin and Myers (2006), consistent with the existence of local incentives to suppress the release of bad news. Thus, a second key attribute of China's stock markets—a heightened risk of large negative stock price crashes—can also relate to the country's weak information environment.

Third, stock prices in China exhibit strong momentum effects. Using data from the Shanghai Stock Exchange's domestic A share market, Kang, Liu, and Ni (2002) and Naughton, Truong, and Veeraraghavan (2008) document the profitability of momentum investment strategies over the periods 1993 to 2000 and 1995 to 2005, respectively. The authors provide evidence that momentum returns arise from the delayed impounding of firm-specific information, and that these portfolio returns are robust to numerous alternative explanations (bid-ask bounce; nonsynchronous trading effects; size effect) and considerations for transaction costs. Subsequent work suggests that some of the documented momentum effects could also be the result of powerful, speculative investors manipulating stock prices through a so-called "pump and dump" strategy (He and Su 2009; Khwaja and Mian 2005). Additionally, momentum effects could reflect the correlated behavioral biases of unsophisticated investors; such an explanation is plausible because Chinese retail investors, who tend to be very sensitive to short-term sentiment effects, are the predominant noncontrolling shareholders in Chinese listed firms (e.g., Choi, Jin, and Yan 2010). Regardless of the cause, the presence of momentum patterns in Chinese price data highlights potential deficiencies in both the information environment and the price formation process for publicly listed firms in China.

Together, this market-based evidence highlights some of the weaknesses in China's information environment. The next two sections will provide descriptive and contextual evidence on the nature of these deficiencies.

4.1.3   Survey Evidence

Each year, numerous country reports and surveys are published that assess the various legal, financial, and political risks associated with investing in foreign (and especially emerging) markets. These reports include the World Bank's "Doing Business Guide," the Heritage Foundation's "Economic Freedom of the World" country reports, and Transparency International's "Corruption Perception Index." As a part of these assessments, the underlying surveys frequently evaluate the country's financial reporting regime, the openness of government about financial policies and budgets, the country's record of protecting investor rights and enforcing contracts, and other aspects of the institutional environment that can affect the supply of and demand for timely and unbiased information. As a principle destination for foreign investment, China tends to be prominently featured in these surveys.

In a seminal survey on global transparency, PricewaterhouseCoopers (2001) assessed five country-level factors that contribute to or diminish the transparency of capital markets and the country's overall economic environment: level of perceived corruption, the legal system, economic policy at the government level, accounting and reporting standards, and the regulatory regime. Out of the original thirty-five countries surveyed by PricewaterhouseCoopers (PwC), China ranked last in overall transparency (an opacity score of 87 out of 100), and was ahead of only North Korea in terms of the transparency of its accounting and financial reporting standards (accounting opacity score of 86 out of 100).

Since the original PwC survey, the Opacity Index has been produced by both the Kurtzman Group (2004) and the Milken Institute (2006 and 2008). These later versions of the survey have been expanded to include a larger set of developing countries and remeasured to capture fundamental changes in these economies. These recent surveys document two important facts about overall transparency in China. First, there has been a gradual improvement in the overall information environment over time; the Opacity Index fell from a score of 50 to 42 (out of 100) over the period 2004 to 2009. This improvement is principally driven by the aforementioned improvements to China's regulatory and legal environment and the implementation of specific exchange-level reporting and auditing requirements. Second, despite the improvement in China's overall score, the country continues to rank as one of the least transparent economies surveyed, ranking thirty-eighth (tied) out of forty-eight countries in the 2009 survey.

Focusing strictly on accounting and financial reporting transparency, similar conclusions are reached by these surveys (see table 4.1). First, China has experienced a significant relative improvement in its opacity score for "accounting and financial disclosure," improving from 56 to 40 (out of 100) over the period 2004 to 2009. This improvement mimics the general global trend toward transparency over the last decade. Second, despite this improvement on an absolute basis, China's accounting opacity score of forty continues to be the fourth-worst among the forty-eight countries surveyed in 2008; only Colombia, Saudi Arabia, and Nigeria fare worse. By contrast, other large emerging economies received accounting opacity scores of 26 (Russia), 29 (India), and 36 (Brazil), while China's Special Administrative Region of Hong Kong received an opacity score of 1.

Other reports offer similar conclusions about the opacity of China's financial reporting environment. For example, the World Economic Forum's *Global Competitiveness Report* (2011) specifically assessed the strength of

Table 4.1   Descriptive statistics on China's accounting, audit, and disclosure standards: Survey evidence

	Opacity index (score)[a]				Global competitiveness report (ranking)[b]	
	2001	2004	2008	2009	2008	2011
China	86	56	41	40	86	61
United States	25	20	20	20	20	40
United Kingdom	45	33	10	11	17	15
Germany	—	17	10	10	14	36
Japan	81	22	21	21	44	35
Brazil	63	40	37	36	60	49
India	79	30	29	29	30	51
Russia	81	40	26	26	108	120
Hong Kong	53	33	1	1	1	12
Malaysia	—	30	29	30	33	25
Singapore	38	50	14	14	7	3
South Korea	90	30	30	30	36	96
Taiwan	56	40	30	30	53	30
Thailand	78	20	21	21	58	56

[a]Score captures opacity in accounting standards and corporate governance practices.
[b]Ranking captures the strength of auditing and reporting standards in the country.

auditing and financial disclosures in 142 countries. Similar to the conclusions drawn from the Opacity Index, China ranked sixty-first out of the 134 countries surveyed in the 2011 report, well below the rankings of key developed economies. By contrast, the other large developing economies were ranked fifty-first (India), forty-ninth (Brazil), and one hundred twentieth (Russian Federation), while local Asian economies Malaysia, Taiwan, and Hong Kong were ranked twenty-fifth, third, and twelfth, respectively.

Together, these surveys identify three important characteristics about China's information environment. First, overall transparency in China has been improving over the last decade in response to better regulation, stronger enforcement actions, and increasing demand from foreign investors. Second, despite these improving trends, overall transparency in China continues to lag at the levels observed in developed economies, such as the United States, United Kingdom, and Japan, the world's largest developing economies, especially India and Brazil, regional economies, such as Singapore, Taiwan, and Malaysia, and China's own SAR of Hong Kong. Lastly, these overall trends and rankings also apply to the financial reporting environment of China's listed firms, thus providing evidence on one dimension of corporate transparency that is likely contributing to the highly synchronized, crash prone, and serially correlated stock price behavior documented in prior research.

4.1.4 Financial Reporting Practices

The preceding survey and returns-based evidence highlights the weak information environment surrounding China's listed firms. At the heart of the weak information environment are deficiencies with respect to the financial reporting and audit practices of China's listed firms. As outlined in section 4.1.1, the reporting requirements of Chinese listed firms mimic those used in most Western markets, and are designed to increase the supply of high-quality financial reports to market participants. Similarly, over the last two decades, market development and deregulation activities have increased the external demand for information about Chinese securities. Yet, despite these regulatory and market changes, the aforementioned surveys continually rank the quality of China's financial reporting practices as low relative to peer countries. These reporting deficiencies, and the adverse reporting incentives surrounding many of China's listed firms, have been illustrated recently by a string of high-profile accounting frauds committed by firms listed on foreign stock exchanges (e.g., Longtop, Media Express, Shangda Tech, Sino-Forest), and by the response of several key market participants to these scandals (e.g., research reports written by Moody's and Fitch). The natural questions are: how do financial reporting and accounting practices in China differ from the rest of the world? And, given that these differences exist, what local institutional factors create this disparity?

Unfortunately, to answer these questions, few studies directly compares the actual financial reporting and disclosure practices of Chinese firms against the reporting practices of other countries within the same study. For example, Bhattacharya, Daouk and Welker's (2003) examination of the link between accounting opacity and cost of capital, Leuz, Nanda and Wysocki's (2003) study of earnings management around the world and Bushman, Piotroski and Smith's (2004) study of corporate transparency around world and Fan and Wong's (2002) examination of earnings informativeness in east Asian countries all include Hong Kong firms in their respective samples, but do not include PRC-listed firms. Similarly, earlier seminal studies on the informativeness of earnings (e.g., Alford et al. 1993) and the properties of accounting numbers around the world (e.g., Ball, Kothari, and Robin 2000) only focus on large, developed economies.[4]

Despite these data limitations, there exists some key evidence on the overall quality of accounting practices in China. The most striking observation about the reported earnings of Chinese firms is the clustering of firm-level ROE realizations around 0, 6, and 10 percent annually (see figure 4.1, panel A). Because the CSRC uses bright-line regulatory benchmarks to

4. One constraint is that numerous cross-country studies exclude communist and former-communist countries from their research design. Additionally, early cross-country studies of corporate reporting and accounting practices excluded China from their databases because of limited data availability during the early 1990s.

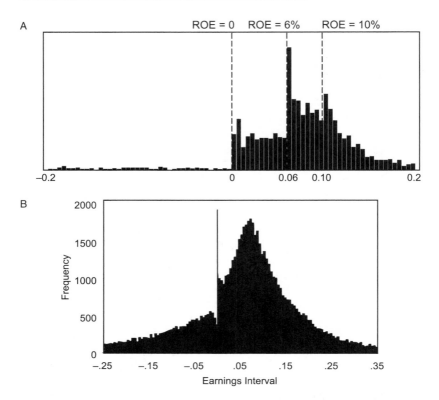

Fig. 4.1   Panel *A*: Distribution of return on equity realizations of Chinese listed firms, histogram of ROE for China's listed companies from 1999 to 2001; panel *B*: Distribution of return on equity realizations for US listed firms

Sources: Liu (2006); Burgstahler and Dichev (1997).

Notes: The distribution of annual net income (Compustat item # 172) scaled by beginning of the year market value (Compustat item # 25 × Compustat item # 199). The distribution interval widths are 0.005 and the location of zero on the horizontal axis is marked by the dashed line. When the interval width is 0.005, the first interval to the right of zero contains all observations in the interval [0.000, 0.005), the second interval contains [0.005, 0.010), and so on. "Frequency" is the number of observations in a given earnings interval.

grant approvals for IPOs and rights offerings and to initiate performance-related delistings, listed Chinese firms have an incentive to manage reported earnings to meet these specific performance benchmarks. As a result, a disproportionate number of Chinese firms report ROE realizations around the CSRC's historical performance benchmarks of 0, 6, and 10 percent. Moreover, there is almost a complete absence of loss-making firms in China. These distributional characteristics are especially striking when compared against a similar distribution of earnings realizations for US listed firms that do not face bright-line regulatory benchmarks (figure 4.1, panel B). Specifically, reported accounting realizations in China are influenced by the CSRC regulatory benchmarks, as evidenced by the concentration of ROE realizations at or above the prescribed regulatory cut-offs; in contrast, capital market pressures to avoid losses appear to be shaping the reporting behavior of US firms, as evidenced by the kink in earnings realizations around zero (e.g., Burgstahler and Dichev 1997). The results are financial statements that frequently do not reflect the real economic condition of listed Chinese firms, especially with respect to key capital market actions.

To achieve specific ROE targets and avoid losses, Chinese firms engage in both accruals-based earnings management and real transactions specifically designed to prop the performance of the listed firms. First, with respect to the use of discretionary accruals, Chen and Yuan (2004) document the booking of excessive non-operating income to meet the ROE requirements for a rights offering, while Aharony, Lee and Wong (2000) document the use of discretionary accruals to inflate earnings in advance of an IPO. Additionally, because the assets of listed state-controlled entities are carved out of local state asset management bureaus, they seldom have a stand-alone history prior to an IPO; as a result, these firms are allowed to report estimates of operating performance when applying for the initial offering, leaving the firm considerable latitude to meet earnings performance benchmarks. Together, these papers, among others (e.g., Chen, Lee, and Li 2003; Kao, Wu, and Yang 2009; Yu, Du, and Sun 2006; Liu and Lu 2007) show that Chinese firms use discretion available in the accrual accounting process to manage reported earnings to meet bright-line performance targets.

More generally, Ball, Robin, and Wu (2001) and Bushman and Piotroski (2006) demonstrate that the loss recognition practices of Chinese firms are less timely than for firms domiciles in other countries, even after the introduction of international accounting standards among listed firms. The limited application of conditionally conservative accounting practices among Chinese firms is striking when compared against the extent of timely loss recognition among the firms domiciled in key developed economies (see figure 4.2) and in large and local developing economies (see figure 4.3). The basic conclusion from these studies is that the accounting numbers of Chinese firms fail to capture deterioration in firm performance in a timely manner, severely limiting the usefulness of these reports for contracting and monitoring purposes. This particular reporting bias is especially problematic among listed state-owned firms, where the timely recognition of economic losses into accounting earnings would enable investors to better monitor managers and majority shareholders in the presence of weak corporate governance and potentially inefficient investment and asset management behavior.

Second, Chinese firms use related party transactions to meet earnings targets and avoid losses. For example, Jian and Wong (2010) document the prevalence of propping activities through related party transactions among China's state-controlled firms to manipulate the firm's earnings. Although the form of these transactions are real (e.g., product sales, raw material

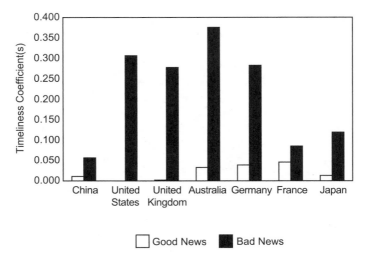

Fig. 4.2   Timely loss recognition practices of Chinese firms versus developed economies

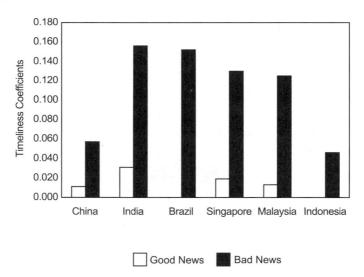

Fig. 4.3   Timely loss recognition practices of Chinese firms versus other emerging economies

purchases, intercompany loans, etc.), the substance of the transactions are designed to facilitate earnings management and, in many cases, tunneling activities. Moreover, Jian and Wong (2010) find that these earnings management effects were most pronounced in those provinces characterized by weak legal institutions and less deregulation of the marketplace, where the likelihood of detection and resultant penalties are expected to be lowest. Similarly, Jiang, Lee, and Yue (2010) document the widespread use of inter-company loans to facilitate the tunneling of resources in state-controlled firms while simultaneously propping up the listed firm's balance sheets.

Together, these papers illustrate alternative mechanisms by which China's publicly traded entities manipulate their reported performance to either meet the aforementioned regulatory requirements, to overstate the value of the firm to potential shareholders, to facilitate the tunneling of resources out of the publicly-listed firm and to hide poor outcomes arising from weak corporate governance. Thus, in spite of recent regulatory actions designed to foster transparency, the financial reporting environment of Chinese listed firms remains opaque. The discrepancy between the strength of China's standards and regulations and the relative weakness of China's actual financial reporting environment is ultimately the result of local institutions and arrangements that create adverse financial reporting incentives. The next section explores in greater detail the impact that China's unique institutional environment has on the financial reporting practices of its publicly listed firms.

4.2   Institutions and China's Information Environment

It is well documented that legal, political, financial, regulatory and cultural institutions exert strong pressures on economic agents and their behavior. In finance and economics, an extensive literature discusses and documents how primitive institutions influence the form of the economy, and the resultant impact the equilibrium set of institutions have on investor protections, financial development, investment behavior, economic growth and wealth. As a key institutional feature that aids in the allocation of capital within an economy, financial reporting practices, and the resultant information environment, are also shaped by these same primitive institutional forces.

In general, institutions associated with stronger investor protections and better economic outcomes are also associated with more favorable financial reporting practices and better information environments. For example, corporate transparency is greater in countries with stronger legal protections and minimal levels of state involvement in the economy (Bushman, Piotroski, and Smith 2004), earnings management is found to be less prevalent in economies with greater investor protection of minority shareholders and less concentrated ownership (Leuz, Nanda, and Wysocki 2003), timely loss recognition practices are stronger in countries with greater investor protections and institutions supporting contract usage (Ball, Kothari, and Robin 2000; Ball, Robin, and Wu 2003; Bushman and Piotroski 2006), earnings informativeness is higher in the presence of less concentrated ownership (Fan and Wong 2002) and stronger investor protections (DeFond, Hung, and Trezevant 2007), and the use of a high-quality auditor is more likely in the presence of strong institutions (Francis, Khurana, and Pereira 2003).

Unfortunately, many developing economies lack the institutional arrangements that create incentives for good governance, high-quality financial reporting practices, and transparent information environment. A weak legal infrastructure that fails to protect property rights will dampen the demand for high-quality accounting information for contracting purposes. These same weak legal institutions will also decrease the expected benefits associated with costly private information acquisition activities and inhibit the trading activities of arbitrageurs.

Additionally, the state's ownership of economic assets and the presence of strong political forces can give rise to adverse financial reporting incentives. In highly political settings, opacity arises to minimize the risk of government expropriation of the firm's assets, to hide inefficiencies and corruption, or to hide the rent-seeking activities of politicians and political cronies. For example, Bushman, Piotroski, and Smith (2004) document that the presence of strong state ownership in the economy and a greater risk of State expropriation creates incentives for opaque reporting practices, Bushman and Piotroski (2006) document that greater state involvement in the economy deters the timely recognition of losses into earnings, and Leuz and Oberholzer-Gee (2007) and Chaney, Faccio, and Parsley (2008) show that politically-connected firms report earnings of lower quality than nonpolitically-connected firms. Additionally, Wang, Wong, and Xia (2008), Guedhami and Pittman (2006), Gul (2006), and Guedhami, Pittman, and Saffar (2009) examine the impact of political forces on the quality of information around privatization events, and find that corporate transparency and the use of a high-quality auditor after privatization is inversely related to the portion of the firm's control retained by the State (and positively related to the extent of foreign ownership in these firms). Given the important role that government entities and politicians have in China's economy, political forces have the potential to exert a significant impact on the information environment of China's listed firms.

The following sections discuss and provide evidence on how China's institutional environment shapes the demand for and supply of information among China's listed firms.

4.2.1   Institutions Influencing the Supply and Demand for Information in China

In the US environment, accounting plays an important contracting role in the governance of listed firms (Watts and Zimmerman 1986). The use of accounting numbers in firms' managerial and debt contracts creates a demand for disciplinary mechanisms, such as the appointment of audit committee and external auditors, to ensure the reporting of high-quality information to all contractual parties, including existing and potential investors in the capital markets (Watts 2006). The stronger the contracting demand for credible information, the higher the accounting quality must be to fulfill this monitoring role.

The contracting role of accounting is first discussed in Jensen and Meckling (1976), who posit that there exists a contractual cost between owner-manager and outside shareholders; this contracting cost is termed agency cost. Accounting is an integral part of the organizational architecture in reducing this contracting cost. In a typical US listed firm, ownership is not concentrated in the hands of an owner-manager or family; instead, ownership is highly diffuse. This diffuse ownership structure creates a serious agency problem because of the separation of ownership and control in the organization. Essentially, the diffuse investors have delegated the control of the firm to professional managers whose interests are not aligned with theirs. This misalignment of interests is less problematic when managers are also part owners of the firm, because their stake in the company creates an incentive to maximize shareholder value. As a result, Fama and Jensen (1983) argue that firms characterized by diffuse ownership have a much stronger need to set up a governance structure that reduces the agency conflicts between professional managers and owners than firms with concentration in ownership. Specifically, firms with diffuse ownership need to appoint independent board members that are given the decision control rights to monitor managers on behalf of the owners. One frequently used monitoring device is an arm's length contract that links the managerial compensation to the firm's accounting performance. In order to validate the credibility of the accounting information, the board also hires external auditors to examine the managers' accounting reports on behalf of the owners (see figure 4.4).

Debt contracts also create a demand for high-quality financial reports in the US environment. Because creditors in the United States (especially bond holders) typically lack board representation and do not have privileged access to firm information, creditors frequently employ debt covenants based on accounting information to monitor the firm. Essentially, these debt covenants are used to trigger the transfer of decision rights from shareholders to creditors in the event of a decline in the financial condition of the firm. The efficacy of these contractual arrangements hinge upon the presence of credible financial accounting information and a judicial system that will enforce the underlying contract. The US strong legal environment, with its strong private enforcement channels, when combined with the prevalent use of public debt, leads to a heightened demand for high-quality financial reports by debt contracting parties. Thus, both the form of the US credit markets and the form of US equity ownership arrangements creates a strong contracting-based demand for high-quality financial reports. Finally, these same strong legal arrangements, namely the presence of a strong US judicial system that enforces contractual rights and an investors ability to engage in private litigation to recover losses, not only supports accounting-based

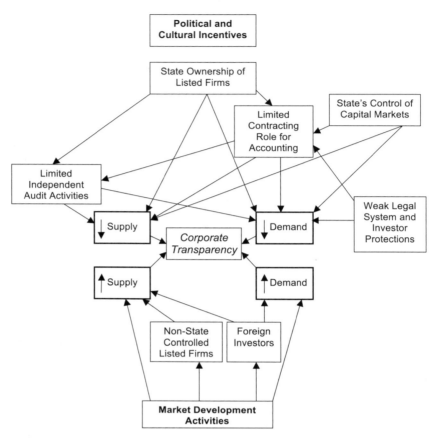

Fig. 4.4   Institutions and the supply and demand for information in China

contracting activity but also increases the benefits of engaging in costly information gathering, interpreting, and disseminating activities and creates a market-driven demand for information among US listed firms.

In contrast to the US environment, there exist a set of local institutional factors that shape the ownership, regulatory, and business environments of the Chinese listed firms. These institutions and related business arrangements, in turn, affect the contracting relationships of the key capital market players and, more specifically, the role and properties of externally reported accounting data for Chinese firms. These institutions and arrangements also influence the incentives of various capital market participants, and together, shape the demand and supply of high-quality financial reporting practices of publicly-listed firms in China. These key institutional arrangements include: State ownership of listed firms; government control of capital markets; weak market institutions and limited protection of property rights; lack of independent auditors; the importance of social networks and political connections. The impact of these institutional arrangements on the reporting practices of China's listed firms is discussed in the following.

Majority of the Chinese Firms Remain State-Controlled after Listing

China set up two stock exchanges in the early 1990s, one in Shenzhen and the other Shanghai, as a way to partially privatize its state enterprises and reform their governance structure to match international standards. However, the central or local government is required to maintain control of these state firms after listing. As of July 2010, the state owns on average 53 percent of the outstanding shares of listed state firms, while the remaining 47 percent of outstanding shares are in the hands of individuals, institutional investors, investment trusts and private firms. In addition, the government has historically given listing preference to state firms; as a result, state-controlled firms make up the majority of the equity market in the two stock exchanges (65 percent of firms with 89 percent of market capitalization).

Because of these ownership arrangements, the contracting role of accounting in a Chinese listed state firm is different from that of a US firm with diffuse ownership. First, concentrated control gives the State (i.e., majority owner) both the incentive and the ability to directly monitor the performance of the firms' managers. For example, the Chinese government retains the rights to appoint key officers such as the chairman and CEO of these state firms (Qian and Weingast 1997); as a result of this control, Fan, Wong, and Zhang (2007) document that 27 percent of the CEOs of listed state-controlled firms have government background. Moreover, as argued by Ball, Kothari, and Robin (2000), the government owners of listed state firms can use private channels and their political networks, instead of public accounting and information reported to the markets, to measure and assess managerial performance, thereby reducing the demand for high-quality external reports. As a result, the demand for high-quality external reports and information for control purposes is significantly lower among Chinese listed firms.

Second, bankruptcy is rare among listed state firms in China. As a consequence, most domestic investors expect the government to bail out state firms that are financially distressed. This implicit insurance against creditor and shareholder losses further reduces outside investors' demand for public information about the financial condition of listed state firms. Instead, investors focus on buying into firms that have strong political support.

Third, profit maximization is not the sole objective of most Chinese publicly-listed state-controlled firms; instead, these firms are also obligated to achieve certain social objectives, such as infrastructure development and full employment targets in the region. Because of these multiple and frequently conflicting objectives, local governments do not solely use firm-level profit information to monitor and assess the performance of the firms' managers. This reliance on other measures of performance reduces the demand for high-quality external financial reports.

Lastly, because the controlling shareholder of a listed state-controlled entity is typically a state asset management bureau, or a holding company owned by the state bureau, listed firms are typically a member of a larger group structure. This structure introduces incentives that both limit the demand for information and suppress the incentive to supply information to the public markets. Specifically, transactions with related entities may rely less on arms-length contracts and, more generally, rely less on accounting-based contracts for enforcement purposes; instead, social norms and political costs are sufficient to compel each party to fulfill the terms of contracts, limiting the demand for credible, audited information from a strict contracting perspective. Moreover, this structure can facilitate propping and tunneling activities via related party transactions, creating an incentive to suppress information about group transactions in the presence of governance conflicts.

In summary, because of the state's controlling ownership in the vast majority of listed firms, the contracting role of accounting numbers in China is very different from that of US firms. This difference reduces the demand for high-quality external financial reports in China relative to the US market. Instead, a greater reliance is likely to be placed on internal reporting mechanisms and performance measures. Unlike their Western counterparts, very little is known about the information and control mechanisms used inside listed state-controlled entities. Future research in this area is warranted.

Government Control of Capital Markets

A unique feature of the Chinese environment is the State's strong control of the capital markets, especially as it pertains to state-controlled entities. Since the creation of the two stock markets in China, the listing process and subsequent share issuances are highly controlled by the CSRC. Furthermore, rather than leaving listing decisions to the market or the firm's managers, the government retains the ultimate power in selecting firms for IPOs and subsequent share offerings. Additionally, the central government has control over the credit market for most listed firms; this control arises because publicly-traded state firms typically obtain the majority of their debt financing from the four largest state banks in China.

The government's control of China's capital markets has two effects on firms' accounting practices. First, due to high information costs, the CSRC uses bright line rules to screen firms for rights offerings and delisting. For example, three consecutive years of losses will lead to delisting for Chinese firms, while return on equity realizations of 10 percent are required for a firm to engage in a rights issuance.[5] And although the use of accounting-based

5. Effective July 2002, firms seeking a seasoned equity offering must have a three-year average return on equity (ROE) greater than or equal to 10 percent and have a ROE greater than or equal to 10 percent in the year directly preceding the offering. Similarly, firms seeking permission of a rights issuance must have a three-year average ROE greater than or equal to 6 percent.

regulations appears to have been effective at screening out many unqualified listing candidates (see Chen and Wang 2007), without a strong market infrastructure to guard against manipulation, and with the CSRC's heavy reliance on these simple accounting targets to regulate the marketplace, listed firms have strong incentives to manage accounting realizations. These incentives result in firms using accounting discretion when measuring firm-level performance, as discussed previously in section 4.1.4.

Second, the Chinese government frequently turns to nonfinancial channels, such as political networks, to obtain information to make capital raising, financing, and listing decisions. For example, Fan, Rui, and Zhang (2008) document that politics influence the decisions of state banks to lend capital to state-owned enterprises, while Du (2011) documents the importance of political connections for firms to gain access to public debt markets. The extensive use of nonfinancial data for capital-raising transactions limits the demand for high-quality external reports in China.

Lastly, the prevalence of debt financing from state-controlled banks minimizes the need for external financial reports to fulfill a debt contracting role. Instead, the government owners of the bank can directly monitor and assess the financial condition of the state-controlled borrower.

Weak Market Institutions and Limited Protection of Property Rights

China was a planned economy prior to the reforms in the late 1970s. Despite the fast economic growth in the past thirty years, the government has retained control in many sectors of the market. For example, the government has the power to appoint key personnel in state firms, grant licenses for operations in a particular location, control and regulate the labor market and influence the supply of input materials and inventory. Thus, it is essential for all Chinese firms to develop and maintain good relations with the government. These political connections, when combined with China's weak legal system and a long tradition of relationship-based transactions in business, mean that the use of accounting numbers to enforce arms-length contracts is much less likely in this transitional economy; instead, these alternative political channels are used to seek enforcement and remedies for nonperformance.

More broadly, the current set of legal and financial institutions do not foster the activities of information intermediaries. First, because of the State's control over the markets and economy, Chinese investors are less likely to rely upon legal protections or information supplied by the firms or financial intermediaries when making their investment decisions. Instead, local investors focus on the firms' political background when choosing investment opportunities, and expect the government to bail but the firm if it experiences financial distress. As such, local investors do not create a demand for high-quality reports. Second, the evidence suggests that both institutional and retail investors in China have a short-term focus and tend to trade on the basis of broad macroeconomic factors and market sentiment; such trading preferences do not create a market demand for high-quality reports about individual firms. Lastly, the weak protection of investor and property rights, along with restrictions on foreign holdings and investment opportunities, limits foreign investment activity and the resultant demand for high-quality financial reports created by foreign investors.

Independence of Local Auditors

In the US environment, external auditors ensure that the managers accurately report the financial condition of the firm to outside investors. In that governance role, it is essential that the auditors represent the interests of the outside investors and remain independent of the managers; as such, the United States has instituted regulations designed to promote the independence of the audit function (e.g., the Sarbanes-Oxley Act). In China, however, the ownership structure of the state-controlled firms, combined with the market for audit activities, adversely affects the governance role of external auditors.

First, as controlling shareholder of a listed state firm, the government can directly communicate with and monitor its managers via internal channels; as such, the demand for external auditors to attest to the quality of public accounting reports is significantly lower in China. As such, the incentive to hire a high-quality external auditor is likely to be concentrated among non-state-controlled entities.

Second, prior to the reform in 1998, almost all the audit firms across China were state audit bureaus. Even today, these audit firms are supervised by their local government and retain many of their old political connections. For example, local finance bureaus, audit bureaus, and CPA institutes are in charge of the licensing of audit firms, the administration of qualifying examinations, and the regulation of audit firms' day-to-day operations (Zhong 1998; Tang 1999). These connections are likely to create conflicts of interest between the managers who are ex-bureaucrats and/or have strong political ties with the local governments and the auditors located in that same local region (local auditors). Moreover, this lack of independence can induce collusion between the local state firms and local auditors to expropriate minority shareholders, resulting in a reduced supply of high-quality financial reports.

Social Networks and Political Connections

As discussed in the preceding sections, social and political connections influence many dimensions of corporate activity in China; as such, any understanding of reporting incentives and China's information environment requires an understanding of the firm's political and social connections. For example, well-connected firms face a lower demand for high-quality external information, as contracts and other business arrangements rely heavily upon the personal reputation of each contracting party. Connected firms may also have an incentive to suppress financial information that either highlights the existence of these relations or casts unfavorable light on related party transactions designed to expropriate the firm's economic assets.

More generally, however, the reporting and disclosure practices of listed firms can be influenced by social and cultural norms that create a preference toward opacity. Corporate reporting activities, like all corporate activities, are executed by individuals whose behavior reflects not just a "value maximization" strategy, but the expected personal rewards and costs that would arise through compliance and noncompliance with social norms and customs. These compliance concerns certainly manifest themselves in the context of the political and social connections discussed previously, but really represent a more general cultural factor that influences corporate behavior in China. Future research is needed to better understand how social and cultural norms shape the incentives of China's executives and capital market participants, and the spillover effect these issues have on China's information environment.

4.2.2   Recent Research on the Supply of and Demand for Information in China

The preceding section outlines institutional arrangements that are expected to influence the reporting practices and information environment of China's listed firms. The following sections summarize recent research findings documenting the impact of these institutional arrangements on observed reporting practices and China's information environment.

Politics and Suppression of Bad News

One dimension of a strong corporate governance regime is the board's ability and willingness to take corrective actions when the firm experiences a deterioration in its performance. Additionally, the board is expected to be forthcoming with bad news to outside investors, whether through press releases, through communication with analysts, or from a financial reporting perspective, through the recognition of economic losses into earnings in a timely manner. In most common law countries, firms generally recognize economic losses into accounting earnings in a timelier manner than economic gains; this conditionally conservative accounting practice thus provides a mechanism that allows board members to closely monitor and discipline managers and to take corrective actions earlier. As discussed earlier, Chinese firms recognize losses into earnings in a less timely manner than firms domiciled in traditional common law countries (Ball, Robin, and Wu 2001; Bushman and Piotroski 2006).

So why are Chinese firms less likely to report bad outcomes in a timely manner? One explanation, put forth by Piotroski, Wong, and Zhang (2001), is that Chinese firms have strong political incentives to suppress bad news.

On the demand side, the Chinese listed firms are under less pressure to report bad news promptly. As discussed earlier, the government ownership of the listed state firms and its control over the capital market weakens the contracting role of accounting, and thus the demand for timely reporting of bad news. On the supply side, the controlling owners of state firms also have political incentives to suppress bad news. Due to the heavy government control in the listed state firms, a large portion of politicians and ex-bureaucrats serve as senior executives and board members. They often pursue political goals or private benefit objectives at the expense of the firms' financial health. Thus, managers and local politicians incur a personal cost by reporting poor performance. Suppression of bad news allows politicians and politically astute managers to hide inefficiencies, expropriation-related activities, and mask the inefficient allocation of resources to achieve political objectives.

Using the crash statistics of share prices in Jin and Myers (2006) and Chen, Hong, and Stein (2001), Piotroski, Wong, and Zhang (2011) document that Chinese state firms control the release of bad news to the markets around three political events: the National Congress of the Chinese Communist Party, provincial-level promotions, and the revelation of provincial-level corruption investigations. The promotion event involves turnover of local governors when they move to a more senior position. The measure of corruption events reflects the exposure of corruption cases involving provincial politicians at or above the bureau level. The results show that state-controlled firms are significantly less likely to experience negative stock price crashes in the years of the National Congress of the Chinese Communist Party (CCP), in advance of political promotion decisions and during the course of corruption investigations relative to nonevent years. This suggests that in China, due to government's control over the capital markets and its ownership of the listed state firms, politics plays a significant role in shaping the information environment of these firms.

Penalties for Accounting Scandals and Relationship-Based Contracting

Another recent study by Hung, Wong, and Zhang (2011) uses penalties associated with accounting scandals to show that accounting has significantly less of a contracting role in China than the United States. In the US setting, Karpoff et al. (2004) and Karpoff, Lee, and Martin (2008a, 2008b) find that the reputation penalty to an accounting scandal is huge, with an average 41 percent decline in share prices for firms caught in accounting scandals sanctioned by the US Securities and Exchange Commission. They argue that a significant portion of the share price decline is associated with the loss in reputation, which leads to loss of potential new contracts or increase in future contracting costs. In contrast to the US experience, the reputational penalty against earnings management is significantly smaller in China. Hung, Wong, and Zhang (2011) find that accounting scandals sanctioned by the CSRC are associated with only about an 8.8 percent share price decline.

The major reasons for such a difference in reputational penalties associated with accounting scandals lie in China's institutional environment. With heavy government influence in the markets, and its weak development in market institutions and legal protection, Chinese firms tend to contract on the basis of social and political networks rather than public accounting information and legal documents; in contrast, US firms rely mainly on arm's length contracts. As such, accounting quality and corporate transparency are essential for various parties to enforce the firms' contracts in the US environment, and an accounting scandal damages the very credibility of the firm's underlying contracting environment. Chinese firms, on the other hand, focus more on their social and political networks in contracting; thus, an accounting scandal has minimal impact on the stability of the firm's underlying contractual relations.

In support of these arguments, Hung, Wong, and Zhang (2011) document that among firms with senior officers that were caught in corporate scandals that damage their ability to contract through political networks (e.g., bribing government officials or misappropriation of state assets), the share prices of these firms dropped by 30.8 percent, which was significantly more than those that were involved in accounting scandals. Because these corporate scandals will likely lead to a bigger disruption of political networks within the firms, they have a much bigger reputational effect on firms than accounting scandals. Hung, Wong, and Zhang (2011) also find that immediately after scandals that severed their political ties, these firms had a much harder time obtaining bank loans, and that there were significant changes in board membership due to changes in political appointees that helped to realign the firms' political networks.

Earnings Management and Related Party Transactions

A common way of measuring the information environment of a market is the level of earnings management among listed firms. Past research has found that Chinese firms have strong incentives to manage earnings. As discussed in the section on China's institutions, the government's bright-line rules for rights offering and delisting, and the weak reputational penalties and legal sanctions against accounting scandals, results in earnings management being prevalent among listed firms in China. There is extant evidence of earnings management in China, ranging from inflating earnings in years leading up to initial public offerings (IPOs) (Aharony, Lee, and Wong 2000), rights offering (Chen and Yuan 2004), and when facing ST (special treatment) status (Liu and Lu 2007).

Besides having strong incentives to manage earnings, the group structure of these listed Chinese firms also facilitates earnings management. Typically, a state firm will only carve out a portion of its assets for listing, leaving the rest in the unlisted parent firm. After the listing, the unlisted parent and the listed subsidiary often continue to trade with each other via related party transactions. The corporate structure of the group that the listed firm belongs to often has multiple layers and many firms in each layer. This complex structure is a result of diversification and vertical integration arising from the lack of developed input and output markets in China.

In a recent study, Jian and Wong (2010) document that the Chinese listed firms use related party sales to their unlisted parents to boost earnings to avoid delisting or qualify for rights offering. Similarly, preliminary research by the authors find that nonoperating related party transactions are associated with a decline in firm performance, while operating related party transactions improve firm performance. Moreover, among private, entrepreneurial firms, these nonoperating transactions increase the likelihood of the firm receiving a modified audit opinion and an enforcement action against it in future years, consistent with these transactions being used for suboptimal purposes. In contrast, state-controlled firms do not experience these adverse audit and regulatory outcomes, perhaps reflective of the benefits of being politically or socially connected.

This research raises a new set of questions on whether and how we should value listed firms in China, and the type of information that should be produced and released to evaluate these firms. For example, should listed companies be considered separate entities from their unlisted parent firms? Since almost all the parents of the listed firms are unlisted, it is difficult for investors to assess the true financial conditions of the listed firms in the market if the health and future performance of the listed company is inextricably linked to the health of the controlling firm or related entities. Should the reporting entity be expanded to include the parent company, or the group of firms controlled by the parent company? Whether and how do the ownership and governance structures affect the valuation of these listed firms in China? The influence of related party transactions, and the group and pyramidal ownership structure, represent several aspects of the information environment of Chinese listed firms that need further research and analysis.

Weak Demand for External Auditing

Prior US research shows that auditor quality can positively influence the information environment of client firms (e.g., Teoh and Wong 1993; Becker et al. 1998). As such, in a move designed to improve both auditing and accounting quality in the Chinese equity markets, the government adopted the international Generally Accepted Auditing Standards (GAAS) for the fiscal year of 1995. DeFond, Wong, and Li (2000) find that the immediate effect of such adoption is that the modified audit opinions go up by ninefold, from 1 percent to 9 percent. This significant increase suggests that Chinese auditors became more stringent when issuing opinions on the quality of their clients' financial statements following GAAS adoption.[6] During this same time period, the Chinese government was attempting to develop a list of Top-10 auditors (based on number of clients or clients' total assets) with superior audit quality. Consistent with the government's desire, DeFond, Wong, and Li (2000) also find that everything else equal, these Top-10 auditors are indeed more stringent, issuing more modified opinions in a sample period of 1993 to 1996. However, after the adoption of the new GAAS in 1995, the market share of Top-10 auditors drops significantly and has remained such for the last decade.[7] So, the obvious question is: Why did the demand for Top-10, higher-quality auditors in China fall after the adoption of the new GAAS?

The reason for such a low concentration of Top-10 auditors again relates to China's institutional environment. As highlighted earlier, block ownership and the likelihood of a government bailout in times of financial distress reduces the demand for the governance role of external auditors. Additionally, the reliance on political networks rather than arm's length contracts further weakens the contracting role of accounting and the demand for high-quality external auditing. Thus, it is unnecessary for state firms to hire Top-10 auditors.

Wang, Wong, and Xia (2008) also propose an alternative explanation for their result that local state firms tend to hire non-Top-10 auditors from the same region (local auditors). Wang et al. (2008) argue that local governments retain substantial political influence over these small local auditors; by hiring local auditors, local state firms can collude with the auditors in managing earnings to meet government targets and/or suppressing bad news for political goals. Wang, Wong, and Xia (2008) report that compared with nonstate firms, local state firms are more likely to hire small local auditors. Moreover, the relative difference in the propensity to hire small local auditors is greater in provinces with more government influence and weaker legal institutions, consistent with political forces shaping the audit choice decision.

4.3   Other Dimensions of Corporate Transparency in China: Information Intermediaries and the Media

Financial reporting is at the heart of a listed firm's information environment; as a result, the preceding sections have focused on understanding financial reporting practices in China. However, other facets of corporate transparency, such as the intensity of information acquisition activities, the strength of the country's information dissemination mechanisms and, ulti-

---

6. Similar evidence on the issuance of qualified reports is found in Yang et al. (2001) for disaffiliated CPA firms in 1997.

7. Wang, Wong, and Xia (2008) document that only 25 percent of the listed firms in China hire Top-10 auditors in 2003.

mately, the extent of informed trading activity, can have a significant impact on the development of a strong information environment. In China, many of these dimensions of corporate transparency are either lacking or not well understood.

Prior research documents a host of economic benefits arising from the presence of strong information intermediaries, such as financial analysts and institutional investors. These benefits range from the more efficient pricing of historical information, greater liquidity, and smaller bid-ask spreads. Additionally, the firm's disclosure practices themselves tend to be intertwined with the presence of information intermediaries; analysts and institutions tend to cover firms with better disclosure practices, and once a relationship is established, these information intermediaries exert pressure on management to supply more information (Gelos and Wei 2004). Thus, firms wishing to obtain the benefits arising from greater analyst coverage and institutional ownership are required to improve their disclosure practices to both attract and retain such coverage.[8] This section will provide evidence on the informational activities of institutional investors, analysts, and the media in China.

4.3.1   Institutional Investors

As sophisticated investors, institutions can improve the efficiency of stock prices through their trades and arbitrage activities. As minority shareholders, institutional investors have the ability to monitor the firm's management and controlling shareholders and exert pressure on management to provide information in ways that neither domestic nor foreign individual investors can. As a result, institutional trading activity and institutional ownership arrangements have the potential to improve the information environment of China's listed firms.

However, weaknesses in China's legal and regulator institutions likely hinder the ability for foreign and domestic institutions from fulfilling these roles. For example, the weak protection of property rights, the limited ability to privately enforce contracts and concerns about corruption, cronyism, and market manipulation will limit expected gains from private information acquisition activities and crowd out informed trading activity. Regulatory and exchange-related frictions, such as restrictions on short selling activity, the existence of daily price movement limits, the lack of intra-day trading, and higher transaction costs hinder institutions from effectively engaging in certain arbitrage activities.[9] Similarly, regulatory restrictions on foreign

8. Alternatively, it is possible that analysts and institutions prefer to follow firms with limited information, which offer the largest benefit to private information acquisition and trading activity. In such a setting, the informed trading activities of institutional investors would serve as a substitute for firm-level reporting and disclosure practices.

9. Current regulations limit the daily downside price movements of listed Chinese firms to minus 5 or 10 percent, resulting in market prices that do not fully reflect extreme negative

ownership and the activities of foreign financial institutions reduce the institution's incentive to serve as long-term monitors and stakeholders of China's listed companies. Finally, the dominance of state-owned firms and their heavy reliance on social and political networks for contracting induce corporate opacity and restrict the role of financial intermediaries in gathering and disseminating value relevant information of these firms.

Empirical evidence on the information acquisition and dissemination activities of institutional investors and their effect on the price formation process is lacking in the context of China's securities markets. Research on the trading behavior of institutional investors in the Shanghai A share market finds that domestic institutions follow momentum/price feedback strategies; such trading behavior is consistent with institutional investors discounting their private information about fundamental valuations when making their portfolio allocation decisions, and instead trading on the basis of market sentiment, information contained in past trades, and general market movements (e.g., Mei, Scheinkman, and Xiong 2005; Tan et al. 2008; Kling and Gao 2008). If that interpretation is correct, this trade-based evidence suggests that the China's weak legal and regulatory environment hinders at least one informational role served by institutional investors. Future research is needed to determine whether, and to what extent, institutional frictions are limiting the arbitrage and information gathering activities of sophisticated domestic and foreign institutional investors in China. Alternatively, to the extent that both institutional and retail investors have a short-term focus and a preference for trading on market sentiment or macroeconomic indicators, it is possible that a greater supply of firm-specific information will result in only minimal changes to behavior of investors and security prices in the Chinese market. Future research examining the trading activity of institutions following the elimination of informational frictions is warranted.

Future research is also needed to understand the governance and monitoring role played by these institutions in the context of China's listed firms. For example, are domestic and foreign institutions (as minority shareholders) able to exert influence in the presence of state control? What if the controlling shareholder is an entrepreneur or family group? Has increased institutional ownership influenced corporate governance practices, disclosure practices, and firm performance? How has the gradual relaxation of restrictions on the activities of foreign institutional investors changed the supply and demand for firm, industry, and country-level information, and how have those changes affected the price formation process? Future research in this area is warranted.

---

information events in a timely manner. The sluggish response of prices to new information introduces a costly friction that can impede the activities of information arbitrageurs. Additionally, the lack of intra-day trading and transaction costs that are about 50 basis points higher than that of more mature markets also reduces the overall efficiency of the marketplace. China Capital Market Development Report (CSRC 2009)

4.3.2   Financial Analysts

The preceding evidence on the behavior of institutional investors suggests that buy-side analysts are not fulfilling a key informational role in China. With respect to the activities of sell-side financial analysts, early research documents that analyst forecast errors for Chinese listed firms are nearly twice as large as those for Hong Kong listed companies, and significantly larger than those of other developed and developing Asia Pacific countries (e.g., Ang and Ma 1999). This pattern is consistent with domestic Chinese analysts grappling with limited information and/or having minimal incentives to gather and produce new information when making firm-level forecasts. Subsequent research focuses on examining analyst forecast accuracy conditional on whether or not foreign investors trade in the given security. These papers find that the relation between forecast accuracy and analyst coverage strengthens in the presence of foreign investor activity, suggesting that either the demands of foreign investors led to greater information production by analysts or that the presence of foreign investment promoted a greater supply of information by the firm. Regardless of the cause, the paper illustrates the type of dynamic interactions that can exist between the presence of foreign investors, changing market regulations, and the information environment of listed firms. Future research is needed to examine the role of politics, development of market and legal institutions, and how ownership structure of Chinese listed firms affect the supply and demand of analyst forecasts in China. Additionally, future studies should seek to understand the forecasting, reporting, and coverage incentives of both domestic and foreign financial analysts in China, the type of new information, if any, that they contribute to the price formation process, and how shifts in China's regulatory environment are changing the incentives of information intermediaries.

4.3.3   Media and Other Information Dissemination Mechanisms

Lastly, the information environment surrounding China's markets and listed firms is shaped by the strength of the country's information dissemination mechanisms. These mechanisms include the aforementioned activities of financial analysts, who through their various investment and industry reports disseminate firm-specific and industry-specific information to a wider set of market participants. More importantly, corporate transparency depends critically upon the role of the media and the Internet to disseminate firm-specific financial information to both domestic and foreign investors.

In this regard, several issues of note arise in China. First, the vast majority of media outlets in the PRC are owned by the State, and to the extent that political incentives prevail, the firm-specific information conveyed through these media outlets is likely to be biased and the supply of information constrained. Moreover, because a state license is required to operate a media outlet in China, the reporting incentives of non-state-owned media outlets are also likely to be influenced by the objectives of the State and local politicians. This lack of independence in reporting would be particularly serious if the news coverage is associated with SOEs that are controlled by the same local politicians. Future research is needed to understand the influence these political pressures have on media coverage and reporting bias in the financial press.

Second, the Internet is a rapidly expanding source for financial information globally. Listed firms post financial information on corporate websites, conference calls and presentations are streamed live and archived on the Web, and both formal and informal news outlets, including financial weblogs and websites, exist to gather and disseminate (and in some cases produce) value-relevant information about listed firms. These outlets often produce independent news coverage because quite a number of them are privately run and escape state censorship. Given the rising importance of the Internet for information dissemination, one must ask whether the "Great Firewall of China" extends into the realm of reporting and disseminating financial information? Recent events involving Google's decision to temporarily suspend operations in China over censorship concerns, for example, suggests that an implicit contract exists between Internet service and content providers and the Chinese government. Similarly, the recent enactment of a regulation that limits the ability of individuals to register domain names is an example of how the government can use regulation to control how information about China's listed firms is disseminated. Whether Internet outlets are important sources of unbiased corporate news to investors in China and whether new regulations will limit their role in generating corporate information are important questions for future research. Research on whether and how political factors influence the flow of firm-specific financial information through China's various media outlets and channels is needed.

4.4 Evolution of China's Information Environment

The preceding sections outline the current information environment in China and highlight the influence that local institutions have on financial reporting incentives. The final sections of this chapter discuss how actual and potential changes in China's institutional and regulatory environment are expected to impact the country's information environment, and the expected consequences associated with changes in corporate transparency.

4.4.1 Potential Consequences from a Change in Corporate Transparency

Prior research documents the potential economic benefits that can arise from strong corporate reporting and disclosure practices at both the firm and country level. The following paragraphs outline the expected consequences in the context of China.

First, prior research using US data shows that firms with better disclosure practices are associated with lower levels of information asymmetry and less uncertainty about future performance, as measured by smaller absolute analyst forecast errors and narrower dispersion of analyst forecasts. The reduction in information asymmetry and estimation risk translates into smaller bid-ask spreads, greater liquidity, and ultimately, lower costs of equity and debt capital (e.g., Barry and Brown 1985; Botosan 1997). Similar relations exist between the quality of reported earnings, information asymmetry, and the firm's cost of capital using both US data (e.g., Francis et al. 2004) and cross-country data (Bhattacharya, Daouk, and Welker 2003).

Additionally, US data shows that firms with more transparent disclosure practices are associated with greater levels of analyst coverage (Lang and Lundholm 1996). To the extent that greater analyst coverage improves overall information gathering, processing, and dissemination activities, the increase in analyst coverage should improve the efficiency of stock prices, reduce information asymmetry, lower trading costs and improve resource allocations. Furthermore, to the extent that greater analyst coverage is positively related to the overall level of investor interest in the firm, greater demand for the securities can increase liquidity, raise valuations, and lower the firm's cost of equity capital (Merton 1987).

Together, the evidence suggests that the credible adoption of transparent reporting and disclosure practices by Chinese firms has the capability of reducing market frictions arising from information asymmetry and adverse selection concerns, potentially lowering trading costs and increasing liquidity for the firm's shares. These shifts are expected to increase the efficiency of market prices and raise firm valuations in the long run. The evidence also suggests that listed Chinese firms could benefit from a reduction in their cost of capital.

The magnitude of this benefit for China's listed firms, however, is debatable. The magnitude and duration of any cost of capital benefit will ultimately depend upon the credibility of the firm's commitment for transparency, the extent that capital is actually being directly raised by the firm in a market setting, and the scarcity of external capital in China. The issue of credibility is straightforward; only a persistent shift in reporting practices has the potential to yield the benefits outlined previously. The suspension of recently enacted regulations or a lack of credible enforcement activities will result in unraveling of these benefits. As for capital raising activities, listed firms in China continue to raise the majority of their external funding from state banks or via politically-influenced channels. If this trend continues, the expected magnitude of the cost of capital benefits from increased transparency will be small or nonexistent. Finally, given the high savings rates in China, nominal costs of capital in China are already low. As a result, the expected cost of capital benefit from a reduction in information asymmetry and liquidity may be economically small in the short term.

Second, in the context of an emerging economy like China, where ownership is concentrated in the hands of the state or a few nonstate owners, greater transparency and stricter disclosure standards have the potential to strengthen corporate governance by improving monitoring and limiting consumption of private benefits by controlling shareholders (e.g., Rajan and Zingales 2003; Stulz 1999; Doidge 2004; Doidge, Karolyi, and Stulz 2004). These governance improvements should result in better asset management and investment decisions for the firm and lower the risk of expropriation by the controlling shareholders. These improvements should produce stronger firm performance, lower costs of capital, higher market valuations, and from the perspective of minority shareholders, larger dividends and greater free cash flows. Consistent with these corporate governance arguments, Bushman, Piotroski, and Smith (2011) show that firms operating in economies with timely accounting loss recognition practices respond to a decrease in growth opportunities more strongly than firms operating in economies with limited loss recognition practices.

Third, strong information systems lower the information gathering costs investors, increase investor protections through the use of enforceable contracts, allow for improved monitoring, and lower the uncertainty faced by foreign investors. Consistent with these arguments, Gelos and Wei (2004) show (using cross-country data) that stronger disclosure practices are associated with greater levels of foreign investment, while Gul, Kim, and Qiu (2010) find that stock price synchronicity in China is inversely related to the level of foreign holdings. Thus, a change in corporate transparency is likely to produce a change in the investment activity of foreign investors. However, the magnitude of this effect is likely to depend upon the objectives of foreign investors; to the extent that foreign investors are purchasing Chinese securities as a means of capturing expected appreciation in the Chinese currency (vis-à-vis the US dollar), or are trading on the basis of macro-trends or investor sentiment, incremental changes in the information environment of listed firms may have only a marginal effect on the level of foreign investment and holdings.

Finally, all of these outcomes are expected to improve the price-setting process in China's markets, ultimately resulting in market prices that will better aid in the allocation of the country's capital toward the most promising investment opportunities. Combined with expected improvements in corporate governance practices, the resource allocation effects arising from greater corporate transparency are likely to produce the largest economic benefits for China over the long run.

In summary, a credible commitment for strong disclosure and financial reporting practices is expected to aid in China's economic development through greater levels of foreign investment and an improvement in the allocation of capital through the more accurate identification of positive net present value (NPV) investment projects and better asset management. Improvements in firm-level cost of capital are possible, but likely to be less important economically in the short term. As will be discussed in the next section, the growing number of nonstate firms and the gradual decrease in the dominance of SOEs in the market will increase both the supply of and demand for corporate transparency. Additionally, as greater amounts of foreign capital flow into the economy, foreign and minority shareholders will demand higher-quality information and audit function to monitor both managers and controlling shareholders, reinforcing the aforementioned benefits.

4.4.2   Expected Impact of Current and Future Institutional Changes on Corporate Transparency and China's Information Environment

China's economy has undergone an incredible transformation over the last several decades, including the introduction of public equity markets and the embracing of many Western-style market arrangements. This market development, along with the arrival of foreign capital, has created a demand for better information about China's listed firms. However, many attributes of the Chinese environment—the State's ownership of listed firms, concentrated ownership structures, a cultural preference for relationship-based transactions, and the role of political connections and incentives—have remained fairly unchanged over this same time period. It is these institutional attributes that have driven a wedge between the market demand for corporate transparency and the listed firm's willingness and need to supply that credible external information for valuation and contracting purposes.

The preceding evidence suggests that, in terms of economic and financial development, China would benefit from an improved information environment and stronger financial reporting systems. However, transparency is not costless. The aforementioned political, legal, and cultural factors create incentives for weak external information systems in China. If the government of China desires an improvement in corporate transparency, it will require a shift in these institutional arrangements. The following subsections discuss the expected impact that different institutional changes would have on the information environment of listed firms given the prevailing incentives for opacity.

Adoption and Enforcement of Credible
Accounting Standards and Regulation

By adopting standards that converge with IFRS, China has benchmarked their accounting standards to global standards. The CSRC has stated in numerous documents and reports that transparency is an important objective for its markets. Given China's desire to improve the information environment of its publicly listed firms, the adoption of International Financial Reporting Standards, International Auditing Standards, and a host of other globally-recognized governance and reporting regulations represent a good first step toward achieving that objective. Unfortunately, internationally accepted accounting standards and regulations alone are not sufficient to improve the information environment; if transparency is desired, the information disclosed must be tailored to the business environment and there must exist credible mechanism to enforce these rules.

Due to the organization and incentive structure of Chinese listed firms, standard setters and regulators have begun to tailor the disclosures of listed firms to provide information about related party transactions and the complex pyramidal and ownership structure of these listed firms. Greater information about these types of transactions and arrangements should allow outside investors to better monitor the activities of the firm; such monitoring should improve corporate governance and allow for the production of more accurate market prices.

More importantly, managers, politicians, and firms will only have an incentive to follow these rules if the costs of noncompliance are sufficiently strong. Prior research shows that the enactment of laws and regulation are insufficient to derive economic benefits. For example, Bhattacharya and Daouk (2002) show that it is the initial enforcement of a country's insider trading law, not the law's enactment, which results in a decrease in country-level costs of capital. Similarly, Bushman, Piotroski, and Smith (2005) show that it is the initial enforcement, not enactment, of those same insider trading laws that results in an increase in the depth and breadth of analyst coverage in an economy. In this regard, a strong central regulator such as the CSRC is in the position to act as the public enforcer, similar to the Securities and Exchange Commission in the U.S. If China begins the process of credibly and impartially enforcing existing securities laws and regulations, then many of the impediments against corporate transparency should fall and the information environment of publicly listed firms will improve over time.[10]

Legal System Reforms

As China continues to reform its legal and judicial system to be free from political influence and corruption, we expect to see an improvement in corporate transparency in China over time. Prior research shows that strong legal systems create an institutional and market environment that promotes and creates a demand for strong financial reporting practices (e.g., Ball, Kothari, and Robin 2000; Leuz, Nanda, and Wysocki 2003; Bushman, Piotroski, and Smith 2004) and attracts foreign investment. These strong legal systems promote the private enforcement of contracts, produce decisions that are made in a fair and transparent manner, and operate independent of political policy objectives and local connections. A credible

10. Moreover, as noted in Allen, Qian, and Qian (2005), IAS-based standards may be counterproductive given current institutional arrangements. Particularly, the inherent discretion imbedded within IFRS, when combined with weak auditing practices and an ineffective judicial system, could actually result in weaker corporate reporting practices vis-à-vis the simpler set of Chinese accounting standards that IFRS is replacing.

shift in China's legal regime will serve to strengthen investor protections in China, creating a climate for foreign investment, arm's-length contracting activities, and the resultant information gathering and auditing activities. Recent events in China, which include the adoption and enforcement of insider trading laws and the first prosecution of a civil servant under these laws, are consistent with credible regulatory and judicial reforms. However, local judicial courts are often under the strong influence of local politicians; this political influence makes enforcement of these new laws difficult. Absent the elimination of these political frictions, regulatory reforms alone will be insufficient to produce significant improvements in the information environment.

Expansion of Market Demand for Information

Regulations and laws (and related enforcement activity) that create market pressures for better corporate governance at the firm level and greater information gathering activities by outside investors are expected to strengthen China's information environment. One approach is the relaxation of rules on foreign investing and ownership in China. Historically, foreign investors have been limited to the B share market in China or the H share market in Hong Kong; however, recent changes in regulation have begun to allow greater holdings by foreign investors. In December 2002, China launched the Qualified Foreign Institutional Investor (QFII) program to allow licensed foreign institutional investors to trade in the A share market. By the end of 2007, fifty-two foreign institutional investors had been granted QFII status, and allocated a quota total US$10 billion. As documented in Gul, Kim, and Qie (2010), greater levels of foreign holdings and the use of a high-quality auditor results in stock prices that are less synchronized in China. More importantly, the introduction of foreign institutions has had a stabilizing effect on China's A share market, with the effects of feedback trading diminishing in the market, consistent with foreign institutions trading on fundamental strategies and information (Schuppli and Bohl 2010). The evidence suggests that continued relaxation of rules on foreign investment activity and foreign ownership is expected to have a long-run positive effect on corporate transparency in China.[11]

The implementation of various governance-related requirements should also produce similar market pressures. For example, Ferreira and Laux (2007) document how better firm-level corporate governance, as measured by the absence or presence of antitakeover provisions, is associated with

11. Similarly, the creation of the Qualified Domestic Institutional Investor (QDII) program in May 2006, which allows licensed domestic institutional investors to invest in overseas markets, will expose domestic investors to the better levels of transparency that exist on most foreign markets. This exposure to foreign practices may increase the demand for better information in the domestic market. As of the end of 2007, fifteen fund management firms and five securities firms have been granted QDII status.

greater transparency (as proxied by stock return synchronicity) through its influence on private information collection activities. Thus, the enactment and enforcement of regulations or exchange rules that effectively promote better governance, such as the insider trading restrictions and independent director requirements already in place, should also increase market pressures for greater corporate transparency.

Finally, the elimination of the exchange and regulatory frictions that prevent effective arbitrage activity would increase the expected gains to private information acquisition and dissemination activities. Combined with the strengthening of property rights arising through better enforcement and a strong judicial system, this increase in expected arbitrage profits will create an incentive for informed traders and investors to enter the market, which will improve the efficiency of the price formation process.

Relaxing State Control of Listed Firms

As shown in our research, one key institutional constraint that leads to the appointment of low-quality auditors is government ownership of listed firms in China. Similarly, state control facilitates propping activities and related political incentives influence the flow of information into prices. As such, any change in the state's role as the principle shareholder for China's listed firms is expected to have an impact on corporate transparency in the long run.

Three recent trends in China are reducing government's influence on the listed firms. First, there has been an increase in the number of privately controlled firms listed in the stock exchanges in China; given that non-state-controlled firms are more likely to seek a high-quality audit, these listing trends bode favorably for an improvement in corporate transparency in the long run. Second, the government has recently been granted permission to freely transfer their state shares to private investors. These private investors will need to rely upon independent auditors to help them monitor the company, and increase the demand for high-quality external financial reports. Lastly, the increase of foreign ownership through New York, London, and Hong Kong listing of Chinese firms, as well as the creation of the QFII program, will also help reduce the government influence over listed companies in China. The gradual erosion of the government influence and control over China's listed firms is expected to improve the corporate transparency in the long run.

4.5   Conclusion

The information environment of China's listed firms is opaque. This chapter has outlined the key institutional arrangements that limit both the demand for and supply of information about China's listed companies. This chapter also raises numerous questions for future research. What are the key drivers of observed improvement in China's information environment over the last decade? What are the key reforms and enforcement events in China, and have these activities had the desired effect on the information environment and the development of China's capital markets? Has the arrival of foreign capital and sophisticated investors into the Chinese market improved the information environment? Who is likely to benefit from greater transparency, and how much priority should be given to the further improvement of the information environment? The answers to these fundamental questions, and their implications, will help China continue along its path of long-term economic development.

Fundamentally, any set of actions that shifts the incentives of managers and local politicians to promote transparency is expected to have a profound effect on the information environment of Chinese listed firms. In this regard, China has taken significant steps in the last several years to change these incentives, as outlined in the preceding section. If the ultimate, long-run objective is to align the reporting and disclosure incentives of politicians, executives, and controlling shareholders with transparency, additional legal and market reforms are needed. Our chapter serves as a vital first step in understanding the important economic links between transparency in China's security markets and the country's institutional environment.

References

Aharony, J., J. Lee, and T. J. Wong. 2000. "Financial Packaging of IPO Firms in China." *Journal of Accounting Research* 38 (1): 103–26.

Alford, A., J. Jones, R. Leftwich, and M. Zmijewski. 1993. "Relative Informativeness of Accounting Disclosures in Different Countries." *Journal of Accounting Research* 31 (Supplement): 183–233.

Allen, F., J. Qian, and M. Qian. 2005. "Law, Finance and Economic Growth in China." *Journal of Financial Economics* 77:57–116.

Allen, W., and H. Shen. 2011. "Assessing China's Top-Down Securities Markets." Working Paper. New York University School of Law. NBER Working Paper no. 16713. Cambridge, MA: National Bureau of Economic Research, January.

Ang, J., and Y. Ma. 1999. "Transparency in Chinese Stocks: A Study of Earnings Forecasts by Professional Analysts." *Pacific-Basin Finance Journal* 7 (2): 129–55.

Ball, R., S. P. Kothari, and A. Robin. 2000. "The Effect of International Institutional Factors on Properties of Accounting Earnings." *Journal of Accounting and Economics* 29 (1): 1–51.

Ball, R., A. Robin, and J. Wu. 2001. "Accounting Standards, the Institutional Environment and Issuer Incentives: Effect of Timely Loss Recognition in China." *Asia-Pacific Journal of Accounting and Economics* 36 (1–3): 235–70.

———. 2003. "Incentives versus Standards: Properties of Accounting Income in Four East Asia Countries." *Journal of Accounting and Economics* 36 (1–3): 235–70.

Barry, C., and S. Brown. 1985. "Differential Information and Security Market Equilibrium." *Journal of Financial and Quantitative Analysis* December:407–22.

Becker, C., M. DeFond, J. Jiambalvo, and K. R. Subramanyam. 1998. "The Effect of Audit Quality on Earnings Management." *Contemporary Accounting Research* 15:1–24.

Berkowitz, D., K. Pistor, and J. F. Richard. 2003. "Economic Development, Legality and the Transplant Effect." *European Economic Review* 47:165–95.

Bhattacharya, U., and H. Daouk. 2002. "The World Price of Insider Trading." *The Journal of Finance* 57:75–108.

Bhattacharya, U., H. Daouk, and M. Welker. 2003. "The World Price of Opacity." *The Accounting Review* 78 (3): 641–78.

Botosan, C. 1997. "Disclosure Level and the Cost of Equity Capital." *The Accounting Review* July:323–49.

Burgstahler, D., and I. Dichev. 1997. "Earnings Management to Avoid Earnings Decreases and Losses." *Journal of Accounting and Economics* 24 (1): 99–126.

Bushman, R., and J. Piotroski. 2006. "Financial Reporting Incentives for Conservative Accounting: The Influence of Legal and Political Institutions." *Journal of Accounting and Economics* 42 (1/2): 107–48.

Bushman, R., J. Piotroski, and A. Smith. 2004. "What Determines Corporate Transparency?" *Journal of Accounting Research* 42 (2): 207–52.

———. 2005. "Insider Trading Restrictions and Analysts' Incentives to Follow Firms." *The Journal of Finance* 60 (1): 35–66.

———. 2011. "Capital Allocation and the Timely Accounting Recognition of Losses." *Journal of Business, Finance and Accounting* 38 (1-2): 1–33.

Chan, L. K. C., N. Jegadeesh, and J. Lakonishok. 1996. "Momentum Strategies." *Journal of Finance* 51:1681–713.

Chaney, P., M. Faccio, and D. Parsley. 2008. "The Quality of Accounting Information in Politically Connected Firms." Working Paper. Vanderbilt University.

Chen, J., H. Hong, and J. Stein. 2001. "Forecasting Crashes: Trading Volume, Past Returns, and Conditional Skewness in Stock Prices." *Journal of Financial Economics* 61:345–81.

Chen, K., and J. Wang. 2007. "Accounting-Based Regulation in Emerging Markets: The Case of China's Seasoned-Equity Offerings." *The International Journal of Accounting* 42:221–36.

Chen, K., and H. Yuan. 2004. "Earnings Management and Resource Allocation: Evidence from China's Accounting-based Regulation of Rights Issues." *The Accounting Review* 79 (3): 645–65.

Chen, X., C. J. Lee, and J. Li. 2003. "Chinese Tango: Government Assisted Earnings Management." Working Paper. Tsinghua University, Tulane University and Columbia University.

China Securities Regulatory Commission. 2008. *Annual Report.* Beijing: China Financial and Economic Publishing House.

Choi, J., L. Jin, and H. Yan. 2010. "What Does Stock Ownership Breadth Measure?" NBER Working Paper no. 16591. Cambridge, MA: National Bureau of Economic Research, December.

DeFond, M., M. Hung, and R. Trezevant. 2007. "Investor Protection and the Information Content of Annual Earnings Announcements: International Evidence." *Journal of Accounting and Economics* 43:37–67.

DeFond, M., T. J. Wong, and S. Li. 2000. "The Impact of Improved Auditor Independence on Audit Market Concentration in China." *Journal of Accounting and Economics* 28:269–305.

Doidge, C. 2004. "U.S. Cross-listings and the Private Benefits of Control: Evidence from Dual-Class Shares." *Journal of Financial Economics* 72:519–53.

Doidge, C., G. Karolyi, and R. Stulz. 2004. "Why Are Foreign Firms Listed in the U.S. Worth More?" *Journal of Financial Economics* 71:205–38.

Du, F. 2011. "Political Connections and Access to Bond Capital: Reputation or Collusion?" Working Paper. University of Southern California.

Durnev, A., R. Morck, B. Yeung, and P. Zarowin. 2003. "Does Greater Firm-Specific Return Variation Mean More or Less Informed Stock Pricing?" *Journal of Accounting Research* 41:797–836.

Fama, E., and M. Jensen. 1983. "Agency Problems and Residual Claims." *Journal of Law and Economics* 26 (2): 327–49.

Fan, J., M. Rui, and M. Zhao. 2008. "Public Governance and Corporate Finance: Evidence from Corruption Cases." *Journal of Comparative Economics* 36 (3): 343–64.

Fan, J. P. H., and T. J. Wong. 2002. "Corporate Ownership Structure and the Informativeness of Accounting Earnings in East Asia." *Journal of Accounting and Economics* 33 (3): 401–25.

Fan, J. P. H., T. J. Wong, and T. Zhang. 2007. "Politically Connected CEOs, Corporate Governance and Post-IPO Performance of China's Newly Partially Privatized Firms." *Journal of Financial Economics* 84:265–90.

Ferreira, M., and P. Laux. 2007. "Corporate Governance, Idiosyncratic Risk and Information Flow." *The Journal of Finance* 62:951–89.

Francis, J., I. Khurana, and R. Pereira. 2003. "Investor Protection Laws, Accounting and Auditing around the World." *Asia-Pacific Journal of Accounting and Economics* 10:1–30.

Francis, J., R. LaFond, P. Olsson, and K. Schipper. 2004. "Costs of Equity and Earnings Attributes." *The Accounting Review* 79 (4): 967–1010.

Gelos, R., and S. Wei. 2004. "Transparency and International Investor Behavior." *Journal of Finance* 42:721–41.

Guedhami, O., and J. Pittman. 2006. "Ownership Concentration in Privatized Firms: The Role of Disclosure Standards, Auditor Choice, and Auditing Infrastructure." *Journal of Accounting Research* 44 (x): 889–929.

Guedhami, O., J. Pittman, and W. Saffar. 2009. "Auditor Choice in Privatized Firms: Empirical Evidence on the Role of State and Foreign Owners." *Journal of Accounting and Economics* 48 (x): 151–71.

Gul, F. 2006. "Auditors' Response to Political Connections and Cronyism in Malaysia." *Journal of Accounting Research* 44 (5): 931–63.

Gul, F., J. Kim, and A. Qiu. 2010. "Ownership Concentration, Foreign Shareholdings, Audit Quality, and Stock Price Synchronicity: Evidence from China." *Journal of Financial Economics* 25 (3): 425–42.

He, Z., and D. Su. 2009. "Price Manipulation and Industry Momentum: Evidence from the Chinese Stock Market." Working Paper. Jinan University, March.

Hung, M., T. J. Wong, and F. Zhang. 2011. "The Value of Relationship-Based and Market-Based Contracting: Evidence from Corporate Scandals in China." Working Paper. The Chinese University of Hong Kong.

Jegadeesh, N., and S. Titman. 1993. "Returns to Buying Winners and Selling Losers: Implications for Stock Market Efficiency." *Journal of Finance* 48:65–91.

Jensen, M., and W. Meckling. 1976. "Theory of the Firm: Managerial Behavior, Agency Costs and Ownership Structure." *Journal of Financial Economics* 3:305–60.

Jian, M., and T. J. Wong. 2010. "Propping and Tunneling through Related Party Transactions." *Review of Accounting Studies* 15:70–105.

Jiang, G., C. M. C. Lee, and H. Yue. 2010. "Tunneling in China: The Surprising Pervasive Use of Corporate Loans to Extract Funds from Chinese Listed Firms." *Journal of Financial Economics* 98 (1): 1–20.

Jin, L., and S. Myers. 2006. "R2 around the World: New Theory and New Tests." *Journal of Financial Economics* 79:257–92.

Kang, J., M.-H. Liu, and S. Ni. 2002. "Contrarian and Momentum Strategies in the China Stock Market: 1993–2000." *Pacific-Basin Finance Journal* 10:243–65.

Kao, J. L., D. Wu, and Z. Yang. 2009. "Regulations, Earnings Management, and Post-IPO Performance: The Chinese Evidence." *Journal of Banking and Finance* 33 (1): 63–76.

Karpoff, J., D. S. Lee, M. Arvind, and G. Martin. 2004. "Penalizing Corporate Misconduct: Empirical Evidence." Working Paper. University of Washington and University of Texas A&M.

Karpoff, J., D. S. Lee, and G. Martin. 2008a. "The Consequences to Managers for Financial Misrepresentation." *Journal of Financial Economics* 88:193–215.

———. 2008b. "The Cost to Firms Who Are Cooking the Books." *Journal of Financial and Quantitative Analysis* 43 (3): 581–612.

Khwaja, A., and A. Mian. 2005. "Unchecked Intermediaries: Price Manipulation in an Emerging Stock Market." *Journal of Financial Economics* 78:203–41.

Kling, G., and L. Gao. 2008. "Chinese Institutional Investors' Sentiment." *Journal of International Financial Markets, Institutions and Money* 18:374–87.

Lang, M., and R. Lundholm. 1996. "Corporate Disclosure Policy and Analyst Behavior." *The Accounting Review* October:467–92.

Leuz, C., D. Nanda, and P. Wysocki. 2003. "Earnings Management and Institutional Factors: An International Comparison." *Journal of Financial Economics* 69 (3): 505–27.

Leuz, C., and F. Oberholzer-Gee. 2006. "Political Relations, Global Financing, and Corporate Transparency: Evidence from Indonesia." *Journal of Financial Economics* 81 (2): 411–39.

Liu, Q., and Z. Lu. 2007. "Corporate Governance and Earnings Management in Chinese Listed Companies: A Tunneling Perspective." *Journal of Corporate Finance* 13 (5): 881–906.

Liu, Q. 2006. "Corporate Governance in China: Current Practices, Economic Effects and Institutional Determinants." *CESifo Economic Studies* 52 (2): 415–53.

Mei, J., J. Scheinkman, and W. Xiong. 2005. "Speculative Trading and Stock Prices: Evidence from China's A-B Share Premia." NBER Working Paper no. 11362. Cambridge, MA: National Bureau of Economic Research, May.

Merton, R. 1987. "A Simple Model of Capital Market Equilibrium with Incomplete Information." *The Journal of Finance* July:483–510.

Morck, R., B. Yeung, and W. Yu. 2000. "The Information Content of Stock Markets: Why Do Emerging Markets Have Synchronous Stock Price Movements?" *Journal of Financial Economics* 58:215–60.

Naughton, T., C. Truong, and M. Veeraraghavan. 2008. "Momentum Strategies and Stock Returns: Chinese Evidence." *Pacific-Basin Finance Journal* 16:476–92.

Piotroski, J., T. J. Wong, and T. Zhang. 2011. "Political Incentives to Suppress Negative Financial Information: Evidence from Chinese Listed Firms." Working Paper. Stanford University and the Chinese University of Hong Kong.

Qian, Y., and B. Weingast. 1997. "Federalism as a Commitment to Preserving Market Incentives." *Journal of Economic Perspectives* 11:83–92.

Rajan, R., and L. Zingales. 2003. "The Great Reversals: The Politics of Financial Development in the 20th Century." *Journal of Financial Economics* 69:5–50.

Roll, R. 1988. "R^2." *Journal of Finance* 43:541–66.

Schuppli, M., and M. Bohl. 2010. "Do Foreign Institutional Investors Destabilize China's A-share Market? *Journal of International Financial Markets, Institutions and Money* 20:36–50.

Stulz, R. 1999. "Globalization, Corporate Finance, and the Cost of Capital." *Journal of Applied Corporate Finance* 12:8–25.

Tan, L., T. Chiang, J. Mason, and E. Nelling. 2008. "Herding Behavior in Chinese Stock Markets: An Examination of A and B Shares." *Pacific-Basic Finance Journal* 16:61–77.

Tang, Y. W. 1999. "Issues in the Development of the Accounting Profession in China." *China Accounting and Finance Review* 1:21–36.

Teoh, S. H., and T. J. Wong. 1993. "Perceived Auditor Quality and the Earnings Response Coefficient." *The Accounting Review* 68:346–67.

Wang, Q., T. J. Wong, and L. Xia. 2008. "State Ownership, Institutional Environment, and Auditor Choice: Evidence from China." *Journal of Accounting and Economics* 46 (1): 112–34.

Watts, R. 2006. "What Has the Invisible Hand Achieved?" Working Paper. Massachusetts Institute of Technology.

Watts, R. L., and J. L. Zimmerman. 1986. *Positive Accounting Theory.* Englewood Cliffs, NJ: Prentice-Hall.

World Economic Forum. 2011. *Global Competitiveness Report*, edited by Klaus Schwab. Geneva: World Economic Forum.

Yang, L., Q. Tang, A. Kilgore, and J. Hong. 2001. "Auditor-Government Associations and Auditor Independence in China." *British Accounting Review* 33:175–89.

Yu, Q., B. Du, and Q. Sun. 2006. "Earnings Management at Rights Issuance Thresholds—Evidence from China." *Journal of Banking and Finance* 30 (12): 3453–68.

Zhong, H. 1998. "Analysis of the Answers to Survey Questions by Chinese CPAs." *CPA News* 1:59–64.

Comment   Li Jin

Joe Piotroski and T. J. Wong study the financial reporting practices and information environment of Chinese listed firms. The chapter follows Bushman, Piotroski, and Smith (2004) to define corporate transparency as the widespread availability of firm-specific information to market participants outside the publicly-listed firm, and categorize country, regional, and firm-level information mechanisms into three broad headings: (1) the corporate reporting regime, which includes the quality of the firm's financial reports and the underlying audit function; (2) the intensity of private information acquisition activities, which includes the depth and breadth of analyst and institutional investor activity; and (3) the strength of dissemination mechanisms, including the role of media and freedom of the press.

Judged by a variety of standards, corporate transparency in China is not satisfactory. At the stock level, Chinese stocks have high synchronicity, meaning less meaningful firm-specific information is incorporated in the stock prices. There is also high crash likelihood, suggesting that bad news often accumulates in the firm for lack of better disclosure, and only later comes out in batches. Survey evidence indicates that while the over-

Li Jin is associate professor of business administration at Harvard Business School.

For acknowledgments, sources of research support, and disclosure of the author's material financial relationships, if any, please see http://www.nber.org/chapters/c12465.ack.

all transparency improves in absolute terms, it continues to lag those in many developed and developing countries. On the surface, Chinese financial reporting standards and practices show trends of improvements, but they still lag behind the rest of the world, particularly as it comes to the actual enforcement of these rules and standards. The lack of sufficient progress is also reflected in the evidences mentioned in the chapter, on the stock market behavior and survey results.

The lack of transparency in China has its deep roots in the unique specification of institutional arrangements in China. The chapter discusses these institutional mechanisms, such as the substantial state ownership of listed firms, the tight government control of capital markets, the weak market institutions and limited protection of property rights, and the use of local auditors whose independence might be questionable.

I very much agree with their assessments, and believe that the chapter laid a solid foundation for a systematic and comprehensive research agenda in understanding the information environment in China. Nonetheless, my role as a discussant is to point out places that evidence is still less than compelling. I will focus on a few issues.

The first is, we could get some additional mileage by reorganizing the impacts of China's institutional features on information production/transparency into the "supply side" and "demand side" of the financial reporting. This might highlight some additional issues that are very relevant for the discussion, but are not sufficiently covered. On the supply side, the question would be: what are the incentives, and conflicts of interests, for the insider/owner to provide timely and accurate financial reporting? The chapter discussed issues such as the lack of accounting standards/execution to push them, the dominant government ownership, and the potential nonprofit maximization objective, which disregard much of the value relevant to private information, and bureaucrats' political needs in hiding bad news, particularly before the important political events. What I would like to see more discussion about also includes insider's desire to manipulate stock price and do insider trading, and the potential collusion of corporate insiders and some perverse outside investors to take advantage of the naivety of the predominantly retail investors, in issuing false/misleading information. On the demand side, we might want to know who are demanding the transparency, and how their behavior is different in China. The chapter points out the dominance of banking system in capital allocation, and the existence and convenience of administrative reporting channel (at least for state-owned businesses). What about the retail investor-dominated market, which is primarily driven by sentiment and not able to consume the financial reports?

The second issue is, some people could question the importance of the improvement of the information environment. In other words, if the Chinese regulatory authority has a number of things to address to improve the efficiency of its capital markets, and only limited resources, how much priority should it give to the further improvement of the information environment? Piotroski and Wong point out a number of benefits. Better transparency can reduce information and transaction costs in an economy, thus improving resource allocation efficiency. It serves as a basis for effective monitoring and corporate governance, in reducing self-dealing, stock price manipulation, and expropriation of minority and outsider investors. It also ensures the smooth functioning of the stock market in avoiding sudden large crashes, which could be disruptive to the financial market. The ultimate results are that corporate transparency is very important in facilitating the development of public capital markets as an alternative channel of resource allocation, in addition to the traditional channel through the banking system. The enlargement of the participation of investors, particularly small domestic investors and foreign investors, would have the additional benefit of broadening the shareholder base, thus potentially lowering the cost of capital. But are these results really true? Who is consuming the information? As detailed in Choi, Jin, and Yan (2010), the average Chinese stock is held by predominantly retail Chinese investors, who are very subject to short-term sentiments. The average turnover of the Chinese stocks can be as high as 1,000 percent in a year, suggesting that the average investors are holding the stock for about one to two months. If those short-term oriented investors rely more on gossips and market-wide signals such as the macroeconomic policy changes, then it is questionable whether they would demand more corporate transparency, and how much they are willing to pay for that. In addition, evidence is emerging that even institutional investors in China are relying more on market sentiment and macroeconomic indicators in their trade decisions (Mei, Scheinkman, and Xiong 2005; Tan et al. 2008; Kling and Gao 2008), again questioning the need of these institutions to gain additional insights through better corporate transparency. The benefits of the enlargement of a shareholder base, particularly the foreign investor shareholder base, might be appealing at first glance. But careful analysis of the situation in China suggest that too much, not too little, foreign capital is flowing into the Chinese capital market, for geopolitical reasons related to the trade imbalance and the perceived "one-sided bet" on an appreciation of the Chinese currency against the US dollar. In this context, the concern of the regulatory body is more likely to be on discouraging the rapid inflow of capital into Chinese companies, rather than encouraging it. The other argument, about the increased crash likelihood due to lack of sufficient information disclosure and the resulting disruption to the capital market and even real economy, can also be questionable if one factor in the reality that Chinese stock market is pretty responsive to the systematic movement of the market environment, such as macro policy. Existing studies, such as Jin and Myers (2006), point out that the withholding of firm-specific information will lead to the higher likelihood of a crash of individual company stocks, rather than a crash of the whole stock market. This will thus limit the concern of the regulatory body. To be fair, one should never understate the importance of corporate transparency, and the improved information environment will certainly facilitate the development of the public equity market, which would provide a potentially much more powerful and efficient mechanism of the allocation of capital within China. But that is something that could be considered along with other means to improve the public capital market efficiency, and reform the market in a balanced way.

Another issue is on the emphasis of the enforcement of the regulations and standards. If we look at the rules and regulations, on the surface China has similar regulations as the mature economies. This might not be surprising, as it is easy for China to copy the wordings in the international standards. But the enforcement might be much harder. Is there a way to measure enforcement and its change over time? I would not be surprised if we could find that the actual change of information environment is closely related to the change of the actual enforcement, rather than the adaptation of the regulations and standards.

Responding to suggestions by many conference attendees (myself included), Piotroski and Wong now added a substantial discussion about the role played by the other two categories of information mechanisms: the intensity of private information acquisition activities, which includes the depth and breadth of analyst and institutional investor activity, and the strength of dissemination mechanisms, including the role of media and freedom of the press. The new evidence there indicating the lack of progress on these two fronts pretty much corroborates their evidence on the corporate reporting regime. This is perhaps not surprising, and it is very much related to the next issue that I want to raise.

An interesting follow-up research question to ask would be: What are the key drivers of the change of information environment and standards in China? One can think of a few different causes (not mutually exclusive): (a) the increase of accounting professionals, both inside the corporations and in the investment community, that enables a more efficient dissemination of information; (b) the increasing pressure of investors, particularly sophisticated investors such as domestic and foreign institutions, that demands such high-quality information; (c) the improvements in the rules and regulations governing the disclosure of corporate inside information, and, perhaps more importantly, the increasingly stringent enforcement of the law; (d) the increase of level of sophistication of investors, both foreign and domestic, and individuals and institutions alike, in demanding more corporate transparency; (d) the gradual easing of the Chinese political system on the tight control of information, particularly information that is viewed as politically sensitive. One could imagine that some empirical analysis could be done to see whether and how the relaxation of each of these constraints can impact the information environment in China. For example, does the high profile prosecution of corporate fraud cases have a meaningful impact on the future disclosure?

In summary, Piotroski and Wong have raised a number of interesting and important issues regarding the development of public equities market in China. However, one needs to be cautious in interpreting the evidence, and further research is required to determine whether and how the features of the institutional and informational environment they identify will spur rapid growth of the local public equity markets.

References

Bushman, R., J. Piotroski, and A. Smith. 2004. "What Determines Corporate Transparency?" *Journal of Accounting Research* 42 (2): 207–52.

Choi, J., L. Jin, and H. Yan. 2010. "What Does Stock Ownership Breadth Measure?" NBER Working Paper no. 16591. Cambridge, MA: National Bureau of Economic Research, December.

Jin, L., and S. Myers. 2006. "R2 around the World: New Theory and New Tests." *Journal of Financial Economics* 79:257–92.

Kling, G., and L. Gao. 2008. "Chinese Institutional Investors' Sentiment." *Journal of International Financial Markets, Institutions and Money* 18:374–87.

Mei, J., J. Scheinkman, and W. Xiong. 2005. "Speculative Trading and Stock Prices: Evidence from China's A-B Share Premia." NBER Working Paper no. 11362. Cambridge, MA: National Bureau of Economic Research, May.

Tan, L., T. Chiang, J. Mason, and E. Nelling. 2008. "Herding Behavior in Chinese Stock Markets: An Examination of A and B Shares." *Pacific-Basic Finance Journal* 16:61–77.

III

Capital Accumulation

Why Are Saving Rates So High in China?

Dennis Tao Yang, Junsen Zhang, and Shaojie Zhou

5.1 Introduction

The spectacular economic growth of China in the past three decades has been associated with an equally remarkable high rate of saving. While the gross national saving as a percentage of gross domestic product (GDP) hovered just a little above 35 percent in the 1980s, the average yearly rate climbed to 41 percent in the 1990s (figure 5.1). Since China's entry into the World Trade Organization (WTO), the growth in aggregate saving accelerated, surging from just below 38 percent in 2000 to an unprecedented 53 percent in 2007. China's national saving rates since 2000 have been one of the highest worldwide, far surpassing the rates prevailing in Japan, South Korea, and other East Asian economies during the years of their miracle growth.[1]

Dennis Tao Yang is professor of business administration at the University of Virginia. Junsen Zhang is the Wei Lun Professor of Economics at the Chinese University of Hong Kong. Shaojie Zhou is assistant professor in the School of Public Policy and Management at Tsinghua University.

The authors would like to thank Julan Du, Joseph Fan, Randall Morck, Leslie Young, and the participants in the NBER Conference on Capitalizing China in Boston, CUHK International Conference on China, and the Tsinghua Conference on Saving and Investment for their constructive comments and suggestions. The authors would also like to thank Jessie Pan for her excellent research assistance. The authors would like to acknowledge the financial support from the Research Grants Council of the Hong Kong Special Administrative Region, China (Project No. CUHK 453008), and the National Natural Science Foundation of China (Project No. 70903039), and the research support from the Hong Kong Institute of Asia-Pacific Studies. Dennis T. Yang acknowledges the research support provided by the Hong Kong Institute of Monetary Research, where he conducted research when he served as a research fellow. For acknowledgments, sources of research support, and disclosure of the authors' material financial relationships, if any, please see http://www.nber.org/chapters/c12068.ack.

1. These saving figures are based on information from the World Development Indicators (WDI). In 2008, the gross national saving rate of China ranked the ninth-highest among 228

The high and rising aggregate saving and thus the low and declining share of consumption in the GDP constitute a central feature of the Chinese economy. High saving is not only closely related to domestic liquidity, investment, economic growth, and income distributions among firms, households, and the government but also to China's international trade and capital flows. With the government's concerted efforts to stimulate consumption and economic growth amid the recent financial crisis, increasing attention has been given on the issue of saving. Despite the bourgeoning literature on the subject, debates continue among economists regarding the underlying causes of China's high rate of saving. Although some progress has been made to understand household saving behaviors, a significant void in research on corporate and government saving still remains. The main objectives of this chapter are to document historical trends in Chinese aggregate saving using multiple data sources, analyze the forces that contributed to the recent rise in government, corporate, and household saving, and assess the prospects for Chinese national savings in the near future.

We start with an overview of the major patterns in Chinese national saving in the past three decades. Drawing data from the World Development Indicators (WDI), China's Flow of Funds Accounts (FFA), and other sources of aggregate statistics, we analyze and compare the aggregate saving in China with that of representative economies and major country groups. A breakdown of aggregate saving into the components of corporate, household, and government reveals major changes and sources of national saving over time. These analyses help define "The Chinese Saving Puzzle," a set of unique features still not well understood in the existing literature of aggregate saving in the historical context of China and in light of international comparisons.

We then proceed to examine the sources and causes of the rising saving of the government, corporate, and household sectors in China, focusing on the period of 1999 to 2007. The sharp rise in government taxes on production and the collection of social security fees and income taxes were the dominant factors that increased the disposable income of the government. As the growth of income outpaced that of government consumption, the saving rate rose rapidly. The analysis of enterprise behavior opens the discussion on data-related issues pertaining to the FFA, the main source of data for documenting aggregate saving in China. We examine the role of firm profitability, labor compensation and dividend, imperfect capital markets, and government policies in shaping corporate saving. Our analysis of household behavior relies on data from the Urban Household Survey (UHS) from six provinces, covering the period of 1992 to 2006. We summarize stylized facts

---

countries recorded in the WDI database. The eight economies with higher saving rates than China are all very small. Saudi Arabia and Singapore are the two economies of significant size with saving rates below that of China, but were nonetheless above 50 percent.

on household saving and explore the factors we believe have driven the recent upward trend in household saving. The role played by unique institutions, policies, and reform processes in China is assessed.

Lastly, based on the foregoing analysis of saving determinants, we argue that systematic forces, such as slower economic growth, moderate export expansion, and government plans to strengthen social welfare and population aging, are already set in to induce a decline in aggregate saving. A saving rate of above 50 percent of the GDP could already be a phenomenon of the past, and China would likely enter an era of a more balanced growth.

5.2   Long-Term Trends in Aggregate Saving

5.2.1   International Comparison

To document the special features of Chinese saving in light of international experience, we make a cross-country comparison of national saving rates using the WDI (World Bank 2010b). The WDI defines gross domestic saving as GDP less the aggregate consumption expenditures based on data from national income accounts. Using this standard definition, we compare China's saving rates for the period of 1978 to 2008 with those of countries from different income groups, BRIC economies (Brazil, Russia, India, and China), and selected developed economies.

Figure 5.1, part A, shows that the rate of aggregate saving in China has remained persistently above 34 percent of the GDP since 1978, the year when systematic economic reforms began. Therefore, high saving in China has been a long-term phenomenon. Since 2000, there has been a surge in the saving rate, reaching a startling 53.1 percent of the GDP in 2007. The saving rates of middle-income and low-income groups have also increased, but at a rate much slower than that of China. In 2006, the latest year with available data on the saving rates of all country groups, the saving rate of China (52.4 percent) was about 3.3 times higher than that of the low-income group (16.1 percent), and 2.4 times higher than the world average (22.1 percent).

China's high saving also stands out among those of the BRIC economies, as shown in part B of figure 5.1. In 2008, the national saving rate in China was 49.2 percent, whereas the rate for Russia was 36.3 percent, India 32.9 percent, and Brazil 19.1 percent. Despite two erratic spikes in Russia's saving series, there has been a recent upward trend in saving for all three countries. Between 1998 and 2008, the saving rate of Brazil increased by 4.1 percentage points, Russia by 14.6 percentage points, and India by 11.9 percentage points.

In contrast to the rising saving observed in the large and fast-growing developing countries, the overall saving rates of industrialized economies have experienced a gradual decline, as seen in figure 5.1, part C. In the early 1990s, the level of saving in China was comparable with that of its rich East

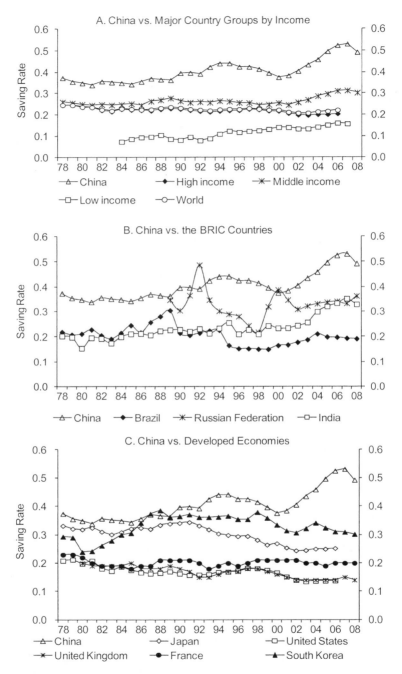

Fig. 5.1   Gross national saving rates of China and other economies, 1978–2008
Source: World Development Indictors (World Bank 2009).

Asian neighbors, Japan and South Korea. However, the saving rate of Japan continually declined after reaching a peak of 34.4 percent in 1991 until it dropped to a three-decade low of 25.2 percent in 2006. The saving rates of the United States, France, and the United Kingdom have either stagnated or experienced chronic decline in the past three decades. Since 2000, the disparity in gross domestic saving rates between China and the major developed countries has widened. By 2006, the saving rate of China was 27.2 percentage points higher than that of Japan and 38.6 percentage points higher than that of the United States. By 2007, the gap in gross saving between China and South Korea grew to 22.1 percentage points, whereas the gaps in France and the United Kingdom increased to 29 and 35 percentage points, respectively.

5.2.2   Components of Aggregate Saving

The high and rising aggregate saving in China can be analyzed by source through the three components: households, enterprises, and the government. Earlier studies that analyzed by sector saving include Qian (1988) for the period of 1978 to 1984, Kraay (2000) for 1978 to 1995, Kuijs (2005, 2006) for 1990 to 2005, and Chamon and Prasad (2010) for 1990 to 2005.

At the inception of reforms in China in 1978, total household saving only accounted for 6 to 7 percent of the GDP, whereas the government saving hovered around 15 to 18 percent of the GDP (Qian 1988; Kraay 2000). Between 1978 and 1984, the household saving continued to rise, and the government saving fell dramatically, maintaining the aggregate saving rate at a stable level. The decline in government savings persisted through the early 1990s.

In 1995, the National Bureau of Statistics (NBS) began to publish the FFA based on the physical transitions of the national income accounting in the Statistical Yearbook of China. With a three-year lag policy, the most recent data available for this chapter cover the period of 1992 to 2007.[2] Whereas the WDI data cover a much longer period, the FFA data have the advantage of reporting the composition of gross domestic saving by household, business, and government, as well as information on incomes and expenditures within each of the sectors. Figure 5.2 presents three interesting observations.[3] First, aggregate saving in China remained at a high level of

2. See He and Cao (2007) and Ma and Wang (2010) for the analyses of Chinese aggregate saving using the FFA data.

3. Yearly saving rates based on the FFA data have noticeable differences from the rates based on the WDI data as reported in figure 5.1, although the long-term trends are generally consistent. Comparing these two data series, we find that from 1992 to 1999, the WDI measure was 2.8 to 6 percentage points higher than the FFA measure. In 1999, their difference amounted to 5 percentage points. Since 2000, however, the difference has become much smaller, except for 2006 when the FFA measure exceeded the WDI measure by 2.9 percentage points. Note that these two measures of domestic saving rates have the same definition—that is, 1 – final consumption expenditure/GDP—and the final consumption includes household consumption and general government consumption expenditures. Although there is little difference in the ratio of government consumption to the GDP in the two data sets, the FFA data report a higher

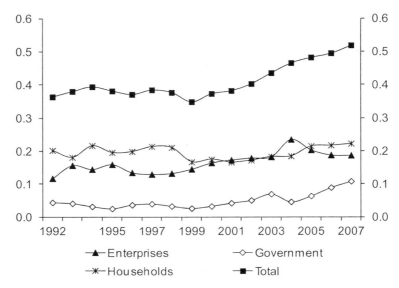

Fig. 5.2   Household, enterprise, and government saving as percentage of GDP, 1992–2007

Source: NBS (1995–2009).

above 34.9 percent of the GDP for the entire period. Second, there was a recent surge in saving rate by almost 17 percent from 1999 to 2007. Finally, all three sectors contributed significantly to the upsurge of the gross national saving. Between 1999 and 2007, the share of corporate saving rose from 14.6 to 18.8 percent of the GDP, the household saving from 16.7 to 22.2 percent, and the government from 2.6 to 10.8 percent. Overall, the largest percentage increase, by 8.2 percent of the GDP, was the saving of the government.

5.2.3   The Chinese Saving Puzzle

In light of the historical trends and international comparisons, we consider the Chinese saving puzzle to have four interrelated aspects: (a) persistently high saving rates between 34 and 53 percent of the GDP in the past thirty years; (b) an outlier in international comparisons, that is, having one of the highest saving rates among all nations since 2000, and an outlier

---

ratio of household consumption to GDP, especially for the periods 1992 to 1999 and 2005 to 2006. Therefore, the disparity in domestic saving rates comes mainly from the differences in household consumption expenditures to the GDP. This disparity reflects in part the content of household consumption in the two data sets. According to FFA statistics, household final consumption expenditure includes not only monetary spending but also in-kind consumption, which could result in higher ratios of household consumption to GDP in the FFA data. In addition, the WDI measure of the final consumption in the GDP also includes any statistical discrepancy in the use of resources relative to the supply of resources, which could contribute to the disparity in domestic saving rates between FFA and WDI data.

in cross-country regressions of saving determination;[4] (c) surge in gross domestic saving by 11 percentage points between 2000 and 2008 based on the WDI data;[5] and (d) household saving as a share of GDP experiencing the highest growth among the three sectors since the inception of reforms in 1978.[6] These observations jointly define the Chinese saving puzzle. We consider it a puzzle because the fundamental forces shaping these special saving patterns are still not well understood.

In what follows, we use the FFA data to investigate the sources and causes of the high and rising government and corporate saving in the period of 1992 to 2007 and use UHS data to examine household saving in the period of 1988 to 2007. The time coverage reflects data availability.

5.3   Corporate Saving

The high corporate and government saving during the earlier years of reform reflects the high-investment and heavy industry-oriented development strategy adopted in the central planning period. Between 1965 and 1977, the gross national saving of China averaged 27 percent of the GDP and had a small component of household saving (Kraay 2000). As the state influence of enterprise accumulation diminished with the introduction of reforms, aggregate corporate saving declined to only about 13 percent of the GDP in the late 1990s. What forces drove up corporate saving by about 6 percentage points of the GDP in the period of 1999 to 2007?

The trend of rising enterprise saving is most commonly documented using the FFA data from the national income accounts of China.[7] As defined by FFA, enterprise saving equals the value-added of both financial and non-financial companies minus labor compensation, production taxes, net asset payments, and net transfer payments.[8] In China, total enterprise saving is equivalent to the "total disposable income" of the business sectors, but the concept is different from either net income or free cash flow in the standard corporate finance literature. It is a concept very close to net income plus

4. Kraay (2000) uses a large sample of countries to investigate the cross-country determinants of saving and finds that economy-wide saving in China is nearly 10 percentage points higher than what would be expected based on standard determinants of national savings.

5. Note that the FFA data reveal a generally consistent trend, although its data coverage ends in 2007.

6. According to Qian (1988) and Kraay (2000), household saving accounted for only 6 to 7 percent of the GDP in the late 1970s. As figure 5.2 shows, however, household saving as a share of the GDP climbed to 22.2 percent in 2007, implying an increase of about 16 percent. In contrast, the combined savings by the government and enterprises stayed roughly the same at about 30 percent of the GDP in the beginning and ending years of the analysis.

7. An exception is Bayoumi, Tong, and Wei (chapter 6, this volume), who examine Chinese corporate saving behavior based on firm level data.

8. More specifically, asset payments include interest payments, dividends, and land rentals, whereas transfers include corporate income tax, social insurance fees, social subsidies, and social welfare payments.

depreciation and amortization. Thus, the formation of fixed capital, capital transfers, changes in inventory, and equity investments are not included in the calculation of enterprise saving.

Using this definition of corporate saving in Chinese statistics, the legacy of the high-accumulation strategy from the central planning and incomplete institutional reforms can partially explain the high enterprise saving in the past three decades. For instance, the suppression of wages, low-interest payments on loans, and low land rentals all tended to raise the disposable income of the enterprises, thus giving them more opportunities to save.[9] These forces of economic planning continued into the reform era despite a gradual decline in the magnitude of the distortions over time. However, aside from these institutional factors that influence the general level of business saving, we argue that several factors have helped elevate enterprise saving in the past decade.

5.3.1   Rising Profitability of Enterprises

The saving capacity of enterprises reflects their profitability. As shown in figure 5.3, the profitability of enterprises has generally improved since the early 1990s. While the nominal firm profits increased more than fifteen-fold from 1992 to 2007, the ratio of profits to industrial value added also improved remarkably, from about 21 percent in the late 1990s to close to 30 percent in 2007. Figure 5.4 provides corroborative evidence that the share of enterprise income in the GDP rose from 13 percent in the late 1990s to above 18 percent in 2007.

The rise in corporate profitability is an outcome of a series of socioeconomic and institutional changes implemented in China throughout the reform period. For instance, the privatization of state-owned enterprises (SOEs) and the growth of private enterprises are found to have induced more innovative efforts and raised the labor and total factor productivity of the corporate sector (Jefferson and Su 2006; Bai, Lu, and Tao 2009). Labor market reforms involving the use of labor-incentive schemes, the relaxation of worker mobility restrictions, and especially the massive rural-urban migration have all contributed to the efficient functioning of firms. In particular, the large flow of rural labor to cities, which was estimated at around 135 million in 2007 (Meng et al. 2010), has helped maintain low labor costs for business, a major factor behind China's emergence as the workshop of the world (Yang, Chen, and Monarch 2010). Moreover, China began implementing a large-scale privatization of SOEs in 1998 with the objectives of improving corporate governance and maintaining the competitiveness of the state sector in the national economy. From 1997 to 2003, the share of SOE workers in urban employment dropped from 54.6 to 26.8 percent as the

---

9. We are grateful to Leslie Young for making constructive suggestions on these arguments as well as referring us to the related literature.

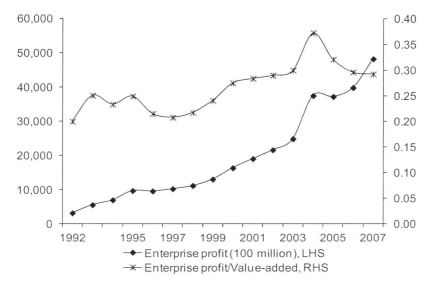

Fig. 5.3   Enterprise profit and value added, 1992–2007
Source: NBS (1995–2009).

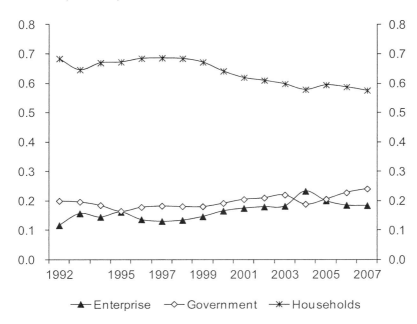

Fig. 5.4   Income distribution among households, enterprises, and government, 1992–2007
Source: NBS (1995–2009).

result of enterprise restructuring (National Bureau of Statistics of China, NBS 1998, 2004). The productivity of the state sector rose, and the competitive pressure also spread to raise the productivity of the nonstate sector.

The rise in corporate saving—that is, 14.6 to 18.8 percent of the GDP from 1999 to 2007—was also attributable to China's remarkable expansion in export associated with its accession to the WTO. Beginning in the late 1990s, with the anticipation of joining the WTO, China's export growth accelerated. The momentum of trade expansion continued after China's accession to the WTO in 2001 as trade barriers and tariffs continued to fall. Between 1999 and 2007, the export growth reached an unprecedented 26 percent per annum (NBS 2008). This expansion in external demand handed China an opportunity to realize its potential comparative advantage in trade. When exports were combined with equally remarkable foreign direct investment (FDI) inflows as well as the imports of sophisticated intermediate inputs, these factors jointly created a powerful force to increase firm productivity and profits.

Trade expansion, and thus increases in corporate revenue, was facilitated by trade policies in China. Since 1998, after the Asian financial crisis, China has initiated a trade-promoting policy of rewarding tax rebates for exports (TRE). Since then, TRE has become an important macroeconomic management policy. The value of the rebate increased substantially after China's accession to the WTO. Figure 5.5 shows that the total volume of TRE increased from 115 billion Yuan in 2002 to 586.6 billion in 2008. The size of these tax rebates was highly significant: in 2006, the total TRE received by exporting firms was equivalent to 10 percent of aggregate corporate saving and about 14 percent of government tax revenue in the same year. The TRE remained at high levels throughout 2004 to 2008. Therefore, the expanded external demand and favorable trade policies both helped raise the corporate earnings of Chinese firms with the accession of China to the WTO.

5.3.2   Costs of Financing, Dividend Payments, and Labor Compensations

While export expansion and tax rebate added directly to the revenue of firms, maintaining the low cost of production also contributed to the rise in the disposable incomes of enterprises. Ma and Wang (2010) find that net interest payments as share of the GDP by the nonfinancial corporate sector dropped by 50 percent between 1992 and 2007. In particular, SOEs financed their loans and paid their debts at interest rates much lower than the prevailing market rates. If SOEs actually paid at market interest rates, their existing profits, and thus their saving, would have been greatly reduced (Ferri and Liu 2009). Moreover, enterprises managed to control labor compensation during the same period. As shown in figure 5.6, the share of labor compensation of employees in the total value added of enterprises declined from

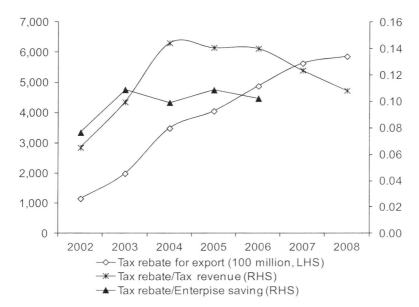

Fig. 5.5   Tax rebate for export in China, 2002–2008
Source: NBS (2003–2009).

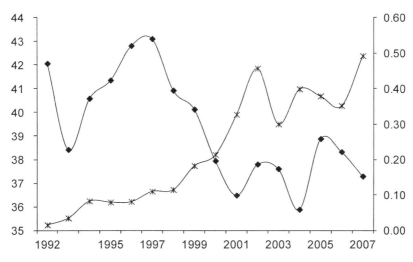

Fig. 5.6   Labor compensation and dividend distributed to households, 1992–2007
Source: NBS (1995–2009).

an average of 41.2 percent in the 1990s to 37.5 percent in the 2000s, helping raise the enterprise saving capacity. Although some stockholders earn dividends, total dividend payments only accounted for a small proportion of the enterprise value added. Despite an upward trend in dividend payments, the ratio of dividend to value added was still less than 0.5 percent by 2007 (figure 5.6). Part of the story is that the Chinese government did not ask SOEs to pay dividends until 2008 even though they had enjoyed improved profits since the state-sector restructuring in the late 1990s. These aggregate statistics appear to be consistent with firm-level data reported in Zhang (2008) that for a large sample of Chinese firms in the period of 1999 to 2003, the average and median dividends to earnings ratios were 0.35 and 0.16, respectively. Lower dividends translate directly to more retained corporate earnings based on the FFA statistics.

5.3.3   Imperfect Capital Markets

Weaknesses in China's financial sector motivated the enterprises, especially small and medium-sized enterprises (SMEs), to rely on their own saving to finance fixed-asset investments. Despite the systematic financial reforms since the middle 1990s, including the reconstruction of nonperformance loans, banks in China still play a limited role in channeling saving from frugal households to the enterprise sector (e.g., Hofman and Kuijs 2006).

Table 5.1 reports the sources of funding for fixed-asset investments in the period of 1995 to 2007. Contrary to the conventional wisdom that bank credits are the main source of financing, the share of domestic loans remained below 21 percent of the total investments throughout the period. Instead,

Table 5.1   **Sources of funds for fixed assets investment (%)**

Year	State budget	Domestic loans	FDI	Self-raising funds	Others
1995	3.03	20.46	11.19	51.88	13.45
1996	2.68	19.58	11.76	47.74	18.24
1997	2.76	18.93	10.63	49.71	17.97
1998	4.17	19.30	9.11	48.81	18.61
1999	6.22	19.24	6.74	49.20	18.59
2000	6.37	20.32	5.12	49.28	18.91
2001	6.70	19.06	4.56	49.79	19.89
2002	7.02	19.67	4.63	50.65	18.04
2003	4.59	20.55	4.43	53.65	16.78
2004	4.37	18.49	4.41	55.35	17.39
2005	4.39	17.25	4.21	58.26	15.89
2006	3.93	16.47	3.64	59.75	16.21
2007	3.88	15.28	3.40	60.59	16.84
2008	4.35	14.46	2.90	64.79	13.50

Source: China Statistical Yearbook 2009.

self-raised funds always accounted for the largest share of contribution to investment. It is worth pointing out that the share of self-raised funds in the total investment increased over time, rising from just below 50 percent in the middle 1990s to 64.8 percent in 2008. In other words, enterprise investment relied more on self-retained earnings, whereas the importance of domestic loans generally declined in the last decade. Therefore, the high saving of enterprises, particularly among SMEs, can be interpreted as reflecting the difficulties in obtaining financing from state banks because of the lack of collaterals required to secure loans.

By 2008, the state budget and FDI contributed to about 7 percent of the total fixed-asset investment. Informal and private financing channels, as represented by the "others" category, accounted for 13.5 percent of the total financing; this share is comparable in size with domestic loans. Therefore, despite the development and commercialization of capital markets in China, formal financing through bank loans is still limited. The weak financial sector creates the incentives for enterprise saving.

5.4   Government Saving

Government in the FFA data refers to all levels of administrative units and nonprofit institutions affiliated with the state and local governments. Table 5.2 presents the data series on consumption, saving, and detailed components of government disposable income. The figures are expressed in nominal terms because selecting price deflators for different variables is prone to arbitrariness, and our primary interest is the changes in yearly saving rates based on current prices. The share of government saving in GDP fluctuated at a level below 4.4 percent in the period of 1992 to 1999, reaching the lowest point at 2.6 percent in 1999. However, the figure had climbed since then, reaching 10.8 percent in 2007.

The government's disposable income, which mainly consists of value added from government production, incomes from properties, taxes on all production, income taxes, and social insurance revenue but minus labor compensations, rose from 1,608.9 billion Yuan in 1999 to 6,308.4 billion Yuan in 2007, as indicated in column (6) of table 5.1. The rise in tax revenues on production, as reported in column (3), was the largest contributor to the growth in government income during this period. The net tax increased by 3058.5 billion Yuan, accounting for 65 percent of the increase in the disposable income of government. The institutional foundation behind the rise in tax revenues can be traced back to the famous 1994 Fiscal Reform in China that managed to reverse a declining trend in state revenues beginning in the mid-1980s. The reform aimed to boost revenue collections and reclaim the majority of the total revenue by the central government (Bahl 1999; Wong and Bird 2008). From having a low share of net revenue in the GDP in the earlier 1990s, the effective tax system, when combined with an

Table 5.2   Sources of government disposable income and saving

Year	Value added in production (1)	Labor compensation (2)	Net taxes on production (3)	Net income from properties (4)	Net current transfers (5)	Total disposable income (6)	Consumption (7)	Saving (8)	Saving as share of GDP (9)
1992	303.7	230.8	385.5	-12.2	92.7	538.9	420.3	118.6	4.4
1993	352.3	271.3	546.0	-17.3	84.5	694.3	548.8	145.6	4.1
1994	422.8	317.1	742.5	-26.5	71.0	892.7	739.8	152.9	3.2
1995	477.8	372.7	842.5	-37.3	81.3	991.6	837.9	153.8	2.5
1996	517.6	364.8	1061.6	-48.4	91.0	1257.0	996.4	260.7	3.7
1997	582.1	427.8	1222.1	-43.0	102.9	1436.3	1121.9	314.4	4.0
1998	678.9	534.3	1375.4	-47.1	39.1	1512.0	1235.9	276.1	3.3
1999	735.1	615.2	1449.8	-52.7	91.8	1608.9	1371.7	237.2	2.6
2000	780.9	637.2	1607.5	-21.5	161.9	1891.6	1566.1	325.5	3.3
2001	911.1	719.7	1836.1	-28.2	230.1	2229.8	1766.5	463.3	4.2
2002	1138.9	876.3	2052.4	-35.1	243.8	2523.6	1912.0	611.6	5.1
2003	1341.9	999.5	2330.5	-54.6	387.7	3006.0	2061.5	944.5	7.0
2004	1420.2	1107.4	2364.1	-69.8	445.0	3052.2	2319.9	732.3	4.6
2005	1564.3	1276.4	2954.2	-25.0	608.1	3825.1	2660.6	1164.6	6.4
2006	1817.3	1369.7	3521.8	-7.9	940.6	4902.1	3011.8	1890.3	8.9
2007	2116.4	1596.6	4508.2	31.6	1248.9	6308.4	3519.1	2789.4	10.8

Note: All figures are in nominal billion Yuan. Total disposable income in column (6) = (1) + (3) + (4) + (5) − (2). Saving in column (8) = (6) − (7).

average annual GDP growth of about 10 percent, resulted in continued rise in government revenue from 1999 to 2007.

The second largest contributing factor to government disposable income is net current transfers. According to more detailed FFA sources not reported in table 5.1, the government collected 1,195.5 billion Yuan of income taxes and 1,081.2 billion Yuan of social insurance fees in 2007, but only spent 1,028 billion Yuan on social welfare payments, social insurance provisions, and other transfers. As a result, the government had a net gain of 1,248.9 billion Yuan in net transfers in 2007, which is an increase of 1,157.1 billion Yuan from the 1992 level, accounting for 25 percent of the growth in government disposable income during the same period. Overall, the combined increase in taxes on production and transfers added to about 90 percent of the growth in disposable income from 1992 to 2007.

Compared with the sharp increase in state income, the total growth of 2,147.4 billion Yuan in consumption is still modest. As a result, government saving increased by 2,147.4 billion Yuan, translating to an 8.2 percentage-point increase in its share in the GDP. This tally is consistent with the popular view of "Nation Rich, People Poor," which is now widely discussed in the public media in China. A piece of corroborative evidence is that the share of household income in the GDP declined from 68.6 percent in 1996 to 57.5 percent in 2007 (figure 5.4). Although this view correctly describes the changes in income positions of the government in the past two decades, China's tax revenue as a percentage of the GDP is still lower than that of major developed economies, such as Japan, Germany, and the United States.

5.5   Household Saving

Household saving in China rose substantially in the past three decades along with economic reforms and fast income growth. As noted earlier, household saving only accounted for 6 to 7 percent of the GDP in the late 1970s but grew to about 22 percent in 2007 based on the FFA data (figure 5.2). In what follows, we use more detailed UHS data to document the major features of the Chinese household saving in the period of 1988 to 2007. In light of these stylized facts, we provide a critical overview of the existing literature and present our views on the main factors behind the rise in household saving in China.

5.5.1   Data and Stylized Facts

The data we use come from twenty consecutive years of the UHS conducted by China's NBS. The computer usable form of data began in 1988; the latest data are from 2007 due to the NBS one-year-lag policy for releasing household surveys. The UHS data record basic conditions of urban households and detailed information on income, employment, demographic characteristics of all household members, and detailed consumption information in each calendar year. Our sample comes from five large provinces (i.e., Liaoning, Zhejiang, Guangdong, Sichuan, and Shannxi) and one municipality (i.e., Beijing). These provinces are representatives of China both in terms of income dispersions and geographical coverage.

Household saving is computed as the difference between disposable income and consumption expenditures on food, clothing, housing services, transportation, communication, entertainment, education, medical care, and other miscellaneous items. We also make use of demographic variables, such as young dependency (i.e., the ratio of children below sixteen to adults aged between sixteen and fifty-five for women and sixty for men) and old dependency (i.e., the ratio of the elderly above fifty-five for women and above sixty for men to the working age population), to determine whether saving varies with demographic structures. We limit our analysis to households whose heads are aged between twenty-five and seventy, and exclude self-employed families due to difficulties in computing family incomes.

Table 5.3 reports the basic summary of statistics on the urban household sample. The average household income grew from 14,918 Yuan in 1988 to 49,061 Yuan in 2007, increasing by more than threefold during the twenty-year period. Likewise, the average household consumption increased substantially, although at a rate slower than income growth. As a result, the rate

Table 5.3   Summary statistics of the urban household sample, 1988–2007

Year	No. of observations	Income (2007 yuan)	Consumption (2007 yuan)	Saving rate (%)
1988	2,869	14,918	14,083	5.6
1989	2,683	14,521	12,905	11.1
1990	2,977	15,456	13,093	15.3
1991	2,998	16,453	14,178	13.8
1992	3,673	18,904	15,885	16.0
1993	3,698	20,208	16,973	16.0
1994	3,713	22,308	18,584	16.7
1995	3,727	22,914	19,212	16.2
1996	3,717	23,651	19,473	17.7
1997	3,704	24,472	20,363	16.8
1998	3,782	25,707	21,430	16.6
1999	3,680	26,364	21,648	17.9
2000	4,077	29,124	23,849	18.1
2001	3,656	31,668	25,090	20.8
2002	9,813	30,166	24,295	19.5
2003	10,906	32,281	25,670	20.5
2004	12,748	36,196	28,377	21.6
2005	14,459	40,312	31,124	22.8
2006	14,204	44,184	33,338	24.5
2007	15,260	49,061	35,862	26.9

Source: CHUS data, 1988–2007.

of urban household saving increased from 5.6 percent in 1988 to 26.9 percent in 2007. These trends are generally consistent with the documented rise in household saving based on aggregate data.

5.5.2   Household Saving by Region and Income Level

Figure 5.7 shows that the Chinese household saving is positively related to household incomes. More specifically, the four lines in the graph indicate the saving rates of four income groups defined by their income quantiles. The saving rates of the lowest income group (0 to 25 percent) fluctuated between 5 and 10 percent in most years, ending at 7 percent in 2007. In contrast, the saving rate of the highest income quantile (75 to 100 percent) began at 10 percent in 1988 and increased steadily and rapidly to above 34 percent in 2007, a level that is 27 percentage points higher than that of the lowest income group in that year. This pattern of higher saving among richer families appears to be consistent with the observations in developed economies (e.g., Dynan, Skinner, and Zeldes 2004). Therefore, for China, the rise in household saving appears to be related to the growing income inequality during the process of economic transition. These patterns imply that income transfers from the rich to the poor can raise the propensity to consume in China today. We will revisit this point when discussing the effects of proposed government policies on household saving in the concluding section of this chapter.

Saving rates by region are presented in figure 5.8, where we take a three-year moving average saving rate for each region to mitigate fluctuations in

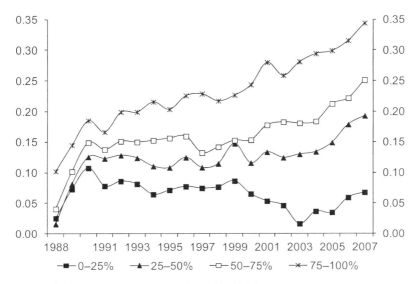

Fig. 5.7   Saving rates by income levels, 1988–2007
Source: UHS data, 1988–2007.

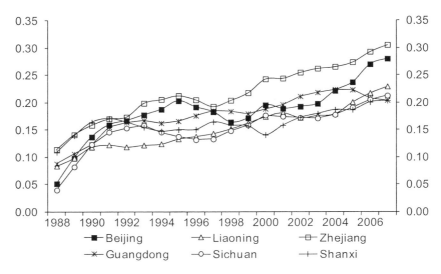

Fig. 5.8   Three-year moving average saving rates by region, 1988–2007
Source: UHS data, 1988–2007.

the measure because of the small size of the sample. The figure reveals that richer provinces, such as Zhejiang and Beijing, have much higher average saving rates than the poor provinces of Liaoning, Sichuan, and Shannxi. The gap in saving rate was initially small in the late 1980s and early 1990s but grew significantly to about 10 percentage points across regions in 2007. Overall, these patterns are consistent with the documented saving rates by income.

5.5.3   Demographic Structures and Life Cycle Saving Profiles

Household saving decisions are pertinently related to their demographic structures. As revealed in table 5.4, family structures in urban China experienced substantial changes in the past two decades. The average size of the household dropped from 3.5 in 1988 to 2.9 in 2007,[10] whereas the average age of the household head increased from 43.2 to 47.3, suggesting the advent of an aging society. The most striking pattern in the table is the sharp decline in child dependency, which is defined as the percentage of households with children below sixteen, from 68 percent in 1988 to 37 percent in 2007. The decline in child dependency is an outcome of the strict implementation of China's one-child policy that began in earnest in 1979.

We plot the saving rates for households of different demographic struc-

10. A household is defined as a residential unit where family members live and have meals together for an extended period of time during the year of the survey. Therefore, family members who live outside the residential unit are not counted as members of a household.

Table 5.4   Demographic structures of the household, 1988–2007

Year	Household size	Age of household head	Schooling of household head	Child dependence ratio	Old dependence ratio
1988	3.5	43.2	10.1	0.68	0.11
1989	3.5	43.8	10.3	0.66	0.12
1990	3.4	44.5	10.3	0.63	0.11
1991	3.3	43.9	10.6	0.64	0.10
1992	3.3	44.7	10.9	0.62	0.10
1993	3.2	45.2	10.9	0.60	0.10
1994	3.2	45.7	11.0	0.58	0.12
1995	3.2	45.5	11.1	0.57	0.12
1996	3.2	46.1	11.2	0.54	0.12
1997	3.2	45.7	11.2	0.53	0.12
1998	3.2	46.0	11.3	0.50	0.13
1999	3.1	46.4	11.3	0.47	0.12
2000	3.1	47.2	11.4	0.44	0.14
2001	3.1	47.3	11.4	0.43	0.13
2002	3.0	47.9	11.4	0.39	0.12
2003	3.0	47.8	11.5	0.38	0.11
2004	2.9	48.2	11.6	0.35	0.12
2005	2.9	48.2	11.6	0.36	0.13
2006	2.9	48.3	11.7	0.34	0.12
2007	2.9	47.3	11.9	0.37	0.11

Source: CHUS data, 1988–2007.

tures in figure 5.9. Persistent increases in saving rates are shown across different types of households, rising by about 21 percentage points in the twenty-year period on average. Since the late 1990s, households with elderly experienced faster growth in saving than the whole sample. Later on, we will discuss that this trend is consistent with the decline in pension incomes for the retired; thus, families with elderly tend to save more to insure smooth consumption. In contrast, households with children tend to save less. This observation is consistent with the fact that costs of children have risen rapidly in recent years. Therefore, for households with middle-aged heads, the increase in their expenditures on raising children appears to have more than offset their higher earnings, thus dragging down their household saving relative to those of other households.

Figure 5.10 presents the age-saving profiles by age of the household head for the periods of 1988 to 1990 and 2005 to 2007. These profiles are perhaps the most important empirical patterns we have documented for the household sector that shed light on the changes in their saving over the two decades. As some age cells contain limited number of observations, we deploy three-age and three-year moving average saving rates to smooth the data series. The 1988 to 1990 age-saving profile reveals a relatively flat "hump-shape," which resembles the typical life cycle saving profiles observed in other econo-

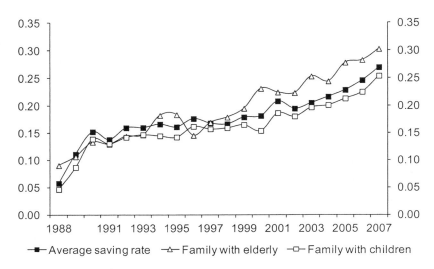

Fig. 5.9   Household saving rates and demographic structure, 1988–2007
Source: UHS data, 1988–2007.

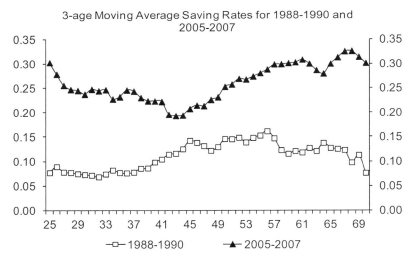

Fig. 5.10   Age saving profiles by age of household head
Source: UHS data, 1988–2007.

mies (e.g., Modigliani 1970). However, the saving profile for 2007 exhibits a dramatic change: (a) saving rates for households of all ages increased substantially, and (b) the profile turns into a "U-shape" over the life cycle; that is, the young and the old saved relatively more than the middle aged. These patterns are consistent with the observations made by Chamon and Prasad (2010) for selected Chinese provinces in the period of 1995 to 2005 and those documented in Song and Yang (2010) and Ge, Yang, and Zhang (2011) using the national sample of UHS data covering the period 1992 to 2007. The two features of increasing household saving and the U-shaped age-earning profiles present a challenge for understanding the determination of household saving in China.

5.5.4   Understanding China's High Household Saving

Given the size of the Chinese economy and the importance of the household sector, considerable research has been devoted to understanding family saving decisions. A number of early studies applied classical models of saving, which originated from the studies of saving behavior in the developed market economies, to the case of China. Among the well-known models are the Keynesian absolute-income hypothesis, Modigliani-Brumberg's life cycle theory, and Friedman's permanent-income hypothesis. These studies, including Chow (1985), Qian (1988), Wang (1995), and Modigliani and Cao (2004), tested alternative hypotheses but ended with inconclusive findings for the saving behavior of the Chinese. One challenging fact that hardly reconciles with theory is that, instead of consuming more to smoothen lifetime consumption, Chinese households continued to save more in anticipation of higher future incomes. Moreover, the age-saving profiles of Chinese households gradually turned into a U-shaped pattern (figure 5.10), which is inconsistent with the hump-shaped profile implied by the life cycle hypothesis.

Habit formation is an alternative theory that can explain the rise in household saving during a period of rapid income growth (Carroll and Weil 1994). The notion of consumption inertia is related to a culture-based explanation to saving behavior. As the Chinese are known to be thrifty, their consumption growth could have lagged behind their income growth during the reform period, thus leading to higher household saving. This argument is supported by the empirical finding that provincial-level variations in household saving over time and space are influenced by the lagged saving rates, a result consistent with the existence of inertia or persistence (Horioka and Wan 2007). However, the empirical evidence is inconclusive. As Modigliani and Cao (2004) argue, the traditional and commonsensical explanation (e.g., why Chinese households are thrifty) counts little, if at all. Indeed, from the 1950s to the mid-1970s, household saving rates in China were below 5 percent, and the sudden spurt occurred during the reform period. Studies based on household data also could not find evidence showing that the current consumption growth is positively correlated with the past consumption growth (Chamon and Prasad 2010). Given that older cohorts usually carry more cultural tradition than younger cohorts, Zhou (2007) rejects the thrifty factor as an important determinant of Chinese household saving. Using the 1988 to 2003 China Health and Nutrition Surveys, he finds that younger Chinese cohorts actually have a higher propensity to save than older cohorts after controlling for other saving determinants.

Demographic changes induced by China's population-control policies could have an effect on household saving through two channels. First, as the nonworking population consisting of the young and the old consumes without producing an income, a rise in their share in the population tends to reduce national household saving. Second, in a developing country without a mature social security system, children often provide old-age support to their parents, and thus children act as an effective substitute for life cycle saving. Motivated by these factors, Modigliani and Cao (2004) use the ratio of employed population to the number of minors up to age fifteen to approximate demographic change. They find that the decline in the young population dependency for the period of 1953 to 2000 increased Chinese household saving through both effects of "less mouths to feed" and old-age security. However, this time-series evidence is not confirmed by panel data studies. Neither aggregate dependency ratio (e.g., Kraay 2000) nor separate accounts of the young and the old dependency ratios (Horioka and Wan 2007) are found to have a significant effect on the household saving rates across Chinese provinces. Applying cohort analysis to data from the UHS, Chamon and Prasad (2010) reach a similar conclusion that demographic structural shifts do not go very far in explaining saving behavior in China.

Competitive saving motive is yet another demographic factor related to the imbalanced sex ratio in China (Wei and Zhang 2011). As the two authors argue, the traditional preference for a son is widespread in China. With restrictive population control policies, many families use the inexpensive type-B ultrasonic technology to detect the gender of fetuses and engage in sex-selective abortion, leading to a severe imbalance in the sex ratio. The intensified competition among men for potential wives stimulates households with a son to spend thriftily to accumulate wealth in order to gain a competitive edge in the marriage market. Building on this idea, Wei and Zhang use provincial panel data (1978 to 2006) to test the effect of sex ratio imbalance on household saving. They show that the imbalanced sex ratio significantly increases household savings, with approximately 68 percent of the increase in rural saving rate and 18 percent of that in the urban rate being attributed to the rise in the sex ratio.

Economic transitions in China not only involved a decline in the size of the state sector but also made a transition from public provision of education, health care, and housing services to private expenditures on these lumpy purchases. The uncertainty associated with the transition could trigger precautionary motives to save. In particular, by the mid-1990s, the Chinese government realized that its gradualist reform policy could no longer manage the mounting losses of SOEs and decided to take more aggressive steps, first allowing the privatization of small and medium SOEs and then, beginning in 1997, moving forward with more aggressive restructuring. The objective was to shut down losing SOEs, establish modern forms of corporate governance, and delink the provision of social services from individual employers. This would be accomplished through the privatization of housing and the shifting of the federal responsibility of health insurance, unemployment insurance, and pension provisions to the local governments, employers, and employees themselves. These aggressive reforms led to mass layoffs in SOEs. From 1996 to 2002, about 32 million workers were laid off from the state sector. Based on the 2001 China Urban Labor Survey and the 2000 Population Census, Giles, Park, and Zhang (2005) estimate that the unemployment rate of urban permanent residents increased from 6.1 percent in 1996 to 11.1 percent in 2002. Using independent population data sources, Knight and Xue (2006) arrive at almost similar estimates, showing that China's urban unemployment rate increased gradually from 7.7 percent in 1995 to 11.5 percent in 2000.

Given the earnings uncertainty and unemployment risk combined with liquidity constraints and incomplete unemployment insurance, Chinese urban households that experienced past income uncertainty appeared to have increased their propensity to save in the period of 1995 to 1999 (Meng 2003). Moreover, the predicted probability of displacement had an even stronger effect on saving for households without unemployed members. Although these findings are robust for the household sample drawn from the specific period, reconciling the findings with the macroeconomic facts is difficult. The reason is that, when the employment uncertainty associated with state-sector restructuring continued to rise and reached its peak in the late 1990s, household saving rate did not increase accordingly but rather fluctuated within a narrow range of 16.2 to 18.1 percent during the second half of the 1990s (table 5.3). Therefore, the precautionary saving motive stemming from employment uncertainty does not seem to explain well the surge in household saving since 2000.

Accompanied with the state sector reforms, budget allocations for education, health care, and housing services declined substantially. For instance, expenditures on health and education only accounted for 2 percent of household consumptions in 1995, but this share rose to 14 percent by 2005. Chamon and Prasad (2010) argue that these rising private financial burdens could induce higher household saving, as younger families accumulate assets for future education spending, older families prepare for uncertain health expenditures, and most people save to prepare for mortgage payments or housing upgrades. Although these are plausible factors, their quantitative effects on savings are difficult to assess. Conceptually, as most of the young adults have already finished their own education, there is no need to save for that purpose; they might have incentives to accumulate assets for their children's education. However, the increase in their saving could be offset by the reduced saving of older families who have to incur higher education costs for their children who are already in school. Similar compositional effects exist for health care and housing expenditures, as higher costs tend to reduce the saving rates of those households that incur higher expenditures in specific years. So far, existing studies have not yet systematically assessed the combined effects on saving across different population groups.

The changes in age-saving profiles between the periods of 1988 to 1990 and 2005 to 2007 shown in figure 5.10 reveal several key features of the saving behavior of the Chinese households. A successful model that resolves the Chinese household saving puzzle should explain not only the rise in household saving but also the U-shaped age-saving profiles over the life cycle in recent years. Two recent studies, Song and Yang (2010), and Ge, Yang, and Zhang (2011), are particularly motivated to explain the stylized patterns of Chinese household savings as shown in figure 5.10. Using the comprehensive data from Chinese UHS covering the period of 1992 to 2007, Song and Yang document three dramatic changes in the life cycle earnings in China's fast-growing environment that are new to the existing literature: (a) there are large upward shifts in the earnings of successive younger worker cohorts, (b) individual age-earning profiles have become flattened during the past two decades, and (c) the aggregate pension replacement rate, which is defined as the ratio of average pension per retiree to average wages per worker in specific years, declined from about 80 percent in the early 1990s to a range of 52 to 58 percent in 2007. Incorporating these features of the Chinese economy into a dynamic optimization model of heterogeneous agents, they show that an otherwise standard intertemporal choice model can account well for the recent surge in household saving as well as the U-shaped age-saving profiles over the life cycle.

Ge, Yang, and Zhang (2011) emphasize the interplay between China's population control policies and saving behavior based on an overlapping generation model. They find that, among several intergenerational linkages, reduced fertility resulting from the implementation of the one-child policy contributed significantly to the recent rise in household saving. Their arguments, complementing the findings of Song and Yang (2010), help explain several special features of household saving in China.

5.6   Prospects of China's High National Saving

The high and rising national saving is a critical component of China's macroeconomic imbalances and is believed by some to be an important contributor to the global saving glut. Indeed, the high aggregate saving rate of about 50 percent of the GDP in recent years not only surpassed the peak saving levels of Japan, Korea, and other East Asian economies during the years of their miracle growth rates, but also has been the highest in the world among economies of significant size. This remarkably high national saving has supported China's high-investment, export-led growth model. As national saving has exceeded the total investment in recent years, and exports have exceeded imports, China's large current account surplus has become an important part of the global imbalances. We show in this chapter that corporate, household, and government sectors have all contributed significantly to the upsurge in national saving in the past decade. The key causes include China's fast economic growth, accession to the WTO accession, rising corporate profits, changes in life cycle earnings, pension system, other provisions of social services, and the demographic transition.

In the aftermath of the global financial crisis, the Chinese economy is facing a series of challenges; responses to these challenges will likely evolve into systematic structural adjustments. After more than a decade of heavy public investments in basic infrastructure, the diminishing returns on similar projects will likely set in, and due to external pressure, China is likely to experience relatively moderate export growth in the future and has no choice but to pursue a more balanced current account. These broad projections imply that China will have to rely increasingly on vigorous domestic demands to assure sustained growth, structurally reforming the previous high-investment, export-led growth strategy. Hence, the transition from a high-saving to a high-consumption regime will be at the center of public attention and policy.

Based on the previous analysis of saving determinants and imminent macroeconomic, demographic, and policy trends into the future, we assert that the Chinese national saving may have already peaked at around 2007. A main reason behind this judgment is the likely slowdown in China's future growth, which is projected at an average annual rate of 8.1 percent for 2011 to 2015 by the World Bank (World Bank 2010a) and an even lower range of 5.37 to 7.27 percent for 2010 to 2020 by the Asian Development Bank (Lee and Hong 2010). The national saving is positively correlated with economic growth (e.g., Carroll and Summers 1991; Deaton and Paxson 2000). Using 2.52 as the growth elasticity of national saving for China for 1978 to 2000 (Modigliani and Cao 2004), the decline in average GDP growth from 9.8 percent in the past decade to 8.1 percent as forecast by the World Bank for the next five years would reduce China's aggregate saving rate by about 4.3 percentage points. Our previous analysis is suggestive of the channels of the effect. Slower GDP growth will mean reduced growth in value-added production tax and reduced income tax for the government, and therefore a lower saving rate if the government's consumption growth is held stable. Our foregoing analysis of corporate earnings suggests that slower GDP growth will also imply reduced capacity for corporate saving.

The corporate sector will likely have a lower saving/GDP ratio in the foreseeable future because of the gradual decline over time in China's gains resulting from its accession to the WTO, the initiation of dividend payments for the state sector, and the pending increase in labor costs. As the largest shareholder, the state did not require SOEs to pay dividends in the past. However, with rising profits after the state-sector restructuring in the late 1990s, the Chinese government started to require dividend payments in 2008. This policy could squeeze corporate saving.

Moreover, reports of labor unrest in China are increasing, including news on labor strikes in Toyota and Honda joint-venture plants and the string of worker suicides at the Foxconn facilities in early 2010. Sentiments favoring the protection of the rights of workers have grown in China as revealed by both media and government sources. By July 2010, eighteen provinces had announced increases in minimum wages by an average of 20 percent. Nationwide increases in the minimum wage will likely spread to nine more provinces by the end of the year. Given the decline in the share of labor income in the GDP (figure 5.4), there have been reports that the Chinese government plans to raise the wages of production workers systematically as a way to boost domestic production and move the economy away from the reliance on exports for growth (Ho 2010). The National Development and Reform Commission, which formulates and coordinates national economic policies, have been developing an income redistribution reform plan that is likely to be incorporated into the twelfth five-year plan for the period of 2011 to 2015. Although we do not intend to analyze the efficiency loss and welfare consequences of implementing such policies, transferring income from high-income to low-income groups under Chinese conditions, ceteris paribus, may indeed lower the average household saving rate because low-income families have higher propensity to consume (figure 5.7). In addition, higher labor costs may suppress the profits of enterprises, thus reducing the capacity of corporate entities to save.

Other evolving forces are also likely to reduce household saving in the foreseeable future. The inevitable slowdown in the growth of labor earnings will likely occur across all age groups in conjunction with a gradual steepening of age-earning profiles, a reversal of what is observed during the period of extraordinary income growth (Song and Yang 2010). Over time, the life cycle earnings in China will converge gradually to the typical earnings profiles observed in more advanced economies. The combined effects of slower earnings growth and the steepening of age-earnings profiles will reduce household saving. As Song and Yang point out, the existing pension contributions under the three-pillared system have fallen far behind the targeted levels. However, in the coming years, the pension system is likely to be improved to meet the targeted provisions better. A more robust retirement system will lead to two consequences. First, with a higher level of pension replacement and thus less retirement risk, individuals will have less pressure to save during their working time. Second, a more complete implementation of the three-pillared pension system will gradually raise the contribution of employers from the current 5 percent of average wages to the policy target of 17 percent wage taxes. This change will again reduce the capacity of enterprises to save.

Population aging in the next several decades will have an effect on aggregate saving as well. According to projections made by the United Nations Population Council, China's dependency ratio, which is defined as the

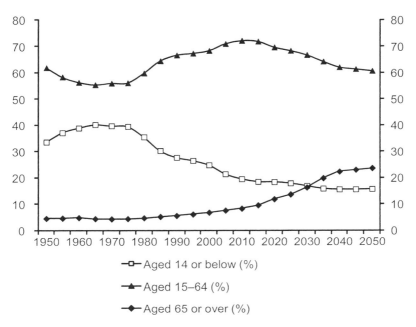

Fig. 5.11   China's long-term population trends (percentage): 1950–2050
Source: United Nations (2009).

sum of the young aged fourteen or below and the old aged sixty-five or above divided by the working population aged between fifteen and sixty-four, has reached the lowest level at 38.5 percent in 2010 (figure 5.11). However, this ratio will rise dramatically to 64.7 percent in 2050, a level comparable to the US figure of 67.7 percent in that year. What drives this rising trend is age dependency: the percentage of population aged sixty-five or above will increase from the current 11.5 percent to an astounding 38.9 percent in 2050, a level higher than that of Japan (37.8 percent) and the United States (21.6 percent) projected for that year. Rising dependency ratio, especially for the old, will likely reduce aggregate household saving through not only the more mouths to feed effects but also the fact that old dependency is generally associated with lower personal saving in high-income economies. This demographic trend has already set in to influence saving, labor markets, and other aspects of the Chinese economy.

The reasons behind the high and rising national saving in China in the last decade are complex. Our medium-term outlook suggests a declining trend in Chinese saving that will help facilitate the transition from an investment-driven growth model to a growth paradigm that increasingly relies on the role of domestic consumption. Radical policy interventions that aim to stimulate consumption, such as the proposed dramatic increases in minimum wage and income-doubling plan for production workers in five years, would involve some risk. Our view is that reliance on the momentum of market and demographic forces, when combined with policies such as building a robust social security system, can help China achieve a successful transition toward a more balanced growth.

References

Bai, Chong-En, Jiangyong Lu, and Zhigang Tao. 2009. "How Does Privatization Work in China?" *Journal of Comparative Economics* 37 (3): 453–70.

Bahl, Roy W. 1999. *Fiscal Policy in China: Taxation and Inter-governmental Fiscal Relations.* South San Francisco: The 1990 Institute, University of Michigan Press.

Carroll, Christopher D., and Lawrence H. Summers. 1991. "Consumption Growth Parallels Income Growth: Some New Evidence." In *National Saving and Economic Performance,* edited by B. D. Bernheim and J. B. Shoven, 305–48. Chicago: University of Chicago Press.

Carroll, Christopher D., and David N. Weil. 1994. "Saving and Growth: A Reinterpretation." *Carnegie-Rochester Conference Series on Public Policy* 40:133–92.

Chamon, Marcos D., and Eswar S. Prasad. 2010. "Why Are Saving Rates of Urban Households in China Rising?" *American Economic Journal: Macroeconomics* 2 (1): 93–130.

Chow, Gregory. 1985. "A Model of Chinese National Income Determination." *Journal of Political Economy* 93 (4): 782–92.

Deaton, A., and Christina H. Paxson. 2000. "Growth, Demographic Structure, and National Saving in Taiwan." *Population and Development Review* 26 (Supplement): 141–73.

Dynan, Karen E., Jonathan Skinner, and Stephen P. Zeldes. 2004. "Do the Rich Save More?" *Journal of Political Economy* 112 (2): 397–444.

Ferri, Giovanni, and Li-Gang Liu. 2009. "Honor Thy Creditors Beforan Thy Shareholders: Are the Profits of Chinese State-Owned Enterprises Real?" The Hong Kong Institute for Monetary Research (HKIMR) Working Paper no. 16.

Ge, Suqin, Dennis Tao Yang, and Junsen Zhang. 2011. "Population Control Policies and the Chinese Household Saving Puzzle: A Cohort Analysis." Working Paper. The Chinese University of Hong Kong.

Giles, John, Albert Park, and Juwei Zhang. 2005. "What Is China's True Unemployment Rate?" *China Economic Review* 16:149–70.

He, Xinhua, and Yongfu Cao. 2007. "Understanding High Saving Rates in China." *China and World Economy* 15 (1): 1–13.

Ho, Chua K. 2010. "Salary Gains to Damp Capital Spending." *China Daily,* June 8.

Hofman, Bert, and Louis Kuijs. 2006. "Profits Drive China's Boom." *Far Eastern Economic Review* 169 (8): 39–43.

Horioka, Charles Yuji, and Junmin Wan. 2007. "The Determinants of Household Saving in China: A Dynamic Panel Analysis of Provincial Data." *Journal of Money, Credit and Banking* 39 (8): 2077–96.

Jefferson, Gary, and Jian Su. 2006. "Privatization and Restructuring in China: Evidence from Shareholding Ownership, 1995–2001." *Journal of Comparative Economics* 34 (1): 146–66.

Knight, John, and Jinjun Xue. 2006. "How High is Urban Unemployment in China?" *Journal of Chinese Economic and Business Studies* 4 (2): 91–107.

Kraay, Aart. 2000. "Household Saving in China." *World Bank Economic Review* 14 (3): 545–70.

Kuijs, Louis. 2005. "Investment and Saving in China." World Bank Policy Research Working Paper no. 3633.

———. 2006. "How Will China's Saving-Investment Balance Evolve?" World Bank Policy Research Working Paper no. 3958.

Lee, Jong-Wha, and Kiseok Hong. 2010. "Economic Growth in Asia: Determinants and Prospects." Paper presented at Finalization Workshop: Long-Term Projections of Asian GDP and Trade, the Chinese University of Hong Kong, July 8–9.

Ma, Guonan, and Yi Wang. 2010. "China's High Saving Rate: Myth and Reality." Bank for International Settlements (BIS) Working Papers no. 312.

Meng, Xin. 2003. "Unemployment, Consumption Smoothing, and Precautionary Saving in Urban China." *Journal of Comparative Economics* 31 (3): 465–85.

Meng, Xin, Chris Manning, Shi Li, and Tadjuddin Noer Effendi. 2010. *The Great Migration: Rural-Urban Migration in China and Indonesia.* Northampton: Edward Elgar Publishing.

Modigliani, Franco. 1970. "The Life Cycle Hypothesis of Saving and Intercountry Differences in the Saving Ratio." In *Induction, Growth and Trade,* edited by W. A. Eltis, M. F. Scott, and J. N. Wolfe, 197–225. Oxford: Clarendon Press.

Modigliani, Franco, and Shi Larry Cao. 2004. "The Chinese Saving Puzzle and the Life-Cycle Hypothesis." *Journal of Economic Literature* 42 (1): 145–70.

National Bureau of Statistics of China (NBS). Various years. *China Statistical Yearbook.* Beijing: China Statistics Press.

Qian, Yingyi. 1988. "Urban and Rural Household Saving in China." *International Monetary Fund Staff Papers* 35 (4): 592–627.

Song, Zheng Michael, and Dennis Tao Yang. 2010. "Life Cycle Earnings and Saving in a Fast-Growing Economy." Working Paper. The Chinese University of Hong Kong.

United Nations, Population Division. 2009. *World Population Prospects: The 2008 Revision Population Database, China.* http://esa.un.org/unpp.

Wang, Yan. 1995. "Permanent Income and Wealth Accumulation: A Cross-Sectional Study of Chinese Urban and Rural Households." *Economic Development and Cultural Change* 43 (3): 522–50.

Wei, Shang-Jin, and Xiaobo Zhang. 2011. "The Competitive Saving Motive: Evidence from Rising Sex Ratios and Savings Rates in China." *Journal of Political Economy* 119 (3): 511–64.

Wong, Christine, and Richard Bird. 2008. "China's Fiscal System: A Work in Progress." In *China's Great Economic Transformation,* edited by Loren Brandt and Thomas Rawski, 429–66. Cambridge: Cambridge University Press.

World Bank. 2010a. *China Quarterly Update.* Beijing: World Bank Office.

———. 2010b. *World Development Indicators 2010.* http://data.worldbank.org /data-catalog.

Yang, Dennis Tao, Vivian Weijia Chen, and Ryan Monarch. 2010. "Rising Wages: Has China Lost Its Global Labor Advantage?" *Pacific Economic Review* 15 (4): 482–504.

Zhang, Haiyan. 2008. "Corporate Governance and Dividend Policy: A Comparison of Chinese Firms Listed in Hong Kong and in the Mainland." *China Economic Review* 19:437–59.

Zhou, Shaojie. 2007. "Essays on Household Consumption and Household Saving Behavior of Chinese Urban Residents." PhD diss. The Chinese University of Hong Kong.

Comment   Leslie Young

Introduction

Professors Yang, Zhang, and Zhou (YZZ) provide useful insights into the question in the title of their chapter. As their work covers a lot of interesting ground in a highly professional manner, I shall not offer a detailed critique. Instead, I shall propose some alternative perspectives on their work that link China's savings rate to fundamental aspects of its modern history and political economy. Specifically, I link China's high savings rate to (a) the social capture of the rents and capital gains foregone by the landlords and capitalists expropriated after 1949, and (b) the recycling of those surpluses into investment by both private companies and state-linked companies. The capital gains on the expropriated assets were massive when China opened up its economy and revalued those assets at world prices. The recycling of the surpluses into investment was massive because China's state-linked corporations effectively have no owners, but their managers now earn both monetary and political credits from good performance. We might say that China's savings are high because of Mao Zedong, Deng Xiaoping, and the "social market economy with Chinese characteristics."

Evidence from the Relative Purchasing Power of National Currencies

A useful perspective on the "revolutionary" origins of China's high savings is provided by the well-known impact of revaluing China's GDP according to Purchasing Power Parity. China's currency stands out from competing countries in enjoying high purchasing power relative to the US$. According to 2007 World Bank figures, 1 yuan buys in China 2.21 times what its US$ equivalent at market exchange rates would buy in the United States. For Brazil, Mexico, and Poland, the corresponding factor is about 1.43.

So Chinese firms could pay $1.43/2.21 = 0.65$ of the salaries in these three countries, yet their workers would enjoy the same purchasing power. The Chinese firms competing with firms from these three countries could capture the difference as higher profits. Yang, Zhang, and Zhou show that profits are mostly saved, rather than being paid out as dividends.

Leslie Young is the Wei Lun Professor of Finance and executive director of the Asia-Pacific Institute of Business at the Chinese University of Hong Kong.

For acknowledgments, sources of research support, and disclosure of the author's material financial relationships, if any, please see http://www.nber.org/chapters/c12458.ack.

Or the Chinese firms could pay more—say, 0.85 of the salaries in the other countries. Then the Chinese workers could consume as much as workers in the other countries, yet save more of their income. Meanwhile, the Chinese firms would face a wage bill equal to only 0.85 of their foreign counterparts, allowing higher profits and savings. If the Chinese firms were competing with US firms, then more savings would be possible.

If a Chinese firm A were producing inputs for another Chinese firm B that exports, then A could charge less than international prices (at market exchange rates). A's profits would be lower than discussed before, but B's profits would be higher. If A were producing goods that were consumed in China, then it could charge less than international prices (at market exchange rates). Then its profits would be lower than discussed earlier, but the cost of living would be lower also.

So, whatever prices of B-to-B and B-to-C transactions in China, Chinese firms and workers would jointly enjoy the additional opportunities to save as just discussed.

Chinese Interest Rates and Dividends

State-related firms can access low-cost loans from state banks; their loans are often forgiven. The resulting advantage over international counterparts shows up as higher profits and/or higher disposable income of the workers. Giovanni Ferri and Li-Gang Liu[1] argue that almost all the profits of state-related enterprises can be explained by favors from state banks.

How could Chinese banks afford to charge low interest rates and forgive loans to state enterprises? They pay low deposit rates. In the past, they were recapitalized by the Chinese state from taxation and seignorage. As China's market economy had grown fast and its immature financial system ensured a low velocity of circulation, it could print a lot of money without triggering inflation.

Yang, Zhang, and Zhou report that Chinese firms pay essentially no dividends. Unlike firms abroad that do pay dividends, they can save and reinvest all the dividends and/or charge lower prices and/or pay higher wages. Whatever the prices of B-to-B and B-to-C transactions in China, Chinese firms and workers as a whole would enjoy additional opportunities to save.

Chinese Rents

The state owns all land, but allows local governments to allocate or sell the use rights and retain the proceeds. The local governments can:

• Charge market rents, and use the proceeds to deliver government services. Then for given government services, China can tax less. This increases the disposable income of workers and firms, which they can

---

1. Ferri and Liu, "Honor Thy Creditors Before Thy Shareholders: Are the Profits of Chinese State-Owned Enterprises Real?" Hong Kong Monetary Authority Paper no. 16/2009.

save. In 2006, sales of land use rights accounted for 35 percent of the revenue of local governments.

- Charge below-market rents to firms (e.g., to attract them to start up locally and pay local business taxes). This increases the profits of firms, which they can save.
- Charge below-market rents to workers. This increases their disposable income, which they can save.
- Use the proceeds from the sale of land use rights to fund new investments. The local government would own these new firms. It typically collects business taxes but refrains from collecting dividends.

Whatever the prices of B-to-B, B-to-C, and B-to-G transactions in China, Chinese local governments, firms, and workers would jointly enjoy additional opportunities to save.

The firms set up by local governments either from land sales or from their legacy of state assets or from reinvested profits need not pay dividends. As previously discussed, this would show up as additional opportunities to save, either by firms or by workers.

Many Chinese farmers pay below-market rents for their land so they can enjoy decent living standards, despite receiving lower prices for their output than their international counterparts. Many Chinese workers enjoy low rents from state housing, low prices of food grown on low-rent state land, and low prices from Chinese firms that can pay low wages and rents so they can enjoy decent living standards, despite receiving lower wages than their international counterparts. And the firms employing them can charge low prices and still earn good profits. In fact, these two points explain the relatively high purchasing power of China's currency that was noted before: costs in rival economies are hiked up by market-driven rents.

The land on the edge of China's cities is being converted to urban use only after substantial economic growth has taken place, so local governments capture the capital gains and use them to fund new firms; that is, these firms are funded from the growth process itself and thereafter added to corporate savings, since they do not pay dividends to the local governments. This contrasts with other countries where land is privately owned: the landlords capture the capital gains. Insofar as they invest these capital gains in firms, they would expect dividends thenceforth.

Behind China's High Savings: Mao and Deng

The previous discussion traces China's high savings to the state assets that were:

- "Liberated" from landlords and capitalists after 1949.
- Built up in the central planning era, when central planners set wages low so that state enterprises enjoyed high profits that could be reinvested to build up state assets.

- Created/maintained through loans from state banks during the transition from central planning (which were often paid off from seignorage).
- Funded from the capital gains on state land as China urbanized.
- Funded by the reinvested profits of state firms.

So we can interpret China high savings as:

- The foregone income and consumption of the landlords and capitalists whose assets were "liberated" after 1949, enhanced by subsequent capital gains and income from the assets that China built up from their contributions—in effect, the foregone consumption of their heirs.
- The foregone income and consumption of workers during the central planning era—enhanced by subsequent capital gains and income from the assets that China built up from their contributions. In effect, the foregone consumption of the capitalists who have been prevented from owning and operating the firms after 1949.
- The social capture of the surplus from the improved division of labor as China's economy developed and grew, as manifested in seignorage, capital gains on state land through urbanization, and the profits of state firms.

Deng's reforms allowed private enterprise, but the state kept its assets or reinvested the proceeds from their sale to create other state assets. State assets had funded social services—health, education, and pensions. Citizens who exited the state economy lost their entitlement to these social services, so they had to save to pay for the services themselves. But the state assets continued to grow in value as the reforms deepened. The citizens of China were the notional owners, but lacked explicit claims. So they saved twice over: as individuals and via the state.

Conclusions: The Political Economy of Savings

China's high national savings are rooted in its institutional structure: the Chinese state has assets growing under the management of state-linked firms but these are not offset by explicit liabilities to its citizens. By contrast, the institutional structure of the United States means that the state has heavy explicit liabilities to its citizens (e.g., their entitlements to Social Security and Medicare) but lacks assets to support those liabilities.

Underlying these contrasting institutional structures are contrasting political economies and political ideals. The Chinese state is owned by the Communist Party, but retaining ownership requires retaining legitimacy. Growing the economy at a high rate confers legitimacy; growing a large proportion of assets under party control provides rewards to the party elite, while keeping taxation low. The US state is legitimized by democratic votes—of the current generation. So democratic politicians tend to shift liabilities to future generations. The current generation trusts the rule of law, specifically, the state's legally-binding promises to fund pensions and health care when it retires. Hence, it feels less pressure to save.

In sum, China saves at a high rate because it is a "social market economy with Chinese characteristics," just as the United States saves at a low rate because it is a democracy under the rule of law.

The Chinese Corporate Savings Puzzle
A Firm-Level Cross-Country Perspective

Tamim Bayoumi, Hui Tong, and Shang-Jin Wei

6.1 Introduction

China's national savings rate, at 50 percent of GDP in 2007, is among the world's highest for any economy of a significant size. This has been said to be an underlying cause of the US housing price bubble during 2002 to 2007 (Bernanke 2005; Greenspan 2009), and by extension, of the current global financial crisis. This illustrates the attention that has been paid to global implications of China's savings issue. It is therefore useful to understand China's high savings rate.

Several authors have noted that a significant part of China's high national savings rate come from its large corporate savings, which by 2007 accounted for roughly half of the national savings. According to Kuijs (2006), what makes China stand out is the high savings by its enterprises. Furthermore, low dividend payments by state-owned enterprises (SOEs), due to a large-scale agency problem, are the primary cause of the large corporate savings. Martin Wolf, an influential *Financial Times* commentator, asserts (*Financial*

Tamim Bayoumi is deputy director of the Strategy, Policy, and Review Department of the International Monetary Fund. Hui Tong is an economist at the Research Department of the International Monetary Fund. Shang-Jin Wei is the N. T. Wang Professor of Chinese Business and Economy and director of the Jerome A. Chazen Institute of International Business at Columbia University, and a research associate and director of the Chinese Economy Working Group at the National Bureau of Economic Research.

We thank Vivek Arora, Olivier Blanchard, Stijn Claessens, Nigel Chalk, Joseph Fan, Randall Morck, David Romer, Ning Zhu, and seminar participants at the IMF, HKMA, Tsinghua University, and NBER Conference on Capitalizing China for helpful comments. We thank Jeanne Verrier for excellent research assistance and Joy Glazener for editorial help. The views in the chapter are those of the authors, and do not necessarily reflect those of the IMF or the NBER. For acknowledgments, sources of research support, and disclosure of the authors' material financial relationships, if any, please see http://www.nber.org/chapters/c12074.ack.

Times, October 3, 2006): "But we must then also ask why China is running such large surpluses. . . . The frugality of Chinese households is not the chief explanation for China's surplus savings. . . . The principal explanation is China's huge corporate savings."

As far as we can see, the first claim—that the large corporate savings rate in China is what drives its high national savings relative to other countries—is based on the flow-of-funds data released by China's National Bureau of Statistics (NBS), which cannot be checked independently by a third party. When it issued revisions to the flow of funds data, the magnitude of the revisions could be large. For example, the recent revision in 2009 changed the Chinese corporate savings in 2003 from 13 percent to 18 percent of GDP, or a revision on the order of US$ 700 billion. The second claim—that a combination of windfall profits received by state-owned enterprises and their low dividend payout due to misgovernance—is based mostly on a hunch, as we have not seen any study that formally compares the profits and dividend practices across Chinese firms by ownership and sector.

In this chapter, we examine these claims by adopting a firm-level cross-country perspective: We compare the savings patterns between 1,557 Chinese publicly listed firms with 29,330 listed firms in fifty-one other countries during 2002 to 2007, and compare state-owned enterprises with majority privately-owned firms within China. Unlike the NBS flow-of-funds data, the financial statements of listed firms are at least subject to independent auditing. The listed firms, collectively, are also an important part of the economy. According to the China Security Regulatory Commission (CSRC, October 4, 2009), the profits of the listed firms' revenues accounted for 37.7 percent of the GDP in 2008, and their profits accounted for 36.3 percent of all enterprise profits. As far as we know, this chapter is the first paper that adopts the firm-level comparative perspective.

Our results cast doubt on the reliability of both claims. First, we find that Chinese listed firms do not seem to have higher gross savings (as a share of total assets) than listed firms in other countries during our sample period. Moreover, the gross savings rate for a typical listed Chinese firm declined from 2002 to 2007, albeit insignificantly, even though China's current account surplus rose significantly over the same period. This is inconsistent with the view that a rise in the corporate savings rate drives China's rising current account surplus. Second, from a comparison of state-owned versus nonstate Chinese firms, we do not find significant differences between these two groups in terms of their savings and dividend patterns. If anything, privately-owned firms appear to have a higher savings rate on average.

The finding that the Chinese corporate savings rates are not much higher than those in other countries is not surprising from the viewpoint of the empirical corporate finance literature in recent years. For example, J. P. Morgan (2005) and the International Monetary Fund (IMF 2005) have noted that corporations in G7 economies have all exhibited a rise in undistributed profits. Bates, Kahle, Stulz (2009) note that a typical firm in the United

States had so much cash holdings by 2005 that it could pay off its entire corporate debt and still have some cash left over. The corporate finance literature does not presume that high corporate savings per se reflect inefficiency or corporate misgovernance. Indeed, Bates et al. hypothesize that it could be a rational (optimal) response to rising working capital needs faced by corporations. Moreover, Fama and French (2001) document a pattern of disappearing dividends in the United States from 1978 to 1999. The fraction of firms paying cash dividends falls from 66.5 percent in 1978 to 20.8 percent in 1999. Part of the reason is a rising population of small firms with strong growth opportunities. Hoberg and Prabhala (2007) argue that a rising risk and therefore an increased need for risk control are the main explanation. Interestingly, the studies that focus on Chinese corporate savings rates appear unaware of this literature and of the fact that the high corporate savings rates in China are part of the global phenomenon.

The firm-level comparative approach in this chapter has its limitations. In particular, it does not account for unlisted firms. It is theoretically possible that both existing claims are correct through the actions by nonlisted firms. We note, however, that most nonlisted firms are private firms. If the savings by nonlisted Chinese firms are much higher than nonlisted firms in other countries, it is unlikely to be driven primarily by the misgovernance issues associated with state-owned firms. A more likely candidate would be financial constraints faced by privately-owned firms. In any case, our results should be interpreted with the caveat that nonlisted firms are not part of the analysis.[1]

Our findings have important implications for policy discussions. First, the existing claims advocate that state-owned firms need to pay more dividends. But if they save for whatever reasons that have led non-state-owned Chinese firms and firms in other countries to save, then forcing them to do less could lower economic efficiency. Second, the existing claims have led to the view that Chinese corporate savings are the primary driver for its large current account surplus, and a reduction in corporate savings would be key to reducing the current account surplus. However, if the Chinese corporate savings rates are actually not much higher than in other countries, then one needs to turn to households and government savings in understanding cross-country differences in national savings. As an analogy, even though the skin is the biggest part of an elephant's body, to understand why an elephant does not run as fast as a leopard, we would not want to focus on an elephant's skin. Similarly, even though Chinese corporate savings is the biggest part of its national savings, it need not be the driver for why the Chinese national savings rate is so much higher than other countries.

---

1. Also, our results examine the level of savings but not the quality of its allocation. Future research can further examine whether Chinese enterprises use their savings more or less efficiently than firms in other countries, along the line suggested in Wurgler (2000) and Durnev, Morck, and Yeung (2004).

The rest of the chapter is organized in the following way. In section 6.2, we analyze savings patterns with macro-level data based on flow of funds or national income accounts. In section 6.3, we turn to firm-level data when we have a much better way to control for various determinants of corporate savings, and can separate gross versus net corporate savings. In section 6.4, we conclude.

6.2   The Patterns from the Flow-of-Funds Data

We start by presenting patterns of corporate savings rates from the flow-of-funds data for China from the CEIC data set from 1992 to 2007 (the latest available data), the same data set used in Kuijs (2006) and virtually all other papers on the topic in the literature. Figure 6.1 presents China's national savings rate (total savings/GDP) during this period, and decomposes it into gross corporate savings, gross household savings, and gross government savings. Corporate savings as a share of GDP rose over time from 11.7 percent in 1992 onwards, peaked at 23.5 percent in 2004, and declined gradually thereafter to 18.8 percent in 2007. The household savings as a share

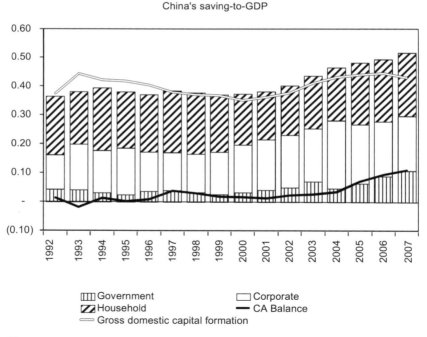

Fig. 6.1   Decomposing China's savings/GDP ratio using the flow-of-funds data

Note: The graph is based on the flow-of-funds data released by China National Bureau of Statistics in 2009.

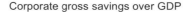

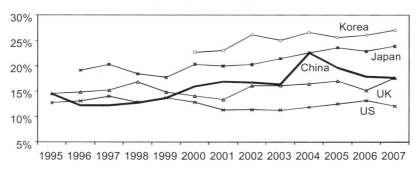

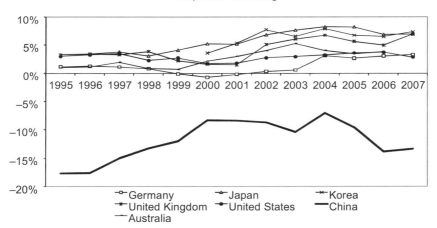

Fig. 6.2   Corporate savings/GDP: China versus selected other countries

of GDP experienced more ups and downs. It became less important than corporate savings in 2003 and 2004, but exceeded corporate savings again after 2005.

In spite of limitations about the flow-of-funds data, it may be useful to perform some simple cross-country comparisons based on the macro data. The top panel of figure 6.2 compares the aggregate corporate gross savings (as a share of assets) from 1995 to 2007 for China, Japan, Korea, Germany, Australia, United Kingdom, and the United States. The Chinese data show a faster increase in the savings rate up to 2004, which then started to decline in the next three years. Note that the corporate savings rates in Japan and Korea are higher than China's in every year during the sample period. In fact, in most years, the Chinese aggregate gross corporate savings rate tends to be lower than the Japanese corporate savings rate by about 5 percent of GDP, and lower than the Korean corporate savings rate by about 10 percent of GDP.

The lower panel of figure 6.2 plots the net savings rates (gross savings/ asset – investment/asset) for the same set of countries. The most striking feature is that China is the only economy in the group that has a significantly negative net savings rate in every single year. This reflects not only the high investment rates in China, but also the greater desire to hoard cash by firms in other economies (rather than to invest or to issue dividends). Overall, what stands out the most is not how much more Chinese firms save than their counterparts in other economies, but how much less they save, conditional on the investment need. (One may argue about whether Chinese investment is more or less efficient than investments elsewhere, but one cannot conclude that the corporate sector in China, on net, has contributed more to its current account than their counterparts in other countries.)

Besides corporate savings, the other two components of national savings are household savings and government savings. Figure 6.3 plots the time series of these two components for China and the other countries. For household savings as a share of GDP, it is clear that China is in a league of its own. It is often higher than the average of the rest of the group by 10 percent of GDP, and higher than the next highest country by 5 percent of GDP. For government savings, China is one of the three highest countries in recent years. For most years, however, Korea has been the clear leader in the government savings rate.

To summarize, even if one takes the flow-of-funds data at face value, it is not clear that China's corporate sector is the biggest contributor to the country's current account surplus, once one adopts a cross-country perspective, especially when one looks at the net corporate savings rate. Both household and government savings must have played a quantitatively important role in driving the current account balance.

6.3   A Close Look at Firm-Level Data

6.3.1   Data and Summary Statistics

We employ data on 1,557 publicly listed firms in China and compare them with 29,330 firms in fifty-one other countries from 2002 to 2007. The data source is the Worldscope. Table 6.1 presents the number of firms for each country in our sample, together with national savings/GDP, investment/ GDP, current account/GDP, and government fiscal balance/GDP, averaged over 2005 to 2007.

A major advantage of examining firm-level data is that we can better control for determinants of corporate savings. An important drawback is that we exclude savings by nonlisted firms. However, if the principal reason

Household net savings

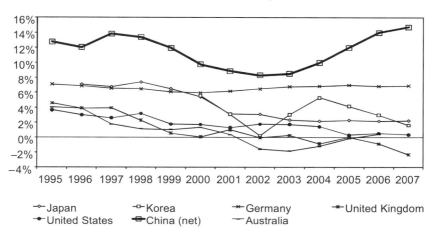

Government gross savings

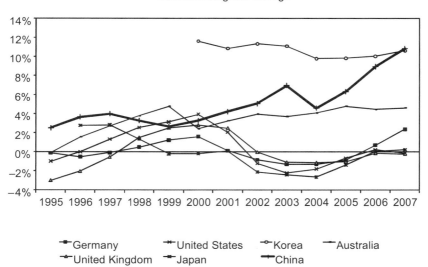

Fig. 6.3   Household and government savings: China and other selected countries

for high corporate savings in China is hypothesized to be the high savings rates of its majority state-owned firms, we have an opportunity to observe this even with publicly listed firms only, since most big state-owned firms are now listed.

Table 6.2 lists the summary statistics for variables on corporate savings.

Table 6.1   **Country coverage and basic information**

Country	No. of listed firms	Current account/GDP	Savings/GDP	Public savings/GDP	Investment/ GDP
Argentina	62	0.02	0.25	0.05	0.23
Australia	1,697	−0.06	0.22	0.06	0.27
Austria	84	0.03	0.25	0.02	0.23
Belgium	128	0.02	0.24	−0.01	0.22
Brazil	276	0.01	0.18	0.03	0.17
Canada	1,656	0.01	0.24	0.05	0.23
Chile	133	0.03	0.24	0.09	0.21
China	1,557	0.09	0.54	0.05	0.45
Colombia	25	−0.02	0.21	0.05	0.23
Czech Republic	18	−0.02	0.24	0.04	0.26
Denmark	132	0.03	0.24	0.07	0.22
Egypt	42	0.02	0.21	−0.03	0.19
Finland	131	0.04	0.26	0.06	0.21
France	820	−0.01	0.21	0.05	0.21
Germany	764	0.06	0.24	0.01	0.18
Greece	294	−0.11	0.11	−0.02	0.22
Hong Kong	834	0.12	0.33	0.05	0.21
Hungary	32	−0.07	0.17		0.24
India	1,792	−0.01	0.36	0.03	0.37
Indonesia	275	0.02	0.27	0.05	0.25
Ireland	79	−0.04	0.23	0.04	0.27
Israel	159	0.04	0.23	0.01	0.19
Italy	248	−0.02	0.19	0.01	0.21
Japan	3,982	0.04	0.28	0.06	0.24
Korea (South)	1,024	0.01	0.31	0.10	0.30
Luxembourg	26	0.10	0.31	0.28	0.21
Malaysia	940	0.15	0.36	0.15	0.21
Mexico	111	−0.01	0.25	0.03	0.25
Morocco	15	0.01	0.32	0.03	0.30
Netherlands	181	0.08	0.28	0.03	0.20
New Zealand	120	−0.08	0.16	0.02	0.24
Norway	217	0.16	0.39	0.20	0.22
Pakistan	113	−0.03	0.18	0.01	0.21
Peru	60	0.02	0.22	0.05	0.20
Philippines	136	0.04	0.19	0.02	0.15
Poland	226	−0.03	0.19	0.00	0.22
Portugal	60	−0.10	0.13	−0.02	0.22
Russian Federation	84	0.09	0.31	0.12	0.22
Singapore	605	0.24	0.44	0.06	0.20
Slovakia	8	−0.07	0.21	−0.01	0.28
Slovenia	12	−0.03	0.26	0.03	0.29
South Africa	357	−0.06	0.14	0.04	0.21
Spain	129	−0.09	0.22	0.05	0.30
Sri Lanka	18	−0.04	0.24	−0.01	0.28
Sweden	362	0.08	0.26	0.03	0.18
Switzerland	210	0.13	0.34	0.04	0.22
Thailand	436	0.01	0.30	0.07	0.29
Turkey	193	−0.05	0.16	0.07	0.21
United Kingdom	2,081	−0.03	0.15	0.00	0.18
United States	7,899	−0.06	0.15	0.00	0.20
Venezuela	16	0.14	0.39	0.13	0.25
Zimbabwe	28	−0.13			

Table 6.2   **Summary statistics on corporate savings and related variables**

	Variable	Median	Mean	Std.	No. of obs.
China	Gross savings/Asset	0.04	0.03	0.18	3,893
Majority state-owned firms	Profit/Asset	0.05	0.05	0.18	3,924
	Dividend/Asset	0.01	0.01	0.02	3,909
	Investment/Asset	0.05	0.07	0.07	3,939
	Net savings/Asset	−0.01	−0.03	0.18	3,891
China	Gross savings/Asset	0.04	0.00	0.34	2,509
Non_State_owned	Profit/Asset	0.05	0.01	0.34	2,525
	Dividend/Asset	0.00	0.01	0.02	2,527
	Investment/Asset	0.04	0.06	0.07	2,540
	Net savings/Asset	−0.01	−0.06	0.33	2,507
Asia	Gross savings/Asset	0.06	0.02	0.36	26,245
(except China and Japan)	Profit/Asset	0.07	0.04	0.36	26,960
	Dividend/Asset	0.00	0.02	0.03	26,329
	Investment/Asset	0.03	0.06	0.07	26,542
	Net savings/Asset	0.01	−0.04	0.38	26,206
All countries	Gross savings/Asset	0.05	−0.18	1.06	125,693
(except China)	Profit/Asset	0.06	−0.17	1.05	128,234
	Dividend/Asset	0.00	0.01	0.02	126,807
	Investment/Asset	0.03	0.06	0.08	127,374
	Net savings/Asset	0.00	−0.24	1.07	124,939
All countries	Gross savings/Asset	0.05	−0.17	1.03	132,812
	Profit/Asset	0.06	−0.16	1.03	135,551
	Dividend/Asset	0.00	0.01	0.02	133,963
	Investment/Asset	0.03	0.06	0.07	134,722
	Net savings/Asset	0.00	−0.23	1.04	132,051

Notes: Due to concerns for outliers, we winsorize all variables at the top/bottom 1 percent (in the sample for all countries) before computing the summary statistics for each group. The min/max values for gross savings are −8.37 and 0.35, respectively. The min/max values for profit/asset, dividend/asset, investment/ asset, and net savings/asset are −8.26/0.39, 0/0.15, 0/0.44, and −8.48/0.30, respectively.

We define firm gross savings as profits minus dividends.[2] Profit is defined as Net Income (WS 01551) plus Depreciation (WS 01151). Dividends are the sum of cash preferred dividends (WS 05401) and cash common dividends (WS 05376). The net savings is gross savings minus capital expenditure (WS 04601). For Chinese listed companies, cash dividends are the product of dividends per share (WS 05101) and the number of common shares (WS 05301, which includes both tradable and nontradable shares). To con-

2. We adopt this definition of firm-level corporate savings to match more closely with that of aggregate corporate savings in the flow-of-funds data. The definition of corporate savings could be different in other settings. For example, if the question is related to a corporation's access to liquidity, then it would be appropriate to include minority stock investment and intercorporate loans in addition to deposit and internal cash as savings. To the extent that these financial assets are liquid and significant, corporate savings may be higher than currently reported under our definition. Also, due to data limitation, we cannot address issues like the contributions to enterprise savings of cross-holdings, subsidiary-to-parent SOE dividends, repos, M&A, plausible tunneling scenarios, foreign direct investment (FDI), and so forth.

duct comparisons across firm ownership, we classify a firm as majority state-owned if the state is the largest shareholder (when nontradable shares are also considered).

We define gross or net savings rate as savings relative to gross asset, rather than savings relative to profit, because firm-level profits can be zero or negative. Table 6.2 reports the summary statistics on the gross savings rate (gross savings/assets), its components (profit rate and dividend rate), investment/asset, and net savings/asset for nonfinancial firms in China and other regions of the world. A few features are noteworthy. First, while the corporate savings rates in Asia are somewhat higher on average than those outside Asia, the savings rates by Chinese firms are not different from those in other Asian economies.[3] Second, within China, there is no significant difference between majority state-owned Chinese firms and majority privately-owned Chinese firms in their median gross or net savings rates.

We can also compare dividend payout practices in table 6.2. An important feature for our purpose is that an average or median Chinese firm issues dividends no less than its counterparts in other countries. The median/mean of dividends over assets is 0.005/0.016 for Chinese firms, compared to 0/0.011 for firms in other countries. The percentage of Chinese firms issuing dividends was 52 percent in 2007, while the comparable number for the rest of the world was 49 percent. In other words, while it is true that many Chinese firms do not pay dividends, it is part of the common corporate practice around the world.[4] In addition, considering that the Chinese economy is growing at a faster rate than most economies in the world, indicative of better investment opportunities in China, the optimal dividend payout in China can be expected to be lower than elsewhere. A second interesting feature comes from comparing the dividends of state-owned Chinese companies with those of non-state-owned Chinese companies. State-owned companies issue slightly larger dividends than non-state-owned companies. In 2007, 56 percent of state-owned companies issued cash dividends, while 45 percent of non-state-owned companies did the same. Hence the mainstream view that state-owned firms are particularly reluctant to issue dividends due to misgovernance is not consistent with the summary statistics.

Corporate savings rates are affected by firm size and other factors. For example, firms in resource sectors may have extra savings due to commodity price booms in the past few years. Also, firms in sectors with an intrinsically higher demand for external finance may also save more. To control for these possibilities, we now use econometric analyses to examine whether Chinese listed firms have more savings.

---

3. The difference in the corporate savings rates between Asia and the rest of the world lies in the mean but not in the median, suggesting that the difference in mean is driven by a few outliers.

4. An article in the *Economist* magazine (Oct 3, 2009) mocked the dividend practices of Chinese firms by noting that "almost 45% of listed companies did not pay a dividend last year," without apparently realizing that the pattern was consistent with corporate practices around the world.

6.3.2   Econometric Specification

We start with a model for gross savings rate:

(1) $\text{Savings} / \text{Assets}_{ijkt} = \beta_1 \, \text{Size}_{ijkt} + \text{China}_k + \text{Sector}_j + \text{Year}_t + \varepsilon_{ijkt}$,

for firm i in sector j of country k at time t. Company size is the total value of book assets measured in current US dollars. Sector dummies are at the three-digit level based on US Standard Industrial Classification (SIC 1987). There are 373 three-digit (nonfinancial) sectors in the sample. Year dummies control for the global trend. Based on this model, we will also check whether gross savings between Chinese state-owned and non-state-owned companies are systematically different.

We perform cross-country comparisons of the components of gross savings: profits and dividends, using the same specification as earlier. Finally, we perform comparisons of investment rate and net corporate savings. To summarize, we conduct a sequence of conditional comparisons, using specification (1), but each component of the following expression as the dependent variable:

(2) $\text{GrossSavings} = \text{Profits} - \text{Dividends}$

             $= \text{Net Savings} + \text{Investments}.$

6.3.3   Corporate Gross Savings

In table 6.3, we report the results from a regression analysis where we control for determinants of corporate savings. We cluster the standard errors at the country level. In column (1), we compare China with the rest of the world. Chinese firms have a higher coefficient of gross savings (as a share of gross assets) than other countries, but are not statistically significant.

We then compare China with each country by adding fifty-one country dummies, except for the United States, which serves as our baseline case. For twenty-one countries with the largest numbers of observations, we plot their coefficients in figure 6.4. We find that, conditional on sector and year fixed effects and firm size, the average Chinese corporate savings rate (0.44) is close to the median of the spectrum. Corporations in India (0.74), Australia (0.63), and the United Kingdom (0.46) all have higher gross savings rates. Meanwhile, these three countries all experienced a current account deficit during the sample period. From 2004 to 2007, the average current account deficit over GDP was –1 percent, –6 percent, and –3 percent for India, Australia, and the United Kingdom, respectively. This illustrates the idea that even with a high corporate savings rate, there need not be a current account surplus.

Figure 6.4 helps to address the power of the test for the China dummy in column (1). In column (1), the coefficient of the China dummy is insignificant, so we cannot reject the hypothesis that Chinese firms behave in the same way as firms in other countries. But a problem of Type I versus

Table 6.3   Corporate gross savings over assets

	Case 1	Case 2	Case 3	Case 4
China dummy	0.0713	0.105**		
	[0.0533]	[0.0491]		
China*time trend		−0.00916		
		[0.00624]		
State-owned dummy			0.00263	0.0270*
			[0.0101]	[0.0159]
State-owned dummy*trend				−0.00665*
				[0.00400]
Firm size	0.223***	0.223***	0.0582***	0.0585***
	[0.0754]	[0.0754]	[0.0181]	[0.0182]
Year = 2003	0.0214***	0.0218***	0.00869	0.013
	[0.00497]	[0.00502]	[0.0101]	[0.0114]
Year = 2004	0.0248	0.0256	−0.0149	−0.00634
	[0.0152]	[0.0155]	[0.0158]	[0.0176]
Year = 2005	0.0171	0.0184	−0.0210*	−0.00842
	[0.0177]	[0.0182]	[0.0114]	[0.0153]
Year = 2006	0.00958	0.0114	−0.0176	−0.00108
	[0.0369]	[0.0381]	[0.0173]	[0.0199]
Year = 2007	−0.0137	−0.0113	0.0109	0.0311
	[0.0434]	[0.0450]	[0.0125]	[0.0188]
Sector fixed effects	Y	Y	Y	Y
Observations	132,801	132,801	6,402	6,402
R^2	0.265	0.265	0.086	0.087

Notes: Standard errors in brackets. Corporate gross savings over assets is winsorized at the 1 percent level. Sector fixed effects are at the three-digit level. Standard errors are clustered at the country level.

***p-value is less than 1 percent.

**p-value is less than 5 percent.

*p-value is less than 10 percent.

Type II errors means we cannot necessarily conclude that the coefficient definitively equals zero either, and the data might be too noisy to allow any conclusion. Figure 6.4 alleviates this concern by estimating the coefficient for each country. We find that China's corporate savings rate is not different from the global average after comparing the magnitude of the China dummy with those of other countries.

So far we look at the average effect over the sample period. In column (2), we examine the trend in Chinese firms' gross savings by interacting the time trend with the China dummy. This interaction is negative (but insignificant), suggesting that the gross savings of Chinese firms did not rise from 2002 to 2007. This pattern of a relatively flat time profile of corporate savings contrasts with the profile of China's current account surplus, which rose gradually from 2002 to 2004 and more dramatically after 2005. This is an additional feature of the data, suggesting that China's corporate savings

Gross Savings

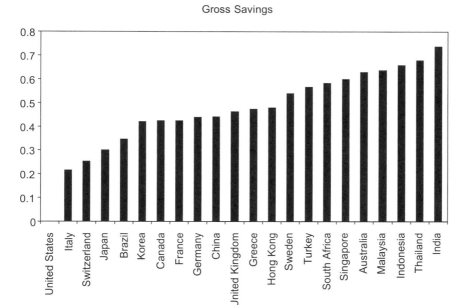

Fig. 6.4   Relative gross savings rates across countries conditional on common sector and year fixed effects and firm size

rates (relative to corporate savings rates in other countries) did not go up in tandem with its rising current account surplus.

We now compare state-owned versus non-state-owned firms in column (3). Conditional on sector and time fixed effects and firm size, there is no significant difference between the two groups, which is consistent with the unconditional pattern in table 6.2. In column (4), we look at the time pattern by adding the interaction of time trend and state-owned dummy. This interaction has a negative coefficient and is significantly different from zero at the 10 percent level. Meanwhile, the state-ownership dummy has a weakly positive coefficient. Taken together, this suggests that state-owned companies have slightly higher gross savings rates than private firms at the beginning of the sample period, but the gap declines gradually to become negligible.

As corporate savings is the difference between profits and dividend payout, we now look at the two components separately.

6.3.4   Decomposing Gross Savings: Profits and Dividends

The patterns of coefficients for profits in table 6.4 are similar to those for gross savings rates. China's firms have somewhat higher profit but not significantly so (column [1] of table 6.4). To find the country-level conditional average dividend rate, we perform a version of the regression in column (1)

Table 6.4   Profits over assets

	Case 1	Case 2	Case 3	Case 4
China dummy	0.0699	0.108**		
	[0.0538]	[0.0499]		
China*time trend		−0.01		
		[0.00601]		
State-owned dummy			0.00486	0.0311*
			[0.0100]	[0.0161]
State-owned dummy*trend				−0.00714*
				[0.00404]
Firm size	0.222***	0.222***	0.0586***	0.0589***
	[0.0744]	[0.0744]	[0.0177]	[0.0177]
Year = 2003	0.0226***	0.0230***	0.00803	0.0126
	[0.00501]	[0.00503]	[0.0101]	[0.0113]
Year = 2004	0.0257*	0.0265*	−0.0135	−0.00438
	[0.0149]	[0.0151]	[0.0159]	[0.0176]
Year = 2005	0.0214	0.0228	−0.0228**	−0.0093
	[0.0172]	[0.0177]	[0.0115]	[0.0153]
Year = 2006	0.0167	0.0187	−0.0197	−0.0019
	[0.0360]	[0.0372]	[0.0173]	[0.0199]
Year = 2007	−0.00411	−0.00144	0.0097	0.0314*
	[0.0405]	[0.0421]	[0.0124]	[0.0188]
Sector fixed effects	Y	Y	Y	Y
Observations	135,540	135,540	6,449	6,449
R^2	0.267	0.267	0.092	0.092

Notes: Standard errors in brackets. Profit is winsorized at the 1 percent level. Sector fixed effects are at the three-digit SIC level. Standard errors are clustered at the country level.
***p-value is less than 1 percent.
**p-value is less than 5 percent.
*p-value is less than 10 percent.

by adding individual country dummies (regression results not reported to save space). We plot the estimated individual country fixed effects in the top panel of figure 6.5. China, while below the median, is not far from it. India, Australia, and the United Kingdom still have higher profit over asset ratios than China.

In column (2) of table 6.4, we compare the trend in China's corporate profits rates during 2002 to 2007 to the global time fixed effects. The coefficient on the interaction between the China dummy and the time trend is statistically insignificant, suggesting that the time profile of Chinese firms' profit rates is not that different from the global trend.

In column (3) of table 6.4, we compare majority state-owned versus non-state-owned firms within China. We find that majority state-owned firms have a similar profit ratio as non-state-owned companies over the sample period. To see the time trend, we add an interaction term between the state-ownership dummy and the time trend. It appears that the majority state-

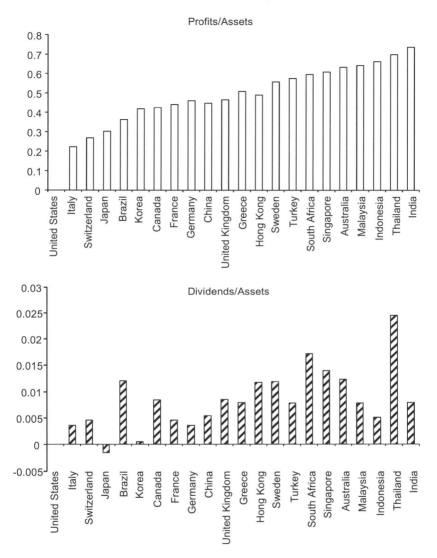

Fig. 6.5   Relative profit and dividend rates across countries conditional on common sector and year fixed effects and firm size

owned firms used to have a higher profit rate than majority private-owned firms, but the pattern reversed in the later part of the sample period.

Now we look at the dividend practices conditional on sector and year fixed effects and firm size (table 6.5). The coefficient for the China dummy is positive but insignificant, suggesting that Chinese firms issue dividends at an amount at least as large as the global average. To find the country-level

Table 6.5   Dividends over assets

	Case 1	Case 2	Case 3	Case 4
China dummy	0.000209	0.00383**		
	[0.00169]	[0.00173]		
China*time trend		−0.000971***		
		[0.000106]		
State-owned dummy			0.00188*	0.00314**
			[0.00107]	[0.00155]
State-owned dummy*trend				−0.000344
				[0.000355]
Firm size	0.00119***	0.00119***	0.00168***	0.00170***
	[0.000287]	[0.000286]	[0.000589]	[0.000596]
Year = 2003	0.000766***	0.000805***	−0.00102*	−0.000799
	[0.000248]	[0.000245]	[0.000612]	[0.000719]
Year = 2004	0.00181***	0.00190***	0.000322	0.000762
	[0.000360]	[0.000368]	[0.000667]	[0.000708]
Year = 2005	0.00278***	0.00291***	−0.00219***	−0.00154*
	[0.000515]	[0.000496]	[0.000836]	[0.000902]
Year = 2006	0.00309***	0.00328***	−0.00245***	−0.0016
	[0.000543]	[0.000515]	[0.000734]	[0.000966]
Year = 2007	0.00334***	0.00359***	−0.00243***	−0.00139
	[0.000586]	[0.000544]	[0.000834]	[0.00114]
Sector fixed effects	Y	Y	Y	Y
Observations	133,952	133,952	6,436	6,436
R^2	0.061	0.061	0.106	0.107

Notes: Sector fixed effects are at the three-digit SIC level. Standard errors are clustered at the country level.

***Significant at the 1 percent level.

**Significant at the 5 percent level.

*Significant at the 10 percent level.

conditional average dividend rate, we perform a version of the regression in column (1) by adding individual country dummies (regression results not reported). The estimates of the individual country effects are plotted in the bottom panel of figure 6.5. There, Chinese firms' conditional dividend payoff rates, on average, lie in the middle: for example, they are larger than those in France, Germany, Korea, Japan, and the United States, but smaller than Thailand, South Africa, Brazil, and Sweden.

In column (2) of table 6.5, we add the interaction term of a time trend and the China dummy. This interaction term is negative and significant but very small (−0.00097), suggesting a moderate decline over the sample period.[5] To gain further insight, we compute the fraction of listed Chinese

5. In October 2008, the China Securities Regulatory Commission (CSRC) required listed firms that applied for refinancing to pay cash dividends annually in an amount no less than 30 percent of its distributed profits over the past three years. As it is outside our sample period, we are not able to test the effect of the policy.

companies that issued dividends in a year. The fraction is 55 percent, 49 percent, 55 percent, 47 percent, 50 percent, and 52 percent, respectively, from 2002 to 2007. In other words, there was a mild reduction in the fraction of dividend-paying firms, but the change is overwhelmed by year-to-year fluctuations. We also compute the average cash dividend per share (DPS) for Chinese firms. The average DPS increased over the years, from 4.74 in 2002 and 4.96 in 2003 to 6.34 in 2006 and 7.47 cents in 2007 (the numbers of shares per company are held constant as stock splits and reverse splits and new shares are adjusted). Note from column (2) in table 6.4, there is a modest (but insignificant) decline in the profit rate of Chinese firms during the same period. In any case, recall from column (2) of table 6.3, there is no significant change in the gross savings rate over time for Chinese firms.

In column (3) of table 6.5, we compare the dividend payout rates between majority state-owned firms and other companies, conditional on the sector and year fixed effects and firm size. Contrary to the mainstream view, we see that state-owned companies issue more dividends. The coefficient on the state ownership dummy is 0.002, significantly different from zero at the 10 percent level. In column (4) of table 6.5, we examine whether and how the difference between state-owned and other firms changes over time. The negative but insignificant coefficient on the interaction term suggests that there might be a narrowing of the gap over time, but the evidence is not statistically significant.

6.3.5   Investment and Net Savings

To understand the corporate sector's contribution to a country's current account, one ultimately needs to look at net corporate savings—the difference between gross savings and capital investments. We now examine China's corporate investments over assets by using the same set of right-hand-side variables for gross savings. In column (1) of table 6.6, the China dummy is positive and significant at the 1 percent level, suggesting that Chinese firms invest more than the global average. To find the country-level conditional average investment rate, we perform a version of the regression in column (1) by adding individual country dummies (regression results not reported). Again, the estimates of the individual country effects are plotted in figure 6.6 (top panel). It is clear that Chinese firms invest more than firms in all other countries save two (India and Canada). From column (2) of table 6.6, Chinese firms appear to decrease their investment relative to assets over time when compared with a global year fixed effects (of generally rising investment).

In column (3) of table 6.6, we compare the conditional investment rate by majority state-owned firms with non-state-owned firms in China. Interestingly, an average state-owned firm invests less than an average nonstate firm. The gap in the investment ratio between state and nonstate firms does not shrink over the sample period (column [4] of table 6.6).

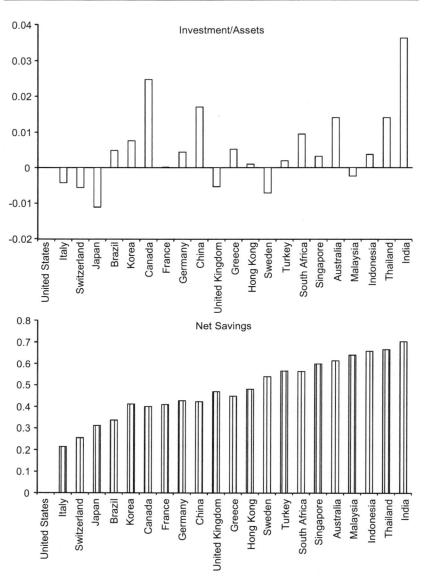

Fig. 6.6   Relative investment rates and net savings rates across countries conditional on common sector and year fixed effects and firm size

We now examine the net savings rate in table 6.7. There is little evidence that Chinese firms have higher net savings as a share of total assets than firms in other countries. The estimated coefficient is positive but insignificant (column [1] of table 6.7). To find the country-level conditional average net savings rate, we perform a version of the regression in column (1) by

Table 6.6   Investment over assets

	Case 1	Case 2	Case 3	Case 4
China dummy	0.0140***	0.0290***		
	[0.00307]	[0.00209]		
China*time trend		−0.00400***		
		[0.000803]		
State-owned dummy			−0.00430**	−0.00476
			[0.00211]	[0.00439]
State-owned dummy*trend				0.000125
				[0.000989]
Firm size	−0.000208	−0.000208	0.00947***	0.00947***
	[0.000258]	[0.000257]	[0.00163]	[0.00162]
Year = 2003	−0.00207*	−0.00191*	0.000921	0.00084
	[0.00104]	[0.00112]	[0.00242]	[0.00258]
Year = 2004	0.00243	0.00278	−3.45E-05	−0.0002
	[0.00175]	[0.00185]	[0.00295]	[0.00332]
Year = 2005	0.00504**	0.00561**	−0.00805***	−0.00829**
	[0.00213]	[0.00223]	[0.00288]	[0.00345]
Year = 2006	0.00750**	0.00829**	−0.0142***	−0.0145***
	[0.00311]	[0.00318]	[0.00260]	[0.00367]
Year = 2007	0.00856**	0.00965**	−0.0120***	−0.0124***
	[0.00361]	[0.00381]	[0.00269]	[0.00444]
Sector fixed effects	Y	Y	Y	Y
Observations	134,711	134,711	6,479	6,479
R^2	0.163	0.164	0.178	0.178

Notes: Sector fixed effects are at the three-digit SIC level. Standard errors are clustered at the country level.
***Significant at the 1 percent level.
**Significant at the 5 percent level.
*Significant at the 10 percent level.

adding individual country dummies (regression results not reported). The estimates of the individual country effects are plotted in the bottom panel of figure 6.6. We see that China's net savings are smaller than more than half of the countries in the sample, including India, Australia, and the United Kingdom. From column (2) of table 6.6, the insignificant interaction term suggests that the gap between net corporate savings in China and the global average has not narrowed over time.

In column (3) of table 6.7, we compare state-owned companies with non-state-owned ones in China. There is no significant difference between the two groups on corporate net savings. Column (4) of table 6.7 suggests that the net savings rate might be higher for state-owned firms at the beginning of the sample. The trend is negative but insignificant. Since there is no difference between state and nonstate firms averaged over the entire sample, we surmise that state-owned firms may have a lower net savings rate than nonstate firms in the latter part of the sample. The insignificant trend term

Table 6.7   **Net savings over assets**

	Case 1	Case 2	Case 3	Case 4
China dummy	0.0596	0.0789		
	[0.0517]	[0.0482]		
China*time trend		−0.00519		
		[0.00578]		
State-owned dummy			0.00694	0.0310**
			[0.00982]	[0.0155]
State-owned dummy*trend				−0.00656
				[0.00405]
Firm size	0.225***	0.225***	0.0491***	0.0494***
	[0.0756]	[0.0756]	[0.0182]	[0.0183]
Year = 2003	0.0229***	0.0231***	0.00766	0.0119
	[0.00494]	[0.00499]	[0.0104]	[0.0116]
Year = 2004	0.0217	0.0221	−0.0146	−0.00621
	[0.0155]	[0.0158]	[0.0158]	[0.0175]
Year = 2005	0.0117	0.0124	−0.013	−0.000604
	[0.0182]	[0.0187]	[0.0118]	[0.0158]
Year = 2006	0.00131	0.00234	−0.00318	0.0131
	[0.0364]	[0.0375]	[0.0176]	[0.0202]
Year = 2007	−0.0235	−0.0222	0.0228*	0.0427**
	[0.0427]	[0.0440]	[0.0129]	[0.0189]
Sector fixed effects	Y	Y	Y	Y
Observations	132,040	132,040	6,398	6,398
R^2	0.264	0.264	0.068	0.068

Notes: Sector fixed effects are at the three-digit level. Standard errors are clustered at the country level.

***Significant at the 1 percent level.

**Significant at the 5 percent level.

*Significant at the 10 percent level.

reflects that year-to-year fluctuations are large (producing a relatively large standard error).

6.3.6   Do Financial Constraints Raise the Savings by Nonstate Firms?

Recall that a key conclusion so far is that within China, private firms do not save less than state-owned firms. One reason that private firms need to save is concern for future financing constraints when good investment opportunities come along.

We now test these arguments. The first question is how to measure external finance needs in a cross-country setting. Following the literature on empirical corporate finance, we use an index for intrinsic dependence on external finance for investment (DEF_INV). Specifically, we construct a sector-level approximation of a firm's intrinsic demand on external finance for capital investment following a methodology developed in Rajan and Zingales (1998):

Dependence on external finance for investment

$$= \frac{\text{capital expenditures} - \text{cash flow}}{\text{capital expenditures}}$$

where cash flow = cash flow from operations + decreases in inventories + decreases in receivables + increases in payables. All the numbers are based on US firms, which are judged to be least likely to suffer from financing constraints (during a normal time) relative to firms in other countries. While the original Rajan and Zingales (1998) paper covers only 40 (mainly SIC two-digit) sectors, we expand the coverage to around 250/373 SIC three-digit sectors (following Tong and Wei 2011).

To calculate the demand for external financing of US firms, we take the following steps. First, every firm in the COMPUSTA USA is sorted into one of the SIC three-digit sectors. Second, we calculate the ratio of dependence on external finance for each firm from 1990 to 2006. Third, we calculate the sector-level median from firm ratios for each SIC three-digit sector that contains at least five firms, and the median value is then chosen, to be the index of demand for external financing in that sector. Conceptually, the Rajan-Zingales (DEP_INV) index aims to identify sector-level features; that is, which sectors are naturally more dependent on external financing for their business operation. It ignores the question of which firms within a sector are more liquidity constrained. What the DEP_INV index measures could be regarded as a "technical feature" of a sector, almost like a part of the production function. To capture the economic concept of the percentage of capital expenditure that has to be financed by external funding, we winsorize the DEP_INV index to range between 0 and 1.

We then interact this DEP_INV index with the China dummy and later with the state-ownership dummy. The results are presented in tables 6.8 and 6.9. Within those sectors with a higher external financial dependence (i.e., higher DEP_INV), Chinese firms have higher gross savings than other countries (column [1]). This is because in these sectors, Chinese firms are making relatively higher profits than their global counterparts (column [2]). A reason might be that Chinese listed firms have relatively lower financing costs. Moreover, within these sectors, Chinese firms issue relatively higher dividends than global counterparts (column [3]), consistent with the argument that Chinese firms may have more access to external finance.

Another possible interpretation on the positive coefficient on the China*DEP_INV interaction term in the profit function is that the contemporaneous profit rate may be a predictor of future investment opportunities. This regression suggests that unexplored investment opportunities are particularly good for Chinese firms in sectors with a higher intrinsic dependence on external finance (column [2]). As a result, these firms also save more (column [1]). To check the validity of this hypothesis, we look at column (3) and find that the investment in these sectors is not particularly

Table 6.8   **Dependence for external finance and corporate savings behavior**

	Gross savings	Profits	Dividends	Investment	Net savings
China dummy	0.043**	0.039**	−0.002*	0.016**	0.029
	[0.018]	[0.018]	[0.001]	[0.003]	[0.019]
China dummy*DEP_INV	0.121**	0.129**	0.005**	−0.007	0.129**
	[0.053]	[0.053]	[0.002]	[0.005]	[0.050]
Firm Size	0.227***	0.225**	0.001**	−0.0002	0.229**
	[0.023]	[0.023]	[0.0001]	[0.0004]	[0.023]
Year = 2003	0.024**	0.025**	0.0008***	−0.0023**	0.026**
	[0.011]	[0.010]	[0.0001]	[0.0008]	[0.011]
Year = 2004	0.027*	0.028*	0.0018**	0.0021	0.024
	[0.015]	[0.015]	[0.0002]	[0.0013]	[0.016]
Year = 2005	0.019	0.023	0.0028***	0.0046**	0.0144
	[0.018]	[0.018]	[0.0003]	[0.0017]	[0.0191]
Year = 2006	0.012	0.019	0.0031**	0.0069**	0.0043
	[0.021]	[0.021]	[0.0003]	[0.0017]	[0.0221]
Year = 2007	−0.013	−0.004	0.0034**	0.0075**	−0.022
	[0.017]	[0.018]	[0.0004]	[0.0016]	[0.0182]
Sector fixed effects	Y	Y	Y	Y	Y
Observations	119,598	121,988	120,589	121,302	118,952
R^2	0.267	0.268	0.059	0.169	0.266

Notes: Sector fixed effects are at the three-digit level. DEP_INV is the dependence on external finance for investment.
***Significant at the 1 percent level.
**Significant at the 5 percent level.
*Significant at the 10 percent level.

higher in China. As a result, all the gross savings show up as net savings as well.

Now we focus on the sample of Chinese firms and include an interaction term of state dummy and external finance dependence. There we find that state companies and nonstate companies have similar gross savings, profits, and dividends payouts, which are not affected by whether they are in a sector with high dependence on external finance or not.

At least for publicly listed firms, there is no evidence that those Chinese firms in sectors that are intrinsically more dependent on external finance issue smaller dividends in order to save more than counterparts in other countries. If corporate savings reflects concerns for credit constraints, the evidence suggests that Chinese firms are not more concerned about credit constraints than their peers in other countries. Publicly traded private firms do not appear to face more credit constraints than their majority state-owned counterparts. Of course, small nonlisted private firms may very well be credit constrained and therefore need to save more. However, this is true everywhere in the world. In any case, the evidence is not consistent with the contention that misgovernance in state firms and favorable price shocks are the primary cause of a high and rising corporate savings rate.

Table 6.9   **Financial constraints for state and nonstate firms in China**

	Gross savings	Profits	Dividends	Investment	Net savings
State dummy	−0.0124	−0.0105	0.00191	−0.00065	−0.0118
	[0.0137]	[0.0138]	[0.00171]	[0.00308]	[0.0131]
State dummy*DEP_INV	0.0426	0.0421	−0.00121	−0.0110**	0.0539*
	[0.0304]	[0.0300]	[0.00279]	[0.00470]	[0.0311]
Firm size	0.0594***	0.0595***	0.00161***	0.00915***	0.0506***
	[0.0193]	[0.0188]	[0.000605]	[0.00171]	[0.0194]
Year = 2003	0.0121	0.0111	−0.00117*	0.00137	0.0104
	[0.0111]	[0.0111]	[0.000613]	[0.00258]	[0.0114]
Year = 2004	−0.0154	−0.014	0.000306	−0.00057	−0.0148
	[0.0176]	[0.0176]	[0.000698]	[0.00314]	[0.0176]
Year = 2005	−0.0179	−0.0202	−0.00257***	−0.00828***	−0.00974
	[0.0125]	[0.0125]	[0.000833]	[0.00306]	[0.0129]
Year = 2006	−0.0178	−0.0202	−0.00275***	−0.0149***	−0.00296
	[0.0193]	[0.0192]	[0.000778]	[0.00267]	[0.0196]
Year = 2007	0.0118	0.0108	−0.00219**	−0.0119***	0.0233
	[0.0138]	[0.0137]	[0.000891]	[0.00285]	[0.0142]
Sector fixed effects	Y	Y	Y	Y	Y
Observations	5,738	5,783	5,769	5,811	5,735
R^2	0.085	0.089	0.094	0.163	0.067

Notes: Sector fixed effects are at the three-digit level. DEP_INV is the dependence on external finance for investment.
***Significant at the 1 percent level.
**Significant at the 5 percent level.
*Significant at the 10 percent level.

6.3.7   Do Politically Connected Firms Save Less?

The savings rates may be uneven across privately-owned firms. One reason may be different degrees of political connection by firm owners, which may result in uneven access to financing. In other words, while private firms may have a more challenging task in accessing finance when they need to than state-owned firms, those private firms with better political connections may need to save less.[6]

We examine this possibility by utilizing a measure of political connection constructed by Fan, Wong, and Zhang (2007). The political connection is a dummy for companies whose chairman is a former government official.

The results are presented in table 6.10. From column (1), it is clear that politically better connected private firms do save significantly less. As columns (2) and (3) reveal, however, the lower level savings does not come from less dividend payout, but instead from a lower profit rate. In other words, firms with better political connection simply perform worse. With a smaller

6. Other corporate governance factors may affect corporate savings too. For example, Morck, Yeung, and Zhao (2008) suggest that enterprise insiders may hide cash from their superiors or successors by tunneling it to tax havens. This could induce the insiders from the beginning to increase corporate savings by reducing dividend payoffs.

Table 6.10   Do politically better connected private firms save less?

	Gross savings/ assets	Dividend/ assets	Investment/ assets	Net savings/ assets
Political connection dummy	−0.485**	−0.0004	−0.0386*	−0.492**
	[0.180]	[0.0028]	[0.0197]	[0.196]
Firm size	0.414**	0.007**	0.00324	0.436**
	[0.123]	[0.002]	[0.0129]	[0.141]
Year = 2003	−0.048	−0.009**	−0.0474**	−0.004
	[0.0320]	[0.002]	[0.0194]	[0.034]
Year = 2004	−0.402*	−0.008**	−0.0711**	−0.371
	[0.225]	[0.002]	[0.0194]	[0.262]
Year = 2005	−0.556**	−0.015**	−0.100**	−0.499*
	[0.233]	[0.003]	[0.0162]	[0.270]
Year = 2006	−0.510**	−0.014**	−0.0988***	−0.422**
	[0.142]	[0.003]	[0.0215]	[0.154]
Year = 2007	−0.454	−0.013**	−0.101**	−0.403
	[0.343]	[0.003]	[0.0242]	[0.358]
Two-digit SIC sector fixed effects	Yes	Yes	Yes	Yes
Observations	1,269	1,276	1,278	1,269
R^2	0.08	0.14	0.09	0.08

Source: Fan, Wong, and Zhang (2007).

Notes: Political connection of a firm is measured by whether the chairman of the company has political connections.

***Significant at the 1 percent level.
**Significant at the 5 percent level.
*Significant at the 10 percent level.

profit, they do not pay smaller dividends or do less investment than firms without a strong political connection. As a result, these firms have a lower gross savings rate and a lower net savings rate.

6.4   Conclusion

Chinese companies maintain a high gross savings rate in absolute terms, and often account for as big a share of GDP as household savings. This has led to the mainstream view that (a) corporate savings in China is a key driver of its current account surplus, and (b) high corporate savings is mainly a result of high savings rates by state-owned firms due to misgovernance.

This chapter casts doubt on both parts of the mainstream view. Using the aggregate flow-of-funds data, we show that corporate gross savings rates are high and have been rising in a number of countries. At least Korea and Japan tend to have substantially higher savings rates by their corporate sectors than China's. Moreover, relative to the investment rate (investment/GDP), China has, in fact, the lowest net savings rate (gross savings rate – investment rate) among the group of major economies. It is the only country that had a negative net corporate savings rate every year during 1995 to 2007.

Micro firm-level evidence could provide better controls for sector and year effects on corporate savings patterns. Once we do that, we see that Chinese corporate savings rates, both gross and net, are not that different from those in other economies.

Overall, the notion that Chinese corporate savings drives its current account surplus is not supported by a careful look at the data. If the corporate savings is not the key driver for China's overall savings, one needs to pay more attention to savings by households and government.[7]

References

Bates, Thomas W., Kathleen M. Kahle, and Rene M. Stulz. 2009. "Why Do US Firms Hold So Much More Cash Than They Used To?" *Journal of Finance* 64 (5): 1985–2021.

Bernanke, Ben. 2005. "The Global Savings Glut and the U.S. Current Account Deficit." The Homer Jones Lecture, St. Louis, Missouri, April 14.

Durnev, Art, Randall Morck, and Bernard Yeung. 2004. "Value Enhancing Capital Budgeting and Firm-Specific Stock Return Variation." *Journal of Finance* 59: 65–105.

Du, Qingyuan, and Shang-Jin Wei. 2010. "A Sexually Unbalanced Model of Current Account Imbalances." NBER working paper 16000. Cambridge, MA.

Du, Qingyuan, and Shang-Jin Wei. 2011. "A Darwinian Perspective on 'Exchange Rate Undervaluation.'" NBER working paper 16788. Cambridge, MA.

Fama, Eugene, and Kenneth French. 2001. "Disappearing Dividends: Changing Firm Characteristics or Lower Propensity to Pay?" *Journal of Financial Economics* 60:3–43.

Fan, Joseph, T. J. Wong, and Tianyu Zhang. 2007. "Politically Connected CEOs, Corporate Governance and Post-IPO Performance of China's Newly Partially Privatized Firms." *Journal of Financial Economics* 84 (2): 330–57.

Greenspan, Alan. 2009. "The Fed Didn't Cause the Housing Bubble." *Wall Street Journal,* March 11.

Hoberg, Gerard, and Nagpurnanand R. Prabhala. 2007. "Disappearing Dividends, Catering, and Risk." American Finance Association (AFA) 2007 Chicago Meetings Paper. October.

International Monetary Fund. 2005. "Awash with Cash: Why Are Corporate Savings So High?" In *World Economic Outlook,* chapter IV, 135–59.

Kuijs, Louis. 2006. "How Will China's Saving-Investment Balance Evolve?" World Bank Policy Research Working Paper no. 3958.

J. P. Morgan Chase & Co. 2005. "The Corporate Savings Glut." June 24.

Morck, Randall, Bernard Yeung, and Minyuan Zhao. 2008. "Perspectives on China's Outward Foreign Direct Investment." *Journal of International Business Studies* 39 (3): 337–50.

---

7. On the high household savings rate, Wei and Zhang (2011) and Du and Wei (2010 and 2011) argue that an inadequate social safety net (via a precautionary saving motive) perhaps plays a smaller role than commonly assumed, and a competitive saving motive triggered by a rising sex ratio imbalance may play a surprisingly important role. In addition, Wei (2011) argues that a portion of the corporate savings rate—those by private firms—may also be triggered by a higher sex ratio, in combination with the financing constraints typically faced by new private firms.

Rajan, Raghuram, and Luigi Zingales. 1998. "Financial Dependence and Growth." *American Economic Review* 88:559–86.

Tong, Hui, and Shang-Jin Wei. 2011. "The Composition Matters: Capital Inflows and Liquidity Constraints during a Global Economic Crisis." *Review of Financial Studies* 24 (6): 2023–52.

Wei, Shang-Jin. 2011. "Is There a Risk of Overvaluing the Risk of the Exchange Rate in Global Current Account Imbalances?" Unpublished Working Paper. Columbia University.

Wei, Shang-Jin, and Xiaobo Zhang. 2011. "The Competitive Saving Motive: Evidence from Rising Sex Ratios and Savings Rates in China." *Journal of Political Economy* 119 (3): 511–64.

Wurgler, Jeffrey. 2000. "Financial Markets and the Allocation of Capital." *Journal of Financial Economics* 58:187–214.

Comment   Ning Zhu

The chapter documents the corporate savings rate at Chinese companies, compares such savings rate with companies from all over the world, and concludes that there is not much difference amid corporate savings between Chinese and international companies.

This is a very important and timely question. From an academic research perspective, understanding whether China's "high" savings rate is driving the legend of Chinese economic development helps understand whether the "East Asian Development Model" works in a broader context and bigger economy. To international economists, more precise understanding of the imbalance in savings rate across countries holds the key to understanding international capital flow and asset allocation.

It is important to point out that the question is also becoming an important one in policy debate and research. During the recent global financial crisis, US Treasury Secretary Hank Paulson made the following comments: "In the years leading up to the crisis, super-abundant savings from fast-growing emerging nations such as China and oil exporters . . . put downward pressure on yields and risk spread everywhere." (see http://www.rothstein economics.com/Paulson.pdf) As a result, it is critical that scholars and policy researchers reach an agreement on whether the Chinese (corporate) savings rate is outstandingly high compared to other countries at similar development stage and if so, what is driving such a high savings rate.

Within China itself, how to stimulate domestic consumption has become

Ning Zhu is deputy director and professor of finance at the Shanghai Advanced Institute of Finance, fellow at the Yale University International Center for Finance, and the Special Term Professor of Finance at University of California, Davis, and at Guanghua School of Management at Beijing University.

For acknowledgments, sources of research support, and disclosure of the author's material financial relationships, if any, please see http://www.nber.org/chapters/c12463.ack.

one of the most important issues in China's attempt to transition into its next-stage development that relies less on export and labor-intensive manufacturing sectors. One crucial step of obtaining this objective is to release the high level of savings from banks into the market. Most of the current efforts have been targeted at promoting consumer finance and stimulating household consumption. However, according some recent studies' claim (i.e., Hofman and Kuijs 2008), China's high savings rate is largely driven by the high savings rate in the corporate sector. If this is the case, it seems that Chinese government policy should be geared toward lowering the corporate savings rate (i.e., through resources tax and dividend tax), instead of reducing household savings and encouraging household consumption.

The chapter produces some novel and potentially provocative findings. Unlike the extant studies, it shows that the savings rate at Chinese corporations is not significantly higher than the savings rate at corporations in other countries. Instead, the findings suggest that the corporate savings rate in China is indeed lower than those in other countries, by almost 20 percent in some extreme years. Such conclusions leave the household savings and government savings as the major reasons for Chinese high savings rate.

One major novelty of the study is that, unlike most extant studies that take a macro-level flow-of-fund approach, the current chapter takes a micro firm-level cross-country approach. Apparently, examining firm level behavior not only has the promise of digging into microeconomic behavior at different firms but also can afford the opportunity to understand how differences in firm characteristics may explain the variations in corporate saving behavior, possibly across different countries.

It is important to point out that there is not a one-size-fits-all criterion for the optimal savings rate at the national level or the corporate level. Apparently, savings rate can fluctuate over economic cycles and depend heavily on the economic conditions that firms go through. As a result, examining savings rate at firm level in a panel-analysis framework provides unique opportunities to control for such variations and the chapter may gain sharper focus on the question of whether Chinese corporate savings rate is higher, by global standards.

Another benefit of utilizing the world scope data is that the data source takes some effort to ensure that the financial data at firm level are somewhat comparable across countries. Therefore, in addition to variations at country level, many of which are endogenous, the current study can also control for some firm level variations across the country, which should make interpretation of the results more precise.

One question that arises in reconciling the findings in the current study and extant literature is that, conceptually, if the micro-level data at firm level are perfectly representative of the macro-level flow-of-fund data, one would expect the two data sources to generate consistent, if not the same, results. After all, the flow-of-fund data are the national-level aggregation of the firm level data. So what can explain the considerable differences between these two approaches?

I think that there are three potentially responsible reasons.

First, as the chapter points out, profits at listed companies make up 37.7 percent of GDP and 36.3 percent of all enterprise profits in China in 2008. Because listed companies tend to be the more successful among all companies, it is conceivable that listed companies may have greater investment opportunities and hence make up a smaller fraction of total savings and investments than their shares in enterprise profits. Hence, it is possible that the listed companies in China are representative of only a minority of Chinese companies when one examines corporate savings rate.

Second, it is worth pointing out that listed companies may display different savings behavior, particularly in the context of Chinese economic transition from their unlisted counterparts. It is commonly believed that unlisted companies are more likely to retain operating cash flow, because of the lack of short-term earnings pressure and lack of short-term shareholder monitoring. Such a pattern may be particularly strong in China because the parent companies of many listed state owned enterprises (SOEs) are themselves SOEs and face relatively weak corporate governance and monitoring. As a result, such parent companies, which make up a large fraction of the GDP, may have the incentives to hold a higher level of savings and retain greater private benefits than their listed subsidiaries.

Finally, even though the chapter has done a very careful job in comparing and contrasting key savings/payout decisions by state-owned enterprises and non-state-owned enterprises, the question still remains as to whether listed SOEs and listed non-SOEs are equally representative of their unlisted counterparts. Because a much larger fraction of SOEs become listed than non-SOEs, the sample of listed non-SOEs tend to be less representative of all non-SOE firms, which indeed make up an increasingly larger fraction of the economy. Because such listed non-SOEs may not fairly represent the bulk majority of unlisted non-SOEs, inferences based on only listed companies may lead to misrepresentative conclusions due to data availability.

In sum, the chapter has made some new and very important discoveries about corporate savings rate in China at the micro level for the first time. Unfortunately, because of the data limitation, the controversy regarding the high level of corporate savings in China would have to be resolved later when more data, especially micro-level corporate savings data for nonlisted companies, become available.

Reference

Hofman, B., and L. Kuijs. 2008. "Balancing China's Growth." In *Debate China's Exchange Rate Policy,* edited by M. Goldstein and N. Lardy. Washington, DC: Peterson Institute for International Economics.

IV

Public Finance

7

Financial Strategies
for Nation Building

Zhiwu Chen

7.1 Introduction

It is hard for historians to ignore the cyclical nature of Chinese history: every forty to fifty years there was a peasant revolt, and every two to three hundred years there was a change of dynasty. For two thousand years, this pattern has continued. Those interested in China's future will naturally ask: Will history repeat itself? What should be done to avoid the cycle?

Of course, different people will have different answers. Given the advances in technology, it may seem that guided missiles, airplanes, and night vision would stifle any peasant revolt today. Centuries ago, before the development of modern warfare technologies, revolting peasants and the government army were evenly matched in terms of weaponry. It was not difficult for revolting peasants to equip themselves with arms similar to their counterparts in the national army. More charged by their determination and passion to revolt, the peasants were a force that could successfully overthrow a dynasty. However, today, the military power of the national army far exceeds that of any peasants'. Historically, insurgents slept during the day and acted at night, but night vision technologies of today have destroyed the difference between night and day; remote regions and mountains used to provide a safe

Zhiwu Chen is professor of finance at the Yale School of Management and visiting professor at the School of Humanities and Social Sciences at Tsinghua University.

The author thanks Peng Kaixiang, Yuan Weipeng, Wei Sen, Liu Guanglin, Long Denggao, Yang Peihong, Li Liming, Li Jian, Li Lingfeng, Wang Jiangwei, and Cen Ke for their suggestions and edits. Diana Wang of Yale College translated the original article from Chinese to English and edited multiple versions of this chapter. The author would also like to thank Joseph Fan, William Goetzmann, Randall Morck, and workshop participants at the NBER conference at the Chinese University of Hong Kong in December 2009. For acknowledgments, sources of research support, and disclosure of the author's material financial relationships, if any, please see http://www.nber.org/chapters/c12070.ack.

base for training and rebuilding by the revolting insurgents, but modern-day airplanes and guided missiles would easily destroy such a base. In the age of modern technologies, any peasant attempt to overthrow the central government would be doomed to fail. The technological asymmetry between government troops and revolting peasants has changed the rules of the game. Historical patterns may be hard to repeat.

From the financial point of view, the rise of modern capital markets may also have broken the cycle of dynastic changes in China. Of course, the reason is not that financial modernization has solved the social problems that fuel peasant rebellions, but it has decreased the probability that such problems would lead to the toppling of government. The role of financial modernization in nation building has been little recognized. While there has been much focus on the benefits that capital markets bring for enterprises and consumers, there is a lack of discussion on the benefits that securities markets—particularly long-term bond markets—have for nation building. In this chapter we will draw from China's recent and more distant past experience, as well as the experience of other countries, to show how financial development can affect a nation's political/economic path.

7.2   Debt-Financed Growth Strategy of Modern-Day China

Let us start with China's economic boom in the past thirty years. Due to financial modernization and development of securities markets, China's public finances in recent years differ significantly from those of Chinese dynasties. The Chinese government of today is not afraid to issue bonds, borrowing from future generations in order to pay for today's expenses. Nor is the government afraid of running budget deficits for the purpose of promoting infrastructure investments and economic growth. Contrary to widely held traditional Chinese beliefs, these new policies have not ushered in a financial meltdown or social instability, but in fact have spurred China's national growth.

Market reforms introduced in the countryside in 1978 pushed China into a period of fast development in the 1980s. The country at that time was in a "catch-up" phase, and the initial boost did not require developed financial markets. The government only needed to loosen its economic control, respect some individual rights, and let the peasants decide what they want to grow and how much output and at what price they want to sell. In 1981 the government initiated the first public debt issuance, bringing forward a portion of future revenue for the present day's spending. That year, the government issued national and foreign bonds worth a total of RMB 12.1 billion, roughly 9 percent of annual government expenditure. No matter the size, for a nation traditionally opposed to government borrowing, the issuing of government bonds at all marked a significant change.

In 1986, the deficit reached RMB 8.2 billion, 3.9 percent of the year's

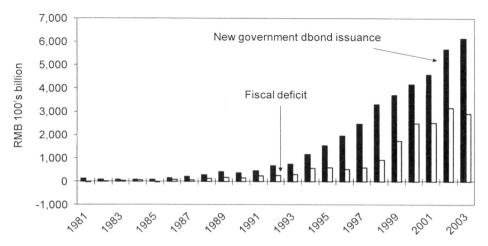

Fig. 7.1   Annual deficit and new government bond issuance
Source: National Statistics Bureau, *Statistical Yearbooks of China,* various issues.

fiscal revenue. As figure 7.1 shows, in that year the size of new bond issues grew by 54 percent to RMB 13.8 billion. By 1988, the deficit reached RMB 13.4 billion, 5.7 percent of public revenue. In 1989, national finances continued to deteriorate, with the government issuing RMB 40.8 billion of new bonds.

Since the mid-1980s, two sectors have been key drivers of China's economic growth: the manufacturing sector (financed mainly through foreign investment) and the construction/real estate sector (financed by government revenue, public bonds, and bank loans to semigovernment entities). Besides foreign direct investment (FDI) and before the recent emergence of the private equity fund industry, bank lending and public bonds have been the two main internal sources of growth financing. In 1989 to 1991 as the economy began to falter, a new bond issue worth RMB 124.5 billion helped put the economy on a recovery path. The result was a rebound in GDP growth from 3.8 percent in 1990 to 9.2 percent in 1991.

In 1994, the fiscal deficit hit a historical record of RMB 57.5 billion, 11 percent of the national revenue. To support the deficit and ensure continued economic growth, the central government in that year issued bonds worth RMB 117.5 billion, marking another historical record.

During the Asian Financial Crisis in 1997 and 1998, a major concern was that China and the global economy would be set back by the turmoil. China responded to the crisis by issuing bonds totaling RMB 331.1 billion in 1998 and RMB 371.5 billion in 1999. In 1998, the fiscal deficit reached RMB 174.4 billion, 15 percent of government revenue. As the Chinese economy was under the pressure from external shocks, public bonds provided the necessary capital for new infrastructure and industrial projects, which served to maintain China's GDP growth at 7 percent, keeping not only China but also the world economy afloat.

By the end of 2004, total government debt outstanding reached RMB 2.9631 trillion, with domestic government debt accounting for RMB 2.8801 trillion and foreign debt for RMB 82.8 billion. The total was 21.6 percent of GDP, below the internationally-recognized warning limit of 60 percent. In 2003, interest payments totaled RMB 300 billion, 14 percent of fiscal revenue.

It should be noted that these debt figures do not include nonperforming loans from state-owned financial institutions such as banks, securities firms, insurance firms, and trust companies. According to some economists' estimates, nonperforming loans for banks alone might, in 2006, have been as high as RMB 4 to 5 trillion, or 29 percent to 36 percent of GDP. With these nonperforming loans included, total government debt might be 50 to 58 percent of GDP.

From 1982 to 2004, public debt grew by an average of 25 percent annually. If the government debt continues to grow at this rate just to sustain China's economic growth, how long will it last before a crisis level is reached? If and when such fiscal deficits had persisted during China's Imperial Age, how would that have affected China? How does the national financing strategy differ between modern-day China and Imperial China?

7.3 Financing Strategy in the Imperial Age: Accumulate Large Silver Reserves

Public finances during the Song (960–1279 A.D.), Ming (1368–1644), Qing (1644–1911), and other dynasties evolved according to a similar pattern. At the start of each dynasty, the imperial court had high government savings. As the dynasty aged, the fiscal surplus weathered away and eventually turned into a deficit. Once the deficit reached an unmanageable state, the dynasty collapsed, followed by a new dynasty repeating the same cycle.

In the past, it was often argued that corruption was behind the financial cyclicality of each dynasty. That is, at the beginning of a new dynasty, corruption was limited and the Imperial treasury enjoyed a healthy surplus. However, as the dynasty aged, ineffective control led to a spread of corruption. Wayward ministers and officials drained the public purse and bankrupt the state. Finally, peasants revolted against the corrupt government officials, leading to the fall of the dynasty. While the lack of effective oversight and political corruption must have been important causes, the imperial financial strategy and the lack of financial markets must also have played an important role in the collapse of each dynasty.

Since fiscal data for the Qing Dynasty are more available, we will look at its financial strategy more closely and compare it to that of today's China. For any emperor or governor, as it is for any household, the greatest fear is that his state would experience an unforeseeable, destabilizing fiscal shock that his state would have no cash at hand to sustain. How can the emperor or his government mitigate such a risk? There are at least two overall national strategies. The first is to save as much as possible and make provisions for "rainy days" (i.e., the "precautionary saving" strategy). The second strategy has two pieces: "borrow and spend," that is, spend as much as possible at the present in order to develop the economy and increase future wealth-generating potential, and borrow money when a fiscal shock occurs to smooth its impact over multiple future years. A version of the "borrow and spend" strategy may even include spending more than today's income by running a deficit and borrowing against the future, in which case the idea is to leverage today's spending with borrowed future cash flows so as to maximize future growth opportunities. These two national financial strategies represent the "spending" versus "saving" debate between two Song Dynasty statesmen, Wang Anshi and SiMa Guang, in which Wang Anshi was arguing for aggressive spending and investing as a way to hedge future shocks, whereas SiMa Guang for aggressive saving as a way to prepare for the future. In the past thirty years, both China and the United States have pursued the "borrow and spend" strategy, though to varying degrees, while the Qing and other dynasties in Chinese history all practiced the precautionary saving strategy in accordance with traditional Confucian values of frugality.

Figure 7.2 shows the Qing Dynasty's National Treasury silver holdings from 1709 to 1850.[1] According to traditional standards, the National Treasury's holdings directly measure the nation's economic strength and sustainability. Then, by these standards, except for the period between the Opium War and the Taiping Rebellion, the Qing should be considered extremely well-off. Its Treasury wealth peaked during Qianlong's reign in the second half of the eighteenth century, when the National Treasury held 70 million taels in 1781 and roughly 60 million taels in 1789. In 1850 the outbreak of the Taiping rebellion drained the Imperial Treasury. Despite the financial burdens brought by military endeavors, the Treasury's silver holdings still managed to grow by 190,000 taels from 1853 to 1863. Though by traditional measures this sum was not high, it still seems quite healthy compared with today's upward-spiraling public debt as it was at least not a deficit. Compared to the $10+ trillion national debt of the United States today, the Qing court's fiscal surplus even during war years may seem excessive. However, the Qing Treasury's high savings was not a sign of vigor nor did its Treasury wealth guarantee the dynasty's future viability. It only reflected the accumulation of past wealth, but not necessarily its future strength. Repeating the aforementioned dynastic cycle, the Treasury condition of the Qing mirrored that of its predecessors: the dynasty's rise coincided with a large accumula-

---

1. Data on Qing government finances is quoted from Zheng (2004).

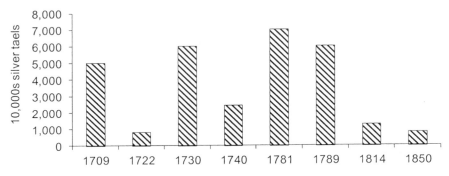

Fig. 7.2   National Treasury's silver holdings of the Qing China
Source: Zheng (2004).

tion of silver, but its Treasury's silver holdings at the end of the eighteenth century did not prevent the dynasty's fall after the nineteenth century.

This can also be seen from China's fiscal balance in the nineteenth and early twentieth centuries. Prior to the nineteenth century and in the era of Emperor Kangxi's reign (1662–722), annual fiscal surplus was on average around 5 million taels of silver. By the latter half of Qianlong's reign (1735–1795), annual fiscal surplus had doubled to about 10 million taels. Figure 7.3 shows the Qing government's annual fiscal surplus from 1838 onward.[2] From this graph, it is apparent that before the start of the Opium War in 1839, the surplus was quite large and exceeded 5 million taels. But, after the Opium War, the Qing government did not necessarily become more aggressive in spending and building national capacity. For example, in 1847, six years after China lost the Opium War, the surplus was still 3.80 million tales. "Precautionary saving" by all means remained the national financial strategy, even at the cost of sacrificing the immediate nation building opportunities. In 1893, on the eve of the first Sino-Japanese Naval War, the Qing government was saving a surplus of 7.60 million taels. Perhaps, not surprisingly, all the savings prevented China from becoming stronger and China lost the naval war to Japan disastrously in 1895, which devastated the Chinese national psyche.

The Confucian way of managing future fiscal shocks through savings today was clearly inefficient for the Qing Dynasty and even insensible. Even after China's defeat in the Second Opium War (1856–1860) and in the face of the Japanese menace, the Qing government continued to save as much as possible, although optimally the Qing court should not only spend all its revenue but also borrow against future revenues and invest at the present

2. Data sources for annual government finances are: Zhang (2003) for the period of 1838 to 1849, Sheng (2002) for fiscal revenue data for 1885 to 1894, Chen (2000) for annual expenditure data for 1885 to 1894, and Tang, Lu, and Niu (1998) for both fiscal revenue and expenditure data for 1896 and thereafter.

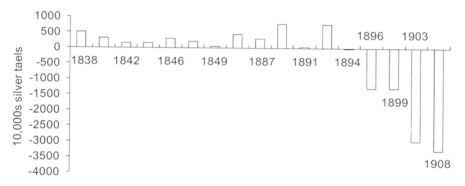

Fig. 7.3   Annual fiscal surplus of the Qing China

Sources: Zhang (2003) for the period of 1838 to 1849, Sheng (2002) for fiscal revenue data for 1885–1894, Chen (2000) for annual expenditure data for 1885–1894, and Tang, Lu, and Niu (1998) for both fiscal revenue and expenditure data for 1896 and thereafter.

to expand future capabilities. Despite the urgency of the times, the Imperial court did not consider forwarding future revenue for the purpose of strengthening the nation right away. Instead, it clung tightly to the notion of saving and shoring the Imperial reserves. The end result was the eventual demise of China's power in relation to other nations.

The Qing finances turned into a deficit at the end of the Sino-Japanese Naval War. In 1896, the deficit reached 12.92 million taels, and 13 million taels by 1899.[3] After the Boxer Rebellion, hefty war reparations forced onto China weighed significantly on national finances. In 1903, the deficit hit 30 million taels. Financial obligations continued to mount on the Qing's budget until the dynasty's collapse in 1911.

7.4   Two Financial Strategies, Two Results

At this point, we can see that the two fiscal strategies pursued by present-day China and the Qing Dynasty have resulted in vastly different results. In accordance with traditional Chinese notions of financial management, the Qing stressed saving and cutting expenditure. For two-and-a-half centuries prior to 1896, Qing finances were basically healthy, with a large annual surplus and much Treasury silver holdings. China should, according to old beliefs, have been strong and mighty enough to face any exogenous shock. However, in reality, putting treasury wealth accumulation above nation building only hastened the demise of the empire.

In contrast, since 1982, the People's Republic of China (PRC) government of today has been running deficits and using the bond markets and bank loans to accelerate investment spending. The deficit in 1982 was RMB 1.8 bil-

3. Data from Tang, Lu, and Niu (1998).

lion, 0.33 percent of GDP, but has grown to RMB 291.6 billion, 2.5 percent of GDP, by 2003. Total government debt has grown from essentially zero to RMB 2.9 trillion. Such a "borrow and spend" strategy of relying on fiscal deficit to drive economic growth would be viewed as symptoms of national weakness according to traditional Chinese values. Yet, China today is actually stronger than at any time in history, including times when the Treasury silver holdings were high. Two distinct financial strategies have lead to two different results. How do we explain this?

In *A Free Nation Deep in Debt: The Financial Roots of Democracy,* James Macdonald (2003) draws a link between public debt and national development. If we use the national treasury holdings data as of 1600 A.D. and divide the nations into two groups, one with rich gold and silver holdings in their treasuries and the other group with nations deep in debt, we find that the nations with large treasury holdings back then are still developing and relatively poor countries today (with Japan as an exception), while these nations deep in debt back then that had to rely on public bond markets to finance their growth are today's democratic nations with developed economies. Around 1600 A.D., the Ming court of China hoarded about 13 million taels of silver and enough grain provisions for nine years' consumption, all to hedge unforeseeable catastrophe shocks. The fear of disasters led to precautionary over-saving and put too much wealth (i.e., gold and silver) in the national treasury. As silver was the main currency at the time, silver hoarding in the treasury not only prevented wealth from becoming productive capital, but also reduced money supply in the economy, stifling potential economic growth. It is thus not surprising that soon after 1600 A.D., the Ming Dynasty collapsed. Around the same time, India's government hoarded 60 million taels of gold, instead of putting the wealth to productive use.

The nation most famous for debt-financed growth today is the United States, as the American national debt far exceeds that of any other country (though the relative national debt level is not the highest). Yet with the help of developed capital markets, large fiscal deficits have not eroded the globally dominating position of the United States, either economically or otherwise. The national financial strategies adopted by the United States and China today stand in stark contrast with that of the Chinese dynasties. National debt per se is not necessarily bad for nation building.

7.5   How Serious Was the Financial Condition of the Late Qing?

It is commonly believed that war reparations from the Sino-Japanese naval war of 1895 and the Boxer Rebellion dealt a fatal blow to the Qing government, making it inevitable to fall. In a major way, the loss in these wars by China was at least partly a consequence of the savings-focused national financial strategy practiced by the Qing and earlier dynasties. But, putting aside for now the question of why China lost in these wars, let us consider the following: How much of a financial burden were these war reparations for China? Would the fate of the Qing Dynasty have been different if China had had a developed financial market?

According to the analysis by Chen Feng,[4] from 1902 onwards, war reparations and the payment of other foreign debt cost the Qing 47 million taels of silver annually. This amounted to 44.7 percent of the annual fiscal revenue in 1903, which was at 104.92 million taels. The deficit in 1903 was around 30 million taels, 28.6 percent of national revenue.

In comparison to today's deficit, how excessive was the 1903 deficit? In 2000, China's fiscal deficit was 18.6 percent of national revenue. From 1999 to 2003, the deficit has fluctuated between 13.5 to 18.6 percent. As a percentage of fiscal revenue, the deficit in the late Qing was higher than that of today's China.

In relation to GDP, both the 30 million taels of deficit and the 650 million taels of war reparations (including both the Sino-Japanese naval war and the Boxer Rebellion) should not have been excessive using today's standards. According to estimates by Guanglin Liu,[5] in 1880 China's GDP was about 2.78 billion taels and total taxation revenue was 3.2 percent of GDP. At this taxation rate, the total fiscal revenue of 104.92 million taels in 1903 translates into a GDP for that year of 3.28 billion taels. Then, the 30 million deficit in 1903 was only 0.9 percent of GNP, far below today's relative deficit level. For example, China's deficit was 3 percent of GDP in 2002, and 2.5 percent in 2003.

Based on the previous estimate, the total war reparations of 650 million taels is equal to about 20 percent of China's GDP of 1903, which is below the relative national debt level of about 22 percent of GDP in 2003. According to this measure, the degree of government indebtedness during the late Qing is actually lower than that of China today.

According to Macdonald (2003), the Netherland's public debt was 1.3 times its national income in 1650, and two times its national income in 1715. Around that time, England's national debt was 80 percent of its national income.[6] These levels of indebtedness were clearly much higher than both late Qing and present-day China's. But their debt did not bring down these nations' government.

A key reason that late Qing China was brought down even with a lower level of indebtedness has to do with China's long-practiced saving-oriented financial strategy, as this strategy had prevented China from developing a domestic bond market and hence limited late Qing China's debt capacity. Without well-developed domestic debt markets, especially without a long-

4. See Chen (2000).
5. Liu (2005).
6. Macdonald (2003).

term bond market, the Qing government did not have the means to smooth the impact of a large fiscal shock and spread the lump-sum war reparation payments over many years. The financial obligations of the late Qing were nothing to be feared. A nation's debt capacity is a function of its debt markets' developedness. Of course, if a nation's financial strategy is to rely on savings and shy away from any government borrowing, its bond market will simply have no opportunity to develop and hence it will not have a developed bond market. In this sense, a debt level that looks relatively trivial using today's standard was enough to bring down the Qing Dynasty, whereas today's China, with much more government debt, is looking strong.

7.6   Levying Taxes to Solve Fiscal Crises

Wars, natural disasters, or manmade disasters often occur suddenly and unexpectedly. Since such events are irregular and unpredictable, they tend to disrupt government finances, often dealing a debilitating blow that few nations can survive. As discussed before, a nation may hedge such risk events by saving preemptively. However, from the previous discussions, we see that precautionary savings may not be enough. From a security design perspective, a fixed-income savings instrument is a bad fit for risk insurance purposes and highly ineffective. It also sacrifices present-day consumption and investment opportunities, preventing the nation from developing, or even expanding, its full potential.

A second option is to buy insurance and other types of hedging product. While such an approach would be far more effective than savings, an insurance market has to exist and be deep enough. But, insurance markets against war and disaster events did not exist and are still not available to nations in their direct forms (except in indirect forms, such as a protectorate arrangement offered by a large empire nation). Under sovereignty for each nation, it is difficult for a transnational insurance corporation to sell insurance to nations and pool their risks together as the corporation would need supernational power to monitor and enforce insurance contracts.

Therefore, other than precautionary savings and cross-national alliances, a nation had and still has only limited options to preemptively hedge future fiscal shocks. Nations were, and are most likely to be, totally exposed. When a major war or natural disaster occurred, the blow to a dynasty was often fatal.

When a major fiscal shock did occur and if the accumulated treasury savings were not sufficient to cover the unexpected expenditures, a deficit resulted and the national government would have three options to solve the deficit problem: raise taxes, debase the currency, or issue long-term debt. In Chinese history, the imperial court always resorted to the first two options because the third option was nonexistent as China never developed a domestic medium- to long-term debt market. Since the first two options were politically and socially dangerous, they typically caused a dynasty to collapse.

Take the Ming Dynasty as an example. During its latter half, national finances had slowly deteriorated to a crisis level. In the mid-sixteenth century, annual deficit fluctuated by 2 to 4 million taels. As the fiscal difficulty continued due to the continuing war in the North, the need to fill the gap became more and more urgent. At the start of 1618 A.D., an official proclamation by Emperor Wanli raised annual taxes by a fixed quota. But that tax raise turned out to be insufficient and did not solve the fiscal crisis. In 1628 when Chongzheng succeeded the throne, the deficit had reached 1.13 million taels, according to Wang Hao.[7] In order to fill the gap, Emperor Chongzheng raised taxes by 3 taels for every *mu* of land, on top of the 9 tael increase ten years earlier during Wanli's reign. The total increase in tax revenue was 1.65 million taels. Not surprisingly, the tax hike only served to enrage the peasants further and led to a sharp rise in peasant revolts, which in turn pressured the court to increase military spending, worsening the fiscal deficit.

As national finances stayed in a crisis, wage payments to soldiers were delayed as a way to provide temporary relief to the Imperial government. In 1620, the first year of Chongzhen's reign, the Imperial court already owed an accumulated total of 5.20 million taels in soldiers' pay. By the tenth year of his reign, the Imperial court was still behind in payments. As a result, the army's morale reached a new low. Losing the support of the army, the Ming Dynasty was unable to forestall its demise. In 1631, events took a decisive turn for the worst as the deficit continued to deteriorate. Without an army, Chongzhen could not quell the peasant revolts, but without cash to pay for soldiers' wages, the military refused to fight. With his hands tied, Emperor Chongzhen decided in 1631 to raise taxes by 2.80 million taels, planting the last seed for ending the Ming Dynasty in 1644.

According to Wang (2001),[8] at the time, Emperor Chongzhen had attempted other solutions including cutting Imperial spending, but all these measures failed to save the dynasty.

The initial mistake of the Ming's early policy was to isolate China from the outside world. By the time Chongzhen was enthroned, the nation's choice set was quite limited and missed important development opportunities relative to Western nations. During that time period, frequent natural disasters in parts of China had also inflicted severe hardship on the peasants. Thus, when Emperor Chongzhen raised land taxes, it is not surprising then that the peasants would revolt.

Levying a onetime tax to solve the fiscal crisis turned out to be a fatal mistake, as it exaggerated the impact of a onetime shock on society and subjected the society to an extreme stress test. The tax placed the financial burden solely on the Chinese peasants who were already living in desperate times. The burden was far too great for the society to shoulder within a short period of time. An alternative would have been to spread the temporary high

7. See Wang (2001).
8. Ibid.

burden over a period of thirty to eighty years, with multiple generations paying for a portion of the fiscal burden each year. However, the necessary financial technologies for spreading the deficit over multiple years—in particular, long-term public bonds—did not exist during the Imperial Ages of China.

The main sources of revenue for the Imperial court have traditionally been taxes on land, salt, customs, and other miscellaneous items. The heavy reliance on taxes may be traced back to the Tang when taxation powers were consolidated by the Imperial bureaucracy. Despite the widespread use of land tax in the Imperial Ages, the Qing in the nineteenth century, like the Ming emperors, found it hard to extract greater revenue from the peasants who were already greatly burdened by natural disasters and taxes.[9] Land tax as a portion of tax revenue decreased, partially replaced by revenue from the Lijin system, a form of transit tax on goods and commodities. The spread of the Lijin system reflected the transfer of central tax authority from the Imperial court to regional authorities as the emperor's power weathered. The Lijin system emerged in Jiangsu province when local leaders took matters into their own hands to raise funds necessary to suppress the Taiping Rebellion during the mid-nineteenth century. The Lijin tax ultimately became a major source of revenue for regional governments.

While the Lijin tax helped fund government expenditures, it demonstrated some of the shortcomings of taxation for additional revenue. First, the Lijin marked a strong state intrusion in local trade and commerce, and the increased transaction costs only served to stifle economic development. The transit tax undermined the local economy also because merchants began circumventing the area to avoid the tax. Second, a significant portion of the tax burden was ultimately placed on the farmers as merchants transferred the costs onto the peasants. By imposing greater regulation over trade, the local authorities constrained economic growth, running counter to the need for larger revenue base. Ultimately, one has to go beyond taxation to find ways to reduce the hurt of a fiscal crisis on the economy and society.

7.7 Policies for Alleviating a Fiscal Crisis

Besides raising taxes, another strategy for addressing a deficit is for the government to print more money. According to Guanglin Liu,[10] the Song Dynasty was a time when the Imperial court centralized its control over the economy, army, and society while greatly expanding its territory. Such actions necessarily required an increase in government expenditures, and the Imperial court soon found itself unable to make ends meet. Faced with

9. See Chen (2000).
10. Liu (2005). In the Chinese history literature, a consensus view is that the Song court succeeded in consolidating much power in the central government's hands. See also Zhao, Liu, and Zhang (2002).

a financial meltdown, the Song's response was to increase money supply, first in the form of iron coins.[11] To pay for the mounting costs of military operations in West Xia, Emperor Renzhong initially ordered an increase in the casting of iron coins, creating a financial catastrophe. As war operations expanded into the western regions, Emperor Songshen institutionalized China's first paper currency, *jiaozi*, that had been in circulation by Sichuan merchants, by spreading its distribution into Hedong and Shannxi and in effect doubling the amount in circulation. The surfeit of paper currency led to rapid inflation and left the economy in shambles.[12]

The development of paper money during the Song Dynasty promoted commercialization and eased fiscal operations. However, through overissuance of paper money, the Song transferred the burden of the fiscal crisis onto the population, grabbing wealth from ordinary people. According to Wang Sheng Duo, during Ningbo's reign the issuance of paper money exceeded 10 million guan. Without a long-term bond market, the Song's financing options were greatly limited. It could see no other alternative but continued to increase circulation beyond 1 trillion guan. The strategy gradually sowed the seeds of its own destruction. It should be noted that while paper currency is one form of public debt, it is technically of immediate maturity instead of long maturity, so it amounts to inflicting the hurt on society right away and offers no ability to spread the burden beyond the present time and over many years.

Even when there was no paper currency in circulation, the Imperial court also used nominally-inflated metal coins to rob the population's wealth. Not only were the Song, the Yuan, and the Ming Dynasties guilty of such actions, but the late Qing and the Republic of China also adopted a similar strategy. In order to resolve the fiscal crisis caused by the Taiping Rebellion in the mid-nineteenth century, the Qing Emperor Xianfeng issued both paper currency and diluted coins. According to Zhang Guohui,[13] while the face values of the copper coins were, respectively, 1,000 wen to 500 wen, the actual values were only 114 wen and 90 wen, allowing the Qing to spend only 115 wen to receive in return 1,000 wen from the population. Using a similar logic of solving fiscal problems via nominal inflation, in 1854, the Imperial treasury began casting metal coins. Between 1853 to 1861, the Qing cast 8.26 million silver taels of metal coins. The excessive casting of coins and printing of paper currency led to rapid inflation. Between 1853 and 1869, the price of sesame oil increased by 3 times, coal by 4 times, tea by 5 times, and candle by 7.5 times.[14] Soaring commodity prices complicated the lives of the Chinese and ate into their wealth. Inevitably, the number of social uprisings rose.

11. Wang (2003), introduction.
12. Ibid.
13. Zhang (2003).
14. Ibid., chapter 2.

The overprinting of paper currency destroyed the economy and cut into the faith in the Qing, ushering the dynasty's demise. Although paper money was invented during the Song Dynasty, money supply abuse eventually made it difficult for paper currency to be trusted and widely circulated. The Imperial court basically destroyed paper currency's potential for stimulating economic growth and industrialization. For more than 800 years since the Song's invention, paper currency never gained full traction until the twentieth century.

Of course, Imperial China was not the only kingdom guilty of debasing the currency to solve a fiscal problem. Ancient Roman emperors addressed a shortage of money by diluting gold and silver coins, effectively inflating the nominal value on the coins—for example, by changing the denomination from 10 to 100 without changing the weight of gold or silver in the coin. Rulers of Western Europe during the Middle Ages used the trick to extract wealth from the people. Throughout the sixteenth century, Spain frequently fell behind its debt payments.[15] Facing intense financial pressures, King Phillip III ordered the minting of *vellon* coins, which were mixtures of silver and copper, to replace pure silver coins. From 1600 to 1626, Spain minted 41 million ducats of debased coins, allowing the royal family to collect a profit of 25 million to 30 million ducats. By 1628, the currency had depreciated by 70%. In 1650, the Spanish King found no other alternative but to increase the printed nominal number on each coin as the Roman emperors had done. As the people began to lose faith in the currency, inflation soared, shattering the economy and leading to the decline of the Spanish empire.[16]

Even though devaluing the currency is less overt than direct taxation, both methods share the same shortcoming: they place too heavy of a short-term burden on the citizens, destabilizing the financial system and damaging confidence in the ruler. Forcing the citizens to accept at debased metal coins or paper money has disastrous long-term consequences, even if the devaluation is temporary. This is why such action is only taken by the most desperate of rulers. Every Chinese dynasty as well as the Republic of China experienced a disastrous consequence of currency overissuance.

Because a nation cannot issue stock shares, which would be one ideal way to address a fiscal crisis (though one could view taxation as collecting money from citizens as "shareholders" except that it is not by citizens' free choice), the best alternative is to issue long-term bonds: the longer the term, the better for smoothing the moment's financial pressure. Long maturity dates (for example, 100 years) spread a onetime expensive or deficit over multiple future years, decreasing the payment burden for any particular year. For example, suppose the government is short of $10 billion. A onetime

15. Macdonald (2003, 136). The loss of credibility from overprinting paper currency also eroded Spain's ability to issue long-term debt.
16. Macdonald (2003, 136).

tax of $10 billion can be hard to take by the population. But, if it issues a perpetual bond of $10 billion at an annual yield rate of 5 percent, the population would only have to pay $500 million a year. While the bond option will require a long-term payment stream and hence the liability lasts forever, the payment pressure for each given year will be more bearable than for the taxation option.

What is the ideal term to maturity for a government bond? This depends on the time span of the benefits created by the debt-funded project. For example, if a bond is used to finance construction of roads that last for ten years, then the bond term to maturity should be as long as ten years. On the other hand, if a war increases the state's staying power and allows the nation to prosper into eternity, a perpetual bond for war operations will let each future generation pay for the war as they will all enjoy the benefit.

In China, the earliest form of government borrowing occurred more than 2,600 years ago during the Warring States Age. At that time, the Qi state's emperor took the advice from Guanzi and borrowed from wealthy households in order to fund war operations. Unfortunately, after the war was over, Guanzi also advised the emperor to default on the loans and the Imperial court did, making it no longer credible for the Qi state to borrow again. After the Qi state, government borrowing had rarely been used, which means that long-term credit markets had not had opportunities to develop during the Imperial Ages of China. On the one hand, both the cultural preference for relying on savings to prepare for future uncertainty and hence the lack of long-term credit market, had pushed the Imperial court to depend on taxation and currency manipulations as a way to get around fiscal crises. That dependence on taxation became a seemingly perpetual tradition of China. On the other hand, once the dependence on taxation had become a familiar and "comfortable" Chinese tradition, long-term public borrowing markets would have even less of a chance to develop and the Imperial court would be made more dependent on taxation than ever. Such a self reinforcing process fueled by the lack of long-term credit markets might have served to strengthen the dynastical cycles.

The fiscal difficulties caused by the Taiping Rebellion in the mid-nineteenth century forced the Qing government to experiment with debt financing again. According to Peng Zeyi,[17] Shanxi, Shaanxi, and Guangdong were the first provinces to issue local government loans. In Shanxi, local authorities asked rich families for funds, issuing a stamped bank note that promised an annual repayment of a portion of the loan. In addition to the promised annual interest, those who lent more than 100,000 taels of silver were awarded with a noble title.[18] In Shanxi, local authorities encouraged its citizens to double their lending amount in return for social advan-

17. Peng (1983, 150–52).
18. See Peng (1983, 150).

tages and political honors. The experiments were relatively successful and later spread to Jiangsu and Zhejiang. The problem arose that once the fiscal crisis was over, each local authority suspended repayments, replacing liabilities with political awards. Reneging on the loans destroyed the Qing government's credibility again and made it impossible for the government to find lenders in the aftermath of the Sino-Japanese Naval War. However, the first set of domestic government loans allowed the Imperial court to at least survive past the Taiping Rebellion.

Essentially, the "domestic government loans" issued in 1853 were similar to the "forced loans" issued in Europe during the Middle Ages. At that time, Western Europe's city-state governments forced the merchant class to purchase bonds in order to raise the funds necessary for war operations or infrastructure projects. These short-term bonds were similar to repayable taxes, not tradable securities.

It is intriguing to ask why long-term credit markets developed in Western Europe prior to modern times but did not develop in China until the end of the nineteenth century. According to Macdonald (2003), Western Europe has had a long tradition of avoiding direct taxation. It started in ancient Greece. "If the inhabitants of the Asiatic empires accepted powers of direct taxation as a matter of course, the Greeks rejected them entirely" (Macdonald 2003, 32). Instead, they relied on voluntary donations and, at times of war and/or large expenditure, on public debt. Macdonald (2003, 37) estimates that from the end of the fifth century to the middle of the first century B.C., there exist more than one hundred records of public debt by the government of Athens. Even in the late Middle Ages and into the Renaissance, Western Europe avoided a fiscal system heavily reliant on taxes due to a strong distaste for direct taxes among the people. In the medieval city-states of Italy, the financial system for public borrowing developed out of the principle that direct taxes were an insult on the free citizens and should be avoided. Forced loans, or repayable taxes, were easier for the people to accept and less insulting than direct taxes.

Public bonds that were collateralized using future fiscal revenue emerged first in 1262 in Venice.[19] For city-states that faced constant warfare and ever-increasing financing needs, debt with maturities less than a year had little use for relieving financial pressure. Financing instruments with small annual payments spread over a long period of time were preferred. In 1470, Florence had so much public debt outstanding that its annual interest payment was 360,000 gold ducats, surpassing previous years' national revenue.[20] In comparison, the Qing government's interest payment in 1903 was only 44.7 percent of fiscal revenue, quite high but not as bad as it was for Florence

---

19. See Chen (2006) for a brief discussion in Chinese and Poitras (2000) for a summary of the experience in English.

20. Macdonald (2003, 88).

more than four centuries back. The financial problems Florence faced forced its leaders to think of a new solution: extending the payment duration (i.e., making the term to maturity longer).

At that time, European governments typically used one or all of three types of financial instruments. The first was life annuities. In this exchange arrangement, the buyer would purchase an annuity after proving his health and be entitled to an annual payment of 5 to 8 percent of the purchase price for each year after a certain age and until his death. Upon his death, the government's obligation would end. For the individual buyer, a life annuity contract offered much needed help as one's remaining lifetime was always uncertain, making it a risk hard to mitigate. For a government, selling life annuities was a good way to raise funds for the present and spread the expenditure pressure over several decades. Thus, it was a win-win financial design. In the fifteenth and sixteenth centuries, life annuities were used widely in the Netherlands and later in England.

The second type of instrument was the dowry fund. With the birth of a daughter, the parents would buy fund shares from the local government. Before the daughter would marry, the government would not pay any interest, but upon her marriage, the government would return both the capital and all accumulated interest from the intervening years. If the daughter would not marry before the age of fifteen or decide to become a nun (which occurred in one out of each four cases), the government would be exempt from the interest payment. The dowry fund was first issued in Florence in 1425 and became popular in Venice and southern European city-states. The typical duration to maturity period was over ten years.

The third type of instrument was long-term or perpetual bonds. These bonds greatly expanded the debt-financing capabilities of European governments.

In 1715, Holland's national debt was twice its national income, while for England it was 0.8 times. Both nations mostly used long-term public bonds to smooth fiscal challenges. For that year, England's public debt was 60 million pounds,[21] of which 16.4 million pounds was perpetual bonds, 12.6 million pounds was bonds with maturity terms of thirty-two and ninety-nine years, and 11.4 million pounds lottery bonds with maturity terms of thirty-two years. For the lottery bonds, the average annual interest rate was about 6.84 percent, but the winners of the lottery would enjoy rates as high as 8 percent a year. The remaining debt was financed by other short-term and long-term instruments. After 1717, interest rates on perpetual and long-term bonds fell to around 4 percent.

The Song, Yuan, and Ming Dynasties were not as lucky as Western European nations. For the Imperial courts, there was no possibility to issue perpetual bonds or bonds with maturity terms longer than one year, which

---

21. Macdonald (2003, 186–87).

might have saved them from collapsing. They were not even as lucky as the late Qing Dynasty. While the war reparations were severe burdens on the Qing, the Qing court at least had the option to borrow from foreign banks. These loans, arranged by HSBC and other banks between 1896 and 1902, were financed by bonds issued in Europe with maturity terms of thirty-six years at annual interest rates of 4 to 5 percent, and they helped extend the life of the Qing Dynasty by several years and also save Manchuria and Shandong from becoming foreign colonies. While public borrowing and especially public borrowing with foreign banks did not rest comfortably with the Chinese population, it was far better than allowing parts of China to be a colony of foreign powers.

Losing the Sino-Japanese Naval War in 1895 left a deep and devastating impact on the Chinese psyche and helped accelerate the financial modernization process. With the establishment of the first modern bank—the China Merchant Bank—in 1898, the finance industry quickly developed. The national debt market truly developed around 1914, soon after the Republic of China was established. Because the government did not find willing foreign lenders in a time of civil unrest, it had to turn more to the internal debt market. Between 1912 to 1926, the Republican government issued twenty-seven public bonds, totaling 612 million yuan.[22] The market continued to expand and deepen and by 1949, the public debt market had fully taken shape. During the 1950s, the bond market ceased functioning, but in 1982 it was revitalized. Helped with the pre-1949 experience in financial market development, the banking sector, stock market, and bond market were quickly restored during the 1980s and 1990s. With the growth of financial distribution networks across the country, public debt financing has continued to expand and is now playing a critical role in China's development.

Currently, the longest maturity term on a public bond is thirty years. Long-term bonds have allowed China to survive the Asian Financial Crisis of 1997 and 1998 and come out of the 2008 global financial crisis stronger. With both short- and long-term financing instruments, China today can avoid the doomed fate of the Imperial dynasties.

7.8   How Long Will China's Debt-Financed Growth Continue?

From our discussions it is clear that long-term capital markets, especially long-term borrowing markets, are crucial for nation building. First of all, they help reduce the pressure for the national treasury to save so the country can invest more of its present income and wealth productively. Second, long-term capital markets allow the government at different levels to convert future fiscal revenues into capital of today, such that once capitalized, the future revenue flows become today's redeployable capital for new infrastruc-

---

22. See Zhang (2001) for details.

ture and other projects. In China's long past history, both cultural resistance to finance and overemphasis on savings served to remove any need to develop long-term financial markets. The lack of financial market development in turn made China's dynastic governments have no choice but attempt to maximize national treasury savings. As a result, China was stuck in a low-development equilibrium, which was fine when every other nation was in a similarly low-growth equilibrium. However, as long-term credit markets started to emerge from the pre-Renaissance to the pre-Industrial Revolution period and really took off during the Industrial Revolution, first city-state governments, and then corporations and entrepreneurs, in Western Europe were able to capitalize future income flows to enlarge today's deployable capital pool and accelerate growth and development speed. China was unaware of such growth-accelerating power of long-term financial markets, until China lost the Opium War in 1842 and the Sino-Japanese Naval War in 1895. It was these losses that forced China to take a serious look at modern financial technologies.

Partly out of need and partly as a result of learning from the West, the Qing Imperial government began to experiment with modern financial markets in the late nineteenth century. After the fall of the Qing in 1911, the Republic of China government continued the experiment in greater scale and breadth. In the 1930s and 1940s, the Republican government benefited greatly from the fast development of the securities markets, including the government bonds market. It practiced a national financial strategy that was heavily dependent on long-term public bonds and administrative control of money supply. A variety of financing options were helpful for the Republican government to spread the costs from fighting both the Anti-Japanese War and the Civil War. However, corruption was so widespread and eventually even a modernized financial market system could not prevent the collapse of the regime.

Since 1982, the PRC government has been relying on government bonds, among other financing strategies, to both fill the annual deficit gap and provide infrastructure investment capital. The national financial strategy of the past twenty or so years has been the opposite when contrasted with the traditional dynastic financial strategy of maximum saving, but is similar to those that have been practiced in Western Europe and the United States for centuries. Its result has been proven positive by China's recent economic success. Therefore, national financial strategy matters.

If the Chinese government continues to depend on public debt to promote domestic demand, thus spurring economic growth, how sustainable is such a policy? How much national debt is too much? This of course is hard to answer, as the answer must depend on institutional and other factors. For example, government debt during the late Qing was about 21 percent of GDP as it is in today's China, but that was enough to bring down the Qing Dynasty, while the PRC seems to be strong at the present.

In comparison, the United States owes $9 trillion in debt, of which $2 trillion is foreign held. Japan's public debt accounts for 170 percent of GDP, Italy's public debt exceeds 120 percent of GDP, and that of the United States is 70 percent GDP. The high level of public debt has not resulted in a fiscal meltdown or social unrest for these countries. However, Asian countries in the 1990s, the Republic of China in 1930 to 1940, and the Latin American nations in the 1980s and 1990s have all suffered social instability arising from excess debt and foreign-held bonds. Why is there a large difference in experience with national debt?

The answer depends on the nature and quality of political institutions. Corrupt institutions and weak checks and balances on political power greatly limit a nation's ability to service debt. The link between institutional quality and debt-financing capacity is seen not only in the present day. In the sixteenth and seventeenth centuries, the Netherland's national debt was much higher than Spain's. In 1650, the Netherland's debt amounted to 1.6 kg silver per capita, while Spain's was only 0.6 kg per capita.[23] The interest rate on Netherland's debt was between 3 and 5 percent, while Spain in the sixteenth century had to pay an interest rate of over 10 percent. The Netherlands did not collapse from high levels of debt. Spain, however, began declining after the mid-seventeenth century. In the mid-eighteenth century, England managed to sustain a much higher level of debt than France. England's per capita debt level far exceeded that of France's. Despite the heavy fiscal liabilities, England's economy boomed and interest rates remained low. In fact, interest rates in England were half that in France for much of the eighteenth century.[24] A major reason behind the difference in financing cost was that after the Glorious Revolution of 1688 a credible government was established in England with the sovereign's power significantly constrained by the Parliament, while France was still under the arbitrary rule of the king. Thus, a country's ability to sustain long-term deficits and its ability to obtain debt-financing at reasonable cost are closely tied to its institutional framework.

Does China's political system offer high enough public debt capacity that China can not only sustain its current debt level for many years to come, but also develop the nation further by issuing more national debt? Will China be able to continue with the current national financial strategy without fundamental political reforms? The answer clearly remains to be determined. But, without a transparent political system, we suspect that China has much more room to increase deficit spending and add national debt.

23. Macdonald (2003, 152).
24. See pages 182–87 of Macdonald (2003) for more discussions on the English and French experience in the eighteenth century.

References

Chen, Feng. 2000. "The Qing Dynasty's Expenditure Policy and Spending Structural Changes." *Jianghan Forum* 2000 (5): 60–70. 陈锋，《清代财政支出政策与支出结构的变动》，《江汉论坛》，2000 年第 5 期.

Chen, Zhiwu. 2006. "On the Rise of the West." *Securities Market Weekly,* September 4. 陈志武，《再谈西方的兴起》，《证券市场周刊》，2006年9月4日.

Liu, Guanglin. 2005. *Wrestling for Power: The State and the Economy in Later Imperial China, 1000–1770.* Cambridge, MA: Department of East Asian Languages and Civilizations, Harvard University.

Macdonald, James. 2003. *A Free Nation Deep in Debt: The Financial Roots of Democracy.* New York: Farrar, Straus and Giroux.

Peng, Zeyi. 1983. *China's Finances and Economy in the Second Half of the 19th Century.* Beijing: People's Publishing House. 彭泽益著《十九世纪后半期的中国财政与经济》，人民出版社 1983年版.

Poitras, Geoffrey. 2000. *The Early History of Financial Economics, 1478–1776: From Commercial Arithmetic to Life Annuities and Joint Stocks.* Cheltenham, UK: Edward Elgar Publishing.

Sheng, Xuefeng. 2002. "Review of the Level and Structural Changes of the Qing Dynasty's Fiscal Revenue." *Beijing Social Sciences* 2002 (1): 75–90. 申学锋，《清代财政收入规模与结构变化述论》，《北京社会科学》2002年第1期.

Tang, Xianxing, Xiangguo Lu, and Jiwei Niu. 1998. "The Late Qing Dynasty's Decline and Setbacks in Early Stages of Modernization." *Literature and History* 1998 (2): 125–37. 唐贤兴，卢向国和牛纪伟，《晚清政府贫困化与中国早期现代化的受挫》，《文史哲》1998年第2期.

Wang, Hao. 2001. "On Emperor Chongzhen of the Song Dynasty." *China Journal of Historical Studies* 2001 (4): 35–51. 王昊，《论崇祯帝》，《史学集刊》，2001年第4期.

Wang, Shengduo. 2003. *Monetary History of the Song Dynasty.* Beijing: Social Science Publishing House. 汪圣铎著，《两宋货币史》，2003年，社会科学文献出版社.

Zhang, Chunting. 2001. "A Brief History of China's Stock Market Development." *Stock Market Review,* 5th issue of 2001. 张春廷，"中国证券市场发展简史，"《证券市场导报》，2001年第5期.

Zhang, Guohui. 2003. *Chinese Finance History, Volume 2.* Beijing: Chinese Finance Publishing House. 张国辉著，《中国金融通史》第二卷，第二章，2003年，中国金融出版社.

Zhao, Xiangbiao, Songlin Liu, and Menggong Zhang. 2002. *A General History of China, Volume 2.* Urumuqi: Xinjiang People's Publishing House. 赵向标，刘松岭，张满弓主编，《中国通史》中卷，2002年，新疆人民出版.

Zheng, Beijun. 2004. *Modern China's Lijin Tax System.* Beijing: China Finance and Economics Publishing House. 郑备军著《中国近代厘金制度研究》，2004,中国财政经济出版社.

Comment   Jiahua Che

In "Financial Strategies for Nation Building," Professor Zhiwu Chen offers us two interesting observations and one brave thesis. The first observation

Jiahua Che is associate professor of economics at the Chinese University of Hong Kong.
For acknowledgments, sources of research support, and disclosure of the author's material financial relationships, if any, please see http://www.nber.org/chapters/c12459.ack.

is that no government lasted for more than three hundred years in imperial China. What can be done to prevent such a cycle of regime change from happening again in modern day China? This is the question that Chen sets out to answer in the chapter. And the answer, according to Professor Chen, is public debt. To justify the answer, Chen offers his second observation: governments in imperial China resorted to either taxes or inflation, but not public debt, to finance government spending. Chen argues that, when a government faces a large negative fiscal shock, using tax or inflation to finance "were politically and socially dangerous," whereas using debt financing would have helped "spread the temporary high burden over a period of thirty to eighty years." To contrast with the experience of imperial China, Chen notes that, since 1982, China has a growing national debt on the one hand and an increasingly strong economy on the other. Borrowing from Macdonald (2003), Chen notes further that countries deep in debt back in 1600 tend to be developed economies today. Chen asserts that making use of public debt can "reduce the pressure for the national treasury to save so the country can invest more," and can allow the government to "convert future fiscal revenues into capital of today." Thus, the thesis from Professor Chen is that public debt helps the nation grow strong.

Chen's thesis offers a refreshing perspective to examine the aforementioned two seemingly unrelated phenomena. It was a pleasure and an inspiration for me to read his article and to contemplate the intriguing observations Professor Chen has brought forward.

Chen points out three advantages of debt over tax in meeting government spending: spreading the tax burden over time, capitalizing on future tax revenues, and reducing the precautionary need for saving for the government. According to Chen, the first one is crucial for a regime to survive a large spending shock; the latter two pave the way for the nation to succeed. Given these great advantages of debt over tax, there is a natural question of why generations after generations of governments in imperial China failed to recognize these advantages, but resorted to debt that ultimately led to their own downfall. While Professor Chen does not elaborate much on this question, two explanations are possible. The first possible explanation is that debt may not enjoy as a great advantage as described. After all, debt postpones tax, and there may be little difference between the two per Ricardian equivalence. Of course, many factors pertinent to imperial China may render the equivalence invalid. Professor Chen can make his thesis more convincing by pinpointing some of these factors.

The second possible explanation is that governments in imperial China did not rely on public debt because they were not able to. One factor Professor Chen may want to consider is the possibility of government default on public debt. If there exists a dynastic cycle, as Professor Chen noted in the case of imperial China, then private agents may not even want to lend money to the regime when a regime is coming to an end. If we add the default factor to Chen's thesis, multiple equilibria become possible. Private agents either lend to the government and, by saving the day, the debt is eventually repaid, or do not lend to the government, in which case the government will collapse, not able to repay any debt should it have borrowed any. In other words, the presence of the dynastic cycle may have prevented public debt from being adopted.

In this case of equilibrium multiplicity, it is natural to further ask which equilibrium is more likely to emerge in the context of imperial China. I think Professor Chen can enrich his thesis by discussing the existing literature related to the dynastic cycle in imperial China, which has attributed the cycle to factors other than the absence of public debt.

Of course, the discussion earlier assumes that the next regime will not recognize the public debt raised by the previous one. I suppose that this is indeed the case for imperial China. However, this is not true for public debt in a modern society. Why there is such a difference is another interesting issue to be addressed to supplement Professor Chen's thesis.

Leaving aside how spending should be financed, Professor Chen suggests that one possible strategy is to "spend as much as possible at the present in order to develop the economy and increase future wealth generating potential." I believe Professor Chen can make his statement more precise if he could elaborate on why, in his view, government spending is more preferable to private spending. These issues are in fact related to his reading of China's economic success during the last three decades, which he attributes to public debt raised by the Chinese government, whereas most students of China's economy would probably have attributed it to the withdrawal of the government's role in the economy.

Finally, I find the chapter to be more relevant for the survival of a dynastic regime than for the building of a nation. Although the two issues may be related, they are not the same. After all, for an extended period of human history, China remained a leading civilization and the largest economy in the world, with the dynastic cycle but without relying upon any public debt.

Reference

Macdonald, James. 2003. *A Free Nation Deep in Debt: The Financial Roots of Democracy*. New York: Farrar, Straus and Giroux.

8

Provincial and Local Governments in China
Fiscal Institutions and Government Behavior

Roger H. Gordon and Wei Li

Provincial and local (hereafter "local") governments in China play an important role in the overall economy. To begin with, local budgetary revenue in recent years is around 8 percent of GDP, extrabudgetary revenue (largely income from land) comes to another 3 percent of GDP, budgetary expenditures are close to 14 percent of GDP, and extrabudgetary expenditures add another 2.5 percent of GDP (see table 8.1). This scale of activity is broadly comparable to that of state and local governments in the United States, where own tax revenue is around 13 percent of GDP and expenditures are 16 percent of GDP. Local governments in both settings have primary responsibility for education, local infrastructure, and local public services.

The similarity largely stops there, however. In the United States, local governments are mainly financed by property taxes and user fees, and state governments by a combination of personal income taxes and sales taxes. In China, until 1994, local governments were mainly financed through a tax on the profits and sales of nonstate firms. Since then, they have received a fraction of the value added tax (VAT) and corporate profits tax collected in

Roger H. Gordon is professor of economics at the University of California, San Diego, a visiting professor at Cheung Kong Graduate School of Business, and a research associate of the National Bureau of Economic Research. Wei Li is professor of economics at Cheung Kong Graduate School of Business.

We would like to express our gratitude for the comments and suggestions that we received from Joseph Fan, Alex Gelber, Hua Li, Zhigang Li, Randall Morck, Bernard Yeung, and participants at presentations at the University of Hong Kong, Beijing Technical and Business University, Tsinghua University, the NBER preconference in Cambridge, Massachussetts, and the NBER-CUHK conference in Hong Kong on "Capitalizing China." We would like to thank Cheung Kong Graduate School of Business (CKGSB) for its hospitality and financial support. For acknowledgments, sources of research support, and disclosure of the authors' material financial relationships, if any, please see http://www.nber.org/chapters/c12075.ack.

Table 8.1   Public finance in China, 1978–2007

Year	Central government				Provincial and local governments			
	Budgetary revenue	Extrabudgetary revenue	Budgetary expenditure	Extrabudgetary expenditure	Budgetary revenue	Extrabudgetary revenue	Budgetary expenditure	Extrabudgetary expenditure
1978	4.8		14.6		26.2		16.2	
1980	6.3		14.7		19.3		12.4	
1985	8.5		8.8		13.7		13.4	
1990	5.3	5.7	5.4	5.6	10.4	8.8	11.1	8.9
1991	4.3	6.3	5.0	5.8	10.2	8.5	10.5	8.4
1992	3.6	6.3	4.3	5.9	9.3	8.0	9.6	7.6
1993	2.7	0.7	3.7	0.6	9.6	3.4	9.4	3.2
1994	6.0	0.6	3.6	0.5	4.8	3.3	8.4	3.1
1995	5.4	0.5	3.3	0.6	4.9	3.4	7.9	3.3
1996	5.1	1.3	3.0	1.5	5.3	4.1	8.1	3.9
1997	5.4	0.2	3.2	0.2	5.6	3.4	8.5	3.2
1998	5.8	0.2	3.7	0.2	5.9	3.5	9.1	3.3
1999	6.5	0.3	4.6	0.2	6.2	3.5	10.1	3.3
2000	7.0	0.2	5.6	0.2	6.5	3.6	10.4	3.3
2001	7.8	0.3	5.3	0.2	7.1	3.6	12.0	3.3
2002	8.6	0.4	5.6	0.2	7.1	3.4	12.7	3.0
2003	8.7	0.3	5.5	0.2	7.3	3.1	12.7	2.8
2004	9.1	0.2	4.9	0.2	7.4	2.7	12.9	2.5
2005	9.0	0.2	4.8	0.3	8.2	2.8	13.7	2.6
2006	9.7	0.2	4.7	0.2	8.6	2.8	14.4	2.6
2007	11.1	0.0	4.6	0.0	9.4		15.4	

Notes: Revenues and expenditures are reported as percentages of GDP and are calculated using data from the 2008 China Statistical Yearbook.

their jurisdictions, and all the revenue from personal income taxes, business taxes, and (until recently) taxes on agriculture.[1]

Chinese local governments also play a much more central role in the local economy than do local governments in the United States, controlling the allocation of land, and in the past, exercising substantial controls over the allocation of bank credit. The initial growth in China at the beginning of the economic reforms in fact is largely attributed to the initiative of local governments in setting up township and village enterprises (TVEs) and other nonstate firms (Gordon and Li 2005).

Oversight over local government in China is also far different than in the United States. In the United States, oversight occurs through both voice and exit. Local officials are elected by residents, so they can be removed from office if residents are not satisfied with outcomes. In addition, local residents can vote with their feet and leave a poorly performing jurisdiction, putting pressure on local officials to keep current residents satisfied. In China, by contrast, neither voice nor exit plays a major role in affecting the incentives faced by local officials. There are no local elections above the village level,[2] so officials face no threat of being voted out of office.[3] The threat of exit is also constrained, since Chinese are subject to the hukou system, a registration system that ties individuals to their current location. In addition, farmers are tied to their land, since there is not a well-functioning market for selling or leasing this land, due to their lack of legal ownership of the land.

If neither voice nor exit serve to provide incentives to local officials in China, what does affect their incentives? Oversight from the central government certainly plays an important role, as emphasized by Xu (2010). Local officials are appointed by higher levels of government and are evaluated by the central government based on a range of criteria. An important source of incentives for local officials in China arises from the implications of their performance for possible promotion to higher positions, or possible demotion (or worse). The central government also mandates that certain intergovernmental transfers from the central government be matched by provincial and local funds and then be used for specific purposes (e.g., education and health care), which constrains the choices of local officials.

In practice, though, local officials still have substantial discretion. For ex-

---

1. See Gordon and Li (2005) and Hussain and Stern (2008) for more discussions on the evolving public finance in China.

2. Since the 1980s, villagers have been allowed to experiment with various forms of self-government, often by electing village management committees, to fill the vacuum left after the demise of the People's Communes (O'Brien and Li 2000). In 1998, village elections and village self-government were codified into law. However, elected village officials often enjoyed little fiscal autonomy. Democratic choice of officials has not to date been extended to higher levels of government.

3. In the official hierarchy in China, village officials are not considered government cadres, even though they are often on the government payroll.

ample, even if monetary expenditures on particular tasks can be monitored, it is difficult to monitor the quality of the resulting services.[4] The country is large, and the resources available to the central government to oversee subnational governments are very limited. Even when oversight exists, the effects of this oversight on the chance of promotion (or demotion) of local officials carries much weight only for the very best and very worst officials, as judged by the observed criteria, since most officials are neither promoted nor demoted. In addition, mandated use of funds, or explicit standards of performance, have the drawback that these standards may not be well suited for many jurisdictions, given the tremendous variation in conditions over a large and diverse country. The information used in making these decisions can also be manipulated by local officials, undermining the effectiveness of these incentives.

In practice, therefore, the quality of the remaining incentives faced by local officials inevitably plays an important role. How well designed are these incentives? The better these incentives are designed, the greater the decentralization of decision making that can comfortably be undertaken. The focus of this chapter is on the range of incentives faced by officials beyond direct oversight from the central government.

Our key hypothesis is that the welfare of local officials is heavily dependent on the amount of government revenue collected in their jurisdiction, minus the amounts they need to spend to provide services to local residents.[5] These residual fiscal profits are under the control of local officials and can easily be used for their personal benefit. The size of these residual profits is affected by the allocation choices made by local officials, so they implicitly serve as an incentive contract. If local revenue depends on the profits of local firms, for example, then officials have a personal incentive to increase these profits.

Given existing tax structures and existing sources of extrabudgetary revenue, what economic incentives do local officials face? What economic choices would local officials then be expected to make, given these incentives? When incentives have changed over time, what changes in behavior would we expect to see? What are the key sources of inefficiency in the allocation of resources by local government forecast based on existing financial

---

4. For example, the national government has ruled that local governments are obliged to provide free education through grade nine. Given the difficulties faced by the national government in keeping tabs on a huge country, any such attempts at oversight have had only modest effect, because, as we shall argue, providing such free education is against the fiscal interests of local officials. Facing this problem, the national government more recently has provided additional national funds to help free students of any remaining fees for education up through grade nine, requiring that local governments provide matching funds of their own for this purpose. The model that we develop here forecasts, though, that local officials have an incentive to provide education only if the resulting fees fully cover the cost. They have no incentive to provide a free education even when the national government finances a fraction of the costs.

5. See White (1975) for a key application to US local governments of this assumption that local officials maximize fiscal profits.

incentives? What would be the forecasted effect of possible fiscal reforms on the efficiency of the allocation decisions made by local officials?

The organization of the chapter is as follows. Section 8.1 summarizes briefly the role of voice and exit in affecting the incentives faced by local officials in the United States, as explored in the past academic literature. Section 8.2 develops an alternative model in which the incentives faced by officials depend on the tax revenue they receive minus whatever they need to spend on local public services. We develop this model using the institutions that have existed in China during the reform period. In section 8.3, we then examine how these incentives changed over the course of the reform period, as the tax law changed and as market reforms were introduced. Section 8.4 then examines the additional incentives faced by officials due to national government control over their possible promotion or demotion. Section 8.5 considers how a range of policy reforms would affect the incentives faced by local officials, and section 8.6 provides a brief summary.

8.1   Traditional Models of Government Oversight

We begin with a summary of the US literature on the forms of oversight of local officials, and why on paper we would then expect to see officials making choices that are largely in the best interests of residents.

One source of oversight is the election process. Each potential official proposes a platform to voters. Voters choose that candidate whose proposed platform provides them the highest utility. If candidates simply care about being elected and voters are homogeneous, then, in equilibrium, each candidate's platform will maximize the utility of voters. Inefficiencies can arise due to differences in the preferences of the median voter compared with the overall costs versus benefits of a project, as emphasized by Buchanan and Tullock (1962). Candidates, though, have their own preferences, and can be influenced by special interests. They are not obliged to follow through on their campaign promises. Voters also face a free rider problem, having no personal incentive to vote or to be informed about the candidates. The quality of oversight through the voting process is therefore uncertain on net. Banerjee and Duflo (2006), for example, find in India that voters provide surprisingly poor oversight over officials.

More central to the literature on fiscal federalism is the Tiebout model. Under this model, officials propose a tax structure and spending package and gain utility from net fiscal profits, defined as any tax revenue left after financing promised expenditures. Residents then choose where to live and firms where to locate, with land prices adjusting to generate an equilibrium residential allocation. Competition among communities, if sufficiently intense, pushes net fiscal profits down to zero, induces officials to provide the package of public services residents are willing to pay for, forces them to finance these expenditures with user fees (or head taxes if all residents benefit equally from the spending), and to provide the services at minimum cost. This competition is most intense if residents are costlessly mobile, if they can carry their income with them, and if there are many competing communities. In equilibrium, when competition is intense, fiscal outcomes should be efficient.

Officials in China, though, are not subject to either voting pressures or much pressure from the mobility of potential residents, given the hukou system. Even though people are not mobile, however, economic activity is mobile: Local firms face intense competition in the (inter)national economy. The aim of this chapter is to make use of the Tiebout framework to explore what outcomes would be expected when officials act to maximize net fiscal profits, as defined based on the existing institutions in China, given that economic activities but not people are mobile across jurisdictions.

8.2   Incentives Created by the Source of Tax Revenue: General Model

In this section, we focus on how the available sources of revenue affect the incentives faced by Chinese officials. Our setup follows the structure of the Tiebout model in that the utility of officials depends on their net "fiscal profits": tax revenue, profits from firms owned by the local government, plus income generated by land rents minus expenditures on public services.

We begin by laying out a general model with the following stylized institutional features. With the hukou system in place, we assume that labor is not mobile across jurisdictions (Wang and Zuo 1999),[6] but it can freely move between jobs within the jurisdiction. We assume for now that capital cannot move across jurisdictions.[7] Land is owned by the local government.[8] Farmers have been given use rights for their plots and must be compensated if the government shifts this land to other uses. Use rights on other land can be allocated, rented, or sold to firms and households for a finite number of years. In the next section, we then relate these more general assumptions to the particular institutions that existed during various time periods under the reforms in China.

Firms can be privately owned or owned by local governments.[9] Privately-owned firms in each industry i located in the jurisdiction face a tax at rate

6. Economic reforms have gradually increased labor mobility, an issue we discuss in section 8.3.

7. Economic reforms have relaxed control over the allocation of capital. In section 8.3, we presume local government control over the allocation of capital until 1994 and market allocation after 1994.

8. The Chinese constitution stipulates that the state owns urban land while rural collectives own rural and suburban land; see http://english.people.com.cn/constitution/constitution.html (accessed on September 23, 2011). The local government, however, effectively exercises ownership rights, subject to the supervision of the Ministry of Land and Resources.

9. In this analysis, we ignore firms owned by the national government, since allocations to these firms are largely controlled by the national government. For simplicity, we also ignore foreign subsidiaries.

τ_i on their profits, denoted π_i, an excise tax at rate s_i on their sales, plus an implicit tax denoted by κ_i on their capital. Here, $\pi_i = p_i(1 - s_i)Q^i - wL_i - (r + \kappa_i)K_i - n_iA_i - u_iG$, where p_i is the output price (which the jurisdiction takes as given), $Q^i = Q^i(L_i, K_i, A_i; G, R)$ is local output produced in industry i using labor (L_i), domestic capital (K_i), and land (A_i), with local infrastructure G aiding production and local regulations R affecting productivity. Here, w is the local wage rate, r is the interest rate charged by banks on loans to the firm (set nationally), and n_i is the implicit rent the government charges industry for use of land, while u_i is a fee (if any) charged for use of G, which at most equals the marginal product of G. Depending on the time period, officials may control the allocation of domestic capital across local firms through their oversight of the local banks. Not only do tax rates differ by industry, but they also may differ by type of firm, with the national government receiving all the revenue from state-owned firms that it controlled, but local governments at times receiving all the tax revenue from both private firms and firms set up by the local government.

For local government-owned firms, the local government receives not only the tax revenue from the firms, but also the after-tax profits, $(1 - \tau_j)\pi_j$. In total, it therefore simply receives the entire pretax profits from these firms. We assume that the local government has designed the incentives faced by firm managers so that they make allocation decisions to maximize the local government's objective function.

Depending on the time period, local officials may also receive revenue from agriculture, both through explicit taxes and through requiring farmers to sell output to the government at a below-market price. Assume for simplicity that the tax revenue from agriculture equals $\sigma p_f F$, where σ is the implicit tax rate, p_f is the market price for agricultural output, and F is the quantity produced, with $F = F(L_f, K_f, A_f; G_f, R_f)$. Here, G_f is another set of public services aimed at agriculture, provided at a user charge of u_f, while R_f represents regulations affecting agriculture.

Farmers have use rights for an area of land A_f^0 without paying explicit rent. If local officials reallocate some of this land to industrial or residential uses, they must compensate farmers by paying them the marginal product of land used in agriculture, an amount we denote by $c \equiv (1 - \sigma)p_f F_A$, where $F_A = \partial F/\partial A_f$ is the marginal product of land.[10] Similarly, the wage rate firms must pay to attract local workers satisfies $w \equiv (1 - \sigma)p_f F_L$. To simplify the subsequent notation, assume that all units of output are redefined so that $p_i = p_f = 1$.

The government provides services to each household, G_h, which the household in part pays for through a user fee u_h. Let n_h denote the rent received per unit of land A_h allocated to housing. Market-clearing rents can be expressed

---

10. Throughout, we use subscripts of a function to denote partial derivatives.

by $n_h = q(A_h, w\Sigma_i L_i)$, where q is decreasing in A_h and increasing in the income of workers.

For simplicity, we start by assuming a fixed total supply of each factor to the jurisdiction, (e.g., $\Sigma_i A_i + A_f + A_h = A^T$), where the superscript T signifies the total amount of a factor available in the jurisdiction. Given the lack of mobility, total factor supplies are clearly fixed for labor and land. For the moment, we assume that the supply of capital to the jurisdiction is fixed as well, based on the deposits under the control of local banks. We also assume that factors are fully employed, so for any given allocation of factors to industries, the agricultural output is simply $F(L^T - \Sigma_i L_i, K^T - \Sigma_i K_i, A^T - \Sigma_i A_i - A_h; G_f, R_f)$.

Assume that firms with $i \in I_p$ are privately owned while firms with $j \in I_G$ are owned by the local government. The objective of officials is to maximize the sum of tax revenue from privately-owned firms, profits from government-owned firms, agricultural taxes, and land rents, minus compensation to farmers and minus the net cost (net of user fees) of public expenditures on local infrastructure and minus the implicit cost of effort expended on regulations:[11]

$$(1) \quad \sum_{i \in I_p} (\tau_i \pi_i + \kappa_i K_i + s_i Q^i + n_i A_i) + \sum_{j \in I_G} (Q^j - wL_j - rK_j) + \sigma F + q A_h - c(A_f^0 - A_f)$$

$$- G\left(1 - \sum_{i \in I_p} u_i\right) - G_f(1 - u_f) - N^T G_h(1 - u_h) - e(R) - e_f(R_f).$$

Here, N^T is the size of the local population. Officials then allocate land and capital and choose how much to spend on each form of public service to maximize expression (1). Local wage rates and labor allocation are determined by the local labor market.

We assume that officials maximize this expression over the time period they are in office, so that each expression implicitly reflects the present value of taxes and expenditures during this time period, and A_f^0 measures the amount of land used by farmers when the official takes office. Decisions clearly are affected by the official's time horizon, since some effects of policy changes show up quickly whereas other effects may materialize only after the official leaves office.[12] We also ignore any agency problems that may exist within the local government, and assume that all decisions are based on the previous objective.[13] Another apparent omission is side payments from firms

---

11. For simplicity, we assume that G and G_f are local public goods, so that costs or quality of service do not depend on the number of users.

12. If the official can "sell" his position to his successor, however, then the price paid can capture these future effects of policy changes, implicitly giving officials a longer time horizon.

13. Since an official may be removed from office if those reporting to him are unhappy with his performance, an official faces a strong incentive to align his interests with those of others in the local government.

or individuals that aim to change government decisions. As argued by Grossman and Helpman (1994), such side payments would ideally be designed so that officials take full account of how their decisions affect the profits/utility of the firm/individual paying the bribe. If a private firm makes such payments, for example, then the official would take into account the effects of any decision on the firm's pretax profits, as is the case for firms owned by the local government.[14]

What decisions are then forecast, given this objective function for local officials? Consider first the allocation of labor to government-owned firms in industry j. The first-order condition satisfies

$$(2) \qquad Q_L^j = w + \sigma F_L - q_L A_h - (1-\sigma) F_{AL}(A_f^0 - A_f),$$

where the subscripts in Q^j and F denote first-order and second-order partial derivatives with respect to capital, labor, and/or land.[15] With full employment assumed, the extra labor allocated to industries has to be taken from agriculture, raising the marginal cost of labor to the government by an amount equal to the foregone agricultural tax revenue σF_L. In addition, extra industrial workers lead to greater rental income from residential housing, and lower compensation payments to farmers due to any drop in the value of land when farmed less intensively.

Note that managers of these firms, if they instead made hiring decisions to maximize after-tax firm profits, would seek a labor force satisfying $Q_L^j = w/(1 - s_j)$. Local governments have financial incentives to force managers of government-owned firms to hire more workers than they would otherwise choose to as long as $w + \sigma F_L - q_L A_h - (1 - \sigma) F_{AL}(A_f^0 - A_f) < w/(1 - s_j)$. This condition holds as long as $s_j > \sigma$. In this case, excise taxes unduly discourage employment in government-owned firms relative to agriculture, while extra government employment provides various added benefits to the government's budget. Managers of government-owned firms certainly claim that they are forced to employ many more workers than they would wish to.

Consider next the allocation of domestic capital to government-owned firms in industry j. The first-order condition satisfies

$$(3) \qquad Q_K^j = r + \sigma F_K - (1-\sigma) F_{AK}(A_f^0 - A_f).$$

Given the local resource constraint, the extra capital can be viewed as coming from agriculture. Now r is paid by the local government rather than by farmers, introducing one cost. The next term reflects the foregone tax revenue from agriculture due to the drop in capital there. The final term

14. Private firms were at times referred to as "wearing a red hat," perhaps reflecting the fact that side payments existed so that local officials treated these firms equivalently to government-owned firms.

15. In general, wage rates can adjust. For simplicity here and later, we ignore changes in wage rates, on the grounds that there has been enough surplus labor in agriculture that any such changes by a local government are too small to matter.

measures the gain due to the fall in land values in agriculture from the drop in use of capital there, resulting in less compensation being paid to farmers for any land shifted out of agriculture to industry.

Efficient allocation of capital requires that $Q_K^j = F_K$. In contrast, we conclude that $Q_K^j < F_K$, implying too much investment in industry than in agriculture on efficiency grounds, as long as r is small and $\sigma < 1$.

Note that investment in agriculture increases when σ increases. With a higher tax rate, the benefits to the local government of investment in the sector rise, leading to additional investment. This counterintuitive result arises because the local government is making allocation decisions based on the implications for tax revenue, rather than having farmers make the decision based on implications for their after-tax profits.

Consider next the allocation of domestic capital to private firms. Compared to allocating capital to government-owned firms, there are two disadvantages to allocating capital to private firms. First, private firms hire fewer workers than the government would like them to, since their hiring decisions are characterized by $Q_L^i = w/(1 - s_i)$, rather than by equation (2). To that extent, private firms make less effective use of extra capital. In addition, the government receives only a fraction of the resulting marginal product of capital equal to $T_i \equiv s_i + \tau_i(1 - s_i) < 1$. For both reasons, the required marginal product on capital allocated to private firms must be higher to compensate for these two offsetting disadvantages to private allocations.

Turn now to the allocation of land for industrial and commercial uses. The first-order condition for land allocated to government-owned firms is

$$(4) \qquad Q_A^j = F_A - (1 - \sigma)F_{AA}(A_f^0 - A_f).$$

By shifting an extra unit of agricultural land to industrial use, the government pays $(1 - \sigma)F_A$ to farmers as compensation and bears a fall in agricultural revenue by an amount σF_A, for a combined opportunity cost of F_A. Allocations are efficient if there are no further considerations, so that $Q_A^j = F_A$. However, leaving less land in agriculture raises its marginal product, so the government needs to provide more compensation to farmers by an amount $-(1 - \sigma)F_{AA}(A_f^0 - A_f)$. While this offsetting effect slows the reallocation of land from agriculture to industry, leading to higher interim values for land in industry than in agriculture, each generation of official inherits a lower A_f^0 and will choose to make further land reallocations as long as $Q_A^j > F_A$. This reallocation continues until officials take office inheriting a value of A_f^0 equal to the allocation they find optimal. At this optimal allocation, we find that $Q_A^j = F_A$. After enough turnover of officials, we can expect land to be allocated efficiently between agriculture and government-owned firms.

Note, however, that each generation of officials acts in its own self-interest, ignoring the effects of its sales on the welfare of other generations of officials. If these different generations of officials could collude, acting as if there were one official in office indefinitely, then as a group they would take into account the effects of land sales on the compensation paid to farmers on all land ever taken out of agriculture, and not just on the land removed from agriculture while that one official is in office. With such collusion, the sales price would be permanently higher for nonagricultural land than for agricultural land. Interestingly, the central government has a policy to preserve at least 1.8 billion mu of agricultural land, ostensibly because of concerns over food security.[16] An alternative motivation could be that this national policy serves as a means of collusion among different generations of officials.

Consider now the first-order condition that arises when officials consider reallocating land from government-owned firms to private firms. Here, we find that $Q_A^i > Q_A^j$ for two reasons. First, while the government receives rent on extra land allocated to private firms equal to the resulting after-tax profits and also receives the extra tax revenue, summing to Q_A^i, it suffers a loss due to the fall in equilibrium land rents: $(1 - T_i)Q_{AA}^i A_i$. The local government, being a monopoly supplier of land, therefore restricts land allocations to private firms in order to drive up rents. Second, the private firm hires fewer extra workers as a result of the extra land than would the government-owned firm, reducing further the value of this land allocation.

For residential land, the government also acts as a monopoly supplier. It compares the marginal revenue it receives to the same types of terms as before, measuring the opportunity cost of the land.

One implicit assumption in the aforementioned derivation is that officials compare the flows of rent in each use. In fact, they need to pay a lump-sum compensation to farmers reflecting the present value of the land in agriculture when land is taken from agriculture. If the trade-off that officials face is between this lump-sum payment to farmers and an increased flow of rents from industry during the limited time period the official remains in power, they would favor leaving land in agriculture. The land use policies and practice since the late 1990s have instead allowed officials to sell use rights to the land for up to 70 years when it is reallocated to industrial or residential uses. Officials therefore compare present values. The respective rents are then divided by a discount rate, giving them much more weight in the previous expressions. The discount rates used by farmers and firms need not be the same, however. In particular, farmers face a harder time acquiring funds, since farmland cannot be used as collateral, unlike industrial or residential land. Farmers' discount rate should therefore be higher, generating a factor favoring a reallocation of land from agriculture to industry. In addition, once land has been sold, changes in rents on this land no longer matter for future officials. In particular, the term in equation (4) capturing changes

---

16. This policy imposes limits on the conversion of agricultural land within each jurisdiction, with opportunity costs that vary greatly by jurisdiction. If rights to develop agricultural land could be traded across jurisdictions, these opportunity costs could be reduced.

in residential rents would now capture changes in rents only on land still owned by the government and changes in value on residential land that will be sold by that official.

What about the choice of expenditures on public services? The choices made by government officials, based on their own self-interest, would be efficient only if local firms and individuals together are left unaffected on net by a marginal change in G.[17] Any benefits to government-owned firms already go in their entirety to the government. The net benefits to private firms, farmers, and workers equal zero, leading to efficient choice, only if

$$(5) \quad \sum_{i \in I_p} (1 - T_i)(Q_G^j - Q_{AG}^j A_i) - (1 - \sigma)F_{AL} dL_G (A_f^0 - A_f)$$

$$- q_L A_h dL_G = \sum_{i \in I_p} (1 - \tau_i) u_i.$$

Here, dL_G measures the reallocation of agricultural labor into industry due to the marginal increase in G, which, we presume, raises the marginal product of industrial labor.

Incentives on officials are therefore efficient only if user fees fully reflect the direct net-of-tax benefits to private firms, farmers, and workers minus any losses they incur due to changes in rents and in compensation payments to farmers. At least for roads with tolls, a firm makes use of these roads to the point where $(1 - T_i)Q_G^i = (1 - \tau_i)u_i$. Efficiency then requires that the remaining terms on the left-hand side of equation (5) equal zero. The remaining terms all reflect losses to the private sector. Governments therefore have too strong an incentive to provide these services and would be expected to provide subsidies to the private firms that undertake these infrastructure investments.[18]

Similarly, the choice of G_f yields an efficient outcome only if the private sector is left indifferent at the margin to any marginal change in provision of public services. This condition holds if

$$(6) \quad (1 - \sigma)F_G + (1 - \sigma)(F_{AG} - F_{AL} dL_{G_f})(A_f^0 - A_f)$$

$$- \sum_{i \in I_p} (1 - T_i)Q_{AL}^i A_i dL_{G_f}^i - q_L A_h dL_{G_f} = u_f.$$

Variable G_f raises the marginal product of agricultural labor and therefore causes a marginal reallocation of industrial workers back into agriculture.[19]

---

17. This statement assumes collusion among different cohorts of officials. Without collusion, since future cohorts of officials benefit if G is increased now, incentives on current officials are efficient only if the private sector loses in present value from added G by an amount equal to the gain to future officials.

18. Note that officials have an incentive to allow private firms to collect higher user fees than are needed for them to break even, in exchange for side payments when the contract is signed. The side payments benefit current officials whereas the higher user fees lower enterprise tax receipts for future officials.

19. The term $dL_{G_f}^i$ in equation (6) denotes the marginal reallocation of labor from agriculture to industry i. Since the reallocation is from industry i back into agriculture, $dL_{G_f}^i < 0$.

For incentives on government officials to be efficient, user fees must fully reflect the net-of-tax benefits to farmers from extra public services to agriculture, plus any net benefits farmers receive through increased compensation for land transferred out of agriculture, plus the net benefits the nonagricultural sector receives from lower rents on commercial and residential property due to a migration of people back to agriculture. If farmers make use of public services until marginal benefits and marginal costs are equal, so that $(1 - \sigma)F_G = u_f$, then efficiency again requires that the remaining terms on the left-hand side of equation (6) sum to zero. All these terms reflect a net benefit to the private sector, implying that the private sector benefits on net from additional expenditures on public services to agriculture. The government, ignoring these benefits, then provides too few such services.

Expenditures on G_h are efficient only if the dollar benefits per household equal their required user fee. In particular, education and health care services would be provided only if costs are fully covered through user fees. This forecast is consistent with the claim we have heard that education and health care have become "commodities" under the reforms, and helps explain why the national government finds it hard to induce local governments to provide these services for free to residents.[20]

Finally, what can we say about regulatory policies? Again, decisions by government officials are efficient only if the private sector is left indifferent at the margin to any changes in regulation. As with public services, the private sector benefits from any increase in after-tax profits, and is affected by any changes in land rents that arise (directly or indirectly) in response to these extra profits. With no extra user fees, though, there is no offsetting price that can adjust so that the private sector can be left indifferent on net. As a result, officials face inadequate incentives to put effort into industrial regulations benefiting private firms, though they would face efficient incentives if there were separate policies for government-owned firms. For similar reasons, there are inadequate incentives to regulate agriculture well.

While local governments in China control the allocation of land and did in past years control the allocation of capital, they do not control the allocation of labor. From their perspective, too much labor ends up migrating to lightly taxed industries away from more heavily taxed industries. As a result, local governments can potentially gain through making use of any further instruments to shift production from lightly taxed to heavily taxed industries. One such instrument is controls over trade between their jurisdiction and the rest of China. In particular, each local government has an incentive to restrict

---

20. In particular, the national government instructed local governments to provide tuition-free education up through grade nine. Local governments seem to have responded simply by reclassifying tuition as "fees." In response, the national government offered to pay a substantial fraction of the cost of education up through grade nine if in exchange local governments covered the rest of the cost, ensuring that education was free to students. Again, according to Wong (2010), local agreement was largely not forthcoming. The national government now pays the full cost of education up through grade nine.

imports in heavily taxed industries and restrict exports in the most lightly taxed industries. By shifting the composition of local production toward goods that are more heavily taxed, government revenue in the jurisdiction increases. Largely, this increase comes at the expense of government revenue in other jurisdictions, who lose export markets for their most highly taxed goods and have a harder time buying elsewhere the most lightly taxed commodities. National prices then fall for the more heavily taxed goods, and rise for the more lightly taxed goods, weakening any further incentive to intervene to restrict trade. These negative fiscal externalities result in an inefficient choice of government policies from the joint perspective of local governments, providing a motivation for the national government to intervene to lessen these trade distortions. Consistent with these forecasts, Young (2000) and Bai et al. (2004) report evidence that local governments restricted trade patterns, leading to too many firms of too small scale in the heavily taxed industries.

8.3 Application of Model to Different Time Periods

We next use this general model to forecast the behavior of government officials during particular subperiods under the reforms in China, and how it should have changed over time.

8.3.1   1979 to 1994

The initial allocation of resources in 1979 favored heavy industries at the expense of agriculture and industries that catered to consumer demands. The government collected revenue with a turnover tax—the industrial and commercial tax—on state-owned firms, by directly controlling the use of state-owned firms' profits, and by taking grain from peasants and leaving them just enough for subsistence. Table 8.2 shows that between 1978 and the early 1980s, government relied primarily on remitted profits from state-owned firms and revenue from the industrial and commercial tax for its revenue. To economize on the cost of revenue collection, the government used price scissors to channel profits and turnover taxes (which were included in official prices) to a few industries located in large cities. Agricultural goods were priced the lowest, followed by raw materials, energy, industrial goods, consumer necessities, and then consumer durables. To capture price scissors, we assume

$$(7) \qquad\qquad p_1^0 \geq p_2^0 \geq \ldots \geq p_I^0 \geq p_f^0 \equiv 1,$$

so the lower numbered industries are higher-profit-margin consumer durables industries. Here, the total number of industries is I, and the superscript ^{0} denotes planned prices. The national government then used its control over the allocation of factors to produce those goods demanded at these prices.

Table 8.2   Tax and nontax revenues as percentages of GDP, 1978–2007

Year	Total	Tax revenue	Tax revenue Industrial commercial tax	Tax revenue Agricultural tax	Tax revenue Corporate income tax	Nontax revenue Remitted SOE profits	Nontax revenue Subsidies to SOEs	Nontax revenue Education fee
1978	31.1	14.2	12.7	0.8		15.7		
1980	25.5	12.6	11.2	0.6		9.6		
1982	22.8	13.1	11.7	0.6		5.6		
1984	22.8	13.1	11.2	0.5		3.8		
1985	22.2	22.6	12.2	0.5	7.7	0.5	-5.6	
1986	20.7	20.3	11.7	0.4	6.7	0.4	-3.2	
1987	18.2	17.7	10.6	0.4	5.5	0.4	-3.1	
1988	15.7	15.9	9.9	0.5	4.5	0.3	-3.0	
1989	15.7	16.1	10.4	0.5	4.1	0.4	-3.5	
1990	15.7	15.1	10.0	0.5	3.8	0.4	-3.1	
1991	14.5	13.7	9.1	0.4	3.4	0.3	-2.3	0.1
1992	12.9	12.2	8.3	0.4	2.7	0.2	-1.7	0.1
1993	12.3	12.0	9.0	0.4	1.9	0.1	-1.2	0.1
1994	10.8	10.6	8.1	0.5	1.5		-0.8	0.1
1995	10.3	9.9	7.5	0.5	1.4		-0.5	0.1
1996	10.4	9.7	7.4	0.5	1.4		-0.5	0.1
1997	11.0	10.4		0.5	1.2		-0.5	0.1
1998	11.7	11.0		0.5	1.1		-0.4	0.1
1999	12.8	11.9		0.5	0.9		-0.3	0.1
2000	13.5	12.7		0.5	1.0		-0.3	0.1
2001	14.9	14.0		0.4	2.4		-0.3	0.2
2002	15.7	14.7		0.6	2.6		-0.2	0.2
2003	16.0	14.7		0.6	2.1		-0.2	0.2
2004	16.5	15.1		0.6	2.5		-0.1	0.2
2005	17.3	15.7		0.5	2.9		-0.1	0.2
2006	18.3	16.4		0.5	3.3		-0.1	0.2
2007	20.6	18.3		0.6	3.5		-0.1	0.2

Source: China Statistical Yearbook 2008, National Bureau of Statistics of China.

Notes: We present only selected categories of tax and nontax revenue that are relevant to our discussion in the chapter. The sum of the parts is therefore smaller than the total.

We can characterize the resulting allocation under central planning as a market allocation subject to a set of excise tax rates, with the highest tax rate on consumer durables and the lowest on agriculture, sufficient to induce firms to produce those goods demanded by consumers at the prices p_i^0.

As part of the initial reforms, local governments obtained control and cash flow rights for new firms they set up or sponsored as well as for existing small and medium-sized SOEs and even some large SOEs. The local government not only received the tax payments from these firms based on the newly introduced excise and profits taxes, but also controlled the use of the firms' remaining after-tax profits. As a result, the objective of local officials was to maximize the sum of pretax profits and land rents, minus the cost of public expenditures on local infrastructure and minus the effort expended on regulations.[21]

$$(8) \qquad \sum_i (p_i^0 Q^i - wL_i - rK_i) + \sigma F - G - G_f - G_h - e(R) - e_f(R_f).$$

This objective is a special case of equation (1), but with no private firms and no income from selling use rights to land for industrial or residential uses.[22] Since the excise taxes used to maintain the initial prices did not affect the allocation decisions of local officials, local governments faced undistorted incentives but prevailing prices that differed sharply from marginal costs. They therefore faced strong incentives to shift production toward goods that had previously faced high implicit tax rates. They were in an effective position to do this, since local officials had control over the allocation of existing bank credit among different firms.[23] While existing industrial workers were guaranteed a planned wage rate, a labor market nonetheless arose since new "contract" workers could be hired at a market wage rate (Gordon and Li 1995).

What do these conditions imply for allocation decisions? The first-order conditions with respect to capital and land satisfy

$$(9) \qquad Q_K^j = \frac{(r + \sigma F_K)}{p_j^0},$$

$$(10) \qquad Q_A^j = \frac{\sigma F_A}{p_j^0}.$$

Conditional on the initial prices, on efficiency grounds the allocation of factors *within* industry should have been efficient, though too much capital and land would be shifted out of agriculture into industry, assuming

21. At least initially, user fees were unusual.

22. Residential housing was provided by each firm for its employees rather than being rented from the local government.

23. We assume that so little land could yet profitably be used in industry or be sold for residential use that $A_f^0 \approx A_f$.

that the interest rate has been set below the market-clearing level. Since the initial prices were not market-clearing prices, however, the resulting allocations led to surplus output in the industries with artificially high prices and shortages in the industries with artificially low prices. The resulting competition among local governments to gain market shares in high-margin industries led to over-capacity and inefficiently small scales in those industries, exposing the incompatibility of pricing under the plan with decentralized decision-making.

These growing surpluses and shortages quickly forced the national government to introduce a dual-track pricing system, whereby a fixed quantity, rationed among firms, must be sold at the original prices, and all further output must be sold at market prices (Li, 1999). With undistorted incentives on local governments and market prices for all marginal transactions, allocation decisions *within* industry should indeed have been efficient. Empirical studies by Gordon and Li (1995), Groves et al (1994), and Li (1997) confirm the efficiency enhancing impact of the reform in the 1980s. It was also documented in Li (1997) that, between 1980 and 1989, more investment did flow to industries that had higher combined taxes and (after-tax) profits per yuan of sales and that product market competition among enterprises did bring about marked improvements in total factor productivity. Competition, however, significantly reduced state-owned firms' profits. Table 8.2 shows significantly smaller remitted profits and the presence of large subsidies to cover state-owned firms' losses in the late 1980s.

However, given that $\sigma < 1$, there would be too little land allocated to agriculture. With $r \approx 0$, there would also be too little capital investment in agriculture, as is apparent in the data. Figure 8.1 shows that the share of capital construction investment allocated to agriculture started from a small 4.5 percent in 1980 and declined steadily to less than 1 percent in 1994. By comparison, the share of capital construction investment allocated to industry remained above 60 percent between 1985 and 1994.

The policies during this period gave local governments a strong financial incentive to encourage the entry and growth of nonstate firms owned by local governments. See figure 8.3 for evidence of a rising share of industrial output produced by nonstate firms between 1980 and 1993. However, since local governments could keep only the tax revenue from private firms, there would be underinvestment and potentially even no land allocated to private firms, unless private firms provided side payments to local officials (implemented perhaps by registering firms as collectives), to compensate for any lost profits from government-owned firms.

What about public expenditures? First, without (much of) a private sector and no land rents, there are no marginal effects on the private sector of any changes in public services to industry, so government incentives lead to efficient outcomes for G as long as changes in wage rates can be ignored. Agriculture would benefit directly from extra services to agriculture, but

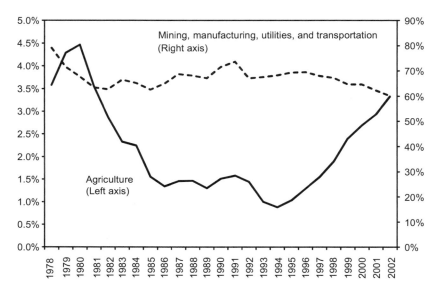

Fig. 8.1   Share of capital construction investment allocated to agriculture and to industry (mining, manufacturing, utilities, and transportation) between 1978 and 2002

Source: National Bureau of Statistics of China (NBS). (From 2003, NBS stopped reporting capital construction investment and replaced it with fixed asset investment, a broader measure of capital formation.)

without user fees, officials have no reason to take these benefits into account, leading to inadequate incentives to provide G_f. Without user fees, there are no incentives to provide G_h to households. Table 8.4 shows that shares of budgetary expenditures on programs that support agriculture, education, scientific research, and social subsidies fell between 1991 (the first year we have available data) and 1993, while shares of budgetary expenditures on capital construction and services to industry, communications, and distribution held steady. Extrabudgetary expenditures, if the data were available, would likely be even more biased toward capital construction than budgetary expenditures.

Finally, what about regulatory policies? With full control over the entire return to improvements in industrial productivity, officials should have invested the efficient level of effort in designing effective regulations for industry. Sharing less in productivity gains in agriculture, they would have invested less effort there. Data in table 8.4 on fiscal support from local governments for agriculture and nonagricultural sectors are consistent with this forecast.

In sum, the reforms starting in the early 1980s offered local officials strong incentives for industrial development. These incentives encouraged officials to pour resources into sectors that the planners had previously restricted.

Our model forecasts an efficient allocation of factors within industry, but an excessive shift of capital and land out of agriculture.

8.3.2   Post-1994

The Chinese government implemented extensive economic reforms around 1994, with many further gradual changes since then. Our stylized summary of the institutions since 1994 are as follows.

The dual track system was phased out by the mid-1990s. Planned prices were largely eliminated. This shift in infra-marginal rents, though, did not change marginal incentives so should not have affected market allocations.

Restrictions on the entry and growth of private firms were substantially eased, resulting in a rapid growth of the private sector. The allocation of factors between private and government-owned firms now becomes a serious choice, making details of the tax system an important issue.

The formal tax structure changed dramatically in 1994. Excise taxes with rates that varied by industry were replaced by: (a) a VAT on mining and manufacturing industries at a uniform rate of 17 percent, with local governments receiving 25 percent of the resulting revenue collected from firms in the jurisdiction;[24] (b) a business tax (an excise tax on service industries), with the revenue going entirely to local governments; and (c) an excise tax on luxury goods and goods with consumption externalities paid to the national government. In addition, the statutory corporate income tax rate fell from 55 percent to 33 percent. The national government received the corporate income taxes paid by financial institutions and firms controlled directly by the national government, while local governments received the corporate taxes paid by local firms.[25] A personal income tax was created, with revenues going entirely to local governments. In addition, the national government took control over the administration of the taxes on firms, largely eliminating the ability of local governments to hide the tax liabilities of local firms from the national government.

The impact of this change in tax structure on the share of budgetary revenue between national and local governments is apparent in table 8.1. From 1993 to 1994, the budgetary revenue of the national government rose from 2.7 percent of GDP to 6 percent, while the budgetary revenue of local governments fell from 9.6 percent to 4.8 percent. And in 1994, table 8.2 shows that state-owned firms stopped remitting profits to governments. In table 8.3, we report tax revenues collected relative to GDP under the new tax regime. The VAT, business tax, and the corporate income tax accounted

24. When first introduced, expenditures on fixed assets were not permitted as a deduction under the VAT. Until 2009, the VAT was production-based rather than consumption-based. In addition, all of the local share of the VAT from a multijurisdiction firm goes to the jurisdiction where the firm's headquarters are located.

25. Since 2002, the national government has received corporate income taxes on all new firms, though local governments continued to keep corporate taxes from existing local firms.

Table 8.3 Tax revenue as percentage of GDP: 1994–2007

	1994	1995	1996	1997	1998	1999	2000	2001	2002	2003	2004	2005	2006	2007
Tax revenue	10.54	9.99	10.05	10.54	10.95	11.66	12.92	14.03	14.27	15.14	16.12	16.77	17.66	19.66
National		7.32	7.07	7.21	7.40	7.91	9.11	9.43	9.51	10.13	11.19	11.59	12.29	13.69
Local		2.67	2.99	3.33	3.55	3.74	3.81	4.36	4.46	4.66	4.93	5.18	5.37	5.98
VAT total	5.53	5.08	5.01	5.01	5.18	5.69	6.27	6.56	6.84	7.47	7.89			
VAT domestic	4.86	4.44	4.31	4.28	4.49	4.52	4.76	5.05	5.27	5.43	5.60	5.81	6.05	6.21
VAT on imports	0.67	0.64	0.70	0.73	0.69	1.17	1.51	1.52	1.57	2.04	2.29			
Consumption tax (CT)	1.07	0.95	0.92	0.92	1.01	0.97	0.90	0.88	0.90	0.90	0.97			
CT domestic	1.04	0.93	0.90	0.90	1.00	0.96	0.88	0.86	0.88	0.88	0.94	0.89	0.88	0.88
CT on imports	0.03	0.02	0.01	0.01	0.01	0.01	0.01	0.01	0.02	0.03	0.03			
VAT and CT on imports												2.29	2.33	2.45
Business tax	1.41	1.45	1.52	1.73	1.94	1.92	1.92	1.93	2.07	2.12	2.25	2.30	2.41	2.62
Corporate income tax (CIT)	1.33	1.26	1.16	1.19	1.03	1.14	1.47	1.96	1.66	1.73	1.97	2.37	2.60	3.07
CIT on foreign firms	0.10	0.12	0.15	0.18	0.22	0.25	0.33	0.47	0.52	0.52	0.58	0.62	0.72	0.78
Personal income tax	0.15	0.22	0.28	0.33	0.41	0.47	0.67	0.92	1.02	1.05	1.09	1.14	1.15	1.27
Other taxes	0.94	0.90	1.02	1.17	1.17	1.23	1.35	1.31	1.27	1.34	1.37	1.35	1.51	2.40
Export rebates	−0.94	−0.92	−1.18	−0.55	−0.53	−0.71	−0.83	−0.99	−1.06	−1.51	−1.38	−1.83	−2.01	−2.10

Sources: Data on taxes come from China's State Administration of Taxation (www.chinatax.gov.cn). Data on GDP are from China's National Bureau of Statistics. In 2005, the State Administration of Taxation changed the categories of taxes in its statistical reports.

Table 8.4   Local government budgetary expeditures by selected programs as percentages of total budgetary expenditures

Year	Capital construction	Agriculture	Culture, education, science	Education	Services to industry communications and distribution	Social subsidies	Social insurance
1991	8.46	9.61	27.19	16.26	1.63	2.91	
1992	8.7	9.39	27.3	15.97	1.72	2.56	
1993	8.47	8.74	25.65	15.34	1.57	2.24	
1994	7.26	8.78	28.22	17.5	1.58	2.33	
1995	8.51	7.95	27.34	16.99	1.42	2.37	
1996	8.8	7.87	26.66	16.61	1.44	2.19	
1997	8.72	7.53	25.63	15.75	1.44	2.1	
1998	10.14	7.26	24.93	15.83	0.98	2.15	1.77
1999	11.75	6.74	23.8	15.44	0.97	1.97	3.6
2000	10.54	6.65	23.64	15.67	1.04	2.03	5.33
2001	12.54	6.23	22.85	15.5	1.06	2.02	5.69
2002	12.37	6.43	23.11	15.93	1.08	2.42	6.29
2003	11.07	5.8	23.2	15.65	1.16	2.87	6.49
2004	10.17	7.54	22.45	15.28	1.35	2.7	6.45
2005	10.64	6.54	21.93	14.83	1.4	2.83	6.28
2006	9.55	6.46	22.04	14.74	1.47	2.96	6.19

Source: China Statistics Yearbook 2007, National Bureau of Statistics of China.

for most of the revenues. Personal income taxes also rose quickly to become the fourth-largest revenue source. Tax revenue rose steadily between 1995 and 2007.

These various tax reforms should have had only limited effects on the incentives faced by local officials when allocating factors to government-owned firms: the only change is that the national government now collects some VAT revenue from these firms, so the local government does not receive quite all of the pretax profits. However, the private sector becomes increasingly important, in part because of a steady push toward selling off control over firms owned by local governments. After a sale occurs, local governments simply receive their share of the taxes collected from these firms, lowering their incentive to allocate resources to these firms.

Another major policy change was to reduce local government's control over the allocation of credit from the banking system, so that loans would be made based on commercial principles. With a commercial market for credit, we then must presume that r becomes a market clearing price. Overall investment in a jurisdiction no longer depends on the amount of bank deposits in the jurisdiction. Some jurisdictions will then be net capital exporters and others net capital importers, leading to a more efficient allocation of capital across the national market.

What can we then say about the relative rates of investment in different types of activity? From the government's perspective, the opportunity cost of investment in a government-owned firm is now simply r, so that investment in these firms continues until $Q_K^j = r$. Private firms would choose to invest until $(1 - s_j)Q_K^i = r + \kappa_i$. Taxes discourage investment in private firms, and to an extent, that differs by industry due to variation in VAT coverage or in implicit tax rates on capital. Investment should therefore fall in a firm once it is privatized. Government firms also have a differential advantage in sectors where private firms face higher tax rates.

Farmers continued to face agricultural taxes, but now can choose how much to invest and will do so until $(1 - \sigma)F_K = r$.[26] In the earlier period, we forecast that $Q_K^j/F_K < \sigma$, assuming $r \approx 0$, but now forecast that $Q_K^j/F_K = 1 - \sigma$. If $\sigma < .5$, we then conclude that capital flows out of government firms into agriculture, following the reforms in 1994. A yet larger shift in capital toward agriculture should have occurred more recently following the elimination of taxes on agriculture. Indeed, as shown in figure 8.1, the share of capital construction allocated to agriculture rose from 1 percent in 1994 to around 3.5 percent by 2001, while the share of capital construction allocated to industry fell from 70 percent to 60 percent. Figure 8.2 also shows that the numbers of tractors per 100 square kilometers of arable land increased rapidly after 1994, and the pace accelerated after 2004 when provinces in China started to reduce and eventually to eliminate agricultural taxes.

---

26. Insecure use rights to the land, however, may inhibit investments in agriculture.

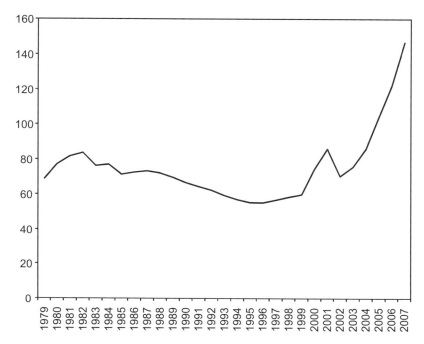

Fig. 8.2   Agricultural machinery: Number of tractors per 100 square kilometers of arable land between 1979 and 2007

Source: National Bureau of Statistics of China (NBS).

When private firms and farmers are left indifferent to adding more capital, however, local governments gain from further capital investment, particularly in private firms, due to the resulting taxes. They can add to the local capital stock by favoring capital-intensive over labor-intensive industries. One way to do this is to continue to restrict imports to the jurisdiction of more capital-intensive products in order to increase demand for local production in these industries.

With the loss of control over the allocation of capital, the remaining control over the allocation of land took on greater importance. Due to the rapid rate of growth in industry and the pressure for large reallocations of land, land allocations became an important issue.

Rather than allocating land specifically to one firm or another, the practice instead has been to auction the land to the highest bidder. The key question is then the amount of land to remove from agriculture and make available for industrial or residential use. Given the institutions prevailing since 1994, we then forecast that too much land would be left in agriculture relative to industry. The excess land in agriculture keeps the auction price high and means that the required compensation to farmers remains low due to the resulting low marginal product of land in agriculture.

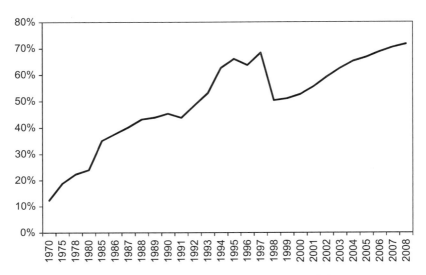

Fig. 8.3   Share of non-state-owned enterprises in gross industrial output
Source: China Statistical Yearbook 2009, National Bureau of Statistics of China.
Note: The large drop in the share in 1998 was a result of a change in sampling methodology
that excludes nonstate enterprises with annual sales less than 5 million yuan.

Due to the restrictions on land available for industrial and residential uses,
urban land rents are artificially high. As a result, land rents have become a
major source of finance for local governments in China. The UBS economist Tao Wang estimated that the national average extrabudgetary revenue
from land auctions is between 17 and 24 percent of total local government
revenues.[27] In coastal cities where property prices have risen sharply since
2003, the contribution of land sales to local government budgets should be
significantly higher. This institution is very much reminiscent of the role
of land controls in place in Hong Kong, where again the government has
limited the allocation of land to industrial and residential uses.

The economic reforms also substantially changed the incentives to finance
public services. Part of the change was the growing use of user fees to finance
infrastructure as well as services to households. Many services (e.g., highways) are provided by private firms, in principle financed fully by user fees.
Since the private sector as a whole loses at the margin from increased services
due to the resulting increases in land rents, local governments gain from
increased services and therefore have an incentive to subsidize private firms
to provide more services. They can do this by allocating extra land to these
private firms, generating an additional source of revenue for these firms.

What can we say about the efficiency of spending on G_f? User fees such

27. Tao Wang, "Understanding Land Transfer and Local Government Debt Problem (in
Chinese)," http://cn.wsj.com/gb/20100225/COL174204.asp, accessed on March 9, 2010.

as road tolls equal the after-tax benefit to farmers from the use of public services, for example, $(1 - \sigma)F_G = u_f$. As seen from equation (6), however, allocations are then efficient only if there are no net effects of the extra public services on land rents. However, any extra services to agriculture benefit farmers due to the increase in compensation paid for land removed from agriculture and also benefit the nonagricultural sector through a fall in land rents there. To that extent, government incentives to provide services to agriculture are insufficient.

The model forecasts that G_h will be provided only if fully financed with user fees. The model omits, though, several complicating factors affecting expenditures on education in particular. For one, more educated workers will be more productive, generating extra VAT revenue, and extra tax revenue from agriculture.[28] In addition, educated workers may be a complement to capital investments, benefiting officials by adding to the taxable capital stock in the jurisdiction. Offsetting these benefits, however, more educated workers may be more likely to leave the jurisdiction (e.g., going off to university), lowering the tax base for the jurisdiction. There would then be stronger incentives to provide education at a price below marginal costs in urban areas, where workers are less likely to leave if they receive better education.

8.3.3   Labor Mobility

Contrary to our previous assumptions, there is some labor mobility in China, even if mobility is clearly restricted as seen from the large differences in wage rates between rural and urban and between inland and coastal residents. Officially, individuals need to change their hukou in order to move, requiring approval of both the new jurisdiction and the old jurisdiction. Mobility therefore requires that the worker as well as both jurisdictions benefit. For a move to benefit both jurisdictions, side payments between the two jurisdictions will normally be needed. However, we often see jurisdictions allowing migrant workers to enter without granting them official residence.[29] Without official residence, however, migrants are not eligible for public services. Our aim in this section is to understand the implications of labor mobility for government incentives.[30]

To begin with, what net benefits does a jurisdiction receive from having workers enter, and to what degree does the answer depend on the skill level of the worker and whether the worker is given hukou status? Making use of expression (1), we can calculate the impact on a jurisdiction from a marginal

---

28. This extra revenue will show up, though, only when these new workers enter the labor force. Officials commonly are reassigned after about three years, and as a result, may ignore most of these benefits.

29. Many coastal provinces in China are home to millions of migrant workers from inland provinces who hold only temporary residency permits.

30. There are in fact experiments under way at the time of the writing of this chapter investigating the economic implications of easing migration restrictions.

increase in the number of workers. The net benefits/costs of having an extra worker consist of several components. First, the extra output increases sales tax revenue. Second, the extra labor force will generate further capital investment, leading to extra tax revenue both directly due to the implicit tax on capital and indirectly through further increases in sales tax revenue. Third, land rents change: industrial land rents go up due to the increases in both capital and labor, residential land rents increase due to the larger industrial labor force, but the compensation that must be paid to farmers for any further land taken out of agriculture also goes up since the value of agricultural land increases. Fourth, the new worker must be provided public services, but pays any associated user fees. If user fees do not cover the full cost of services, reflecting, for example, the pressures from the national government to provide free education, then the jurisdiction loses to the extent that the worker needs such services. The demand for services is reduced substantially if the worker is not allowed to shift hukou to the jurisdiction.

The size of these net gains will vary by jurisdiction and by type of worker for a variety of reasons. The gain in sales tax revenue depends on the industrial composition of the jurisdiction. For example, if the jurisdiction is mainly agricultural, then their gains are small given that agriculture is no longer taxed. The gain is also larger in jurisdictions with a high local wage rate, since then the marginal product of labor is higher, leading to larger increases in sales tax revenue. The increase in capital investment would normally be larger the more capital intensive the key industries in the jurisdiction are. Capital intensity should be higher in part when the local wage rate is higher. To the extent that capital and skilled labor are complements, then skilled labor attracts more capital, leading to a greater increase in tax revenue from capital. The increase in industrial land rents would normally be greater the larger the increase in capital and labor, while the higher compensation to farmers for their land is less important in more urban jurisdictions.

What migration do we then expect to see? Workers will want to move to jurisdictions that provide them higher utility. We assume that their utility can be expressed by $U(w, q, G_h, u)$: Utility should be increasing in the wage rate, falling due to higher land prices, and higher when the package of public services and user fees is more attractive. In order to attract workers, a jurisdiction faces an incentive to provide cheaper housing and more attractive public services. To the extent that communities gain from extra workers, competition can force down the price of public services and housing below the values we forecast earlier.

When will the old and new jurisdictions together agree to shift the migrant's hukou? Without a change in hukou, the old jurisdiction normally loses from the migration. Consequently, with unrestricted migration, the resulting rate of migration can be excessive since neither the migrant nor the new jurisdiction takes these losses to the previous jurisdiction into account. If the previous jurisdiction does not receive compensation, however, jurisdictions that are threatened with a loss of residents can create barriers to migration, for example making it difficult to transfer agricultural land.

The new jurisdiction per se has an incentive to avoid making a side payment to the old jurisdiction. Only migrants who receive a change in hukou are eligible for public services, providing a further incentive on the new jurisdiction not to seek to change the worker's hukou. However, without a change in hukou, workers face a higher implicit price for public services, perhaps because their best option is to leave their family in their old jurisdiction where services continue to be available. Because of these higher costs, workers would be willing to migrate only if other aspects of the new location are more attractive (e.g., wage rates are higher). Given the added costs beyond the marginal costs of the services when the family is divided between two locations, there should be a feasible agreement between the two jurisdictions to change the worker's hukou. This agreement may even involve the old jurisdiction compensating the new one for the provision of public services to the worker's family. This pressure to change hukou status is limited, though, if the migrants do not place much value on the resulting public services, compared to the cost of these services.

We have heard anecdotes of jurisdictions trying to prevent entry of unskilled workers. Why might this be? Industries vary in their relative demands for skilled versus unskilled workers. The industrial composition of the jurisdiction should then in equilibrium adjust so that demands for different skill levels match supplies. Given that some industries pay more in taxes than others, a jurisdiction would then want to adjust the skill composition of its labor force to match the desired skill composition of the more heavily taxed industries. If skill-intensive industries are more heavily taxed, as seems plausible, then jurisdictions have an incentive to increase the ratio of skilled to unskilled workers, by preventing the in-migration of unskilled workers. For example, the government of Zhongshan, a city in Guangzhou province, started to implement a scoring system to screen nonresident applicants. The system assigns 80 points for a college degree, 90 points for a graduate degree, 10 points for owning property in the city, and one point for each 50,000 yuan investment in the city for up to 10 points. The city government would offer a migrant worker and his dependents basic medical care if he has a cumulative score at or above 60, job training if his score reaches 70, equal access to public services that hukou-holders are entitled to if his score reaches 90, and hukou if he accumulates a score of 100 or above. The scoring system makes transparent the preference of the local government for skilled migrant workers.

8.4   Incentives Generated by Promotion and Retention Procedures

The previous model can easily be extended to a setting with multiple levels of government, with higher levels of government affecting the incentives faced by lower levels of government not only through the design of local tax structures but also through the promotion criteria for local officials. The higher-level officials care about the impact on their own fiscal surplus of decisions made by lower-level officials. To internalize these externalities, the future job of lower-level officials can depend on the level and growth rate of national tax revenue generated in their jurisdiction.

Over time, the national government has made increasingly explicit its mechanism for judging the qualifications of local officials for possible promotion. As forecast by the previous extension of our model, promotions are in fact based heavily on the level and rate of growth of national tax revenue from the jurisdiction. The preferences of other top officials in the jurisdiction are also taken into account. How do these added incentives affect our prior results?

Previously, the objectives of local officials reflected the local net fiscal profits they controlled while in office. National promotion policies induce officials to give some weight as well to national tax revenue. The national government collects 75 percent of the overall VAT payments, increasing the importance of sales tax revenue. It collects all of the corporate tax revenue from new firms and from state firms, tending to equalize the incentives local officials face to aid one category of firm compared to another. The national government, though, does not collect any revenue from agriculture, so the added incentives increase the weight placed on industry compared with agriculture. Since the VAT does not allow deductions for capital, promotion incentives create yet more of an incentive to favor capital-intensive industries over other sectors.

Having promotion decisions depend on the preferences of other top officials in the jurisdiction helps address any agency problems in the jurisdiction. In a hierarchical structure, officials at any given level in the hierarchy require the support of those in the next lower level. Given these links at each level of the hierarchy, even the top official implicitly needs to worry about the preferences of the lowest ranked officials. While leading to an alignment of interests among all officials, however, this structure does not in itself create any reason to care about the welfare of nonofficials, supporting our omitting the utility of residents from the objective function for local government officials.

The national government also affects the incentives faced by local governments through its control over the allocation of intergovernmental transfers of funds. Funds are in part allocated based on geography, going particularly to inland provinces. Since residents lose access to any benefits resulting from these transfers if they leave the jurisdiction, these transfers result in less migration of workers from inland regions that receive greater per capita transfers. Since we forecast excessive migration previously, transfers can then help ease the resulting misallocations.

8.5   Alternative Policies and the Resulting Incentives for Local Officials

Since promotion standards and centralized allocations of funding cannot easily be tailored to local conditions, these interventions inevitably lead to misallocations. The interventions may still improve on outcomes to the extent that local officials face poorly designed financial incentives. To the degree that financial incentives were altered so as to lead to more efficient decentralized allocations, the central government would face less pressure to intervene directly. How then would the inefficiencies generated by current sources of finance for local governments be affected by plausible changes in the tax structure?

Under existing incentives faced by officials, outcomes are inefficient on many dimensions. Governments make use of their controls over the allocation of land to keep prices high for industrial and residential uses, and low for agriculture. Since any movement of resources from agriculture to industry generates more tax revenue, officials will make use of their control over public services and regulations to aid industry relative to agriculture. They will make use of their regulatory powers to favor more highly taxed (often the more capital-intensive) local industries. To finance public services with user fees, the required fee must equal the average cost of the service per user in order to break even. But the service is used efficiently only if the fee also equals the marginal cost per user. High tolls on the roads, for example, unduly discourage usage and inadvertently encourage truckers to overload their trucks. Migration of workers is limited, leading to dramatic differences in wage rates across locations, suggesting large inefficiencies from the misallocation of workers. Along each dimension, what policy changes might lead to more efficient decentralized allocations?

Taxes avoid favoring one industry over another (for a given local population) only if the taxes collected are the same for each worker, regardless of the industry in which a worker is employed. This equalization of taxes paid per worker would exist under a variety of alternative tax structures. In principle, it arises with a consumption-based VAT, since here taxes paid depend on each worker's consumption expenditures but not on the industry where they are employed.[31] A retail sales tax creates equivalent incentives, but also can have a high evasion rate due to the many small retail firms that are hard to monitor and due to the ease of cross-border shopping. A third alternative is to confine such a consumption tax to those goods that can easily be monitored, including, for example, residential housing, ownership of a car, and a range of other goods such as electricity consumption and phone

---

31. In practice, though, a consumption-based VAT is hard to enforce, since it is very difficult to monitor the flow of goods into and out of the jurisdiction. It would also be difficult to monitor trade within a multijurisdictional firm, given the use of transfer pricing.

usage. Differential rates by form of consumption induce a misallocation of consumption across commodities, but the efficiency costs here are normally second-order. Under these alternative tax bases, revenue does not depend on the industry in which a worker is employed. Revenue also increases as income per capita and the population in the jurisdiction rise, giving officials an incentive to raise per capita income and to attract new residents. For these reasons, it is not surprising that the principal sources of tax revenue among local governments in the United States are a property tax and a local retail sales tax (that covers in practice around a third of overall consumption).

What policy alternatives might lead to a more efficient allocation of land? Since officials are compensated heavily based on the price differential of land in alternative uses, they face strong incentives to shift land to higher-value uses. Officials shift land too slowly on efficiency grounds to take advantage of their market power. However, due to the turnover of officials, each generation of official will choose to transfer additional land to higher-value uses. As long as this transfer occurs through a sale rather than a lease of land, the resulting drop in rents on inframarginal units sold by previous officials is borne by past buyers rather than by the government. According to equation (4), allocations therefore converge toward one with $Q_A^j = Q_A^i = F_A$ as the additional transfers by each generation of official $(A_f^0 - A_f)$ converge toward zero. Misallocation of land therefore seems to be primarily a transition problem in the absence of any mechanism through which different generations of officials could collude, acting as if there were one official in office indefinitely.[32]

One other current source of inefficiency arises from the high user fees for public services. When the average cost exceeds the marginal cost for a service, as should be the case for highways, for example, then the services are underutilized. Even when the marginal and average costs are equal, as could be true for education, users may face binding liquidity constraints that prevent them from undertaking an investment in human capital even if the eventual rate of return is very high. As seen previously however, officials have no incentive to provide these services unless doing so generates enough extra revenue to cover the costs.

What alternatives exist? Mobility is the mechanism emphasized in the Tiebout model to induce officials to provide the efficient level and composition of services. To the extent people are mobile, officials are pressed to adopt policies that attract potential residents and induce existing residents to stay. With intense competition, policies end up maximizing the utility of residents and are efficient. To attract additional residents, the key means available to officials is to reduce the price and increase the quality of public

---

32. However, as we discussed earlier, a policy of the central government that preserves at least 1.8 billion mu of agricultural land could be serving as a means of collusion among different generations of officials to keep the value of nonagricultural land permanently higher than agricultural land.

services. The residual costs of the extra public services can then be financed out of the other taxes paid by the new residents.

A natural fear if restrictions on mobility are relaxed is that cities with high wages will quickly develop shantytowns on their periphery. To some degree this occurs already, due to the temporary residents who lack hukou status. An alternative to the hukou procedure for limiting the population of a city is to restrict residence to those who own or have signed a lease for a registered housing unit in the city, and perhaps meet occupancy restrictions (number of people per square meter).[33] People can then move freely, and property values adjust as jurisdictions become more or less attractive. Competition among jurisdictions for residents still creates incentives on officials to provide higher quality public services, even if the population remains unchanged, since a more attractive jurisdiction attracts higher income residents, who consume more and so pay more in consumption taxes. Property values also rise, leading to greater property tax payments.

One factor inhibiting mobility is the lack of a market for farmland. Those working in agriculture then face the potential loss of much of the value of this use-right to the land if they migrate. Only if the utility gain is large enough, given these hurdles, will those currently working in agriculture move. With easier transfers of use rights, there would be greater mobility and more pressure on officials to provide the efficient level of public services.

8.6 Conclusions

The Chinese economy has benefited dramatically from the decentralization of decision making to individual firms and workers, regarding what to produce, how to organize production, and where to work. The question focused on in this chapter is the feasibility of an equivalent decentralization within the government. China, like the United States, has a federal system of government, with national, provincial, county, municipal, and village levels of government. Given the huge size and diversity of the country, it is difficult for the national government to make allocation decisions for all of these different levels of government, just as it was difficult for the national government to make allocation decisions for all of the many firms in the economy. To what degree can decentralized decision making within the government lead to more efficient outcomes? This can occur only to the degree that the economic incentives faced by local officials are designed appropriately.

In this chapter, we examined the economic incentives faced by local officials in China over the course of the economic reforms. In doing so, we made use of a number of the standard presumptions in the Tiebout model. In particular, we assumed that local officials benefit from the tax revenue received by their jurisdiction plus any income from renting or selling land

---

33. Enforcement of occupancy restrictions will likely be difficult, however.

minus the costs of public services. Given these financial incentives, what allocation decisions do we expect local officials to make? The behavior of local officials forecast by the model, to our mind, corresponds closely to the stylized facts we see in the data. If we accept this model as a valid characterization for how officials behave, then the model provides a mechanism to help guide the redesign of these incentives in order to induce officials to allocate resources more efficiently. Potential reforms were discussed briefly, though many others may also reduce the inefficiencies that result under current incentives.

References

Bai, C.-E., Y. Du, Z. Tao, and S. Y. Tong. 2004. "Local Protectionism and Regional Specialization: Evidence from China's Industries." *Journal of International Economics* 63 (2): 397–417.
Banerjee, A., and E. Duflo. 2006. "Addressing Absence." *The Journal of Economic Perspectives* 20 (1): 117–32.
Buchanan, J. M., and G. Tullock. 1962. *The Calculus of Consent.* Ann Arbor: University of Michigan Press.
Gordon, R. H., and W. Li. 1995. "The Change in Productivity of Chinese State Enterprises, 1983–1987." *Journal of Productivity Analysis* 6:5–26.
———. 2005. "Taxation and Economic Growth in China." In *Critical Issues in China's Growth and Development,* edited by Y. K. Kwan and E. S. H. Yu, 22–40. Burlington, VT: Ashgate.
Grossman, G., and E. Helpman. 1994. "Protection for Sale." *American Economic Review* 84:833–50.
Groves, T., Y. Hong, J. McMillan, and B. Naughton. 1994. "Autonomy and Incentives in Chinese State Enterprises." *Quarterly Journal of Economics* 109:183–209.
Hussain, A., and N. Stern. 2008. "Public Finances, the Role of the State, and Economic Transformation, 1978–2020." In *Public Finance in China: Reform and Growth for a Harmonious Society,* edited by J. Lou and S. Wang, 13–38. Washington, DC: The World Bank.
Li, W. 1997. "The Impact of Economic Reform on the Performance of Chinese State Enterprises, 1980–1989." *Journal of Political Economy* 105 (5): 1080–106.
———. 1999. "A Tale of Two Reforms." *Rand Journal of Economics* 30:120–36.
O'Brien, K. J., and L. Li. 2000. "Accommodating 'Democracy' in a One-Party State: Introducing Village Elections in China." *The China Quarterly* 162:465–89.
Wang, F., and X. Zuo. 1999. "Inside China's Cities: Institutional Barriers and Opportunities for Urban Migrants." *The American Economic Review* 89 (2): 276–80.
White, M. J. 1975. "Suburban Zoning in Fragmented Metropolitan Areas." In *Fiscal Zoning and Land Use Controls,* edited by E. S. Mills and W. E. Oates, 31–100. Lexington, MA: Lexington Books.
Wong, C. 2010. "Fiscal Reform: Paying for the Harmonious Society." *China Economic Quarterly* 14:22–27.
Xu, C. 2010. "The Institutional Foundation of China's Reform and Development." Working Paper. University of Hong Kong.

Young, A. 2000. "The Razor's Edge: Distortions and Incremental Reform in the People's Republic of China." *The Quarterly Journal of Economics* 115 (4): 1091–135.

Comment   Zhigang Li

Gordon and Li adapt the Tiebout framework to the institutional setting of China to model the decisions of its local governments. The model generates rich and important predictions, which are broadly consistent with the stylized facts of China. The Gordon-Li framework makes it possible to systematically analyze a number of economic phenomena in China, and to diagnose and improve the efficiency of the fiscal system.

I first summarize the major features of the chapter. I then discuss competing theories and the feasibility of empirically distinguishing them from the Gordon-Li model.

Main Features

In the Gordon-Li model, local officials share the objective of the governments they serve, which is to maximize the local fiscal revenue net of the cost of public services. The model accommodates rich and realistic sources of local fiscal revenues and items of expenditure. This facilitates analyzing distortions in the resource allocation between agricultural and nonagricultural production, and between capital-intensive and labor-intensive industries. The model has important implications for the efficiency of the tax system, for example, that efficiency could be increased by replacing the production-based VAT in China with a consumption-based VAT. Another important source of efficiency loss explicitly analyzed in the chapter is the different objective functions, due to taxes, of state-owned and non-state-owned firms.

Even with its realistic features, however, the model is highly simplified. Except for the fiscal revenue, other incentives for local officials are not considered. For example, the model does not include the promotion incentive provided by upper-level governments, which may be relevant (Xu 2010). Moreover, the model assumes that tax rates are exogenous even though the effective rates may be endogenous: local governments can affect the actual tax rates through various preferential tax schemes, such as establishing special industrial zones. In addition, in the Gordon-Li model prices are exog-

Zhigang Li is assistant professor of economics at the University of Hong Kong.

For acknowledgments, sources of research support, and disclosure of the author's material financial relationships, if any, please see http://www.nber.org/chapters/c12464.ack.

Table 8C.1   Predictions of Gordon-Li model and their empirical relevance

Predictions	Empirical relevance
1. Local governments force state-owned firms to increase employment.	Consistent
2. Local governments allocate less credit and land to private firms than to government-owned firms.	Consistent
3. Overinvestment in industry as compared to agriculture.	Consistent
4. Local governments convert less land from agricultural to industrial or residential use than they should, thus keeping land prices high in the urban areas and low in the rural areas.	Unavailable
5. Local governments oversupply infrastructure that benefits industries but undersupply public goods that benefit agricultural production.	Consistent
6. Local governments have inadequate incentives to supply public services or to implement regulatory policies that benefit local private firms.	Consistent
7. Local governments may use local protectionism to intervene in interregional trade.	Consistent
8. More capital-intensive regions are more likely to provide hukou to skilled labor.	Unavailable

Note: Empirical relevance here simply means that the stylized facts of China are consistent with the model predictions. The predictions have not been rigorously tested.

enously set. Although endogenizing prices may not affect the static analysis of allocation efficiency, it could affect the implications of a tax reform.

Despite the potential complications due to the omitted factors, the predictions of the Gordon-Li model fit well with a number of stylized facts about China. Table 8C.1 summarizes the major predictions of the model. Some of the predictions have been suggested by earlier research, but some are original. For example, the model implies that regional governments have an incentive to convert less land from agricultural to industrial or residential use than they should. As a result, land prices are high in the urban and low in the rural areas.

Alternative Models

Can other models of regional government generate similar predictions as in the Gordon-Li framework? It is possible. An example of this is a model in which the decision of local government officials is affected by the central government. The central government may impose a list of "targets" for local governments to achieve (Tsui and Wang 2004). To motivate local government officials to fulfill those targets, the central government may introduce certain rewards, such as the promotion of officials based on their performance. Xu (2010) formalizes how a promotion scheme can provide incentives for local officials. Aware of this influence of the central government, in section 8.4 the authors extensively discuss its implications that are *different* from those by their model. Here, in addition, I would like to draw readers' attention to *similar* predictions of the different models. For example, as the list of "targets" typically includes fiscal revenue, this target system can motivate local officials to behave as if they are maximizing tax revenue.

The policy implications of the two models may differ. The behavior of local government officials would be more sensitive to the change of the central-local relationship under the promotion incentive than under the revenue-maximizing incentive. Moreover, the efficiency implications may also differ by model. Hence, it is important to be able to determine whether it is the centrally provided incentives or the local governments' own incentives that have been the main driving force of their behavior.

In addition, corruption revenues may also be a relevant incentive for officials. For example, the Gordon-Li model predicts that local governments may convert less agricultural land to urban use because local officials stay in position for limited periods. Anecdotal evidence, however, suggests that local officials have a strong incentive to convert farm land to industrial and residential use. This might occur because the private benefits to local officials (e.g., bribery) from the land conversion dominate the incentive to maximize local fiscal revenue.

Suggested Further Tests

Given the rich predictions of the Gordon-Li model, it is possible to test its relevance by testing its unique predictions. One possible way to do so is to identify major tax reforms and test their impacts as predicted by the Gordon-Li model. A key condition of this test is that at the same time as the tax reform, there should not be a major change in the central-local relationship or the target system to avoid their confounding effects.

To illustrate, consider a prediction of the Gordon-Li model as follows. The 1994 tax reform would change the incentive for local governments to invest in agriculture: low investment before the reform and high investment afterwards. Since the target responsibility system evolved gradually for the mid-1980s and became fully developed by 1995, one would need to identify some regions in which the target system developed early and changed little around 1994. The agricultural investment in these regions can then be investigated to test whether it significantly increased after the tax reform, as the Gordon-Li model implies.

Other Comments

One assumption required in the Gordon-Li model to achieve efficient outcomes is that regional public investments do not have spillover effects on other regions. This might be violated, for example, in the case of transport infrastructure investment. In a recent study, Li and Li (2010) find that the highway investment in China has a strong effect on the inventory holding of firms in neighboring provinces. In this case, the choices that are efficient for regional governments may not be efficient nationwide.

In comparing stylized facts about China to model predictions, the authors typically use national aggregates. On several occasions, it would be more consistent with theory to present more disaggregated information. For example, figure 8.1 in the chapter shows the variation of investment in agriculture over time. As the Gordon-Li model focuses on the behavior of regional governments, a more relevant diagram would show the investment by local governments. It is important to distinguish between investment by the regional and central governments because the fiscal ability of the central government also changed significantly due to the 1994 tax reform. Separating the investment by the regional and central governments may thus reduce the confounding effects of the changing fiscal capacity of the central government.

References

Li, Han, and Zhigang Li. 2010. "Road Investments and Inventory Reduction: Firm Level Evidence from China." Working Paper.
Tsui, Kai-yuen, and Youqiang Wang. 2004. "Between Separate Stoves and a Single Menu: Fiscal Decentralization in China." *China Quarterly* 177:71–90.
Xu, Chenggang. 2010. "The Institutional Foundation of China's Reform and Development." Working Paper. University of Hong Kong.

Contributors

Franklin Allen
The Wharton School
University of Pennsylvania
3620 Locust Walk
Philadelphia, PA 19104

William T. Allen
New York University School of Law
NYU Stern School of Business
44 West Fourth Street, 9-53
New York, NY 10012

Tamim Bayoumi
International Monetary Fund
700 19th Street, NW
Washington, DC 20431

Jiahua Che
Department of Economics
The Chinese University of Hong Kong
9/F, 10/F, Esther Lee Building, Chung
    Chi Campus, Shatin
Hong Kong

Zhiwu Chen
School of Management
Yale University
135 Prospect Street
New Haven, CT 06520

Joseph P. H. Fan
Department of Finance
The Chinese University of Hong Kong
Room 1204, 12/F., Cheng Yu Tung
    Building, No. 12 Chak Cheung
    Street
Shatin, N.T. Hong Kong

Roger H. Gordon
Department of Economics 0508
University of California, San Diego
9500 Gilman Drive, Dept. 0508
La Jolla, CA 92093-0508

Li Jin
Harvard Business School
Baker Library 343
Soldiers Field
Boston, MA 02163

Wei Li
Cheung Kong Graduate School of
    Business
3F, Tower E3, Oriental Plaza, 1 East
    Chang An Avenue
Beijing 100738, China

Zhigang Li
43/F, IFC II, 8 Finance Street
Central, Hong Kong

Qiao Liu
Guanghua School of Management
New Guanghua Building, Room 349
Peking University
Beijing 100871 China

Randall Morck
School of Business
University of Alberta
Edmonton, Alberta
Canada T6G 2R6

Joseph D. Piotroski
Graduate School of Business
Stanford University
Stanford, CA 94305

Katharina Pistor
Columbia Law School
435 West 116th Street
New York, NY 10027

Jun "QJ" Qian
Finance Department
Carroll School of Management
Boston College
Chestnut Hill, MA 02467

Han Shen
Davis Polk & Wardwell LLP
The Hong Kong Club Building
3A Chater Road
Hong Kong

Zheng Song
Booth School of Business
University of Chicago
5807 S. Woodlawn Ave
Chicago, IL 60637

Hui Tong
International Monetary Fund
700 19th Street
Washington, DC 20431

Shang-Jin Wei
Graduate School of Business, 619 Uris
    Hall
Columbia University
3022 Broadway
New York, NY 10027

T. J. Wong
School of Accountancy
The Chinese University of Hong Kong
Room 1502, 15/F, No.12, Chak Cheung
    Street
Shatin, N.T., Hong Kong

Chenggang Xu
School of Economics and Finance
903 K. K. Leung Building
University of Hong Kong
Pokfulam Road, Hong Kong

Dennis Tao Yang
Department of Economics
The Chinese University of Hong Kong
Shatin, N.T., Hong Kong

Bernard Yeung
NUS Business School
National University of Singapore
Mochtar Riady Building, BIZ 1, 6-19
15 Kent Ridge Drive
Singapore 119245

Leslie Young
Department of Finance
The Chinese University of Hong Kong
Room 1206, 12/F, Cheng Yu Tung
    Building
No.12, Chak Cheung Street, Shatin,
    N.T., Hong Kong

Chenying Zhang
The Wharton School
University of Pennsylvania
2435 SH-DH
3620 Locust Walk
Philadelphia, PA 19104

Junsen Zhang
Department of Economics
The Chinese University of Hong Kong
Shatin, N.T., Hong Kong

Mengxin Zhao
School of Business
University of Alberta
2-32C Business
Edmonton, Alberta
Canada T6G 2R6

Shaojie Zhou
Room 318, School of Public Policy and
    Management
Tsinghua University
Beijing, China 100084

Ning Zhu
Shanghai Advanced Institute of
    Finance
Datong Plaza, 211 West Huaihai Road
Shanghai, P.R. China 200030

Author Index

Acemoglu, D., 25, 128
Aghion, P., 25, 175
Aharony, J., 149, 169, 213, 225
Alford, A., 211
Allen, F., 11, 14, 28, 43, 64, 87, 114, 115,
    126, 127, 128, 129, 130, 131, 135, 150,
    172n32, 206, 235n10
Allen, W. T., 180
Allesandria, G., 132
Ang, J., 230

Bahl, R. W., 261
Bai, C.-E., 256, 350
Ball, R., 211, 213, 215, 219, 223, 235
Banerjee, A., 341
Barry, C., 232
Bates, T. W., 284
Baumol, W. J., 13
Bebchuk, L., 180
Becker, C., 226
Beltratti, A., 120
Berkowitz, D., 202
Berle, A. A., 38
Bernanke, B., 283
Bertrand, M., 6
Bhattacharya, U., 211, 232, 235
Bird, R., 261
Blades, D., 15
Blanchard, O., 175
Bo, Z., 42
Bohl, M., 236
Bortolotti, B., 120

Botosan, C., 232
Brandt, L., 77
Brown, S., 232
Brumberg, R., 16
Buchanan, J. M., 341
Burgstahler, D., 212, 213
Burkart, M., 127
Burns, J. P., 42
Bushman, R., 201, 211, 213, 215, 216, 223,
    233, 235, 242

Cai, Y., 82
Cao, S. L., 131, 269, 270, 273
Cao, Y., 253n2
Carew, R., 58n27
Carroll, C. D., 269, 273
Chamon, M., 16, 17, 253, 268, 269, 270, 271
Chan, K., 104n27
Chan, L. K. C., 206
Chaney, P., 216
Chang, E., 173
Chang, L., 169
Chang, R., 136n42
Chatusripitak, N., 101
Che, J., 175
Chen, D.-H., 168, 319
Chen, F., 321n4, 324n9
Chen, G., 154, 155n3
Chen, J., 206, 224
Chen, K., 221, 225
Chen, M., 184
Chen, V. W., 256

Chen, X., 213
Chen, Z., 318n2, 328
Chia, R., 56, 57
Choi, J., 244
Chow, G., 269
Chu, Y., 113
Chung, S. P.-y., 66n4
Cifuentes, R., 136
Claessens, S., 127
Clarke, D., 125, 155n3, 172n32, 184
Coase, R. H., 13
Coates, J. C., 180
Cohen, A., 180
Cull, R., 125

Dai, X., 159
Daouk, H., 211, 232, 235
Deaton, A., 273
DeFond, M., 215, 226, 227
Demetriades, P. O., 144
Demirgüç-Kunt, A., 70, 77
Deng, J., 183n44, 184, 184n45
Deng, Y., 8, 12, 108, 113, 113n30, 114
Dichev, I., 212, 213
Djankov, S., 126, 127
Doidge, C., 202, 232
Du, B., 213
Du, F., 221
Du, J., 106
Duflo, E., 341
Durnev, A., 206, 285n1
Dynan, K. E., 265

Easterbrook, F., 180, 181
Edwards, S., 13

Faccio, M., 216
Fama, E., 285
Fan, J. P. H., 18, 92, 107, 124, 168, 173, 175, 198, 211, 215, 219, 221, 305
Feldstein, M., 69n7
Ferreira, M., 236
Ferri, G., 258
Ferrucci, G., 136
Firth, M., 106, 154, 155n3
Fischel, D., 180, 181
Fogel, K., 25, 189
Francis, B. B., 168
Francis, J., 216, 232
Franks, J., 118
Freeman, R., 4
French, K., 285

Fukuyama, F., 25, 28
Fung, P., 106

Gale, D., 28, 114, 115, 126, 127, 130, 131, 135
Gao, L., 229
Garnaut, R., 92
Ge, S., 269, 272
Gelos, R., 228, 233
Giles, J., 271
Goetzman, W., 66n4
Goodfriend, M., 135
Gordon, R. H., 22, 175, 339, 339n1, 352, 353
Green, S., 149
Greenspan, A., 283
Greif, A., 126, 127
Grossman, G., 345
Groves, T., 353
Guedhami, O., 216
Gul, F., 207n2, 216, 233, 236
Guo, D., 145
Guo, F., 113
Gyourko, J., 108, 113, 113n30, 114

Haber, S., 13
Hall, P. A., 57
Harvey, C., 56, 57
Hasan, I., 168
Hayek, F., 7, 13, 27
He, X., 253n2
He, Z., 208
Heilbrunn, J., 6
Heilmann, S., 43, 44, 44n9
Hellman, J., 175
Helpman, E., 345
Herring, R., 101
Ho, C. K., 273
Hoberg, G., 285
Hofman, B., 309
Hoggarth, G., 130
Hong, H., 206, 224
Hong, K., 273
Horioka, C. Y., 270
Howson, N., 173, 175
Hsieh, C.-T., 28
Hu, R., 175
Huang, H., 181, 190n47
Huang, J., 173
Huang, Y., 6, 42
Huang, Y. S., 113
Hung, M., 215, 224, 225

Hussain, A., 339n1
Hwang, C.-Y., 120

Jacques, M., 5
Jefferson, G., 256
Jegadeesh, N., 206
Jeng, l. A., 114
Jensen, M., 22, 131, 217
Jian, M., 213, 225
Jiang, G., 215
Jin, L., 11, 206, 207, 208, 224, 244
Johnson, S., 128
Jun, H., 92

Kadushin, C., 56
Kahan, M., 180
Kahle, K. M., 284
Kaminsky, G., 132
Kane, E., 84
Kang, J., 208
Kao, J. L., 213
Karolyi, G., 202, 232
Karpoff, J., 224
Kato, T., 106
Khanna, T., 1, 4
Khurana, I., 216
Khwaja, A., 208
Kim, J., 207n2, 233, 236
Kirby, W., 66n3, 127
Klenow, P., 28
Kling, G., 229
Knight, F., 13
Knight, J., 271
Köll, E., 66n4
Kortum, S., 114
Kothari, S. P., 211, 215, 219, 235
Kraakman, R., 180
Kraay, A., 253, 255, 255n4, 255n6, 270
Kramarz, F., 6
Kuijs, L., 253, 260, 283, 286, 309
Kuznets, S., 12

Labonte, M., 65n2
Lakonishok, J., 206
Landry, P., 5, 6, 24
Lang, L., 127
La Porta, R., 7, 119
Lardy, N. R., 37, 43
Laux, P., 236
Lee, C. J., 213
Lee, C. M. C., 215
Lee, D. S., 224

Lee, J., 149, 169, 213, 225
Lee, J.-W., 273
Lee, T. V., 66n3
Leigh, L., 43
Lequiller, F., 15
Lerner, J., 114
Leuz, C., 211, 215, 216, 235
Levine, R., 70, 72n9, 77
Li, B., 82
Li, H., 6, 371
Li, J., 213
Li, K., 124
Li, L., 339n2
Li, S., 226, 227
Li, W., 22, 175, 339, 339n1, 352, 353
Li, Z., 371
Liao, L., 120, 131
Liebman, J., 69n7, 171n30
Lipton, M., 180
Liu, B., 120
Liu, G., 155n3, 321n5, 324n10
Liu, K., 16
Liu, L.-G., 258
Liu, M.-H., 208
Liu, Q., 197, 198, 212, 213, 225
Long, C., 106
Lopez-de-Silanes, F., 7, 119
Lu, J., 256
Lu, X., 318n2, 319n3
Lü, X., 6, 15
Lu, Z., 213, 225

Ma, G., 258
Ma, Y., 230
Macdonald, J., 20, 320, 321, 321n6, 326n15, 326n16, 328, 328n20, 329n21, 332n23, 332n24, 334
Macgregor, R., 2, 5, 8, 24
Maclean, M., 56, 57
Maddison, A., 15
Mandanis, H., 37n1
Martin, G., 224
Martin, M., 41
Mayer, C., 118
McMillan, J., 126
Means, G., 38
Meckling, W., 131, 217
Meghir, C., 25
Mei, J., 104n27, 229, 244
Meng, X., 256, 271
Menkveld, A., 104n27
Merton, R., 232

Mian, A., 208
Michie, R., 118
Milhaupt, C. J., 53n23, 53n24, 171n30
Mills, C. W., 57
Modigliani, F., 16, 268, 269, 270, 273
Monarch, R., 256
Moore, G., 57
Morck, R., 11, 13, 19, 20, 25, 159, 206, 207,
    285n1, 305n6
Morrison, W., 65n2
Murphy, K., 7, 13
Murrell, P., 125
Myers, S. C., 11, 206, 207, 208, 224, 244

Nakamura, M., 19
Nanda, D., 211, 215, 235
Naughton, B., 41, 45, 56, 172n32
Naughton, T., 208
Nee, V., 1, 16
Ni, S., 208
Ning, Z., 92
Niu, J., 318n2, 319n3
North, D., 24

Oberholzer-Gee, F., 216
O'Brien, K. J., 339n2
Olson, M., 13, 28
Opper, S., 1, 16, 175
Oura, H., 130
Ouyang, Y. A., 135

Panunzi, F., 127
Park, A., 91, 271
Parsley, D., 216
Paxson, C. H., 273
Peng, Z., 327n17, 327n18
Pereira, R., 216
Perkins, D., 82n11
Piotroski, J., 201, 208, 211, 213, 215, 216,
    223, 224, 233, 235, 242
Pistor, K., 51, 51n16, 52, 53, 53n23, 53n24,
    175, 206
Pittman, J., 216
Podpiera, R., 43
Prabhala, N. R., 285
Prasad, E., 14, 16, 17, 70, 135, 253, 268,
    269, 271

Qian, J., 11, 64, 91, 93n23, 126, 127, 128,
    129, 132, 150, 172n32, 235n10
Qian, M., 11, 64, 126, 127, 150, 172n32,
    235n10

Qian, Y., 61, 175, 219, 253, 255n6, 269
Qiu, A., 207n2, 233, 236
Qiu, Y., 82

Rajan, R., 11, 26, 128, 135, 202, 233, 303
Ranciere, R., 130
Rawski, T., 82n11
Reinhart, C., 132
Reis, R., 130
Richard, J. F., 206
Robin, A., 211, 213, 215, 219, 223, 235
Rock, E. B., 180
Roll, R., 206, 207
Rosenstein-Rodan, P., 7, 19
Rossi, S., 118
Rui, O., 106, 124, 221

Saffar, W., 216
Saporta, V., 130
Schankerman, M., 175, 229
Scheinkman, J., 104n27, 244
Schooner, H. M., 37n1
Schumpter, J., 13
Schuppli, M., 236
Sehrt, K., 91
Shen, H., 172, 184, 206
Shen, Y., 162
Sheng, X., 318n2, 319
Shih, V. C., 42, 43
Shin, H. S., 136
Shleifer, A., 7, 13, 119, 127, 180
Sing, T. F., 113
Skinner, J., 265
Smith, A., 211, 215, 216, 233, 235, 242
Smith, T., 6, 27
Song, L., 92, 272, 273
Song, Z. M., 61, 269
Soskice, D., 57
Spence, J. D., 6
Stanislaw, J., 1
Stein, J., 91, 206, 224
Stern, N., 339n1
Stigler, G., 12
Storesletten, K., 61
Strahan, P., 91, 93n23
Strasburg, J., 58n27
Stulz, R., 127, 202, 233, 284
Su, D., 208
Su, J., 256
Subramanian, G., 180
Summers, L., 180, 273
Sun, P., 155n3

Sun, Q., 213
Sun, X., 168

Tam, K., 155n3
Tan, L., 229, 244
Tan, W., 149, 166, 169
Tang, X., 318n2, 319n3
Tang, Y. W., 222
Tao, Z., 256
Taylor, M., 37n1
Teoh, S. H., 226
Thesmar, D., 6
Thurow, L., 188n46
Tiebout, C., 21, 22
Titman, S., 206
Tobin, J., 10, 11, 26
Tong, H., 303
Tornell, A., 130
Trezevant, R., 216
Truong, C., 208
Tsai, K., 125, 126
Tsui, K.-y., 370
Tuan, J., 160, 181
Tullock, G., 341
Turner, Lord A., 52

Valasco, A., 136n42
Vandenbussche, J., 25
Veblen, T., 7
Veeraraghavan, M., 208
Vishny, R. W., 7, 13

Wan, J., 270
Wang, F., 342
Wang, J., 221
Wang, Q., 216, 227, 227n7
Wang, S., 323, 323n7, 325n11
Wang, X., 12, 15
Wang, Y., 188n46, 258, 269, 370
Watts, R. L., 216, 217
Wei, S.-J., 17, 70, 135, 228, 233, 270, 303, 307n7
Weil, D. N., 269
Weingast, B., 219
Weitzman, M. L., 144
Wei Yu, 173, 174, 175
Welker, M., 211, 232
Wells, P. C., 114
Westerman, F., 130
White, M. J., 340n5
Whiting, S., 125
Willett, T. D., 135

Williamson, R., 127
Wilson, J., 25
Wolfenzon, D., 13
Wong, C., 261
Wong, S., 106, 173, 175
Wong, T. J., 18, 107, 149, 168, 169, 175, 198, 208, 211, 213, 215, 216, 219, 223, 224, 225, 226, 227, 227n7, 305
Woo, W. Thye-, 12, 15
Wu, D., 213
Wu, H. X., 15
Wu, J., 108, 113, 113n30, 114, 213, 215, 223
Wurgler, J., 10, 26, 285n1
Wysocki, P., 211, 215, 235

Xia, L., 216, 227, 227n7
Xie, Z., 159, 183
Xiong, W., 104n27, 229, 244
Xiu, S.-y., 169
Xu, C., 6, 125, 128, 144, 339, 369, 370
Xu, L., 154, 155n3, 159
Xue, J., 271

Yan, H., 244
Yang, D. T., 256, 269, 272, 273
Yang, F., 20
Yang, J., 15
Yang, L., 227n6
Yang, Z., 91, 104n27, 213
Yao, Y., 92
Yergin, D., 1
Yeung, B., 11, 13, 25, 159, 206, 207, 285n1, 305n6
Young, A., 350
Yu, Q., 213
Yu, W., 9, 11, 159, 206, 207
Yuan, H., 225
Yue, H., 124, 215

Zeldes, S. P., 265
Zhang, C., 330n22
Zhang, F., 225
Zhang, G., 318n2, 319, 325n11
Zhang, J., 269, 271, 272
Zhang, S., 120
Zhang, T., 18, 107, 175, 198, 208, 219, 221, 223, 224, 305
Zhang, X., 17, 270, 307n7
Zhao, L., 124
Zhao, M., 124, 305n6
Zheng, B., 317n1
Zheng, Y., 197, 198

Zhong, H., 222
Zhou, L.-A., 6
Zhou, N., 188n46
Zhou, S., 269
Zhu, X., 77

Zhu, Y., 120, 197, 198
Zilibotti, F., 25, 61
Zimmerman, J. L., 216
Zingales, L., 11, 26, 128, 129, 202, 233, 303
Zuo, X., 342

Subject Index

Page numbers followed by *f* or *t* refer to figures or tables, respectively.

Accounting scandals, penalties for, 224–25

Advancement, corporate, international comparison of, 56–58

Agriculture Bank of China (ABC), 67; IPO of, 87

Auditing: independence of, and information environment, 222; practices, China's information environment and, 211–15; weak demand for external, 226–27

Bad news, politics and suppression of, 223–24

Bankers, market socialist, 11–12

Banking crises, 130–32

Bank of China (BOC), 51, 54, 67, 67n5

Bank of Communications (BComm), 38; IPO of, 87–90

Bankruptcy laws, 68, 91–92

Banks: aggregate evidence on deposit and loans of, 74–77; analysis of nonperforming loans of, 77–86; breakdown of loans by, 78t; comparison of deposits for, 76t; efficiency of state-owned, 86–93; Hui Jin and, 41–42; international comparison of total bank credit extended to private/hybrid sectors by, 77f; IPOs of, 87–90, 88t; ownership of, 38–41, 39–40t; privatization process of, 87–91; sources of Chinese deposits for,

75f; state-owned and private, 95–96t. *See also* Financial system, of China

Big Four banks, 77

Blackstone, China Investment Corporation and, 58–59

Board of Directors, 105–6

Board of Supervisors, 105–6

Bond markets, of China, 101–3, 102t

Bonds, government, 326–27

Bubbles, 131

Capital, market socialist, 14–17

Capital account liberalization, 132–33

Central Discipline and Inspection Commission (CDIC), 42

Central Financial Work Commission (CFWC), 43–44

Central Hui Jin Investment Ltd. (Hui Jin), 38, 46; ownership of China's banks and, 41–42

Central Organization Department (COD), 44

Chief executive officers (CEOs), market socialist, 6–7

China: bond issuance and, 315–16; debt-financed growth strategy of modern-day, 314–16; economic boom of, 314; economy of, 3; financing strategies of dynasties of, 316–19; financing

China (*continued*)
strategies of Qing dynasty and present-day, 319–20; future of debt-financed growth in, 330–32; global ambitions of, 51–56; history of government borrowing in, 327–28; market reforms and, 314–15; per capita GDP of, 3; public finance in, 337t; sectors driving economic growth of, 315. *See also* Local governments
China Aviation Oil Company (CAO), 53
China Banking Regulatory Commission (CBRC), 37–38, 68
China Construction Bank (CCB), 54
China Development Bank (CDB), 38
China Insurance Regulatory Commission (CIRC), 37, 48–50
China Investment Corporation (CIC), 41, 42, 44, 49–50, 52, 69; Blackstone and, 58–59; Morgan Stanley and, 58–59
China National Offshore Oil Corp (CNOCC), 6
China National Petroleum Corp (CNPC), 6
China Petroleum and Chemical Corp (SINOPEC), 6
China Securities Regulatory Commission (CSRC), 37, 68, 107, 151, 154, 164; corporate governance and, 205–6; dual mandate of, 165–66; as gatekeeper, 166–68; goals of formal governance activities of, 177–78; IPOs and, 168–69; listing of private firms and, 161–63; role of, in corporate governance, 176–78; transparency and, 204–5
Chinese Communist Party (CCP), 2; business enterprises and, 5–6; CEOs and, 6–7; control of banks by, 41–42; control of economy by, 24; control of financial system and, 44–45; control of human resource management by, 36; corporate governance and, 173–75; promotions and, 5–6; reliance of compensation and promotion incentives by, 24. *See also* Human resource management (HRM)
Chinese Communist Party Organization Department (CCP OD), 2, 25; key positions of SOEs appointed by, 174
Chinese courts: institutional contributions of, 182–83; shareholder suits and, 183–84
Chinese Financial Futures Exchange (CFFEx), 160

Civil Service School, 7
Code of Corporate Governance for Listed Companies (CSRC), 176–77
"Commanding heights," 1, 2, 5
Commercial bonds, absence of substantial market for, 163–64
Common stock, types of, issued, 103–5, 104t
Company Law, 68, 183
Competition, in China, 16; as corporate governance mechanism, 126
Contagion, financial, 136–37
Corporate governance: alternative mechanisms, 127; competition as mechanism for, 126; CSRC role in, 176–78, 205–6; formalization of, 37–42; government and party involvement with internal, 173–75; international comparison of advancement and, 56–58; introduction, 35–37; market socialist, 7–11; mechanisms, of Listed Sector, 105–7; reputation, trust, and relationships as mechanisms for, 126–27; role of Chinese Communist Party and, 56; role of "internal," 178–82; state role in, and shareholders, 175–76
Corporate saving, 255–61; econometric model for gross, 293–99, 294t; financial constraints and, 302–4; net, 299–301; politically connected firms and, 305–6; profits/dividends and, 295–99. *See also* Saving
Corporate scandals, 107
Corporate transparency, defined, 201. *See also* Transparency
Corruption, government, 128
Crises: avoiding, and financial system, 65; banking, 130–32; currency, 135–36; financial markets and, 130–37; fiscal, 322–30
Cui Guangqin, 49
Currency crises, 135–36

Debt-financed growth, 320
Debts, market socialist, 19–20
Deng Xiaoping, 12, 152, 203
Derivative lawsuits, 183–84; shareholder problems of collection action and, 184–85
Disciplinary tender offers, 180–82
Disclosure practices, China's information environment and, 211–15
Dowry funds, 329

Earnings management, information environment and, 225–26
Elites, international comparison of, 56–58
Enterprise savings, 16
Entrepreneurs, market socialist, 12–14
Equity futures contracts, 160

Fiduciary duty of loyalty, 183
Financial analysts, information environment and, 230
Financial contagion, 136–37
Financial crises, 130; banking crises, 130–32; market crashes, 130–32
Financial markets, of China, 96–98; asset management industries, 115–18; bond markets, 101–3; corporate governance mechanisms in, 105–7; crises and, 130–37; institutional investors and, 121; liberalization of, 132–33; range of products and, 121–22; real estate market, 107–14; regulations and, 118–19; sale of government shares in listed companies and, 119–20; stock markets, 98–100, 118; training of professionals and, 120–21; twin crisis and, 135–36
Financial reporting practices, China's information environment and, 211–15, 227–28. *See also* Information environment
Financial system, of China: avoiding crises and, 65; formalization of, 37–42; international comparison of, 71t; introduction, 63–66; overview of, 70f; review of history of, 66–70; size and efficiency of, 70–74. *See also* Banks; Corporate governance
Fiscal crises: policies for alleviating, 324–30; taxation for solving, 322–24
Foreign currency reserves, sterilization of, 133–35
France, 27
Fu Chengyu, 6

Governance. *See* Corporate governance
Government bonds, 326–27
Government borrowing, history of, 327–29
Government saving, 261–63; sources of, 262t
Growth Enterprise Board (GEB Board), 162–63
Guo Shuqing, 54

Household saving: data and stylized facts, 263–65; demographic structures and, 266–69, 267t, 268f; by region and income level, 265–66, 266f; understanding China's high, 269–72
Hui Jin. *See* Central Hui Jin Investment Ltd. (Hui Jin)
Hukou reforms, 23
Human resource management (HRM), 35–36; Central Financial Work Commission and, 45t; China's governance regime and, 58–59; Chinese Communist Party and, 42–45; comparative perspective of, 56–58; future of, 51–56; global governance and, 58–59; scale and scope of, and China's financial system, 45–51, 47f. *See also* Chinese Communist Party (CCP)
Hybrid Sector, 1, 13–14, 64–65; discussion on mechanisms in nonstandard financial sector, 125–30; listing of firms from, 120; market forces and, 119; state/listed sectors vs., 122–25; survey evidence on, 125; trading of companies from, 103

Iceland, 52–53
Index futures, 160
Industrial and Commercial Bank of China (ICBC), 9, 37, 51, 67; IPO of, 87
Information environment: accounting scandals and, 224–25; characteristics of China's, 210; as determinant of efficiency of resource allocation decisions, 202; earnings management and, 225–26; evidence from stock prices and, 206–8; evolution of China's, 231–37; expected impact of current/future institutional changes on, 234–37; financial analysts and, 230; financial reporting practices and, 211–15; independence of auditors and, 222; institutional investors and, 228–29; institutions and supply of and demand for information, 215–23, 218f; Internet and, 231; listed firms and, 203–4; local politicians/leaders and, 203; media and, 230–31; research on supply of and demand for information and, 223–27; social and political connections and, 222–23; standards/regulations and, 204–6; State's control of capital markets and, 220–21; suppression of bad news and, 223–24; survey evidence and, 208–10;

Information environment (*continued*)
weak demand for external auditing and, 226–27; weak demand for information and, 221–22. *See also* Financial reporting practices
Initial public offerings (IPOs): of banks, 88t; China Securities Regulatory Commission and, 168–69; feasibility of and benefits of disclosure-based system for, 169–70; mandatory information disclosure for, 169; pricing of, 168–69
Institutional investors: financial markets and, 121; improving information environment and, 228–29; securities markets and, 160–61
Insurance industry, 93–96
International Financial Reporting Standards (IFRS), 205
Internet, information environment and, 231
IPOs, of banks, 87–90

Jin Liqun, 49

Landsbanki (Iceland), 52
Law on State Owned Assets (SOA Law), 38
Lenin, Vladimir, 1, 2
Lijin tax system, 324
Liu Mingkang, 106
Local governments: alternative policies and resulting incentives for officials of, 365–67; budgetary revenue of, 337; Chinese vs. US oversight of, 339–40; financing of, 337–38; general model application to different time periods for forecasting behavior of officials, 350–63; general model of incentives created by tax revenue sources for Chinese officials, 342–50; incentives generated by promotion and retention procedures and officials of, 363–64; role of, in local economies, 339; traditional oversight models of, 341–42
Long-term (perpetual) bonds, 329
Lou Jiwei, 49

Management buy-outs (MBOs), 9
Margin sales, 160
Market crashes, 130–32
Market forces, market socialist, 2–29
Market for corporate control, 180–82
Market socialism, 2n1, 3; achievement and potential of, 4–5; bankers and, 11–12;

CEOs and, 6–7; Chinese characteristics, 5–23, 24; corporate governance and, 7–11
Media, information environment and, 230–31
Millionaires, market socialist, 12–14
Ming Dynasty, financing strategy of, 316, 320, 323–24
Ministry of Finance (MoF), 38
Morgan Stanley, China Investment Corporation and, 58–59
Mutual fund industry, 115–18, 116f

National Council of the Social Security Fund (NCSSF), 38, 69, 161
National income accounts, 15–16
National Security Fund (NSF), 52
Nation building: financial modernization in, 314; introduction, 313–14. *See also* China
New industries, funding of, 114–15
Nonperforming loans (NPLs), 64, 65; analysis of, 77–86; comparison of, and government debt, 80–81t. *See also* Banks
Nonstate financial intermediaries, growth of, 93–96
Non-state-owned enterprise sector, 1
Nontradable shares, 154

Opacity Index, 209–10

Paper currency, 325–26
Party School, 7
Peasant revolts, 313–14, 323
Pension system, 69
People's Bank of China (PBOC), 37–38, 42–43, 46, 50–51, 67
People's Construction Bank of China (PCBC), 67
People's Republic of China (PRC). *See* China
Perpetual (long-term) bonds, 329
"Poison pill" securities, 180
Private equity, 114–15
Private firms, listing of, 161–63
Profits, market socialist, 17–19
Promotions, 5–6
Provincial governments. *See* Local governments
Public finance, market socialist, 21–23
Public Offering Review Committee (PORC), 166

Qing Dynasty: financial condition of, 320–22; financing strategy of, 316–19

Qualified domestic institutional investor (QDII) funds, 117

Qualified domestic institutional investors (QDIIs), 161

Qualified foreign institutional investor (QFII) funds, 116–17, 154

Real estate markets, 107–14

Relation-based contracting, penalties for, 224–25

Rural Credit Cooperatives (RCCs), 67

Saving: components of Chinese aggregate, 253–54; corporate, 255–61; corporate profitability and, 256–58; future prospects of China's high national, 272–76; government, 261–63; household, 263–72; political economy of, 281–82. *See also* Corporate saving

Savings rates: of China, 15–16; Chinese savings puzzle and, 254–55; of enterprises, 16, 18; firm-level data and summary statistics for, 288–92; household, 16–17; international comparison of Chinese, 251–543; introduction, 249–51, 283–86; patterns from flow-of-funds data, 286–88

Securities markets, of China: access and, 161–63; assessing growth of, 185; characteristics of, 151–52; enforcement and, 170–71; future development steps for, 186–88; institutional investors and, 160–61; likelihood of investor-initiated protection in, 189; likelihood of more efficient, 189–91; product innovation and, 160; secondary role of legal infrastructure in, 188–89; share segmentation system of, 152–55

Shanghai Stock Exchange (SHSE), 64, 67, 67n6, 98, 149–50, 154, 155, 219; concentration, liquidity, and pricing efficiency of, 157–60

Shareholders: inability to participate in disciplinary tender offers and, 180–82; right to sue and, 182–85; right to vote and public, 178–80; state role in corporate governance and, 175–76

Share segmentation, 152–55

Shenzhen Stock Exchange (SZSE), 64, 67, 67n6, 98, 149–50, 155, 219

Short sales, 160

Small and Medium Enterprises Board (SME Board), 162–63

Socialist market economy. *See* Market socialism

Song Dynasty, financing strategy of, 316, 324–26

State Administration for Foreign Exchange (SAFE), 41, 46, 52, 116

State-owned Asset Supervision and Administration Commission (SASAC), 38

State-owned enterprises (SOEs), 2; Chinese Communist Party Organization Department (CCP OD) appointment of key positions in, 174; growth in market for shares of, 155

Stock markets, 26; listing of firms from Hybrid Sector and, 120; overview of, 98–100; publicly listed and traded companies of, 103–7; recent performance of, 118; tradable vs. nontradable shares, 105t; types of common stock issued, 103–5, 104t. *See also* Financial markets, of China

Stock options, 106

Su Shulin, 6

Tender offers for corporate control, 180–82

Township and Village Enterprises (TVEs), 9, 13, 65

Transparency: CSRC and, 204–5; expected impact of current/future institutional changes on, 234–37; potential consequences of change in corporate, 231–34; survey evidence on global, 209–10

Trust and Investment Corporations (TICs), 67

Twin crisis, 135–36

Tycoons, market socialist, 12–14

Urban Credit Cooperatives (UCCs), 67

Venture capital, 114–15

Voting rights, of public shareholders, 178–80

Wang Yilin, 6

Wei Liucheng, 106

Xiao Gang, 54